In a celebrated career spent between London, Paris and New York, MICHAEL PEPPIATT has written regularly for *Le Monde*, the *New York Times*, the *Financial Times, Art News* and *Art International*, which he re-launched as publisher and editor from Paris in 1985. He is the author of more than twenty books, including the definitive Francis Bacon biography, *Anatomy of an Enigma*, as well as the memoirs *Francis Bacon in Your Blood* and *The Existential Englishman*. He has also curated numerous landmark exhibitions, most recently 'Francis Bacon: Man and Beast' at the Royal Academy of Arts.

BY THE SAME AUTHOR

Francis Bacon in Your Blood

The Existential Englishman

GIACOMETTI

IN PARIS

Michael Peppiatt

BLOOMSBURY PUBLISHING
LONDON • OXFORD • NEW YORK • NEW DELHI • SYDNEY

BLOOMSBURY PUBLISHING
Bloomsbury Publishing Plc
50 Bedford Square, London, WC1B 3DP, UK
29 Earlsfort Terrace, Dublin 2, Ireland

BLOOMSBURY, BLOOMSBURY PUBLISHING and the Diana logo are trademarks of Bloomsbury Publishing Plc

First published in Great Britain 2023
This edition published 2024

A catalogue record for this book is available from the British Library

ISBN: HB: 978-1-5266-0095-0; TPB: 978-1-5266-0096-7; PB: 978-1-5266-0099-8;
EBOOK: 978-1-5266-0097-4; EPDF: 978-1-5266-7236-0

2 4 6 8 10 9 7 5 3 1

Typeset by Newgen KnowledgeWorks Pvt. Ltd., Chennai, India
Printed and bound in Great Britain by CPI Group (UK) Ltd, Croydon CR0 4YY

To find out more about our authors and books visit www.bloomsbury.com and sign up for our newsletters

Contents

Introduction

A LETTER TO ALBERTO GIACOMETTI

My life seemed to have come suddenly into focus. Since leaving university in 1964, I had found a pleasant but precarious existence as a part-time English teacher and publisher's reader in Barcelona. By the time I returned to London, keen to begin a 'proper' career, I found that all the attractive jobs in journalism had been snapped up, so I pieced together a living with translation work, which included elusive prose poems by Henri Michaux, then little known in Britain. Under parental pressure, I put in for an editorial position advertised in *The Times* that I did not really want because it meant uprooting myself again to live abroad, this time in Paris. To make sure that I stood no chance among the many eager candidates who applied, I was offhand and flippant during the interview with the editor, who had come to London especially. The strategy backfired, however, since my rudeness was misread as a sign of ability, and I received a letter confirming my appointment and enclosing a one-way ticket to the Gare du Nord.

Just before leaving London in January 1966, I went to say goodbye to Francis Bacon, whom I had seen regularly since I first interviewed him for a student review three years earlier.

'Now who do you know in Paris?' Bacon asked me as we made our way through a bottle of Krug in his studio.

'Well, no one really,' I said. 'Just the editor at *Réalités* magazine who's offered me the job.'

More than ever, it seemed a bad idea to be going to Paris at all. On the few occasions I had stayed there, the city had seemed cold and snobbish, making me feel very much the awkward young foreigner. In London, on the other hand, I was at home. I shared a basement flat in Chelsea with two friends I had been close to at university, I had a few favourite pubs and there was a girl I had recently fallen in love with.

'What about Giacometti?' Bacon asked, popping the cork on another bottle. 'The thing is, there is something terribly sympathetic about him. And he knows absolutely everyone in Paris.'

'Well,' I said, taken aback by a name famous enough for me to recognise. 'I can't just turn up on Giacometti's doorstep and tell him I thought I should say hello.'

'No, of course not,' Bacon replied firmly. 'I'll write a letter of introduction and you can take it to him once you're over there. I think you might get on very well.'

He padded round the studio until he found a paint-splashed copy of *Paris Match* lying on the floor, tore out the pages at the centre, then sat down, concentrating intently as he wrote a few lines over them.

I folded the double page, putting it carefully into my inside jacket pocket. We then went out for a lavish evening on the town and I, for one, got happily drunk.

Once I had arrived in Paris, I carried the letter to Giacometti around with me for several days, waiting for an opportunity to deliver it. I call it a 'letter', but in fact it was just a brief message in French, scrawled in Bacon's big, sloping hand in green felt-tip pen across a photo-reportage on the war in Vietnam.

'Cher Alberto,' the letter read. 'J'espère que vous allez bien. Je voudrais présenter un grand ami à moi Michael Peppiatt qui arrive maintenant vivre à Paris. J'espère vous voir bientôt Alberto.'*

Francis Bacon
7/1/1966

I found Giacometti's address easily enough because his studio was already something of a landmark. From the photographs I had seen

*'Dear Alberto, I hope you are well. I would like to introduce a great friend of mine Michael Peppiatt who has come to live now in Paris. I hope to see you soon Alberto.'

in catalogues it looked like a disused cave inside, filled with discarded bits of plaster and other junk, except that, as if growing out of the mess underfoot, rows of plaster heads and clumps of figures, varying in size from very tall to very small, were massed together in the minuscule space. The walls looked curiously alive because Giacometti had etched so many skeletal studies and notes on their crumbly surfaces. I knew I should go there and deliver the letter as soon as I had settled into my junior editor's job at *Réalités*.

A French girl at the office told me I could rent the one-room flat her parents owned in Alésia. I had been moving from one dingy hotel to another almost daily, and I accepted the offer as soon as I had seen that the flat on rue du Moulin-Vert was clean and pleasant enough. The street turned out to be literally a stone's throw from Giacometti's studio. I walked past his building to make sure and, if you went into the dank alleyway leading off the little courtyard in front, you could see the name 'GIACOMETTI' painted in small white capitals on the first door on the left.

Pierre Vauthey, Alberto outside his studio on rue Hippolyte Maindron, 1956

For several minutes I stood in front of the door, with Bacon's letter still stowed in my inside jacket pocket, wondering whether I shouldn't knock there and then. At the same time it occurred to me how irritated Giacometti might be to have a new visitor of little interest turning up just as he was trying to finish another of those tall, brittle figures that had so impressed people in London at his Tate show the previous summer. He and Bacon had seen a lot of each other around the opening of that show, during big, boozy dinners at Wheeler's in Soho and L'Etoile in Fitzrovia, surrounded by their mutual friends Isabel Rawsthorne, Michel Leiris and David Sylvester. I think Lucian Freud was there, too, and George Dyer, Francis's new boyfriend. Standing there irresolute and confused, I suddenly wished I had met Giacometti back then. It would have made things so much easier.

The alleyway, which had other damp, dilapidated, studio-like structures on either side, was completely silent – a silence that seemed to grow deeper, more ominous, as if the buildings were listening in while I hesitated. It was an icy January day, but I was beginning to feel uncomfortably warm, with my face flushing, as though simply being there had become acutely embarrassing. I raised my hand to knock on the door. But I couldn't. What if Giacometti was exhausted and still asleep, I wondered. What if he was with someone, a model or an important collector, or even a lover, and I interrupted him? Would he fling open the door in a rage and tell me to scram? Surely the best thing would be to slip away before anyone noticed.

Like a thief trying to leave the scene of the crime, I slunk back along the narrow passage and down the quiet street, regaining my anonymous new digs with relief. I'll try again tomorrow, I told myself. I'll go in the evening when Giacometti, who works mostly at night, is bound to be up and about. And I did, several times, but the same paralysing shyness and shame at trying to impose myself on a world-renowned artist overcame me. 'Terribly sympathetic' as he might be, Giacometti had better things to do than chitchat with an obscure young man.

Once I began my first full week at *Réalités*, I found out what several other editors in the building seemed to have known for some time. They laughed at me, the new boy. It had been all over the newspapers, they said. Giacometti had died in Switzerland several days ago. His Paris studio would have been empty and locked. I could have knocked and knocked. Giacometti hadn't been there. He had left Paris a couple of weeks before I arrived.

Giacometti was dead.

MY GIACOMETTI

It could have ended there. Most missed opportunities do. You chase after all kinds of things, in every direction, when you are young – a passion for Antonioni or Borges, new love, the discovery of Italy, surf-boarding or jazz. Then the trail peters out, other interests take over and you move on. But I couldn't move on. Once I heard that Giacometti had died, my immediate reaction was to gather up all the obituaries I could find about him, as if he were a famous, long-lost relative I had just discovered. As I read more about his strange life and his even stranger fame, achieved against extraordinary odds and almost against his own will, my feeling of personal loss grew stronger. If I had met Giacometti and talked to him in his studio, I was convinced, my life would have been radically changed. Giacometti and I might never have become close, not even in the improbable father/son way in which my friendship with Bacon had developed. To begin with, there was a full forty-year gap in age between us (almost to the day, since he was born on 10 October, and I on 9 October), as well as an even greater divide in background and experience. But I sensed that, since I was already intrigued by him and his work, I might have been lucky enough to form a special relationship with him, writing about him, meeting the people around him, interviewing him and allowing his conversation and his existence to overflow into mine, as Bacon's had done.

After a few weeks in my new job, with cheerful new colleagues, my situation felt less dire than I had feared. In the gloomy basement office just next to the canteen where the English edition of *Réalités* had been relegated, an enjoyable expatriate camaraderie prevailed. We all worked in the same, big room, and the banter rarely stopped; towards lunchtime, we took bets on what the *plat du jour* would be to decide who paid for the first round of drinks after work. Among more mundane editing tasks, the job allowed me to research and write about art across the centuries, from Egypt and China to Patinier and Pisanello, Bonnard and Balthus. Yet the sensation that I had missed a far greater opportunity never went away. The pine bookshelves in my room in Alésia began to fill up with whatever printed material on Giacometti I could glean from the range of second-hand booksellers that abounded all over Paris. My greatest satisfaction during those early, still lonely months came from sifting through the dark recesses of various *libraires* and discovering the slim, tattered catalogues of historic Giacometti exhibitions – of Galerie Maeght's May 1954 show of his paintings, for example, or, wonder of wonders, of the exhibitions that Pierre Matisse had put on in his gallery in New York.

From these hauls of paper, what struck me most were the gritty black and white photographs, not of Giacometti, who remained remarkably photogenic even in his scruffiest, most plaster-caked clothes, but of the artist's refuge, his lair, his shell. I had come so close to seeing the studio, circling obsessively around it, and now I saw it as the embodiment of everything I had missed within its prehistoric-looking walls: tiny heads, blobs of clay, tall, knobbly figures reaching upwards like ladders to the sky, early sculptures and recent canvases, body parts, an arm here, a foot there, unidentified fragments everywhere in the overflowing, ankle-deep mess where closely cross-hatched drawings had been trampled underfoot amid a mix of books and newspapers and disused tools and,

Scheidegger, inside Alberto's studio, 1958

of course, plaster. Plaster bits were dispersed as far as the eye could see, powdering the air and collecting even on the one natural object in the studio, a spindly tree that had fought its way up miraculously through the beaten-earth floor.

Even though I knew by now that 46 rue Hippolyte-Maindron was a broken-down, rickety, insalubrious hovel, with little heating, no running water and a roof that leaked, the studio grew and grew as I collected more photographs of it, taken at every period, from every angle. I also began wondering about all the people, many of them still alive, who were closely connected to Giacometti and had spent time with him there. A few of them, I realised – as I began to establish myself, shakily enough, as an English art critic based in Paris – I already knew. I came across his widow, Annette, early on, through her assistant, Julie Burns, whom I had met at a party in the Marais; but although always amiable Annette appeared overburdened by her new role as head of her late husband's estate. I got on easily enough with Diego, Alberto's brother and right-hand man, who would tell me stories about the early days in Paris, then lapse into a companionable silence. Then, of course, there were his dealers, the extravagantly coiffed Aimé Maeght, and his erstwhile artistic director, Louis Clayeux, whom I saw often at art events and other artists' studios, as well as the reserved, gruff Pierre Matisse, whose taste I respected even though he struck me as belonging to another epoch until I visited him in New York, where he seemed more relaxed and approachable. I also got to know Jacques Dupin, the poet whose harsh, vivid imagery impressed me, and who had written the very first book on Giacometti. Jacques became a friend, although I always remained slightly in awe of him, as I did of anyone whose art or writing I admired; no one made Giacometti come more memorably alive than he did in a few graphic anecdotes. The other writers who had come to the fore as experts on Giacometti I saw as a matter of course, although both, sensing perhaps that I might one day be snapping at their heels, kept their distance: David Sylvester, whose magnum opus on his sculptor hero was to remain in gestation for decades, and James Lord, whose familiarity with the great names of the Paris art world was enviable but whose haunted look made me ill at ease.

Among Giacometti's many friendships with writers, the one that lasted longest was with Michel Leiris, who had written a review of Giacometti's work in 1929 and remained an ally until the sculptor's death. During the

1970s I was invited to work with Leiris on a translation of the interviews that David Sylvester had done with Francis Bacon. I spent many mornings at the Café des Deux Magots with the distinguished, elderly writer who introduced me courteously in the preface to the book as an '*Anglais parisianisé*' and his '*co-équipier*'. Over long lunches after our translation sessions (for me, the best French lessons imaginable), Leiris reminisced about the writers and artists he had been close to in Paris from the early 1920s on and often recalled his fond admiration for Giacometti and his world. Through Bacon, I also met Isabel Rawsthorne, whose fraught affair with Giacometti fascinated me; but I was too intimidated by her imperious presence and extended, sibylline utterances to ask any questions, let alone intimate ones. Another long-time companion of Giacometti's, the Greek-born publisher Tériade, was, on the contrary, the easiest of people to chat with, and in the course of an interview I did with him for the *New York Times* I was able to reconstruct the background to *Paris sans fin*, the series of Giacometti's lithographs of the city that Tériade brought out after the artist's death.

Unlike many artists, Giacometti tended to get on well with his fellow painters and sculptors. He developed unswerving admiration for several of his elders, notably Matisse *père*, Derain and Laurens, while maintaining a lively friendship with Balthus. When the opportunity arose at *Réalités* to interview Balthus in Rome in summer 1967, I ventured to ask him about the early days with Giacometti in Paris while not forgetting to keep my main focus trained on Monsieur le Comte Balthasar Klossowski de Rola, as he quaintly styled himself, and the restoration he had undertaken of the fabulous Villa Medici. Another painter I came across from time to time was André Masson, who (although he was too modest to say so) had given Giacometti his first, decisive leg-up into the Paris avant-garde in the mid-1920s, introducing him to many of the writers and artists who remained loyal friends throughout his life. As for the photographers who burnished his and the studio's reputation, their number was legion, from Brassaï to Henri Cartier-Bresson, both of whom I was fortunate to know well and who shared their memories freely with me of a man and an artist whom they considered head and shoulders above everybody else they had ever met.

My growing devotion to Giacometti advanced not only through the excitement of coming closer to the world he had inhabited, but also through a time of dark despair. After living in Paris for a couple of years, I had collected most of the available Giacometti literature, and the folder of photographs had grown so fat that his studio now looked like, not a single, shabby room, but an entire universe that the whole of Alésia could barely contain. The tiny cell had proliferated into an infinity of spaces, all different yet all interconnected. As in some endlessly expanding realm, each photograph provided an extra facet of information, a fresh angle on an entity that could never be fully circumscribed. What had proved far more difficult was to see Giacometti's work in the flesh. Although I had come across a few individual sculptures here and there in museum displays, there had been no major exhibition devoted to his oeuvre while I had been in Paris until a commemorative retrospective curated by the art historian and museum director Jean Leymarie opened at the Musée de l'Orangerie towards the end of 1969.

Giacometti was dead, but he came more fully alive than ever for me during that show. Winter had closed its grip around the city, reducing its contours until the people bent against the wind and the withered, leafless trees in the Tuileries looked like so many variations on Giacometti's skeletal forms. Pared back to the bone, the sculptures seemed in turn to have sucked their spindly substance from the thin glacial air. Caught in an unhappy love triangle that had spiralled out of control, I knew that my fragile bearings in Paris were lost and I could see no way out of a doomed situation. I began visiting the exhibition regularly, religiously, standing awestruck before the striding bronze figures that I named the 'survivors' because they had endured an eternity of winters, grim and shriven but alive. Slowly I took solace from them, thinking that if they still stood and strode I too might survive. Outside in the Tuileries, the grey sky pressed down, the fountains had iced over, all nature was dead. But now I had a glimmer of hope. Giacometti had been there before me. Having thought I could not go on, I saw now that perhaps I could. Thereafter my attachment to Giacometti grew into the bedrock of my existence.*

*That attachment took on a further, more professional dimension when I returned to London in the mid-1990s and Giacometti's major collectors in England, Robert and Lisa Sainsbury, asked me to curate an exhibition based on the works they had donated to their foundation at the University of East Anglia. Since they had begun collecting shortly after the war, and since at the time that period in Giacometti's work interested me most, I chose 'Giacometti in Postwar

ALBERTO GIACOMETTI IN PARIS

For years I have been thinking about how I might make a new, valuable contribution to the formidable store of literature on Giacometti. When my biography of Francis Bacon[1] came out nearly thirty years ago, I felt the time ripe to make a similar commitment to Giacometti, the other major artist to have transformed my life. In the mid-1990s, however, James Lord's biography[2] was still regarded as definitive, and publishers were reticent about undertaking a new approach. In the intervening years, Giacometti's reputation has continued to soar. Not only have exhibitions of his work proliferated across the globe, with the prices of individual pieces soaring on the art market, but two Giacometti foundations have been promoting and protecting his renown, one established in Zurich before the artist died, and another later in Paris, where a separate Giacometti Institute, containing a research library and a recreation of the artist's studio, opened in 2018. Few artists have benefited from such extensive, official representation, which continues to burnish the Giacometti legend.

The writing on Giacometti has kept pace with these developments, with a cascade of new catalogues, monographs and essays, including detailed studies devoted to highly specialised or minor aspects of the artist's career. Some of these publications have proven rewarding, while others remain repetitive and peripheral. In 2017, a new biography appeared by Catherine Grenier, who had been appointed director of the Fondation Giacometti in Paris three years earlier. With unparalleled access to the Giacometti archives, Grenier produced the most rigorously accurate summary of the artist's life and work to date, which stands as a corrective to Lord's looser, lusher version. Most recently, the Fondation Giacometti announced plans to create a fully fledged Giacometti Museum to house the nearly 10,000 works that it holds as well as an art school and the artist's reconstituted studio. The site chosen is the

Paris' as my theme. The catalogue came out in a French-language version when the works were exhibited at the Fondation de l'Hermitage in Lausanne. A subsequent show was organised in 2010 at the Eykyn Maclean Gallery in New York. This time, the theme, 'In Giacometti's Studio', stemmed directly from my original fascination with that unique space, and the exhibition travelled to the Bucerius Kunst Forum in Hamburg and the Museo di Gallarate, Milan. In 2018, I was privileged to co-curate the 'double-bill' exhibition, 'Bacon/Giacometti' – my two tutelary deities – at the Fondation Beyeler outside Basel.

former Invalides train station built, with its underground annexes, for the Paris Exposition in 1900 on the spacious Esplanade des Invalides.

Thus interest in Giacometti might be said to stand at an all-time high. Conscious of the wealth and quality of writings about Giacometti – and here I should like to cite not only Jean-Paul Sartre, Jean Genet and Yves Bonnefoy but, *inter alia*, Reinhold Hohl, Valerie Fletcher and Thierry Dufrêne – I felt nevertheless that a full exploration was lacking of the sculptor's unusually intimate association with Paris during its intellectual revolutions before and after the war, including the many outstanding writers, artists and other personalities with whom he associated there.

In my own mind, the symbiosis between Giacometti and his adopted city was so complete that it had become impossible to think of one without the other. Not only did Giacometti find his place rapidly at the forefront of the artistic and literary ferment that set Paris apart in the 1920s and again in the 1940s, he also partly shaped the way others came to see the city. Giacometti's images – a Surrealist object, a 'Walking Man', a 'Standing Woman', a sketch of leafless trees or a café interior – speak unmistakably (like the harshly lit, poetically ill-fated films of Marcel Carné) of a specific Paris at a specific time. His tentative figures could not have emerged anywhere other than from the grey air and crumbling stone of the capital's humbler areas, nor could Paris claim its full identity without those images, now so intimately woven into the city's fabric that they still haunt the boulevards and cafés of Montparnasse and Saint-Germain. Loping through the backstreets or among the regulars propping up a low-life bar, you even expect, if you are steeped in the lore of those times, to find the dishevelled figure and luminous gaze of Giacometti himself.

That said, I no longer wished to undertake a full-scale biography of the artist. With the information currently available added to fresh research, I realised that any attempt at a complete survey would require the scope and detail that John Richardson brought to his multi-volume (although eventually uncompleted) homage to Picasso. Worthy though the quest seemed, I sensed that the specific story I wanted to tell of the artist's relationship to his chosen milieu would be smothered under the mass of biographical information. Part of Giacometti's fascination is that he eludes being pinned down, above all by what is not essential. Like his finest drawings, he is both there and not there. When you seek him out, he is as much in the silence of the surrounding blank sheet of paper as in the spectral outline of a face. What is left out in the rarefied Giacometti realm is as telling as what remains.

My approach, based on a paring down rather than an accretion, would mostly omit the artist's early development – from an idyllic childhood in the Val Bregaglia, through a Swiss education in Schiers and Geneva, to his first forays into Italy – as well as the extended trips home to Stampa and Maloja that remained a constant in Giacometti's life and essential to his wellbeing. The Swiss background has been amply described elsewhere, as have the formal details of his artistic development, period by period. That said, *Giacometti in Paris* takes the artist's early years into account whenever they become relevant to its theme, and stylistic analyses of the artist's breakthrough works and their contexts remain fundamental throughout, with pride of place at every phase in the artist's career. The story told here, however, is primarily an attempt to explain, or at least to suggest, how a certain person, a certain place and a certain time combined to create such an unusual, penetrating vision of mankind, hopefully conveying all the while a living likeness of the sculptor and his world.

Simple and straightforward as my project seemed at first, I soon grew aware that other influences were at work as I wrote. First there was my abiding fascination with the time immediately prior to my birth – the period during which my parents came of age and the world as I would know it came into focus. That whole pre-war epoch, no longer the present but not yet altogether the past, has persisted throughout my life like a background, the landscape I was born into and think of as my roots. Then, what drew me especially to the more general theme of Paris before and after the Second World War was not only that both periods witnessed amazing bursts of creativity, style and irreverence but also that the latter period had immediately preceded my own obscure arrival in the city.

The stars of that post-war epoch were just departing the stage then, leaving their spangled aura of cocktails and jazz, revolutionary politics and art, passionate lives and loves behind. They were what, when I arrived in the mid-1960s, I had just missed, and the Paris that I found and needed to adapt to existed quite tangibly in their shadow. Giacometti having just disappeared, almost all his famous contemporaries had either already joined him or were to die over the following few years, leaving behind a void that seemed unlikely to be filled again with a comparable range of creative and intellectual talent.

Since I stayed in Paris for almost thirty years after Giacometti's death, I was especially fascinated by the idea of mapping out every relevant point at which he had interacted with the city: how he had coped with its particular pressures, how it had formed him, and how in turn, despite being a foreigner who always retained his Swiss nationality, he had created a Paris in his own image. To confirm this design, foolishly and dramatically, I walked in his steps, bent against the wind and the rain, frequenting the same bistros and cafés, from the Coupole and the Dôme to the Rosebud and the Falstaff, from Chez Lipp and the Flore to the Palette and the Petit St-Benoît; in this respect, my greatest triumph was having lunch with Diego at one of the brothers' old haunts in Alésia and hearing him complain that the boeuf bourguignon had been so much better when he and Alberto had enjoyed it there in the 1920s.

The Paris I encountered thus seemed a pale reflection of the glory days that Giacometti had known, and so the genesis of this book can be traced back to not one but two failures: having missed meeting him in his studio, then having missed the city at the height of its cultural achievements. But I take comfort from the fact that, in Giacometti's world, failure is accepted not only as inevitable but as the essential prerequisite for any worthwhile endeavour. Delving into the Giacometti lexicon, I have also attempted to be as concise as this sweep of cultural history allows, aiming at the extraordinary, condensed expressiveness that the artist himself achieved. A reductive mode not being my natural forte, I have nevertheless allowed myself the odd touch of colour when it invigorates the dominant palette of greys; and while limiting the narrative to ascertainable fact, I have occasionally taken a degree of poetic licence to suggest Giacometti's own inner dialogue, based on the numerous interviews he gave as well as the unusual, posthumous closeness to him that has taken root and grown in me for sixty years.

Rather than a conventional biography, *Giacometti in Paris* is an intimate portrait of an exceptional artist in Paris during its last decades as the undisputed art capital of the world. A double portrait, in which a gifted individual and a magical city confront and reflect each other. A mirror held up to one of the most poignant lives and arresting visions of the twentieth century.

PART ONE

(1922–44)

1

Magic City (1922–26)

When he arrived in Paris for the first time on the morning of 9 January 1922, Alberto Giacometti had already been travelling for several days. Just after the Christmas holidays, he had said goodbye to his family in the Val Bregaglia, high up on the Swiss-Italian border, and begun the long journey down to Zürich and on to Basel, the main crossing point from Switzerland into France. Like his ancestors, Alberto[*] had been brought up in a village enclosed by towering mountains, cut off from the outside world, above all during its harsh winters, where people communicated mainly in a local Italian-based dialect known as Bregagliot that varied from one isolated village to the next.

Barely twenty years old, the young artist was nevertheless undaunted by the trip ahead. He had already studied for a while in Geneva[†] and lived for most of 1921 with an uncle and his family in Rome, visiting the city's museums, drawing tirelessly, and falling in love. For a boy brought up in the Alps, he could consider himself a seasoned traveller, speaking fluent Italian as well as serviceable German and French. Now, however, the stakes were higher. Still unsure as to whether he wished to develop his precocious talents as a painter or a sculptor, Alberto knew

[*]Alberto Giacometti himself preferred to be called 'Alberto', once telling Pierre Matisse, his dealer in New York, that he did not like his family name. Certainly, most of the people around him, including local tradesmen, cab drivers and café waiters, called him 'Alberto' or 'Monsieur Alberto'. I refer to him as Alberto throughout this book for this reason, but also because it distinguishes him clearly from his brother Diego.
[†]Unimpressed by the art schools in Geneva, Alberto rapidly grew bored and restless.

that by leaving his secure background to plant himself at the source of modern art,* where the most significant artistic discoveries and careers were made, he would be changing his life for ever.

When the question had first been mooted by his parents – Giovanni, a successful regional painter, and Annetta, his matriarchal wife – Alberto himself had not been particularly keen on following his father's footsteps by studying in Paris. With the contrarian streak in his nature already to the fore, the young man decided that he preferred Vienna, then still basking in its *fin de siècle* glow, where he imagined his reasonable, but not lavish, allowance in Swiss francs would go further because of the favourable exchange rate. He also toyed with returning to Rome, which he remembered fondly not only for its ancient monuments and artistic treasures but for the easy-going prostitutes with whom he had enjoyed his first sexual experiences. But once his sensitive, caring father stopped insisting that his eldest son study in Paris, Alberto soon came round to the idea. There were, after all, distinct advantages to being at the hub, not only of modern art, but of everything that was stimulating, fashionable and provocative. This fabled city had been the centre of creativity in Europe before the Great War, and now it had resumed that role as if by right.

The only problem to have arisen so far on the journey was the bureaucracy in Basel where it took several days to process the visa Alberto needed to enter France. Luckily his younger brother, Diego, had come to keep him company, but the wait grew so frustrating that Alberto began to dream every night of a vast train arriving at breakneck speed to carry him off to parts unknown. Once he had boarded the steaming locomotive and the Swiss border had flown past, the reality turned out to be less glamorous, with hard seating rather than the plush upholstery and wagons-lits he had caught sight of in first class. But comfort was never to mean much to a youth inured since birth to the harshness of mountain life. As the night train rumbled through the dark, dense forests of eastern France, Alberto could sense that the trip was really under way and his dream coming at least nearer.

Alberto was travelling light. He disliked accumulating possessions, and his modest suitcase contained mainly underwear and a change of clothes.

*Where else, after all, did one find the very greatest artists – Proust, Joyce, Picasso and Stravinsky – all dining together as they did in a grand Parisian hotel in May 1922, very shortly after Alberto arrived in the city?

He had already gone through a brief, dandyish period in Rome, so the high-buttoned jacket and bow tie came with him, if only to reassure the Parisians he was about to mix with that he had already ventured beyond the mountain fastnesses of south-eastern Switzerland. After much ribbing from his family during Christmas at home, though, the fashionable cane and long cigarette holder he had sported in Rome were left behind. Slim and of barely middling height, Alberto's wiry physique gave off an impression of coiled alertness and energy. Framed by unruly, dark curls, his head looked slightly too large, too dominant, for his body, but his features were pleasant and well defined, with that expression of being constantly surprised by life that he had caught so well in his accomplished *Small Self-Portrait* painted the year before. To the outsider, the young Swiss traveller would have come across as reserved, but once he began to talk his enthusiasm, warmth and natural charm came through, lighting up his face and hinting at unusual depths of character.

Dozing fitfully through the night, Alberto would not have exchanged more than the odd pleasantry with the other passengers. Everybody in his carriage seemed intent on what the next chapter in their lives might bring, and none more so than Alberto as he watched the fields under snow give way to scattered towns and eventually the lugubrious suburbs of Paris. As the vast silhouette of the Gare de Lyon, one of the city's nineteenth-century 'cathedrals' of travel, hove into view, Alberto could only compare it to the old Termini station he had known in Rome, with its prominent obelisk and ornate architecture. Yet the Termini hardly boasted the same sense of bustling modernity or, indeed, a prestigious Belle Epoque restaurant like the Train Bleu where, Alberto had heard, wealthy patrons dined off lobster and champagne before taking the overnight train to the Côte d'Azur.

Curious about every detail of his new surroundings, Alberto wandered through the soaring iron and glass halls, savouring the romance of railway travel, with its young couples meeting and embracing, embracing and parting. Then he lingered on the concourse outside, catching his first real glimpses of the city. Much of ancient Paris had been swept away when Baron Haussmann was instructed by Napoleon III to drive spacious boulevards across the old streets to connect the main monuments and facilitate traffic as well as, when necessary, the swift deployment of troops to keep the city's unruly population in check. Since the latter had grown considerably by the middle of the nineteenth century, new housing was urgently needed, and the increasingly industrialised capital required better transport and communications with the rest of the far-flung, underdeveloped country. That was why the Gare de Lyon, like the city's other main stations, had been constructed.

Some sixty years later, the sweeping – many called them brutal – changes were still noticeable, stamping Paris with a new identity. Flanked by trees on wide pavements that encouraged pedestrians to saunter and sit at the numerous café terraces, all the boulevards were lined by large,

Albert Harlingue, the Strasbourg Saint-Denis crossroads, Paris, 1922

uniform apartment buildings that rose six floors above the street. Shops or cafés often occupied the ground floor, with a mezzanine provided for storage or living quarters above the premises. Then came the so-called 'noble' floor, with its larger, more heavily decorated windows and wrought-iron balconies, which was especially sought after in the days before lifts had been installed. The other floors behind these mainly bland and monotonous façades then decreased in prestige, landing by landing, up to the attic, where servants, students and the less fortunate members of society were lodged, often in exiguous rooms without running water or any other facilities beyond a narrow bed, a washstand and, with luck, a dormer window that looked out over the rooftops of Paris.

But that early Monday morning was bitterly cold, and even Alberto, accustomed to the dark, freezing winters of his mountain valley, needed to walk briskly to keep the January weather at bay. He was in any case happiest walking and looking – staring even with a sudden intensity, as if he were seeing things for the very first time, which people found unnerving and sometimes complained about. Whenever he came across a side street blackened with age that had escaped Haussmann's renovation, Alberto took to it instinctively, marvelling at the sense, almost the smell, of time that its walls exuded. Having crisscrossed a warren of these ancient passages, he was suddenly confronted by a majestic bridge leading over the Seine. Even on this, his first day in the city, Alberto knew that whatever would interest him in Paris was not to be found on the Right Bank. Clamping his hat closer to his mop of curls and bending against the icy wind that whipped off the water, he changed his suitcase from one hand to the other and crossed over the bridge with a mounting sense of elation, breathing a self-conscious sigh of relief as he arrived at the other side. Now he stood on the promised land, the Left Bank, where everything would come into perspective. It was here that artists were meant to be, and sooner or later he would find the Latin Quarter and then the mecca towards which he knew painters and writers from all over the world were being drawn in droves: Montparnasse.

With these rough bearings in mind, Alberto moved more purposefully westwards along the banks of the Seine, glancing from the fast-flowing, greyish water to the Jardin des Plantes' huddle of leafless trees and wintry flowerbeds on the other side of the broad thoroughfare. Further on the *bouquinistes* were just arriving to lay out their displays of second-hand novels, obscure memoirs and dog-eared, pre-war magazines, but the quayside was already alive with people on their way to work, on foot and in carriages or taxi cabs with uniformed chauffeurs; many of these drivers, as Alberto knew from the newspapers, were White Russians who had once owned and driven their own automobiles. This was a spectacle the young artist was never to tire of whenever he walked through Paris: the mixture of elaborate horse-drawn carriages, reminiscent of the previous century, and the men pulling their own carts, piled precariously high with tools or bricks or produce, through the latest motorcars – the Peugeots, Renaults and Charrons, spiced up by the odd delectable Delage sports coupé. Cutting through these and adding to the overall spectacle were the boulangerie vans, delivering France's most staple food across the capital, and the stately autobuses, their open-back platforms tightly packed with passengers finishing a cigarette before hopping off with a well-practised, casual flourish. The rumble of carriage wheels and hooting of klaxons mingled with irate cries and the revving of engines. At every crossroad, the whole cacophonous symphony was conducted by an authoritative gendarme in navy blue cape and kepi.

The variety of people was even more fascinating and swiftly analysed by the young man's keen eye. Even Alberto, not yet aware of the subtle class distinctions that existed among Parisians, had no trouble in distinguishing the bourgeois from the workers. The difference was frequently underlined by the very hats they wore, with the lower classes attired almost to a man in cloth caps, and everyone else, from office employee to wealthy rentier, in headgear ranging from homburgs and trilbies in winter to a straw boater or Panama in summer. These conventions were even followed by avant-garde rebels such as filmmaker Luis Buñuel, who arrived in Paris in 1925 and later recalled wearing 'gaiters, a waistcoat with the fashionable four pockets, and a bowler hat'.[1] Where the sleek gentleman wore silk shirts and well-cut pinstripe suits, workers stood out by their coarse linen, tell-tale overalls and battered leather boots. This one clearly delivered coals while that youth's blood-spattered apron identified him as a butcher's apprentice.

Complex as his attitudes towards women and sexuality turned out to be, Alberto remained devoted to female beauty and elegance, and the Parisiennes who now surrounded him fully lived up to their reputation for avant-garde extravagance and drop-dead chic. Cleverer than the men in disguising their social status, many a seamstress or housemaid fingered their strings of pearls, their boas and cigarette holders with the insouciance of an heiress or a rich man's wife as they sat chatting, smoking and laughing at the little marble-topped café tables. Trudging past these alluring creatures in their distinctive cloche hats and breathing in their perfume, Alberto would not yet have been able to tell one pair of bee-stung lips from another, but the flat-chested '*garçonne*' look* and sporty, almost mannish attire so many of them affected, certainly struck home because he had heard talk about Paris as a cosmopolitan hotbed of Sapphism. The whole notion of same-sex love, in men or in women,

*Coco Chanel's 'little black dress' became all the rage from 1926 onwards.

came to intrigue him with its whiff of scandalous unconventionality and the courage it required to accept and practise its forbidden ways. Years later, Alberto would concur with his friend Michel Leiris when the distinguished writer (and possibly repressed homosexual) declared that 'perversions are above all a way of becoming more human'.

For all his mountaineer's stamina, Alberto was beginning to feel the strain from a night spent on the train and the suitcase that had begun to drag on him heavily, but he pressed further along the Left Bank, fascinated by the long barges piled high with coal, sand or wine barrels that slid past on the swollen Seine, and by the stately, ancient townhouses lining the quays of the Ile Saint-Louis. When the unmistakable silhouette of Notre-Dame de Paris suddenly filled the horizon with its massive towers, he let out an involuntary cry of excitement and stopped to take in the outlines of its huge roof and the succession of flying buttresses that leapt outwards like unleashed beasts about to crash into the river below. What transfixed Alberto most was the rose window, so much

Joseph-Philibert Girault de Prangey, the rose window of Notre-Dame Cathedral, 1841

larger and more magnificent than in the photographs he had seen in his father's library at home. It was like a vast, resplendent eye, a magnificent creation of faith that had witnessed the city's tumultuous history from the Middle Ages right up to the Great War and its aftermath that could still be felt throughout France. It was the eye of Paris and, as Alberto gazed at it, he felt not only entranced by its scintillating patterns and colours but deeply scrutinised by it himself.

The happy-go-lucky mood passed, leaving Alberto suddenly, uncomfortably, self-conscious. For the past couple of hours he had been wandering the streets like any carefree traveller, revelling in the sights and sounds of the city – the waiters swooping around the café tables with their trays of drinks held high, a short-lived spat between two pampered poodles, a stout lady in a wide-brimmed hat dodging comically through the heavy traffic to join a friend on the far pavement. Exhaust from the traffic was laced now with the thinner, penetrating aroma of coffee and the watery dankness of the Seine. Alberto breathed it in deeply – this was his first real smell of Paris. Everything he had seen and felt intrigued and amused him, but in the end none of it really concerned him. He would just be passing through, always passing through, and he didn't expect or really want anything more. He would stay a few months to study, as he had agreed with his parents, and his recent dissatisfaction with art school in Geneva had left him all the more eager to learn, to work hard, to understand and, above all, as he himself put it, 'to shine the light' on his own inner self and what he wanted from life. But not to settle, not to find comfortable lodgings – not to fit in and plan for stability and a lucrative career.

He thought back to the eye of Paris which had stopped him so abruptly and commandingly in his tracks. It knew as well as he did that there could be no settling down now, not after the terrible moment a few months ago when he had seen a man die before him, almost in his arms. He had never been face to face with death before, and the shock of being alone in a hotel room in the Alps with a cultivated older companion, a Dutch archivist called Pieter van Meurs, who had invited him on a trip to Venice, then died in his presence a couple of days after they had set out together. Van Meurs had spent his last night crying and writhing in agony from acute kidney disease. It had been terrifying. Once Van Meurs was dead, Alberto had wanted to quit the hotel immediately, leave the whole horror behind. But the policeman sent to investigate the death located a suspicious red mark on the chest of the dead man and detained Alberto for questioning, only eventually letting him go once natural causes had been confirmed.*

Life as Alberto had known it until then – a young man's life, full of promise, of discovery, pleasure and laughter – fell apart. He had seen death up close and how it moved, swiftly, without warning, turning a living person into an inanimate thing, its mouth hanging open, in a trice. This did not prevent him from continuing the trip to Venice alone, using the one thousand Swiss francs he had stolen from his father as a 'precaution'; no doubt he had wanted to ensure that, if he and Van Meurs fell out, he would not be destitute. He tried to blot out the terror – and perhaps the guilt – he felt by haunting certain cafés and pursuing as many girls as he could, then settling for the services of a prostitute. His fear was reflected in the dark, silent canals and intensified by the ancient façades behind which so many generations had lived and breathed before. In this city, eroding and sinking into its own history, death could come at any moment, to anyone. There was no way around it. From now on, he had no choice but to keep moving, from room to room, and always with a light on, burning through the night. It was the only way to wake up again in the morning. The only way to keep death at bay.

The wind whipping off the Seine felt even colder. Footsore, and with a suitcase that seemed much heavier, Alberto started to look more urgently for the boarding house where he would spend his first night. He was not going to stop some stranger and ask, though, because he always took pride in finding his own way wherever he was, even if that meant getting lost from time to time. His mother had taught him to be as strong and independent as she was, although he – in ways of which he, her eldest and favourite child, was barely conscious – remained totally and uniquely dependent on her; and even when he was abroad, contact with her, and her approval, was to dominate every turn he took. It was so natural, so ingrained, that he never questioned or thought

*How did the red mark the police discovered occur, and why should they have detained Alberto? Had Van Meurs made a pass at the attractive young man and been violently, even fatally, repulsed? It is most unlikely, yet the reasons for Alberto's detention have never been fully ascertained.

about the dependency, even though it was to colour all his relationships with women, causing him unconsciously to flee steady commitments while elevating streetwalkers into goddesses.

Like other *pensions de famille* and little hotels where Alberto was to lodge briefly over the following few months, the modest establishment where he spent his first few nights in Paris rented out small rooms with basic amenities and little privacy. At the start, before he began to find his way around the Left Bank, Alberto took the half-pension on offer and sat down with the other *pensionnaires* for breakfast and dinner, filling up in between on half a baguette and a piece of cheese. Post-war rationing was still in force, with strict limits on both bread and meat, unless you had friends on the make and on the take who could sell you the extra mound of butter or leg of lamb. Wine, the other great French staple, proved less of a problem since the country produced it in such quantities, and its qualities had been so lauded that it had been doled out in liberal daily doses to the French troops to keep their spirits up during the recent conflict. Although naturally sociable beneath his reserve, Alberto soon tired of these awkward repasts and lost no time in rooting out the best cheap cafés and bistros in the area where he could be fed anonymously.

After a spell in another boarding house just off rue Mouffetard, Alberto found lodgings at the Hôtel Notre-Dame by the Seine on Quai Saint-Michel, then at the Hôtel de la Paix, not far from boulevard du Montparnasse on the more staid and bourgeois boulevard Raspail. These small hotels, less comfortable than they would be today, had the great advantage that they let students draw and paint in their rooms as long as they kept them clean and paid the rent on time. They also gave them the freedom to come and go as they pleased, which was particularly important for Alberto since he had already located certain interesting streets nearby, notably the shadowy rue Delambre, where prostitutes gathered in the doorways at night, providing him with the kind of quick, unsentimental transaction that was to become a lifelong habit. Brought up in Calvinist Switzerland, Alberto was surprised at first to find how easy-going relationships between men and women seemed in Paris, with casual flirtations starting in the bus or on café terraces with all the world to see. Despite his talent for creating scandal, the young Buñuel, who became a good friend of Alberto's, recalled a similar reaction: 'When I went to France for the first time in 1925, I was shocked, in fact disgusted,

Henri Manuel, Antoine Bourdelle in his workshop with a model, around 1900

by the men and women I saw kissing in public, or living together without the sanction of marriage. Such customs were unimaginable to me; they seemed obscene ... with rare exceptions, we Spaniards knew of only two ways to make love – in a brothel or in marriage.'*

Nocturnal prowls apart, Alberto had a strong sense of duty: he never forgot that the prime motive for his being in Paris at all was to study, and the Académie de la Grande Chaumière, the well-established art school where he had enrolled in the life drawing and sculpture class of Antoine Bourdelle, was as close to his hotel as rue Delambre, if not as instantly seductive. Bourdelle, who had very slightly altered his unfortunate birth name of Bordelles ('bordellos' or 'whorehouses'), had once been a principal assistant to Auguste Rodin and, by the time Alberto joined his class, he was nearing the end of a distinguished career as, alongside Aristide Maillol and Charles Despiau, one of

*Buñuel was also struck by the fact that there were some 45,000 artists living in Paris, mostly in Montparnasse, and that, owing to the devaluation of the French franc against the peseta at that time, he was able to drink champagne like water.

France's most recognised sculptors. He also enjoyed a reputation as an exceptional teacher, attracting pupils (including a young Henri Matisse) to the Grande Chaumière from all over the world. Bourdelle's teaching method consisted mainly of weekly correction sessions, when he would appear in a grey smock and deliver long, lofty monologues to his students – on topics such as the primacy of the intellect over the visual – while moving through the maze of modelling stands where their recent efforts were displayed. A photograph of the time shows the elderly, grave-looking master posing among his mainly female students attired in similar smocks gathered around a naked model. Characteristically, a sturdily independent, smockless Alberto stands like the proverbial bad boy, half-cropped, at the back of the teaching studio.

Bourdelle's own work was deeply influenced by Rodin's fluid naturalism, but around 1900 he had established his own style which combined a classical sense of symmetry and realism with the purified forms of Art Deco. As an independent artist, his aesthetic interests ranged far wider than his grandiloquently classical sculpture – which included numerous busts of Beethoven – might suggest, since they extended from Mesopotamian and Egyptian sculpture to non-Western art and even Cubism. In these influences Bourdelle saw a healthy corrective to the overbearing legacy of the last century's academic *pompier* painters such as William-Adolphe Bouguereau and Jean-Léon Gérôme. Although Alberto grew increasingly irritated by his teacher's didactic verbosity, comparing it unfavourably to the more natural, hands-on instruction he had received from his father since boyhood,* he followed Bourdelle's classes regularly for the next three years, then began to drop in occasionally over the following two years until he tailed off completely. As gratified as he had been when Bourdelle singled out his prowess at drawing in front of the whole class, Alberto openly contested his negative view of working from a model, which remained central to the younger artist's practice throughout his life; he was also unimpressed by what he saw of his master's own work. 'Bourdelle did not give me much,'[2] he later claimed, yet comparisons

*Albrecht Dürer's dictum – 'Art is embedded in nature; he who can extract it, has it' – was instilled in Alberto early on when he began working under his father's eye. Indeed, Alberto had been named after Dürer, as his brother Diego was after Velázquez.

have been drawn between the older artist's tall, slender figure of *Madeleine Charnaux* (1917) and Alberto's *Women of Venice* (1956), as well as the experiments they both made with polychromy. Certainly, Bourdelle's insistence on the primacy of drawing and the relevance of the art of the past left its mark on Alberto, confirming two of his lasting, core beliefs.

On Sundays, when the Grande Chaumière was closed and museum entry was free, Alberto made regular excursions over the Seine to the Louvre. Although he seldom strayed far from Montparnasse, he took every opportunity to spend time in this vast, sombre palace and explore a collection of art and antiquities that rivalled even the treasures he had discovered in Rome. The Louvre was to become a second home for Alberto, a public treasure house where he could study and sketch undisturbed the artistic achievements of the past. Question Bourdelle's opinions and attitudes as he increasingly did (while remaining exultant in his letters home whenever his teacher commended his recent efforts), Alberto's admiration knew no bounds as he walked down the Louvre's Grande Galerie, where he could marvel at the succession of masterpieces concentrated in the museum's extraordinary vistas. Used to copying works in reproduction by Dürer and Rembrandt that had fired his imagination ever since he was allowed into his father's studio at home, the young student soon set himself up to copy some of the Louvre's sublime masterpieces from the original, including Cimabue's *Virgin Surrounded by Angels*, Mantegna's *Saint Sebastian* and a magnificent Titian *Self-Portrait*.*

Having paid homage to the Italian masters, Alberto allowed himself to be drawn into the further recesses of Louis XIV's former home, making a beeline for the sculpture and paintings of ancient Egypt which, like many artists, he considered the greatest artistic achievement of all time. He sketched Egyptian figures and heads obsessively, copying not only what he saw in the Louvre but works he found reproduced from other major collections. At that precise moment, all things Egyptian were very much in the news since Tutankhamun's nearly intact tomb had

*Alberto continued to copy the work of past masters, from the Egyptians to Cézanne, throughout his life. Some of the best examples to have survived are reproduced in Luigi Carluccio, *Giacometti: A Sketch Book of Interpretive Drawing*, New York, 1968.

been discovered in November 1922. Alberto was also fascinated by the museum's thin, stylised and mostly female Cycladic 'idols', but it was Sumerian art that came as the great revelation – in particular a head of Gudea, the legendary ruler of Lagash, dating back more than two thousand years before Christ. With its pronounced frontality and fixed, blank stare, the sculpture cast a spell over Alberto, who not only sketched it obsessively but bought a plaster cast of it from the Louvre. The head remained with him, either on his desk in the studio or under it, and he regularly referred to the cast as a prototype, a point of comparison with whatever sculpture he had under way. In later life Alberto frequently commented on the lasting influence this ancient head exercised on him:

> Along with Egyptian sculpture, Sumerian sculpture has great style. I very much admired it for years and it was one of my great discoveries when I saw Sumerian works in the Louvre for the first time. For at least one whole winter I went every Sunday and looked at nothing else … For me they were … the closest to reality. The construction of the head seemed truer to me than Roman portrait busts which are not visual but conceptual art.[3]

Alberto also borrowed a human skull, drawing and painting it with characteristic obsessiveness rather than attending his courses at the Grande Chaumière throughout most of a desolate, depressed winter. But however rooted he was in the great tradition of Western and ancient art, the young sculptor remained open to a whole world of artistic styles, from Byzantine mosaics to the African and Oceanic art much admired in Paris since Derain and Matisse, Picasso and Ernst had begun collecting it and incorporating some of its powerful motifs into their work.[*] Once he had come across the dusty displays of such art at the Musée de l'Ethnographie du Trocadéro (renamed the Musée de l'homme in 1937) and seen other pieces in art dealers' windows – the influential gallerist Pierre Loeb became an enthusiastic collector – or picked up by friends in flea markets, Alberto was deeply struck by the direct expressive force pulsating from the masks and other so-called 'primitive' objects. Although he was never to become a collector like

[*] In 1929, the influential *Cahiers d'art* devoted their second issue to Oceanic art.

many other artists, he did buy a handsome Kota reliquary figure* from Serge Brignoni, a fellow Swiss and one of his friends at the Grande Chaumière, which took pride of place on his desk. The influence of non-western imagery on Alberto's own sculpture was absorbed early on, freeing him from his instinctive adherence to classical tradition in the formative pieces that the young artist was to produce later, such as *The Couple*, introducing a dialogue between the sexes explored in several subsequent sculptures and leading directly to one of his early, noted successes, *Spoon Woman*.

Alberto's first few years in Paris were marked by periods of intense homesickness, normal enough in a young newcomer to the city, but exacerbated by his aloofness and the regular intervals when he returned to Switzerland for a stint of national service in the mountain infantry corps or to the Val Bregaglia for Christmas and, above all, the summer. Although his mountain upbringing had prepared him for a solitary existence, he welcomed these periods back home and the visits his father paid to Paris, revisiting old haunts from his student days in the 1890s and, sportingly enough, joining Alberto's fellow students in their classes at the Grande Chaumière.

Meanwhile, Alberto's domestic arrangements had taken a notable upturn. Archipenko, the Ukrainian sculptor, allowed him to sublet his spacious studio just behind Montparnasse, at 77 rue (later avenue) Denfert-Rochereau, with its view over the Observatoire gardens, while he was away in Berlin. Alberto was overjoyed to have a real Parisian atelier of his own for the first time (and not least since the peppercorn rent of 100 francs a year left his monthly allowance of 1,000 francs per month virtually intact). 'I've often tried to imagine you in your studio,' his mother wrote to him from Stampa. 'I can see you putting coals into your stove with a big mess all around. I'd like to make your bed for you, I'd probably be cross with you while loving you nevertheless.'[4] The new arrangement was unfortunately not to last because, when Archipenko emigrated to the United States not long after, Alberto was obliged to find new premises.

*Used to protect the bones of ancestors, these figures played a pivotal role in initiation ceremonies in Gabon.

He moved again in January 1925, this time to a smaller, low-ceilinged working space on the upper floor of 37 rue Froidevaux, a hangar-like building recently transformed into makeshift studios that looked out onto Montparnasse Cemetery. Its previous occupant, Marcel Duchamp, had found the studio 'impossible and cold', but once again the low rent left enough of Alberto's allowance over to pay for models to come occasionally to pose for him there. Never one to complain about discomfort, Alberto might have found solace in seeing Brancusi's *The Kiss*, a sculpture he admired, and indeed the only avant-garde sculpture in a public place in Paris, sited among the graves.* The radically simplified, proto-Cubist forms of Brancusi's sculpture, combined with its emotional, erotic content, had a marked impact on Alberto, who saw in the older master a model of what a modern sculptor could achieve. Like the more traditional Bourdelle, Brancusi had been a student in Rodin's studio, where he had stayed only two months, having concluded that 'nothing grows in the shade of great trees', a conviction that fuelled his breakaway stylistic experiments.

By this time, the young Alberto was beginning to find his feet, at least in the small area he frequented around the Vavin crossroads, with its two imposing brasseries, La Rotonde and Le Dôme, and another big, smart-looking café, Le Select, further down boulevard du Montparnasse. With his knack for being in the right place at the right time, Alberto had chosen to live and study in Montparnasse just as its reputation as the centre of avant-garde art was being reaffirmed almost daily. As if to prove the point, another famous brasserie, La Coupole, was to open with great fanfare opposite Le Select in December 1927, providing a large terrace and a huge restaurant for everyone who was anyone in the arts, as well as their many admirers and hangers-on. In a few years, La Coupole was synonymous with Montparnasse and everything that was new in Paris, and for Alberto it quickly turned into a club, where he could drop in and be sure to find people he knew or chat to the waiters and catch up on local gossip.

If close friends had at first proved elusive, Alberto began to talk more openly with a few of his fellow students, occasionally dining with them at a tiny, modest Italian restaurant called Chez Rosalie on

*This is one of several versions of *The Kiss* (c. 1907–08), widely referred to as the 'first modern sculpture' of the twentieth century.

rue Campagne-Première originally much favoured by Apollinaire, Max Jacob and Modigliani. The meals cooked and served by Rosalie, a former artist's model, consisted mainly of minestrone and spaghetti with tomato sauce, but they were filling and the conversation was often boisterous and good fun. Alberto felt all the more at ease in this company because none of the students were French, so he wasn't embarrassed by his own faltering command of the language, which did not become fluent for another couple of years. In fact, he was taken aback by how few French students there were at the Grande Chaumière, the most noticeable one being Pierre Matisse (son of the famous painter, himself a former student), who later became Alberto's doughty New York dealer. He also bemoaned the difficulty of getting to know French people: it's like 'running into a wall', he said. Other students found him by turns warm and communicative, then distant and self-absorbed: a serious, self-critical 'genius' who would either go very far or go mad. With his long arms and large hands, they joked, Alberto could also scratch his knees without needing to reach down.

Despite his continued incursions into the seamier side of French life, Alberto formed other, more respectable relationships with the opposite sex. Letters continued to arrive from his cousin Bianca in Rome who, despite her initial rejection of Alberto's advances, had come to see him in a rosier light now that he was far away. When they met again in Switzerland, she allowed him to carve his initial, a small capital A, into her arm with a penknife, drawing blood in the process; their passion for each other was never assuaged sexually, however. Back in Paris, Alberto also began an intense liaison with Flora Mayo, an American art student from Denver, that lasted – with flare-ups over Alberto's diffidence and Flora's infidelities – until she left France in 1929. The quasi-caricatural plaster *Head* that Alberto produced of Flora in 1926 unerringly reflects the ambiguities of their affair; meanwhile, its touches of polychromy – red lips, blue eyes, blonde hair – can be traced back to the young artist's interest in Egyptian art and his desire to bring painting and sculpture together again. The relationship made Alberto all the more conscious of his complicated feelings and notably the difficulties he had in reconciling the brute urge of sex with the emotional need for tenderness and understanding. A recent encounter with a prostitute whom he had taken to his studio left him triumphant: 'It's cold! It's mechanical!', he exulted in a notebook at the time. Later, he continued to talk about his sexual preferences frankly and openly, even in interviews:

> I've always felt very deficient sexually. That's why, when I arrived in Paris in 1922, I kept avoiding love affairs. It's also why I've always preferred going with prostitutes. The first woman I had was a prostitute. It suited me. The whole idea of 'love' with its muddled, sticky mix of feeling and physicality has always bothered me. With a prostitute, having sex is clearly mechanical, with no emotions involved ... You see, when you have problems with impotence, prostitutes are ideal. You pay, and it doesn't matter whether you can do it or not. She couldn't care less.[5]

Driven partly by performance anxiety, Alberto's attitude to women recalls what Sigmund Freud termed the Madonna–whore complex that he believed existed in men who struggle to reconcile arousal and emotion (sex and love) and so seek sexual contact exclusively with women they already consider to be debased, while reserving admiration, even devotion, for women they consider to be pure. This misogynistic binary defined Alberto's romantic encounters throughout his life. But the key difference between his attitude and Freud's formulation is that Alberto did greatly, even obsessively, admire many of the prostitutes he knew, not least for their sexual freedom, which represented the antithesis of his Protestant, bourgeois, no-sex-before-marriage upbringing.

A stabilising factor as Alberto ricocheted between the facility of bought love and the complexities of shared love in his life in Paris was the arrival of Diego, his tough, taciturn younger brother. Diego's tendency to veer towards making easy money from such illicit activities as smuggling contraband cigarettes had sufficiently worried Annetta, the boys' mother, to ask her eldest son to take his semi-delinquent sibling in hand and try to get him back on the straight and narrow. Since the rue Froidevaux studio, while within easy walking distance of the Académie, was too small for both boys to live in, Alberto found Diego a cheap room nearby, thereby confirming what would be, alongside his devotion to his mother, the most stable relationship in his life as well as in his career. The two brothers had always been unusually close, with Diego agreeing to serve as Alberto's model even (albeit unwillingly and with tantrums) as a child. Like the entire Giacometti family, Diego recognised Alberto's exceptional talent from an early age, and he did more than his own share of household chores so that his elder brother could concentrate on making pictures. This was the role Diego would continue to play more faithfully and consistently than any of Alberto's other regular models. He would also undertake all the more practical tasks of building the armatures for sculptures and making the bases for them as well as overseeing their casting into bronze at the foundry and applying the most suitable patinas to each new work.

In the short term, it proved difficult to keep Diego out of trouble: he had a natural talent for getting involved in whatever shady scheme promised to provide for his pleasures. Strikingly good-looking, with a taste for sharp suits and gangsterish fedora hats, Diego had already established himself as a ladies' man and knew (unlike his brother) not only how to show a girl a good time but also how to sustain a stable emotional relationship, as he did with a long-term, live-in girlfriend called Nelly Constantin.[*] But once the brothers had evolved their close working routine, Diego avoided or countered anything that might threaten it, deepening the fraternal bond by taking on such extra responsibilities as advising on works that Alberto had under way as well as on his brother's relations with dealers and other art world business matters.[†] In the meantime, Diego continued to sit for his demanding brother, who liked to keep to a strict pattern of drawing a full-length figure in the morning, either at the Grande Chaumière or (if he could afford a professional model) in his own studio; then, in the afternoon, Alberto would concentrate on modelling busts. Neither brother strayed often from their Montparnasse 'village': going to Montmartre seemed like a major excursion, Diego remarks in a letter home, while Alberto adds that 'on the rare occasions I cross the Seine, it feels as if I've come back to Paris after a long absence and all the commotion takes me by surprise, as if I were seeing it for the first time. Here we are almost … in the countryside.'[6]

[*]Long referred to simply as 'Nelly' in Giacometti literature, new research has established that a Nelly Constantin was living with Diego Giacometti at 51 bis, rue du Moulin-Vert, the building at the far end of the rue Hippolyte studio complex.

[†]Samuel Beckett, who became a close friend of Alberto's, once compared the relationship between him and Diego to that of Vincent and Theo van Gogh.

Amid the disruptions and adjustments that forging a new life in a new city entailed, there was one that preoccupied Alberto more deeply and constantly than any other. He wanted 'to shine the light' on himself, which in his terms meant finding not only what kind of person he was but, above all, what kind of artist he could be. He had absorbed neo-Impressionism from his father, who was heavily influenced by earlier painters such as Seurat and Gauguin and who used dazzling colour combinations, small divisionist dots of paint and classically informed compositions. With his father Alberto was able to discuss not only his own aspirations but some of the crazier sounding aspects of the avant-garde: most notably Dada, the movement that encouraged extreme manifestations of the absurd and had originated in staid if relatively cosmopolitan Zurich. From boyhood, Alberto had applied himself diligently to copying every image that fired his imagination, from Snow White in her coffin and other fairy tales to the engravings of Old Masters. He tackled one subject after another, showing off his skills. 'I thought I was great,' Alberto said later, recalling his prowess at the age of ten. 'I thought I could do everything with the wonderful techniques of drawing, that I could copy absolutely anything and that I understood it better than anyone else.'[7]

But even for a young man as fluent in every classical mode as Alberto became after his idyllic apprenticeship in his father's studio, Paris presented a bewildering kaleidoscope of styles, with new '-isms' being bandied around, and usually mocked – on café terraces and in art schools as well as in the newspapers. After Alberto began to abandon observational processes in 1925, this array of artistic directions suddenly opened up to him; he would in the following years sample, or at least take some inspiration from, almost all of the major currents in modern art.

Fauvism, faint echoes of Expressionism and Cubism had already unfurled like so many waves over the city's intellectual horizon, to be followed by Constructivism, Orphism (a purely abstract offshoot of Cubism) and Futurism. Most significantly, the tsunami of Surrealism, welling up out of a radical rejection of the recent war-torn past, was about to be unleashed on an unsuspecting public. As he was searching for himself and for his style, Alberto remained unusually receptive to what was in the air but also highly selective, enthusing about certain trends and artists as well as dismissing others and debating the overall aesthetic confusion of the times in his regular letters home. 'I see a lot of modern stuff,' he wrote to his parents in January 1925, 'but it's a bit like the Tower of Babel. There are so many different things, going off in all directions, that it's difficult to get a clear overview.'[8]

Both son and father, united above all in their admiration for the great classical masters and for Cézanne, had rejected Dada 'nonsense' out of hand. But early on in his Parisian existence Alberto had established a number of contemporary cultural heroes, notably the older painters André Derain and Georges Braque and the sculptor Henri Laurens, to all of whom he was to pay his respects and later write admiring tributes.[9] Also very much in evidence were two other émigré sculptors whom Alberto ran into in the group exhibitions to which he was beginning to contribute occasionally, as well as in the big Montparnasse cafés: Jacques Lipchitz and Ossip Zadkine. Both invited the budding young artist to their studios and showered him with advice, and both would later claim to have had the more decisive impact on Alberto's increasingly successful development, with Lipchitz even referring to him as his 'pupil'. Alberto produced a number of sculptures under their influence in 1926–27, including the impressive bronze *Cubist Composition (Man)*. As is typical of Cubist works, the ambiguity of the forms is juxtaposed with the literal nature of other signs, with the abstracted shapes of the figure's body elucidated by a carved circle on the face denoting its eye. Even if the young sculptor quickly moved on from this approach, the achievements of Cubism – its innovative simplification of forms and use of the relations between different elements to concoct reality – would significantly influence Alberto's interwar work, as it would almost all twentieth-century art.

By the following year Alberto had already changed course by combining his admiration for Brancusi with his deepening interest in both African and Cycladic art to create seminal works like *Spoon Woman* (which Lipchitz claimed Alberto had deliberately predated to make it look more 'advanced' than his own work). Another sculpture from this period, *The Couple*, makes the non-western influence especially clear; the two flat, upright forms appear like totems, with their genders efficiently clarified by discrete symbols. Exhibiting these radically simplified forms at the vast Salon des Tuileries in April 1927 brought Alberto a new degree of recognition, enabling him to stand out

Horst Tappe, Jacques Lipchitz, 1970

from the rank and file.* Here Alberto's work was already being presented beside some of Paris's more prominent contemporary artists, a point he did not fail to underline in a letter to his doting family: 'I am in the Salon's most modern room which this year they've put in the middle, near the big, sculpture room. I think it's the most interesting room, the one that makes the biggest impression. In the middle there's a sculpture by Brancusi in polished metal. On one side there's a Zadkine, and I'm on the other side. On the wall there are some big pictures by Léger and Gleizes, amongst others.'[10] In the same letter, Alberto comes back to Brancusi's *Bird in Space*, calling it 'the best thing' in the Salon, indeed the only thing better than his *Spoon Woman*, then criticises it for being overly worked, with 'its beautiful metal polished like a mirror', while dismissing Brancusi himself for being 'already old, with a white beard'. He was nevertheless sufficiently impressed by the gleaming sculpture to make a drawing of it in his sketchbook next to his own *Spoon Woman* which, melding influences from Brancusi and Lipchitz to the large figure

*There were some two thousand other entries at the Salon.

spoons used in Dan (Ivory Coast) ceremonies, he rightly considered to be his most accomplished sculpture yet.

Never one to withhold praise for his son, Giovanni congratulated Alberto in a letter, saying, 'it was my dream to conquer Paris, but now it is you who is doing it with your sculpture'.[11] The new works marked how far Alberto had already distanced himself not only from his flirtation with Cubism but from the academic precepts of Bourdelle, whose florid statuary would have seemed by comparison even more rooted in the traditions of the late nineteenth century. Bourdelle, one of the founders of the Salon, was reportedly not best pleased by certain Modernist contributions, commenting acidly, 'one does something like that at home, for oneself, but one does not show it'.

Picasso had already taken up a prominent position in Alberto's pantheon of admired artists, to the extent that he wrote to his parents saying that he thought Picasso's work the 'best modern things I've seen since I've been in Paris', adding proudly that he had recently been introduced to the poet Max Jacob and stressing how close the latter was to Picasso. The two artists were not to meet until 1931, but Alberto, like so many artists in Paris, followed Picasso's development closely, making a point of attending the exhibitions put on by his exclusive dealer, Paul Rosenberg, who had rented an apartment for Picasso to live and work in with Olga, his ballerina wife, next door to his gallery on posh rue La Boétie. Alberto could not have failed to be impressed that Picasso, by now approaching mid-career, appeared to be the name on everyone's lips in the art world while enjoying an enviably privileged lifestyle.

Twenty years younger and less self-assured and flamboyant than the Spaniard, Alberto was just beginning to feel out what direction his life might take. Not unlike Picasso, he had been devoted to art and to his own singular talent since early childhood, but his interests were notably varied. As his French improved and he became more familiar with Paris and its distinct, codified ways, he began to emerge from his shell and take a more active part in not only the artistic but also the political discussions that were often begun with friends at the Grande Chaumière and continued in the Montparnasse cafés afterwards. Alberto's interest in literature had always been strong, and he had been encouraged both at home and at school to read widely. As with art, his curiosity was boundless, and he ranged effortlessly between classical and contemporary, novels and poetry, history and philosophy, including such demanding (and fashionable) world views as Hegel's. Alberto also began writing, not only a voluminous correspondence back home, but ideas and reflections that came to him between bouts of work in the studio or in idle moments when he could no longer focus on drawing or modelling. This was an interest that was to grow impressively over the following years, leading to highly personal, imaginative texts that were published in the leading avant-garde reviews.

Alberto's desire to make his mark was predicated strictly on his own terms. Admire Picasso as he did, he already knew that, even if he could, his temperament would not allow him to follow the latter's well-publicised road to success. At the same time he was growing increasingly conscious of the need to carve out his own path. 'I never wanted to play the artist and make a career,' he admitted later. 'I was in the position of a young man who sort of makes a few tries to see what happens. As long as my father supported me I never even thought of making art my career. But about 1926 or 1927 my father said I should try to stand on my own two feet.'[12] Independent by nature, Alberto did not need telling twice.

To be twenty-five years old and free in the most enticing city in the world made other claims even on as serious-minded a student as Alberto. Like any young person let loose in the metropolis with a little spare cash, Alberto dedicated himself sometimes exclusively to the pursuit of pleasure. When he could no longer stomach Mère Rosalie's spaghetti, there were plenty of inexpensive local bistros where he and Diego could tuck into the more substantial, traditional French dishes they enjoyed, such as boeuf bourguignon and blanquette de veau. When a new month's allowance came in, Alberto ventured further down boulevard du Montparnasse to La Coupole, which everybody in Paris was curious to see after some two thousand people had flocked to the opening of its fashionable Art Deco interior, spilling out onto its spacious terrace to show off the latest fashions, chatter animatedly and drink house champagne. Being mountain-bred and cautious with their money, the brothers perhaps avoided the new brasserie's celebratory seafood platters on crushed ice, plumping instead for a more homely choucroute.

Opposite, the other pillar of Montparnasse life, Le Select, had fast become a central rendezvous for the city's queer men – the 'sons of Sodom', as they were poetically described – who also congregated at Magic-City, a huge dance hall on rue de l'Université famous for its extravagant masked balls. If Alberto wanted to indulge his youthful curiosity further, several establishments, such as Le Monocle, founded by the colourful, cross-dressing Lulu de Montparnasse, also catered to lesbians. Brassaï, the photographer who excelled in capturing the secrets of Paris by night, shows us many a willowy lipstick lesbian being swept round the dance floor by ambiguous-looking partners with close-cropped hair and wearing sober, manly suits. Others in full tuxedo gaze out at these antics from the bar, their world-weary allure offset, naturally, by a monocle.

Throughout Alberto's early years in Paris, the city was known not only as the undisputed capital of the arts but as an unusually tolerant haven for deviants of every stripe as well as anyone else partial to or driven by the pleasures of the flesh. Paris breathed freedom and creativity, and many foreigners, notably Americans, who could afford to flocked to the city to enjoy its liberality. Alongside Montparnasse's thriving café life, various hotspots sprang up to cater for this 'Lost Generation' of writers, artists and assorted thrill-seekers. The Jockey* became the place where Parisian celebrities such as Marcel Duchamp, Dada founder Tristan Tzara, Jean Cocteau, Ezra Pound and Man Ray, as well as Kiki de Montparnasse, artists' model and muse, could rub shoulders with expatriates while watching others feverishly dance the foxtrot and shimmy in varying degrees of undress, while 'Abbé' Ernest de Gengenbach – Satanist and defrocked priest, one-time Surrealist and well-known Montparnasse eccentric – let rip to the jazz music wearing a cassock dyed in outrageous hues and decked out with a red carnation. The Jockey was later replaced by the Jungle Club, undergoing a notable change of décor, while the bar at the Dingo Club, run by a retired boxer from Liverpool, counted Picasso among its clients and brought Ernest Hemingway and F. Scott Fitzgerald together for the first time, just after *The Great Gatsby* had been published.†

*Alberto mentions the Jockey, wondering whether to take a girlfriend there, in one of his early letters. This club is not to be confused with the exclusively aristocratic club of the same name at the other end of town which counted Alberto's early patron, Charles de Noailles, as one of its members until he was excluded for having financed Luis Buñuel's scandalous film *L'Age d'or*.

†In more sober moments, Fitzgerald and Hemingway would get together at the modest but essential meeting place for all English-language writers in Paris: Sylvia Beach's lending library and bookshop, Shakespeare & Company, not far away on rue de l'Odéon.

Alberto would not be a regular at such international high jinks – he was still too young, too insecure and too needy – but like any good 'Montparno', as people living in the area were called, he was already beginning to think of it as 'his' *quartier*, his village even, because everyone knew everybody else, at least by sight and by reputation. The latest local news – bars or exhibitions opening, scandals and divorces, books or manifestos being published – swiftly did the rounds. And although he was yet to become a nightbird, Alberto did occasionally get mixed up with the Montparnasse jet set, as when he was invited by Caresse Crosby, known not only as the 'godmother' of the Lost Generation in Paris but also as the inventor of the 'modern bra', to celebrate her birthday along with other artists at the Canard amoureux.

What haunted Alberto now and throughout his life was not high society, although he later had his notable moments there; nor, being already hooked on cigarettes and coffee, was he especially drawn to alcohol or opium, the latter then the drug of choice, but to the grand, inexhaustible mystery – the fleeting shadow under a streetlamp, the alluring silhouette cooing in the doorway – of prostitutes. Unsure of his ability to perform the sexual act fully, satisfactorily, as he might be, he spent many a night crisscrossing the 'hot' streets of Montparnasse around rue Delambre and its tributaries full of little hotels where rooms could be rented by the hour, in search of the ideal woman, both 'goddess' and 'whore', with whom he felt so much more himself and at ease than with any 'normal' girl. This chase, stalking the streetwalker like an exotic animal until she found a new client and disappeared 'upstairs', left the young man both crushed and elated, cursing himself for not carrying off the prize but secretly relieved that he was not to be put to the test, then carrying on, spotting a new prey, obsessed by the illusion of intimacy, release, happiness.

In thrall to the truth, as much about himself as the world he was trying to understand and record, Alberto made no secret of his obsession. 'All my walks, my wanderings, across Paris at night were in search of prostitutes,' he freely admitted. 'I was obsessed by prostitutes, other women simply didn't exist, only prostitutes attracted me and dazzled me, I wanted to see them all, know them all, and night after night I set off on my long, lonely trails.' A fascination for these creatures of the night never left him. Unlike the other women he was to meet socially, they were mysterious,

Brassaï, sex worker in Paris, 1932

unknowable. Alongside the mysterious, unknowable domain of art, they were to remain his touchstone and obsession.

Towards the end of 1926, the need to be independent – to 'stand on his own two feet', as he put it – caught up with Alberto. Like Duchamp before him, he was finding his miserable studio increasingly irksome, not least because of its view onto the Montparnasse Cemetery, where in summer a luminescent blue gas could be seen hovering ominously over the graves. Like any self-respecting sculptor, he needed a ground-floor space to facilitate delivery of materials and transport of finished work as well, he hoped, as visits from interested art dealers and potential collectors. Talk at the Grande Chaumière often centred around who had just left or found a great new space, and after visiting a couple that were available Alberto settled without much conviction on a room in a rickety building in Alésia, a modest *quartier* just behind the glamorous cafés and 'American' bars of Montparnasse.

It was to be a temporary solution, after all. The whole damp, ramshackle building at 46 rue Hippolyte-Maindron, where not only artists but varied artisans had tried to eke out a living, looked as if it might collapse during a storm, and the studio itself was too run down and too poky – smaller than either of Alberto's previous two spaces – for anyone to want to stay there for long. It was no better than a 'hole', Alberto said dismissively, but he said it with a certain sly satisfaction. Given the chance, Alberto loved being contradictory. So, here he was, a promising young sculptor eager to gain attention and become his own man, burying himself in a dump where no one would want to set foot. Poor Alberto, people around would say, with all his lofty artistic dreams! But there was another reason, deeper than the pleasure of paradox. As a child, Alberto loved to crawl into the smallest openings in the mountainsides and hide there. In an early autobiographical text, 'Yesterday, Shifting Sands', he describes how 'what gave me the greatest joy was when I could crouch in the small cave at the back: it was barely big enough for me: all my dreams had come true'.[13] The darker and deeper the nook, the safer he felt. At some level, he sensed, this studio was like those tight mountain caves. He would be protected there, free to live and work without outside interference, on his own terms alone. In any case, it would only be for a while. Then he would move on again. He would always move on, never stay anywhere for long and accumulate habits and possessions. He later proclaimed that he would 'rather live in hotels, cafés, places where people come and go'.[14] Seeing the Dutchman Van Meurs die before his eyes had made any notion he might 'settle' impossible – ridiculous. What could be the point? We would all die, and any of us might, at any moment. No one would want to stay in the rue Hippolyte studio anyway. It was a dump, just a 'hole' that he and Diego would crawl into, just like they had as children in the Val Bregaglia.

On 1 December, Diego helped his brother load their possessions, consisting mostly of Alberto's sculptures, paintings and materials, onto a simple wooden handcart and trundled it a short mile into the anonymous, grey hinterland behind Montparnasse. Once there, they surveyed their new home and their faces slowly creased in a smile, as if sharing a silent joke. How horrified their mother would be if she knew! The Giacometti boys were tough and clever, and they had come through all sorts of scrapes together. But to take on a dump like this and make it work might have been just a step too far.

2

Rue Hippolyte (1926–30)

For anyone determined to keep moving, never settling anywhere, the studio at 46 rue Hippolyte-Maindron* seemed ideal. Run up out of builders' oddments on the ground floor of a hodgepodge of artisans' workshops and zinc-roofed lean-tos, its general air of decay and desolation had 'short stay' written all over it.† Rather than an artist's studio, it looked like the sort of place that locals might once have used to get their kitchen chairs re-caned or a pair of old boots patched up and, at one point, a cobbler did indeed ply his trade there. The interior was small and dank, with a beaten-earth floor and neither running water nor electricity, although that would hardly surprise someone from Val Bregaglia, where most peasant dwellings also lacked such basic amenities. Gas jets, introduced by Baron Haussmann in the previous century, gave out what dim, flickering light was available after nightfall. The communal toilet was located in the little alleyway outside the studio, and a nearby tap provided water for washing or cooking. Since Alberto seldom washed and never cooked, that was hardly a problem. Back inside in the studio, however, the high, rotting roof let the rain in from an ever-varying number of cracks and holes.

*The street takes its name from a worthy but now forgotten nineteenth-century sculptor.
†The only other influential artist believed to have taken a studio in the building was Jean Fautrier, who arrived in 1923 and left in 1926, before Alberto moved in. Recent research has confirmed that, at various times, Victor Brauner, Stanley Hayter, Yves Tanguy and Zao Wou-Ki were also resident in the studio complex.

Even at a time when artists might be used to harsh living conditions, the new space on which Alberto was about to sign the lease was not only primitive, making his two previous studios look almost comfortable, but gave out all the wrong signals for a sculptor trying to make his way in the fickle, fashionable capital of France. The private joke the brothers had shared of taking on such a run-down place soon wore thin once the realities of domestic life in the studio began to hit home. The worst was the extreme cold, which even two lads accustomed to long mountain winters found challenging. But they had a family reputation for resilience to defend: their grandfather, also called Alberto and a baker by trade, had been known to put his bread in the oven, run up the mountainside in all weathers to slaughter a cow and be back in time to take his perfectly baked, golden loaves out. Both boys were loath to complain about hardship, yet Alberto could not refrain from sending the following report home: 'The water is frozen everywhere. As soon as we are up, we get the fire going, and it's only then that I can think of how I should get myself properly dressed and washed.'[1] That was the way he began the day: first dressing (and always donning a tie, however shabby his clothes grew) and only then washing.

In another letter, Alberto also mentioned the leaky roof and his fear that he might wake up one morning to find his bed covered in snow.

rue d'Alésia

A degree of consolation came from knowing that both Georges Braque and Henri Laurens, whom he liked and respected, lived not far away, albeit in far more convenient and salubrious conditions. As time passed and the weather turned increasingly nasty, both he and Diego would move out and spend a night or two in one of the small local hotels, a favourite being the Hôtel Primavera on nearby rue d'Alésia, built over the old Chemin des Boeufs. They also took some comfort from the fact that sufficient greyish daylight filtered through the large, grimy studio window and that the ceiling, although damp and dangerous, was high enough to allow for a narrow mezzanine balcony to complete the décor. Reached by a steep staircase, this shelf-like, wooden embellishment provided just enough width for Diego to bed down on. He would have preferred it if Alberto hadn't insisted that keeping the light on all night was the only way he could get to sleep, but this was one of his brother's foibles and soon accepted as part and parcel of their shared existence. Alberto himself had a narrow cot downstairs, closer to the one other luxury, a pot-bellied coal stove that, when lit during the day, gave out as much smoke as heat. Every now and then, once Diego had found slightly less basic lodgings in a nearby hostel, others down on their luck, such as the poet Jacques Prévert,* would spend the odd night up on the balcony, thankful to have some kind of a roof, leaky or not, over their head.

When Alberto signed the binding lease to rent these lowly premises, what instinct was he following? He was no Modigliani, no Soutine, nor one of those others who had flocked to Montparnasse, predestined by their temperament to suffer, to be spurned for all their sacrifice to art and die an early death. He came from a solid, affectionate Swiss family, wholly supportive of his artistic ambition, where he had not been ill-treated from birth like so many of the *artistes maudits* who haunted the streets of Paris with their vacant eyes, empty bellies and burnt-out hopes. Dutiful and studious, Alberto had enrolled at a leading art school, where he had done his best to conform, to please, at least in as far as his will and the deeply rebellious streak that ran through him would allow.

But times were tough and as the *années folles* ran their course, they were about to get tougher. The application for a bursary from the Swiss government that Alberto had put in had been declined, a rejection for

*Prévert also wrote songs, including '*Les feuilles mortes*' (Autumn Leaves) as well as screenplays for film director Marcel Carné, notably *Le Jour se lève* (Daybreak) and *Les Enfants du Paradis*.

which he never forgave his mother country. But times are always tough when you want to make a career in something as unpredictable as art, even if your loyal family is still providing you with an allowance. In taking on such a dump, about as far a cry from Picasso's plush setup on rue La Boétie as you could get, Alberto seemed to be deliberately raising the odds for success against himself. The young man's contrariness has already been acknowledged, but in opting for such disadvantaged quarters when he might have chosen something less extravagantly impoverished, he was not just indulging his taste for paradox but taking a more controversial stance. He had – he knew, his parents knew, his fellow students knew – talent to burn. In art, he could turn his hand to anything, and then to its opposite, copying everything with ease, adopting and adapting all styles and modes convincingly. If there was a problem, it was precisely this facility. Alberto needed all the difficulty he could get to have something worth pitting his talents against. Only failure – what he could not achieve – interested him; only the possibility of repeated failure created conditions demanding enough to stretch him fully; only by failing would he ever begin to engage in the struggle that separates the real artists from the mediocre, the half-hearted, the easily satisfied. And if, however latent it remained for the moment in this vigorous, ambitious young man, failure – continuous, vertiginous failure – was to be his aim, what better stage could there be to play it out than the rotting timbers and putrid atmosphere of what the brothers were to refer to thenceforth simply as 'rue Hippolyte'?

Plumping for this tumbledown site as the centre of his existence turned out to be a stroke of genius so well disguised that Alberto himself did not at first realise it. He joked about the place, repeatedly calling it no more than a 'hole', or his 'grotto', so small and unsatisfactory that he would be moving out, moving on, in short order.

Then, imperceptibly, the longer he stayed, the larger the 'hole' seemed to grow, accommodating all his sculptures, past and present, all his paintings and drawings, most of the latter stuffed under his bed or strewn and trodden into the bits of plaster and other detritus lining the floor. Paradoxically, the 'hole' seemed to make so little claim on him that gradually it wrapped itself around him, making itself indispensable. In time, it became his entire existence, and its restricted sphere helped him focus on what had always mattered most: his own inner development. 'Small rooms discipline the mind,' as Leonardo da Vinci remarked from his own experience, and the flimsy perimeter of rue Hippolyte was to foster that condition admirably. What Alberto could not have foreseen, although he had sensed it subconsciously, was that the space would become his shell, the place where he could withdraw from the outside world and be most profoundly himself.

Rue Hippolyte was to have all kinds of other advantages and attractions. While favouring the work he would do there, the studio would itself be transformed by it, and its makeshift appearance drew an extraordinary longevity from what was created within its crumbling walls. Alberto's art, with its persistent echoes of the past, took the transient structure into another dimension of time. Ultimately, that such haunting sculptures should emerge from these disinherited surroundings became a contradiction in itself that enhanced not only the genesis of the work but its extraordinary success. This unlovely space was to become an essential part of Alberto's myth, the symbol and the stage of his achievement.

At first sight Alésia, Alberto's new neighbourhood, recalls Gertrude Stein's withering description of her hometown of Oakland, California, that there is 'no there there'. The area was very much a suburb throughout much of the nineteenth century, giving out onto a hinterland of fields, farms and forests where Parisians rarely ventured. Major changes to this rustic spot came once the Gare de Montparnasse (originally known as Gare de l'Ouest) opened in 1840, with the railway bringing in a steady stream of workers and families from the provinces, notably the Massif Central. The wine trade flourished, with cheap cafés and drinking counters springing up all over the area, some of them run by the same family for generations. Peasants hailing from the Auvergne continued to wear their traditional blue linen smocks as the Basques did their shepherd's berets, and milk was delivered on a horse-drawn float until well into the 1940s.

Humble and low-key as Alésia was to remain, it proved an ideal environment for the Giacometti brothers, who liked the feeling that it was cut off like a forgotten suburb of the city. Its rickety labourers' cottages with their scruffy backyards and patches of garden had evolved around the turn of the century into a warren of backstreets cut into different sections by acacia-lined, Haussmann-like avenues, many of them still following the route of the country lanes they replaced. With its inhabitants ranging from working-class artisans to minor officials and indigent artists (including Juan Gris, the American writer Henry Miller and the Surrealist painters Yves Tanguy and Victor Brauner), the warren was the heart of this hinterland, and it fascinated Alberto and Diego by the variety of small shops, from timber yards to furniture repairs, that had sprung up there. 'It was a paradise when we arrived,' Diego was to reminisce much later. 'You could get any work you wanted done then: welding, marble cutting, gilding. Or any tools you needed made for you. There was a man who came down the street to sharpen knives on his grindstone and another who tuned old pianos! People still kept animals in their little gardens, and you could buy things like fresh goat's cheese. And of course the food you found in all the little bistros was proper, traditional French food. It was a lovely life.'[2]

That life was lived much more on the outside than in the wealthier *quartiers*, with neighbours' quarrels and love affairs being broadcast from one dwelling to another and often carried on in instalments in the shops and on the street. Compared to similar working-class areas further south, in Toulouse or Marseilles, for instance, there was a notable absence of colour. Everything appeared to have taken on a permanent shade of grey: the sky, the streets, even the clothes and the people, recalling the monochrome spectrum of Alberto's models in plaster and dampened or drying clay. And yet, the drab palette teemed with life. There were market days, bringing fresh farm produce and unfamiliar faces, as well as neighbourhood celebrations where local wits vied with each other to crack the most risqué joke in '*parigot*' slang. Accordion players and other itinerant musicians frequently passed through, and cafés often staged impromptu dances, mostly women dancing together, with the menfolk smoking and looking on until the odd ladies' man or sharp dresser from Montparnasse made an appearance in the mainly vain hope of sweeping them off their feet into bed. With the craze for Bakelite radios still a way off, entertainment was mainly confined to what was going on in the bistros and bars.

Close to the Giacomettis' new abode was the Moulin Vert, once an open-air drinking spot, or *guinguette*,* where wine was cheaper, and

*Similar establishments existed all over the area, with the Moulin de la Mère Saguet having counted Delacroix and Victor Hugo among its regular customers.

now the best place to eat in the area, where the brothers sustained themselves occasionally with a steak frites or something less expensive such as tripe or grilled pig's feet. Since they had neither the wherewithal nor the inclination to prepare food themselves in the studio, they went out to eat and drink, even for a cup of coffee, their main ports of call being the bistros on rue Didot and rue d'Alésia where they could always get a sandwich and a drink or a simple dish of the day. Le Gaulois, an unremarkable café-tabac on the crossroads between rue d'Alésia and rue Didot, was also a good standby where Alberto could stock up on cigarettes to go with his regular fix of black coffee; its bar became such a staple in his life that he later made it the subject of an evocative drawing. Similarly, a quick glass of *vin ordinaire* and a little local gossip could be had at any moment of the day at the *café-bougnat*, run by a certain Monsieur Touati, on the corner of rue Hippolyte and rue du Moulin Vert. The *bougnat*, traditionally a peasant hailing from the mountainous Auvergne in central France, had become a feature of most areas of Paris, providing not only inexpensive wine and spirits directly from the producer but also household fuel. Once Alberto and Diego had drunk their drop at its sooty counter, they could haul back a sack of coal to fire up the pot-bellied stove in the studio.

For grander occasions, when the brothers wanted to escape Alésia and its grubby streets, the Auberge de Venise on rue Delambre, where the classier local prostitutes conferred with their pimps, was a favourite. But Alberto was never overly interested in or fussy about what he ate, and when a small brasserie called Les Tamaris, run by an ex-convict and frequented by the shadier elements in the area, opened nearby, it became his local canteen; he ate the couscous there at all hours without bothering to brush off the plaster that stuck to his clothes and lodged in his hair. At Les Tamaris he could relax, chat with all sorts of other punters or read, as he did intently every day, his newspaper. It was only later that the owner acknowledged that, to his lasting regret, he had thrown away the scores of sketches and doodles that the eccentric artist left behind (as he also did at the Dôme and the Coupole) on the disposable paper tablecloths.

Once Alberto started prowling round the area at all hours, he was drawn to its nightlife, and soon there was no after-hours establishment, from bars and cafés to bordellos, that he had not sampled. He had

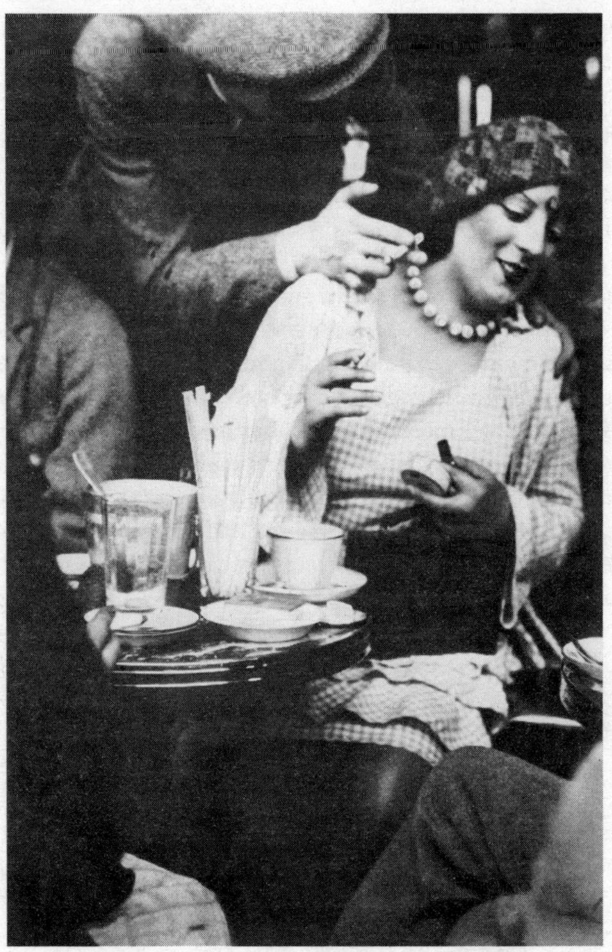

Kiki de Montparnasse in the Café du Dôme, 1929

never cared for dancing – indeed, as a youth in Switzerland, whenever he felt attracted to a girl he would ask Diego to dance with her while staring meaningfully at her from the sidelines – but he enjoyed all kinds of nightclubs. Very much in vogue at the time was the Bal Blomet, renamed the 'Bal Nègre' by the Surrealist poet Robert Desnos, because it regularly hosted black American jazz musicians and performers who had begun to attract enthusiastic crowds, including some of the leading Parisian artists and intellectuals. The area was already well known for the lively complex of artists' studios, hardly more salubrious than Alberto's, that existed almost next door to the 'Bal' on rue Blomet; two of the talented group living there, André Masson and Joan Miró, were shortly to become Alberto's close friends. All fashionable Paris, from Josephine Baker (formerly of the Plantation Club in New York's Harlem, and now a success in Paris) and Maurice Chevalier to Ernest Hemingway and Kiki, the artist's model and ubiquitous 'It' girl of Montparnasse, flocked to the Bal Nègre to listen to the potent new rhythms and jive the night away; not for nothing was this frenzied period in Paris remembered as the 'Jazz Age', causing even the otherwise severe-looking Piet Mondrian to throw lozenge abstractions to the wind and really get down to the intoxicating sound. Later, the dance hall regularly drew other bosom companions, above all Jean-Paul Sartre, Simone de Beauvoir* and Albert Camus. Maurice Merleau-Ponty, the leading phenomenological thinker, then in hot pursuit of Juliette Gréco, the leading Existentialist chanteuse, durably

La Coupole, around 1930

*In Simone de Beauvoir's 1960 autobiography, *La Force de l'âge* (The Prime of Life), she described evenings spent at the Bal: 'I enjoyed watching the dancers and drank rum punch, and the noise, the smoke, the effects of the drink and the music's pulsing beat overwhelmed me as I watched one handsome, laughing face after another pass by. My heart started beating faster as the uproarious last dances exploded around us. This surge of cheerful, festive bodies seemed closely bound up with my own urge to live.'

impressed Alberto as much by the originality of his philosophical stance as the suppleness he displayed on the dance floor.

Another regular treat for the Giacometti brothers was the cinema, above all American cinema, to which Parisians had been flocking in growing numbers as an escape from the traumatic memories of war. As an intensely visual person, Alberto was enthralled by the moving image and lost no opportunity to see new films as they came to the city's thriving movie theatres, some of them huge, such as the Grand Rex, an Art Deco palace on the *grands boulevards*, or exotic like the neo-Egyptian Louxor and the Pagode, imported piece by piece from the East. The young artist knew the recent European classics such as Fritz Lang's *Metropolis* and Abel Gance's *Napoleon*, but he also enjoyed popular cinema (as he did popular literature, enjoying 'Série Noire' detective novels quite as much as obscure philosophy*). He certainly never missed a 'Charlot', or Chaplin, film, having been won over by the sweeping success of *The Kid* and *The Gold Rush*. As he was finding his feet in his new *quartier*, Alberto would have been intrigued to hear that the first 'talkies', notably *The Jazz Singer*, starring Al Jolson, were being released. He was also enthusiastic about the first films in colour, remarking at the time that, impressive as they were, the art of painting had nothing to fear from their technical prowess. A taste for popular culture in no way ruled out more 'highbrow' entertainments and, as his letters to his parents attest, Alberto also occasionally sampled classical concerts, avant-garde plays and, of course, various Salon and museum exhibitions.

Meanwhile, Alberto was working out where to store the works he had brought with him and how best to dot his meagre possessions around the studio floor. For all the neglect and chaos he appeared to live in, everything around him had to correspond to a certain order of his own making. He might allow fully worked drawings to fall to the floor and get mixed up in the heaps of clay and plaster underfoot, but his socks and shoes had to be precisely lined up beside his bed if he were to get the least wink of sleep. Accordingly, his working table and wicker chair, his *Spoon Woman* and his Kota reliquary were moved round endlessly until

*Some sixty of these detective novels, many of them containing notes and sketches, were found in the studio after Alberto's death.

they had been angled into the ideal spot, just as the sculpture stand or his raincoat required specific siting, even if such arrangements looked random to everyone else. This manic, if harmless, obsession extended outside the studio, and Alberto was never happy sitting at a café table until he had repositioned ashtray and drink, cigarettes and newspaper, in an exact symmetry of his own devising.

Having become used to his brother's whims (or '*bizarreries*', as their family called them) since he had sat for the first sculpture Alberto made of him at the age of twelve, Diego went along with this manic behaviour without demur, just as he fell in with the strict working routine that Alberto imposed on himself and anyone else who came into his professional life. In the early days at rue Hippolyte, this tended to be a simple division of drawing from a model in the morning and working on a sculpture in the afternoon. Drawing became as natural as breathing, and it continued even at mealtimes – on books, newspapers or any scrap of paper that came to hand.

As their first spring at rue Hippolyte approached, the brothers warmed to the anonymity and unpretentiousness that living in Alésia allowed. Being taciturn but neighbourly, and living as sparsely as day labourers, they fitted in seamlessly, and locals joked that you could always tell where the brothers were in the area from the plaster footprints their boots left on the street. If they needed a hand to patch up the roof or get a spot of welding done – as they certainly did – they knew which door to knock on. For Alberto, the fact that here was a place where he was able to get down to work with minimal disruption and the right, practical backup, would always be the main issue. Temporary though it was meant to be, from this point on he referred to the studio as '*chez moi*', while Switzerland, the mother country, now became exactly that: '*chez ma mère*'. His mother Annetta appears to have acknowledged that Paris was Alberto's territory, and after her husband's death she never visited him there, even for the openings of his exhibitions.

Alberto might have looked as if he were turning his back on success by burying himself in an obscure section of the 14th *arrondissement*, but its uncompromisingly workmanlike atmosphere appeared, on the contrary, to encourage further breakthroughs by helping him to focus single-mindedly on the struggle ahead. In truth, having barely finished his studies at the Grande Chaumière, Alberto was still in search of a direction that would allow him to develop his prodigious gifts fully. With the broad range of styles on offer in Paris during the second half of the 1920s, his natural versatility enabled him to explore and drift between numerous approaches for several years before he established his own obsessive, unalterable quest. As naturalism had given way to Cubism, *Spoon Woman* and his other tribal-inspired sculptures led to the 'Plaques', a series of faintly dimpled flat pieces so severely simplified as to appear virtually abstract, which Alberto produced in the winter of 1928–9. Pieces from this series, such as *Gazing Head*, play with the fine line between abstraction and mimesis, testing the limits of representation. Here Alberto finds a form which verges on abstraction while still bringing to mind its subject. This may be seen as a natural aim for an artist who became so frustrated with sculpture's inability to exactly represent reality. Here he delights in the very elasticity of representation – even the inability of forms *not* to depict something of the world. Indeed, one might argue that *Gazing Head* derives from Alberto's continuing portraits of his father which involved making increasingly reduced forms resemble the gentle Giovanni. Even though some examples appear as traditional portrait busts, one example from 1927 is radically simple, made up solely of etched lines on a disturbingly flat face. The formation of Alberto's individual style can be traced, then, through a meeting of two worlds: the experimental formalism of Parisian avant-gardes reconciled with his enduring desire to represent something of the world.

Despite this teetering on the edge, the young artist would never be tempted by complete abstraction, aware though he was of the recent work of Mondrian, whom he knew as a fellow habitué of the Dôme. Life itself seemed already too unfathomable, indeed too 'abstract', and reality too fleeting; moreover, abstraction's heyday and the great abstraction/figuration divide was still some way off. Far from spontaneous or seamless, this extreme transition was achieved through a complex process of trial and error that Alberto would undergo at every major, critical stage of his development. Looking back at that period of radical change from his maturity, Alberto gave a succinct account of how demanding the process had been. It also provides an intimate glimpse into the contradictory workings of his mind:

> In order to work out these plaques I began to model from memory as much as possible of what I'd seen. In other words, I began to analyze a figure – the legs, the head, the arms – and all of it seemed false to me. I didn't believe in it. To get closer to my idea, I had to sacrifice more and more, limit myself – leave off the head, the arms, everything. So what was left of the figure was only a plaque, and that didn't happen on purpose and didn't satisfy me, just the opposite. It was always disappointing that what I really mastered in terms of form reduced itself to so little!
>
> It took a long time before I arrived at these plaque sculptures. A whole winter long I worked on them and other things of the same kind. Here I should add that I began two or three motifs in different ways, but the same thing came out in the end ... did I actually want to make something I saw in things, or express the way I felt about them? Or a certain feeling for form that is inside you and that you want to bring outside?[3]

Yet whether it is in his handling of volume or the repetition of motifs, such as the scarification marks taken from tribal art, one can detect the same sensibility running through and uniting the diverse, radical transformations. On this evidence, Alberto's greatest obstacle would seem to be his own ability to take up diametrically opposed stylistic stances: from convincingly classical, rounded, plaster heads of his father to frontal, almost caricatural representations of him in bronze, from Cubist constructions to the shallow indentations of the serenely simple, enigmatic 'Plaques' that were to catapult the young sculptor to his first moment of fame. It is fascinating to note that even in this period of formal experimentation, when he relied substantially on his imagination, Alberto continued to work in a more observational idiom when he returned home to Stampa and modelled portraits of his family. While the portraits he made in this period vary in style a great deal, it is still as if he led a kind of double life as an artist, between nineteenth-century naturalism in rural Switzerland and the radical experimentation and eroticism of rapidly modernising Paris.

Full of variety and genuine invention, the Paris art world of the late 1920s nevertheless revolved around a clearly defined inner circle, as did the corresponding literary world with which it interacted – in

Robert Desnos [left] and André Masson, around 1940

a culture in which artists and writers had worked hand in hand since Baudelaire wrote about Manet and Bonnard illustrated Verlaine.* That inner circle included André Masson, a young artist who had already made his mark on the avant-garde by experimenting with 'automatic' drawing; that is, images that supposedly flowed from the unconscious without mediation or control. These morbidly violent works had been partly inspired by the importance that the newly formed Surrealist movement, in thrall to Freud's major discoveries, accorded to the depths of the psyche in all fields of creativity. Masson was five years older than Alberto, and that, as well as being reassuringly French and naturally sociable, had helped him to manoeuvre more adroitly than most around the caste-bound Paris art scene. Masson was also unusually generous to other artists, and since he liked Alberto immediately and admired his recent work he took him under his wing, as he had the budding writer Michel Leiris.

One of Paris's most enterprising young art dealers, Jeanne Bucher, whose gallery on the Left Bank had already presented work by Picasso, Juan Gris, Mondrian and Masson himself, visited Alberto in the studio

*Examples of this kind of collaboration abound, but certain come to mind immediately, such as Picasso's illustrations for Pierre Reverdy's *Le chant des morts*, Braque's for Apollinaire, Miró for Eluard's *A toute épreuve* or Nicolas de Staël's for his poet friend René Char. Giacometti, of course, made engravings for many of the poets he knew, and in turn many writers, from Breton to Sartre and Genet, wrote extensively about him and his work.

and decided to include two of his 'Plaques' in her ongoing show of Massimo Campigli, one of a group of painters known as the 'Paris Italians' with whom Alberto had begun to associate. The more rough-and-ready art world of the day comes into focus once one discovers that her apparent foresight was prompted by the recent sale of two Campiglis which left a gap in her gallery that she was keen to fill, a fact that initially made Alberto reticent about accepting. When the two works, *Gazing Head* – with its single vertical and horizontal groove – and *Figure* were put on show in June 1929, they made an immediate impression on other avant-garde artists and writers, but also on Vicomte and Vicomtesse de Noailles, the most daring and sophisticated avant-garde art collectors and patrons in Paris, who added the enigmatic *Gazing Head* to their impressive collection. As Alberto enthusiastically reported to his parents, 'Within eight days everything was sold and I had several offers from other dealers on my desk'; he also mentioned that he thought of Masson, who proved 'very, very friendly' towards him, as the best painter currently at work in Paris.

In the event, however many 'offers' there were, Alberto signed a one-year contract with Pierre Loeb, the dealer whose Galerie Pierre on rue des Beaux-Arts was soon to be the main hub for Surrealist art exhibitions. Loeb would pay Alberto a basic monthly salary of 1,500 francs and cover whatever material costs he had in making his sculpture in return for the right to acquire, exhibit and sell the artist's entire production for a year. No doubt impressed by the favourable reaction of both collectors and critics to Alberto's recent show, Loeb also offered to cover half the annual rent on any studio that Alberto fancied up to 8,000 francs. Since the rent at rue Hippolyte only came to 4,500 francs, finding another, more expensive studio would have been very tempting to a less self-willed and contrary figure.

Pleased by his protégé's success, the amiable Masson did Alberto the even more signal favour of introducing him to his friends, a sign of confidence and support rare between artists, and even rarer between artists in Paris. From knowing few people outside his fellow students and complaining how difficult it was to meet the French, Alberto found himself surrounded by some of the best and brightest young painters and writers in the city. As he put it laconically in an interview years later: 'I saw Masson at an exhibition, the same day meeting the majority of the friends I still have today, that is, Masson, Bataille, Leiris, Desnos, Queneau, and many others.'[4] Once he had broken through what had appeared to be a 'wall' between himself and other artists – the 'many others' included Jean Arp, Max Ernst and Joan Miró, whose studio on rue Blomet had been next to Masson's – all boundaries seemed to melt away. The breakthrough had occurred because of his striking talent as a sculptor, but it did no harm that Alberto was not only young and eager but attractive and, when he emerged from his reserve, charming, with a wry sense of humour and an ability to hold his own in any conversation. He also possessed a gift for friendship and a strong sense of loyalty, not only to his peers and those who might bolster his career, but to neighbours and, not least, some of the streetwalkers he had encountered on his nightly prowls.

Of the impressive roster of writers who began to gather around Alberto during this early success, Georges Bataille and Michel Leiris would have the most immediate impact. In the literary and political turbulence of the times, Bataille stood out as the most radical figure, with a devouring conviction that the only way to reach the sacred lay through complete identification with the profane – a literary movement and a permanent revolution of ideas of his own, prominent among which was a fascination with base materialism and transgressive eroticism. How could one fail to see, Bataille asked, that the idealism of the Greeks and of subsequent Western civilisation attempted to conceal the basic contradictions of life, namely its incoherence and savagery – in a universe, moreover, that has revealed itself as futile and formless as, in his vivid definition, a gob of mucus? A fervent Catholic in his youth, Bataille had originally considered entering the priesthood before instead specialising in numismatics at the Bibliothèque nationale, a career which allowed him the freedom to devote his restless energy to a range of unconventional intellectual inquiries, including his theory that everything in the world is a 'parody' of something else, leading to such memorable dicta as 'coitus is a parody of crime'.[5]

Having been attracted to Surrealism at the outset, Bataille withdrew after a sharp doctrinal dispute with the movement's leader André Breton (who called Bataille a 'sexual pervert' before skewering him more pointedly as 'an excremental philosopher obsessed by degradation and decay'). Bataille went on to group other dissidents from the movement

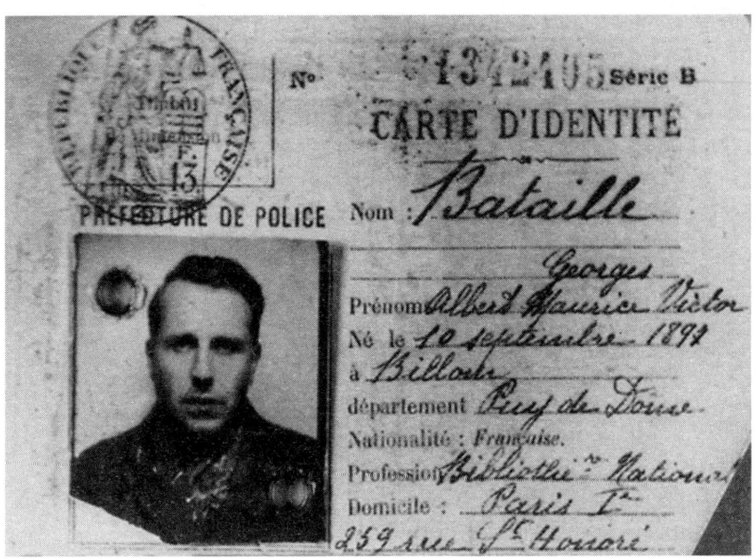
Série B
CARTE D'IDENTITÉ
PRÉFECTURE DE POLICE
Nom : Bataille
Prénom Georges Albert Maurice Victor
Né le 10 septembre 1897
à Billom
département Puy de Dôme
Nationalité : Française.
Profession Bibliothèque Nationale
Domicile : Paris Ier
259 rue St Honoré

Georges Bataille's identity card, 1940

around the influential but short-lived review *Documents*, financed by the art dealer Georges Wildenstein. With its eclectic mix of essays on archaeology, jazz and ethnography, not to mention photographic studies of the big toe (exemplifying Bataille's notion of anti-artistic 'baseness'), severed hooves and the 'ominous grandeur' of slaughterhouses, *Documents* remains 'a war machine against received ideas', as provocative as its principal founder intended. Alberto kept a full run of the subversive publication in the studio throughout his career.

Leiris, a more moderate fellow dissident, had a parallel career as an ethnographer, later joining the staff at the Musée de l'homme, where Alberto had visited the outstanding tribal collections. But, like Bataille (whom he later nicknamed 'Bataille the impossible'), Leiris was first and foremost a writer, with a marked autobiographical bent and a lasting connection to art that extended from Picasso and Miró to Giacometti and Bacon. Along with his close friend and mentor Masson, Leiris succeeded in maintaining a wide circle of literary and artistic friends among both the dissident and the orthodox Surrealists, the divisions in the Parisian intellectual world being often more porous than the vociferous character of their debates suggests: Breton might well doff his hat courteously to a passing foe (unless he slapped his face) and elaborately kiss his wife or mistress's hand, just as he might banish errant members from the group, then welcome them back to the fold once they had acknowledged the error of their ways. Leiris initiated his lifelong relationship with Alberto by writing the first article devoted to his work, which *Documents* published in September 1929. For all the mythical overtones it has acquired since, this early, short text is very much that of a young writer championing a young artist (both were born in 1901) and based more on sudden enthusiasm and generalised defiance – inspired by the truculent tone set by Bataille – than on stylistic analysis or aesthetic perception. 'There are moments that we may call *crises*,' Leiris wrote, 'and these are the only ones that count in life. I like the sculpture of Giacometti because everything he does is like the petrification of one of these crises.'[6] Amusingly and revealingly, Leiris also notes in his diary at the time: 'I finished the essay on Giacometti but I couldn't give a damn about all that. I want to be a demon lover or a cool gigolo.'[7]

Leiris's instinct was right, nonetheless, and by stating how directly and meaningfully Alberto's recent works had affected him (as opposed to most art, which he describes as 'more boring than rain'), he compares their power to that of 'true fetishes that one can idolize' and then proceeds to do so in rapturous words: 'Some of these sculptures are hollow like spatulas or empty fruits. Others are perforated and the air passes through them, moving grids interposed between the inside and the outside, screens gnawed by the wind, the hidden wind enveloping us in its immense black vortex, those incredible moments that leave us raving.' Leiris chose to illustrate his text with images of recent works that Marc Vaux had photographed in Alberto's studio. One of these shows three white 'Plaques' sculptures encircling *Man and Woman* (1928–9), in which the schematic male form points a sharp, lance-like protuberance into the wide, concave female figure. In retrospect, that particular configuration can be seen as recording a key shift in Alberto's focus, with the subtle play of full and hollow, light and shade in the 'Plaques' giving way to a strident sexuality that was no doubt latent but had never surfaced so clearly. The emphasis on erotic violence and physical aggression would now grow as Alberto moved closer towards joining the Surrealists, tentatively – much as one might before espousing a new religion.

Man Ray, Michel Leiris, around 1930

The combination of up-and-coming writer with up-and-coming sculptor proved particularly persuasive, since Leiris's prescient remarks came at a time when Alberto's reputation was already beginning to take root. One might note, for instance, that in the same issue of *Documents* the Galerie Pierre took an advertisement already listing Giacometti's name in its 'stable' of artists alongside Braque, Miró, Picasso and Soutine; Pierre Loeb had not been slow in taking the initiative. Meanwhile the Swiss writer and fellow 'Montparno' Charles-Albert Cingria went out of his way to praise the young sculptor: 'For a few years now I have been marvelling at the persistence with which chance brings me into contact with a young man who has a head like an Etruscan sculpture … the sculpture-wunderkind all Paris is talking about. A very important person whose name I don't want to keep repeating [Jean Cocteau] seems to have singled him out. Someone else has pipped him to the post, however: the Surrealist (not Surrealist at all at the moment, like so many others), Michel Leiris.'[8]

Tongue in cheek as it might sound, this kind of acknowledgement could hardly fail to brighten the lonely existence Alberto had led until now, seeing only a handful of his former fellow students, his taciturn brother and the occasional prostitute. If jubilation erupted in rue Hippolyte, the event would have been duly celebrated at the Coupole. Elated as he was by his sudden success, Alberto also felt its destabilising effects, and he was glad to have the tacitly deflating presence of the silent Diego by his side.

Further success now appeared inevitable. Accompanied by his friend the illustrator-cum-designer Christian Bérard, Jean Cocteau had indeed put in an appearance at Jeanne Bucher's gallery and rhapsodised about Alberto's 'Plaques'. That the leading *arbiter elegantiae* of most things cultural in Paris had been impressed constituted a major accolade for any emerging artist. Conscious of his power to make or break reputations, and forever in search of *bons mots*, Cocteau noted his reaction to their mysterious indentations in his diary: 'I know sculptures by Giacometti that are so solid yet so light that they look like snow that has retained the footprints of a bird.'*

Art publishers of the importance of Christian Zervos, who founded the influential *Cahiers d'art* in 1926, were quick to single Alberto out as a rising star. A co-founder and editor of *Documents*, the German-born art critic Carl Einstein, had also taken an immediate interest in the young sculptor's work from the moment he saw it at the Galerie Jeanne Bucher in 1929, where visitors included De Chirico and Léger. Ottilia, Alberto's sister, was in Paris at the time, and in a letter to their parents she communicates the sense of excitement surrounding her brother's sudden triumph: 'The other evening we met up with Einstein and all the leaders, and they were really, really friendly to Alberto, you could see they were very interested in him.'[9] Einstein, who was

*'*Je connais de Giacometti des sculptures si solides, si légères, qu'on dirait de la neige gardant les empreintes d'un oiseau.*' Cocteau also included the note in *Opium* (1930), his subsequent account of detoxification. For his part, Alberto had seen and liked Cocteau's play *Orphée*, first put on at the Théâtre des Arts in Paris in 1926.

in contact with such leading art dealers as Daniel-Henri Kahnweiler, Georges Wildenstein and Alfred Flechtheim, gained renown for his expertise in Cubism as well as African art.* Having advised Alberto to sign up with Pierre Loeb, Einstein also suggested he should promote his work by choosing the best photographers to take pictures of his recent achievements. Alberto had noted how effective Marc Vaux's shots of his new sculpture and studio had been, and he began approaching other talented photographers, such as Jacques-André Boiffard and Man Ray, both of whom photographed the young sculptor's already cluttered studio to brilliant effect. Man Ray, the only major American artist to have joined the Surrealists, later left a striking pen portrait of Alberto:

> Giacometti, the sculptor, gave one the impression of a tormented soul. Always dissatisfied with his work, feeling that he had not carried it far enough, or perhaps too far, he'd abandon it in his heaped-up little studio, and start on an entirely new formula. He could talk with lucid, voluble brilliance on many subjects. I liked to sit with him in a café and watch as well as listen to him. His deeply marked face with a greyish complexion, like a medieval sculpture, was a fine subject for my photographic portraiture.[10]

Many of Alberto's new acquaintances tended to align themselves with one specific intellectual group and political conviction. In the half-dozen years that Alberto had now spent in Paris, Surrealism had gained ground spectacularly not only as a concept and a way of being but now, increasingly, as a quasi-militant movement. From its timid beginnings centred around *Littérature*,* a small but belligerent literary magazine founded in 1919 by three writers (André Breton, Paul Eluard and Philippe Soupault), Surrealist thinking had begun to move away from the absurdist nihilism of Dada towards a more active spirit of change and exploration – what Breton called a 'total liberation of the spirit' – incorporating such radical new departures as psychoanalysis.

*Einstein's most influential book, *Negerplastik*, had been published as early as 1915.

*The title *Littérature*, taken from Verlaine's line 'All the rest is just literature', was deliberately ironic since the magazine's main aim lay in denouncing the hollow, fatuous writing widely accepted, above all by the previous generation, as 'literature'.

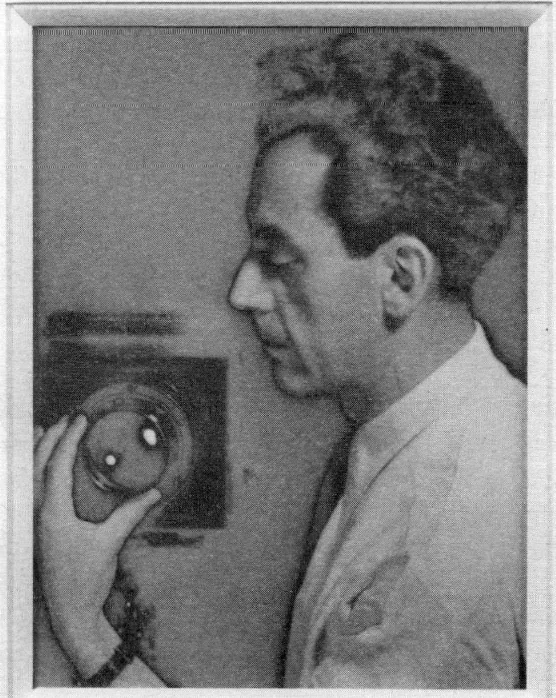

Man Ray, Self-portrait, 1930

Breton himself had studied medicine with the intention of becoming a neuropsychologist, and he had travelled specially to Vienna to meet Freud. He had recently published *Nadja*, his semi-autobiographical account of a brief, haunting love affair that sets out certain attitudes and a tone that were adopted by other budding Surrealist writers. This strangely compelling memoir ends with the famous line 'Beauty will be convulsive or will not be at all', which was taken up as a battle cry for the new movement as it developed under Breton's domineering influence. The notion of 'convulsive beauty' is characteristic of his approach since it relates to the way in which romantic desire breaks down conformity and psychological coherence. The term can be paired with another major Surrealist idea, 'the marvellous', that Breton uses to describe the sensational realm of experience that becomes accessible once the human mind is freed from the shackles of reason and rationality. All of these Surrealist concepts centre around the unconscious (a realm

Jacqueline Chaumont and René Crevel in Tristan Tzara's Dadaist play, *Coeur à gaz*, 1923

of the psyche highlighted by Freud and his followers) as a very real, and tragically suppressed, aspect of life that can be used to combat the conventions, injustices and sheer tedium of bourgeois society.

Apart from the originality and brilliance of his approach, the breadth of his culture and the scope of his imagination, Breton was equally gifted as a poet and pamphleteer, self-publicist and political activist, orator and art collector. To quote Alberto himself on Breton's complex nature, in a letter he wrote to Breton but decided not to send: 'One doesn't know to whom one is writing, you are many people, yes many, in at least four, plus several other, dimensions.'[11] A leader of men and assiduous wooer of women, Breton had imperious good looks and proven physical courage, putting himself at considerable risk in the various demonstrations, public outbursts and scandals that accompanied the Surrealist movement's constant battery on French society's accepted ideas. On top of those qualities, Breton exerted a personal magnetism that alone won him support from the most diverse quarters, and Alberto was one of a wide range of gifted artists and writers to fall under the spell of his personality.

At the same time, Breton's domineering self-assurance as well as his capricious changeability of views and direction as self-appointed leader had won him a formidable array of enemies (although divergences and alliances, whether theoretical or political, shifted constantly amid the pre- and post-war Parisian intelligentsia). A number of these original adherents to the movement who now vehemently proclaimed their dissidence had realigned themselves around the review *Documents* and regularly struck blows against Breton's personal authoritarianism and intellectual ideals (he had joined the French Communist Party in 1927), proclaiming the superior validity of Bataille's 'base materialism', which rejected the lofty sentiments of the natural nobility of mankind held by the previous pre-war generation. In the last issue of *La Révolution surréaliste* at the end of 1929, Breton published his Second Surrealist Manifesto, praising his supporters while excoriating those who had left the group, thus betraying him and his doctrine. At this the 'dissidents', headed by Bataille and Leiris, shot back a pamphlet entitled '*Un cadavre*' (with Breton photographed wearing a crown of thorns on the cover), with various texts criticising the movement's delusional 'idealism' and likening its self-appointed 'Pope' to a 'castrated lion'.

Alberto followed every shift in these intellectual in-fights. Initially his sympathies had been with his new, disaffected friends and benefactors Masson, Leiris, Bataille and Einstein. Highly individualistic though he remained, there was no way that a young artist like Alberto could not take sides to some extent in these polarised times. But he remained primarily involved in his own aesthetic problems and would never become as passionately engaged as Bataille or Breton in public intellectual debates, even if he enjoyed discussing them from the sidelines. While he did passionately espouse some left-wing causes, one senses that the hard-headed, mountain-bred Swiss in him retained a robust scepticism towards the more advanced, not to say fanciful, positions taken by his revolutionary comrades. Like certain other foreign artists in Paris and notably Max Ernst, by remaining less involved Alberto was able to follow his own, judiciously middle way for a good while, taking an alert interest in both extreme factions without falling out with either.

Whether it was the Bataille group or the Breton group, the adherents made deliberate attempts to antagonise the public, and the bourgeoisie in particular, frequently attracting not only severe strictures (which were quite easily rebuffed) but also real physical risk. When the young, frail Michel Leiris revolted against his own classically bourgeois background and, at a moment of national outrage against the killing of some French soldiers,

UN CADAVRE

Il ne faut plus que mort cet homme fasse de la poussière.
André BRETON (*Un Cadavre, 1924.*)

PAPOLOGIE D'ANDRÉ BRETON

MORT D'UN MONSIEUR

AUTO-PROPHÉTIE

'Un Cadavre', a pamphlet written against Breton by dissident Surrealists including Leiris and Bataille in 1930

shouted 'Down with France' in Montparnasse, he might well have been lynched by the irate crowd that began beating him up, had not the gendarmes intervened, taken him down to the commissariat and beaten him up further.

Some of the deliberate provocations during this period succeeded by creating scandals, newspaper headlines, shocked debates in the Assemblée nationale and police crackdowns. Others, however skilfully orchestrated, did not. One of the most famous, *Un Chien andalou*,* the short film made by Luis Buñuel and Salvador Dalí, is also one of the most characteristic events of the time in which revolutionary intellectuals and the Paris *beau monde* met and, rather than clash bloodily with lasting consequences

*The title was taken from the Spanish saying: 'When an Andalusian dog howls, someone has died.'

for all, got along just fine. Yet every attempt to outrage had been made in the picture, with deliberately meaningless sequences leading from a woman's eye being sliced with a razor to dead donkeys on grand pianos with bewildered priests roped to them and the palm of a hand crawling with ants. Aristocrats and art patrons mingled with Picasso, Le Corbusier and a whole phalanx of Surrealists who enthused about the merits of the film – as did the owner of the Left Bank cinema where it played, alternating Wagner and tango dance music, to packed houses for eight months. Buñuel, who had filled his pockets with stones to throw at what he thought might be a violently hostile audience, described the film as 'nothing other than a desperate, impassioned call for murder' and was mortified by its worldly success, even though it won him and Dalí their spurs as enthusiastically co-opted members of the Surrealist clan.

The *Chien andalou* screening brought together a significant microcosm, reflecting an essential truth about the rarefied atmosphere of the world in which Alberto was making his way and which, with all too much haste, he was to make his own. It unmasked the uneasy alliances struck between art and fashion, established wealth and left-wing fervour, entrenched attitudes and radical change. In retrospect, it is easier to make out the shadow of the Wall Street crash falling over Europe, slowly exacerbating political tensions which, on that evening in the Studio des Ursulines cinema, stood out in full relief. Foregathered at one extreme was the Vicomte Charles de Noailles, scion of one of the oldest aristocratic families of France, and his Vicomtesse, the immensely wealthy and artistically perceptive Marie-Laure, a descendant of the Marquis de Sade; at the other, the rabidly anti-bourgeois, anti-clerical Luis Buñuel, himself the heir to bourgeois parents who had made a fortune in Cuba. In the middle, ready to shift their ground according to the circumstances, stood the endlessly amiable, ubiquitous Jean Cocteau, cruelly lampooned as the '*grand couturier des arts*', and the more sinister but at least equally talented Salvador Dalí, subsequently branded for life as '*Avida Dollars*' in a memorable anagram by André Breton. For that brief moment there was a truce, but *L'Age d'or*, Buñuel's next venture, wholly financed by the Noailles,* hit home, creating a scandal and violent scenes fomented by the far-right Camelots du Roi and Jeunesses Patriotes. The right-wing press denounced the new

*It says much about Paris around 1930 that, after financing the film, Charles de Noailles was ostracised by many of his social class, as previously noted, and expelled from the aristocratic Jockey Club.

film as 'the most repulsive corruption of our age … the new poison which Judaism, Masonry, and rabid, revolutionary sectarianism want to use in order to corrupt the people'. In the scuffles that ensued, the paintings lent specially to enhance the opening, including works by Arp, Dalí, Man Ray and Tanguy, were ripped off the walls, vandalised and trampled underfoot.* Breton had undoubtedly found his Surrealist filmmaker.†

As *Un Chien andalou* was titillating *le tout-Paris*, Alberto learned that his erstwhile professor Bourdelle had died. It had been only a couple of years

Anna Riwkin, Breton, Dalí, Crevel, and Eluard [left to right], 1935

*One of these, *Invisible Sleeping Woman, Horse, Lion* (1930), a key Surrealist work by Dalí, was thought to have been irretrievably damaged, but some fifty years later it resurfaced, heavily restored, in a bequest to the Centre Pompidou in Paris.

†Buñuel remained a committed Surrealist, paying an independent and clear-sighted homage to the movement in his memoirs: 'All of us were supporters of a certain concept of revolution, and although the surrealists didn't consider themselves terrorists, they were constantly fighting a society they despised. Their principal weapon wasn't guns, of course; it was scandal. Scandal was a potent agent of revelation, capable of exposing such social crimes as the exploitation of one man by another, colonialist imperialism, religious tyranny – in sum, all the secret and odious underpinnings of a system that had to be destroyed. The real purpose of surrealism was not to create a new literary, artistic, or even philosophical movement, but to explode the social order, to transform life itself.' Buñuel, *My Last Sigh: The Autobiography of Luis Buñuel*, p. 107.

since he had stopped going to his classes at the Grande Chaumière, but the chasm that now separated the teacher's sculpture from the student's can be gauged by looking from *Apollo Meditating with the Muses*, the frieze which Bourdelle had created for the façade of the Théâtre des Champs-Elysées, to the latest experiments under way at rue Hippolyte. Aeons seem to divide these reinterpretations of the Parthenon frieze from the minimalist, almost featureless 'Plaques' that Alberto was fine-tuning. But if the near-abstract works were resolutely modern, they were also unfathomably ancient. In their challenging blank nudity, endless centuries of artistic development have been washed away, like white marble under water, so that the present suddenly reappears in a shape and simplicity going back three thousand years to the shores of pre-classical antiquity. Where Bourdelle's frieze, in its direct homage to classical art, looks tired and lifeless, Alberto's 'Plaques' announce a moment of rebirth and a new beginning.*

Man Ray, Galerie surréaliste, 1927

*It is not difficult today to dismiss Bourdelle's grandiloquent work, but it is worth recalling – *O tempora, O mores!* – that he was revered in his own time and continues to be honoured by a substantial Musée Bourdelle, with his original studio, a massive collection of his art and a sculpture garden, in a street named after him near Montparnasse.

Unlike lesser artists who might have settled down to making ever-more ingenious variations on the 'Plaque' theme, not least since they had proved saleable, Alberto decided that his pleasing Cycladic-inspired series had already reached its limited potential. Other, more immediate concerns were crowding in on his imagination, of which the most pressing, not surprisingly in a healthy young man, was sex. If there is one subject that preoccupied Giacometti throughout his entire career, it could reasonably be stated, outstripping any interest in artistic invention or philosophical inquiry, it was the relationship between man and woman and the primal, driving force of sex. Alberto's obsession with it was compounded by the fact that, as he sportingly acknowledged, he was not very good at it. The desire was certainly there, and however much he enjoyed the company of gay men, he was robustly heterosexual, chasing the alluring shadows that excited him so intensely as they flitted between street and rented room.*

Alberto's next major sculpture – and everybody who saw it instantly had a fair idea of what it was about – addressed that very problem. A large ball, engorged with longing, swings as if magnetically over a narrow groove, so nearly caressing it yet doomed to miss it forever by a millimetre. It was a small monument to unrequited desire, an objectification of suspended orgasm, a brilliant transposal of what we might call Alberto's 'shortcoming'. *Suspended Ball* also worked as a metaphor for a generalised state of pent-up frustration, and the Surrealists, with their heightened interest in sexuality, provocation and the general shocking of public opinion, were not slow to apprehend the sculpture's importance.

In April 1930, Alberto exhibited for the first time at the Galerie Pierre – which Pierre Loeb had established within spitting distance of the imposing Ecole des Beaux-Arts – alongside Miró and Arp. As well as presenting his 'Plaque' sculptures, including a marble version of *Gazing Head*, he also introduced this enigmatic new structure that was to prove a turning point both in his oeuvre and in his career: *Suspended*

*Alberto remained keen on finding more conventional female company, but he lacked confidence. In a letter dated 27 November 1929 to his youngest brother, Bruno, he jokes: 'At dinner tomorrow I will be seated next to one of the most beautiful and elegant women in Paris, but since she is almost six foot tall, I don't fancy my chances. We'll see. In the cafés it's always the same faces in the same places the whole time!' SIK-ISEA Archives, Zurich, 274. A. s.1.97.

Ball attracted immediate attention, not least because Loeb placed the original plaster version in the gallery's front window, just in front of a canvas by Miró featuring a shooting star.

Salvador Dalí picked up right away on its references to endlessly deferred coition (although Alberto may not have intended such a precise interpretation) and gave it an enthusiastic review in the Surrealists' new periodical, *Le Surréalisme au service de la révolution*:

> Symbolically active objects … depend on the delusions and fancies that arise through the functioning of subconscious desires … A wooden ball with a female groove floats suspended on a violin string over a moon-scythe form whose blade almost touches the groove. The observer feels instinctively moved to slide the ball along the blade of the scythe which, because of the shortness of the string, is only partially possible …[12]

Surrealist poet René Crevel gave a parallel account of how the new work had impressed him:

> You set into motion this wooden ball which Giacometti has marked with a female indentation and watch it gliding above the edge of an elongated fruit made of the same material but with a male form: both are at the end of their tether, they are both crazy about each other, and this excitement communicates itself to the viewer, even if one would hitherto hardly have thought it possible; for these are nothing more than two pieces of smooth boxwood, which – if the string should halt the motion of the ball – can never sink into the Nirvana of satisfaction.[13]

Most significant of all, Breton's attention was immediately drawn to the way *Suspended Ball* seemed to tap so revealingly into the unconscious mind, to the extent that he actually acquired the sculpture (keeping it in his collection for the rest of his life) and visited rue Hippolyte to meet the young sculptor. For his part, Alberto had already formed a positive impression of Surrealism – describing it in a letter to his parents as 'the only movement where something is really going on'. The Surrealists seemed to be exploring the most interesting and radical themes, and he realised that his *Suspended Ball* had come about partly because of their emphasis on the importance of dreams and the unconscious. Breton also struck him by his regal self-assurance and charisma as well as by his elaborate sense of courtesy. If Alberto did not succumb to the mellifluous poet's invitation to join the Surrealist ranks right away, it was because he felt that he would be betraying the friendships he had already formed with Masson, Leiris and Bataille – by now well established as the movement's most prominent dissidents. He was unusually scrupulous in decisions of this kind, worrying whether he was acting out of self-interest alone. But the situation was nothing if not fluid, with in-fights and rapprochements, adhesions and resignations, taking place regularly between the two groups.

Alberto had already realised that he was not one of life's joiners, and, since he had never really thrown in his lot with the dissidents, he would never fully subscribe to 'orthodox' Surrealism, keeping in with both sides and synthesising their views, much as he had done with the variety of artistic styles that had greeted him on his arrival in Paris. In any case, all important decisions were put on hold because, coming out of the Galerie Pierre, Alberto suddenly doubled over with an intense, prolonged pain in his stomach and fell into a state of exhaustion, brought on partly no doubt by the anxieties of having his work on show and being thrust into the limelight. Incapable of working, he consulted Dr Théodore Fraenkel, an old friend of Breton's who was well known in both Dada and Surrealist circles, then took to his bed for several weeks. Since the pain did not abate, Diego called in another doctor who diagnosed appendicitis. If Paris was the uncontested centre of all his artistic endeavours and ambitions, Switzerland remained the place where Alberto retreated when he was worn down or ill. He was operated on in a hospital not far from the family home, and the surgeon told him afterwards that further delay in removing his appendix might have proved fatal. Shaken by this near encounter with death before he had even turned thirty, Alberto stayed with his parents for the rest of the summer, drawing strength from a Val Bregaglia carpeted with mountain flowers.

By the autumn of 1930, Alberto was back in Paris, fully recuperated and anxious to make up for lost time. Although he did not join the movement officially until 1931, he began attending various Surrealist gatherings right away, participating in their joint activities and publishing texts influenced by their experiments with automatic writing. Although still somewhat sceptical of certain Surrealist convictions and practices, he had not only officially joined the ranks of the avant-garde but was also on his way to becoming one of its major protagonists. From having been an outsider, the novice Swiss sculptor found himself at the heart of the biggest cultural revolution of the times. Decisively, and almost too rapidly for comfort, a new chapter was beginning, one that would prove central to Alberto's life in Paris and his entire subsequent career.

3

A Fantastic Palace at Night (1930–33)

Encircled by huge mountains the sky goes dark in winter and for months no light reaches the floor of the Val Bregaglia. Those brought up there expect hardship, and they are not likely to have their heads turned by the gloom momentarily lifting or a sudden thaw in the bitter weather.

Success had taken Alberto unawares, but the more he downplayed it, treating it as a fluke, the more it appeared to seek him out. As he woke in the morning in his lugubrious lair, made ghostly by the pale, flickering lights kept on through the night, even he felt obliged to count his blessings. Events had happened so fast that Alberto craved the quiet of the studio to sort them out into some kind of pattern. He lay there for a moment, almost warm for once under the bedclothes, listening to the rain pattering on the roof and dripping onto the floor. It had been less than ten years since he had arrived in Paris, and much of that time had been spent as a lonely foreign student trying to make his way in what seemed to be a closed circle where you might spot the odd group of acknowledged artists and writers in the bars and cafés, and perhaps even get a nod or a greeting, but never actually be one of them. And now, in the space of what seemed like a few months, he had gone from a couple of chance encounters with André Masson and Carl Einstein to being one of the most promising new artists in town. It wasn't only the shows and the notable sales (who else from Bourdelle's class had found their way into the most coveted avant-garde collections?), but a whole new world of influential people, including the leading Surrealists and their avowed enemies, grouped around Bataille, as well as such silver-tongued taste-makers as Jean Cocteau. Without warning, everything had changed. From feeling an outsider, Alberto reflected, it was if he had always lived in Paris.

Nowadays, whenever he was not hard at work trying to bring a complex new construction into existence, Alberto seemed to be mostly in their company, and sometimes en masse, as not long ago when the whole variegated bunch turned up for the screening of Buñuel's film *L'Age d'or*, at the venerable old Cinéma du Panthéon. As with *Un Chien andalou*, Dalí had been involved in the original screenplay, but the two Spaniards had quarrelled violently and fallen out. Eventually Buñuel made the film alone, financed by the Vicomte de Noailles, who also funded the film *Le Sang d'un poète* for Cocteau – with whom his wife, Marie-Laure, had once had an (inevitably) brief affair. Most of the Surrealists, both 'orthodox' and 'dissident', attended, as well as more established writers such as André Gide, and numerous prominent artists, including Picasso, Brancusi and Duchamp. Then Dalí had thrown in a firecracker, denouncing the film as an attack on Catholicism that linked Jesus Christ to the Marquis de Sade and, as previously recounted, a major scandal ensued.

That incident had hardly been isolated, since Alberto's new friends sought to disrupt a society they considered not only corrupt but responsible for the futile war that had so recently ravaged Europe. Breton was old enough to have experienced the horrors of war from the psychiatric ward in a hospital where he had served as an orderly, and the memory of it fed his fanatical devotion to Surrealism. The sons were rising up against their fathers, surviving on a heady mix of artistic innovation and revolutionary fervour. Combining Freudian revelations with Marxist analysis, the Surrealist way of thinking advocated a complete revolt against established norms and promised total freedom, not unlike Communism, as long as it followed the constantly changing dictates – even caprices, as some like Bataille would say – of its leader.

One such whim was a preference for the colour green. Breton dressed quite elaborately with jacket, waistcoat and tie, all in grassy or mossy hues, and he liked to surround himself with variations on that colour, writing in green ink, for instance, and having certain titles of his publications decked out in letters of green. Accordingly, when the Surrealists organised their meetings, as they frequently did, it was considered appropriate to drink crème de menthe or green Chartreuse. When Alberto began joining these key meetings, it is also significant that, while the rank and file sipped their verdant concoctions, he ordered a defiantly non-green cognac. The young man who had boldly questioned his professor Bourdelle, who had recently written a note admonishing himself not to 'be influenced by anything', was clearly not always going to toe the party line, even as the bonds of friendship and mutual admiration drew him closer and closer to Breton.

Fascinated as he was by all the intellectual and artistic commotion he found around him, Alberto was, as we have seen from his attitude to orthodox Surrealism, not a joiner; or if he did join in espousing many of Surrealism's main tenets for a period of some years, it was always (not unlike his amorous relationships) with an implicit 'get-out' clause. If he ever committed to anything outside the absolute singularity of his own personality and vision, it was certainly to Surrealism, then still in the first flush of its controversial brilliance. He was also in his first flush, and without any of the cynicism he later adopted towards

Man Ray, Charles and Marie-Laure de Noailles, Jean Cocteau, Georges Auric [left to right], around 1928

subsequent intellectual fashions, including Existentialism. Moreover, he was exploring numerous directions at this juncture, from an interest in Hegel, Sade, Lautréamont and other Surrealist saints to the seductive upper reaches of the Parisian *beau monde*.

Charles and Marie-Laure de Noailles held a unique position at the crossroads of high society and modern culture. Charles's lineage stretched back to the Crusades, while Marie-Laure had inherited her father's collection of Old Masters along with a banking fortune. The couple became renowned for encouraging and financing new directions in all the arts, from music to architecture, and the parties they gave in their vast mansion, decorated by Jean-Michel Frank on the place des Etats-Unis (now the Musée Baccarat), have become the stuff of legend. Portrayed by Dalí and Balthus, the rather plain Vicomtesse also delighted in shocking her primmer guests by showing them the original manuscript of Sade's *120 Days of Sodom*, which she kept in a phallus-shaped leather case. What 'Marie-Laure' (as she was known even to people who had never met her) did and said at her fabled soirées and costume balls still cuts the ice in certain fossilised Parisian circles.

Alberto, who also made a small plaster head of Marie-Laure (later cast in bronze), was immediately drawn to the couple once they acquired his *Gazing Head*, as any young artist would be by such an early, significant sale. Their wealth and sophistication so impressed him that he wrote home eagerly to report that on 'Saturday I went to see a marquise in a palace with enormous rooms. I would never have believed that such luxury even existed,'[1] and, in a letter to his youngest brother, Bruno, that on 'Sunday I went to a reception where there were many very well-known people and it amused me, and anyway I stayed in a corner drinking cocktails'.[2] Seated between the Vicomte and Vicomtesse at lunch, Alberto was struck by the silver plate, the marble table and the liveried footmen standing behind each chair.[3] These glimpses of Alberto's new 'high life' provoked not only pride in the rustic family home but also a salutary ribbing from his father, Giovanni, who replied: 'We are most impatient to hear Alberto speak to us about his new acquaintances and to tell us about his invitations to princesses and marchionesses. We too will put on white gloves to receive him.'[4]

Although Alberto's forays into the Noailles' lavish receptions and fancy-dress evenings dwindled once the novelty wore off, he and Diego were invited to work on a monumental sculpture for the garden of the couple's new summer residence, designed and built in reinforced concrete by the architect Robert Mallet-Stevens, at Hyères on the Côte d'Azur. Having chosen a huge block of pale stone from a quarry in Burgundy and had it transported to the Noailles' villa, Alberto and Diego laboured on it sporadically for two years. Standing nearly ten feet high, the statue-like piece suggests a huge, disembodied leg bent slightly at the knee when seen from a certain perspective, but its aspect changes as the viewer moves around it, so that the whole sculpture, now rarely exhibited, remains shrouded in an enigmatic aura. No doubt the Noailles, like the rank and file of the Surrealists, welcomed its incongruity, looming up in all its threatening erectness in their Mediterranean garden, as one more proof of their fearless modernity.

The Noailles came up with another, more playful idea – somewhat in the tradition of past *grands seigneurs* – to amuse their guests at a musical event they were organising in Hyères. Happy to please his lavish patrons, Alberto painted a huge giraffe on a wooden panel: its spots were designed as removable panels that would turn out to contain various poetic phrases and puns courtesy of Luis Buñuel (one spot described a vast orchestra playing *Die Walküre* in a basement, another 'Christ laughing hysterically'). The two artists installed it in the villa's garden in the spring of 1932 before the guests arrived. '… before going into dinner,' Buñuel recalled, 'each guest was allowed to climb a ladder and read the spots. After coffee, Giacometti and I wandered back into the garden only to discover that our work of art had vanished without a trace. Had this been one scandal too many? (I still have no idea what happened to it, and, oddly enough, Charles and Marie-Laure never mentioned it to me).'[5]

Enigma, usually with violent or fearful undertones, proved to be the key element of Alberto's work throughout this period. *Disagreeable Object*, dating from 1931, might be described as an oversized, spike-sprouting phallic form or a punitive dildo with no obvious purpose beyond its ability to puzzle and perturb; beyond that, the work defies categorisation, as indeed the artist intended. Fellow Surrealist Man Ray, who became almost as ubiquitous on the Paris arts scene as Cocteau, was quick to photograph this half-alarming, half-spoofy object, adding to its enigma brilliantly by presenting all nineteen inches of it clutched like a child to the naked breast of a beautiful woman.* *Disagreeable Object to be Thrown*, made in the same year, exudes a similar sense of indefinable menace coupled with the patent purposelessness of its shallow hollows and sharp protuberances.

These 'Moving and Mute Objects', as Alberto himself described them beside a series of seven relevant sketches in his first published piece of writing,† reflect both the sculptor's personal fears and sexual fantasies – fetishes, indeed, as Leiris had suggested – as well as his sly, black humour. (It is worth pointing out here that, like Alberto, Leiris openly confessed to problems with impotence.) In referring to them as he often did as 'objects without bases', Alberto was also suggesting that these curious pieces, which were neither decorative nor utilitarian, stood outside the bounds of 'art', challenging all previous definitions of what constituted a sculpture. As such, they perfectly catch the Surrealist fascination with the mysterious ambiguity of discarded objects, as well as their conviction that real works of art were 'found' objects dredged up, ready-made, from the unconscious. At one point, Alberto and Breton combed through various stalls at the flea market in Saint-Ouen together to find items (a metal mask and a wooden spoon that ended in a little carved shoe) that sparked off a stream of suggestively random associations.

The whole tenor of Alberto's work in the early 1930s is a response to the challenges of Surrealist invention and freedom, although he was soon aware of its equally constrictive, dogmatic aspects (drinking crème de menthe being the least of them, given Breton's homophobia). Alberto's enormous versatility and skill as an artist was ably seconded by Diego and a Basque artisan named Ihitsague, who carved many of the first versions of the works in wood from Alberto's designs before they were cast in bronze. Yet there is nothing in Alberto's work and life, as all those who have written about him would surely attest, that is not complex, filled with further, half-hidden events, touching on other experiences and meanings. And much of the tension and anguish, the violent sexual implications and only half-humorous

*The woman in question was called 'Lili' (full name Emilie Carlu), and she also posed in another memorable photograph with Kiki de Montparnasse (aka Alice Prin) behind Alberto's later Surrealist masterpiece, *The Palace at 4am*.

†In *Le Surréalisme au service de la révolution*, no. 3, 1931. The sketches of the seven Surrealist objects are framed by an 'automatic' prose poem written by Alberto.

intimations of dread lead back to a woman who remains half in shadow, but excruciatingly present to the artist during their long, tortured affair.

For years she was known to posterity only as Denise, but more recent research has revealed her full name as Denise Maisonneuve. Alberto most likely met her in one of the dubious bars that had become his regular nocturnal haunts in Montparnasse. Denise certainly liked to drink and took to it unreservedly, as she did to ether, when things in her life were going awry. As a working-class girl with no advantages beyond her looks, she made her way by whatever expedients came to hand. Alberto appears to have been one of them, since she lived at least partly off the meagre sums of money he stumped up for her. But they clashed and quarrelled constantly before breaking up and being reunited dramatically over a period of some four years, unable to live either together or apart. If Alberto's sculpture called on deep reserves of black humour and panic, it was due as much to this passionate, on-off liaison as his new adhesion to Surrealism and the rich imagery of the unconscious. Where Denise was inclined to fits of despair, Alberto retreated into his all-too-real fear of emotional commitment. The violent rows were shot through with jealousy, Alberto because she continued an affair with a boyfriend who sold fruit off a market stall (memorably nicknamed 'Dédé le raisin', or 'Andy the Grape'), Denise because he continued to frequent prostitutes. Denise also wanted to be taken back to Switzerland and presented to Alberto's mother, a request that he, the respectful son under the matriarchal thumb, adamantly refused.

To add to the couple's problems, Alberto's obsessive fascination with sex workers knew no bounds once Le Sphinx, a luxury brothel, opened in Montparnasse in 1931. Situated conveniently close to the big brasseries, this elegant establishment on boulevard Edgar Quinet called itself a 'Bar Américain' and, with its restaurant and dance floor open to all, it looked like any other large, refined café apart from being decorated throughout in the 'Egyptian fashion' – or what was briefly called the 'Nile style'. The women who worked there, about seventy in all with up to three punters a night (but limited to two on Sundays), were reputedly not obliged to consort with anyone they did not fancy, and clients were welcome to drop in for a drink and a chat among friends

James Boswell, *Le Sphinx*, 1937

without being expected to proceed further. Indeed, some patrons came in with their wives and even their children, although one wonders what the latter made of all the half-naked ladies flitting to and fro. Regulars came to include Samuel Beckett (sometimes accompanied by Alberto), Ernest Hemingway, Henry Miller and Jean-Paul Sartre, who had no hesitation in bringing Simone de Beauvoir with him. All tastes were catered to, including the 'love that dare not speak its name', allowing Marlene Dietrich to carry on her affair with French actress Madeleine Sologne freely there. But even in a city where bordellos of all kinds were commonplace, from Le Chabanais, once favoured by Edward VII,* to the brisk-sounding 'Le One-Two-Two', the Sphinx stood out for its relaxed atmosphere, more like a club than the furtive establishments (lovingly recorded by Brassaï) that Alberto had known hitherto.

One of its clients, Julien Levy, an art dealer who was to put on a show of Alberto's Surrealist sculpture in his New York gallery in 1934, wrote a tribute to the Sphinx in his memoirs:

> The atmosphere was half-nude, very carnival, pretty and amusing. The artists in the neighbourhood had developed a habit of coming to the Sphinx at aperitif time in the late afternoon, just

*The portly royal kept a special chair there, built to facilitate sedentary lovemaking.

> for the pleasure of having a glass of wine and chatting in this rather unusual atmosphere. The girls were not at all averse to this, enjoying being treated to a drink by the artists and having a chat before their professional clients came in, usually later in the evening. This became a habitual indoor café for the 'in' group. It was nice, and clean, and fun, and the girls were pleasant and pretty, something rather unusual for the everyday, or rather every-night, cathouse in Paris.[6]

For a man who doubted his ability to accomplish the sexual act satisfactorily and who, in any case, lived most intensely through his eyes, the Sphinx was a godsend. Quite clearly, Alberto was powerfully drawn to women, and any suggestion that he was also sexually attracted to men – because he became friends with such well-known homosexuals as the poet René Crevel, or, later, the writer Jean Genet – seems unlikely.[7] Such attraction as existed was probably prompted by his sympathy towards unorthodox sexual and moral behaviour, even though, much later on, he confided to Francis Bacon: 'Whenever I'm in London, I feel homosexual.'[8] At the Sphinx, he could surround himself with prostitutes (who, he admitted early on, 'attract and amaze me',[9] and who were to become one of his favourite artistic subjects) without feeling obliged to do more than buy a few drinks, chat with anyone who was around and absorb the whole tolerant and ultimately very human atmosphere; in his notebooks, he sometimes jotted down remarks he heard made here or at other brothels. Above all, Alberto could give himself over to the excitement of watching how the sexes intermingled, with the girls gliding through the rarefied, pink-lit spaces before deciding upon which entranced client they would confer their favours.

While his evenings at the Sphinx afforded Alberto a welcome respite from the tensions of his relationship with Denise, a chance incident in Montparnasse was to shake him to the core. In early April 1932, he had been drinking at Le Dôme with friends, including Tzara and a young artist called Robert Jourdan, when a few of them moved on with Alberto in tow to find somewhere discreet to enjoy a hit of opium. Diego, who was sitting with his own friends at a nearby table, made it clear that he did not like the idea but, although he usually took his brother's advice into account, Alberto was not in a mood to back down. Unusually handsome but not homosexual, Jourdan had been taken up by Cocteau and Bérard who had introduced him to the drug. Since he had brought plenty of opium dross with him that evening, one of the young women with them suggested going back to her flat. There they tiptoed past her sleeping children to a bedroom where they all ingested the substance. Alberto dozed off almost immediately under its stupefying effect – as he tended to on the few occasions he took drugs – and soon everyone was fast asleep.

Alberto came to early the following morning to find himself lying fully clothed on a bed in a strange room. Jourdan lay next to him, also still dressed. At first Alberto thought Jourdan was still sleeping, but his body was completely inert. He wasn't even breathing, and when Alberto touched his hand lightly he found it limp and cold. To his horror, he realised that Jourdan was dead. Once again, as on that morning with Van Meurs in the hotel in the mountains, he was trapped in a strange room with a dead man. Keeping on the move, keeping the light shining through the night, had done nothing to avert death. Intentionally or otherwise, Jourdan had overdosed. Fear and guilt flooded through Alberto. Was this his fault, his curse? Was he doomed to have people die around him? He had to get away as quickly as possible. Next door the two little girls were still soundly asleep. Unnoticed by anyone, he made his way down to the street and found a cab to take him back to the security of rue Hippolyte.

To Alberto's relief, he found Diego, who was as reassuring as his taciturn nature allowed. The story did not end there, of course. Having been notified of the death, the police called Alberto in for cross-examination; as in the case of Van Meurs' death, he was under investigation. Since Jourdan's father, a high-ranking civil servant, intervened, the details of the case were hushed up, and Alberto was cleared of any suspicion. But the shadow of the death remained, darkening the predicament into which a rackety love life – however flatteringly it seemed to echo Breton's recently published love story, *Nadja* – had already plunged the newly fêted artist. As always, only one recourse was available: to work, to plan, to draw and to make new sculptures.

If keeping the lights on could not keep the fear of death at bay, then art would.

By its very title, *No More Play* (1932) sounds a warning note. Alberto had turned thirty, become embroiled in a tumultuous love affair and had woken up early one morning to find himself lying next to a corpse.

It was time to review his place in the universe: to absorb his already considerable experience of life and confront his deepest fears and desires, stretching his experimental sculpture as far as it would go. *No More Play* is a rectangular slab of white marble about the size of a game board with numerous indentations in it.* It resembles certain African games like Bao that Alberto would have seen in ethnographic collections. As recent research suggests, it also harks back to the little graves depicted in Hell in Fra Angelico's *The Last Judgement*.[10] Significantly, both sources would indicate that Alberto had strayed far from the Surrealist-approved procedure of finding images ready-made in one's unconscious (prized though tribal culture had become), with the artist still calling unrepentantly on his rich store of art-historical images. In the centre of the board, one of the graves contains a tiny skeleton, while two isolated figures, one apparently female and motionless, the other with arms upraised, stand on either side. It is tempting to link the skeleton with Jourdan's death and the figures with Alberto and Denise, as if transfixed in a game over which they have no control. At all events, Denise clearly overshadowed Alberto's imagination, to the extent that he confessed to Breton in the summer of 1933 that he was unable, in good, orthodox Surrealist fashion, to make anything that was not connected to her (Breton was to make a similar confession about his future wife, Jacqueline Lamba, in *L'Amour fou*). But it is most unlikely that Alberto himself would have accepted such a simplistic, biographical interpretation of this or indeed any other work, even though they often appear to cry out for this kind of elucidation.

Another outstanding example of Alberto's foray into transgressive subject matter – and his radical transposition of sculpture from its lofty pedestal to the dirty floor – is *Woman with Her Throat Cut*, also made in 1932. Here, Alberto has given free rein to a murderous passion in which a female form appears to have been not only raped and murdered but stripped to its skeleton and left, like the disquietingly

**No More Play* was first made in plaster, and it was photographed by Man Ray for an article by Christian Zervos in *Cahiers d'art*. A copy of this original version was given to Zervos by Alberto, who also donated a copy of the edition in marble to a sale to help bankroll the financially beleaguered *Cahiers d'art*. Generous as these gestures were, Alberto could not have been unmindful that to have a publication as influential as the *Cahiers* behind him would serve his career well.

large, complex insect it resembles, to die on the ground. It is worth noting that the Surrealists were fascinated with certain insects and their sexual practices; both Breton and Eluard bred praying mantises, and Dalí is known to have observed their mating ritual, in which the female eventually devours the male, with complicit glee. Once again, since we know of Alberto's fury at Denise's infidelities (while no doubt making light of his own uninterrupted whoring), obvious clues to deciphering the complex figure lie conveniently to hand – even though suggestions that Alberto might have been working out some Jack the Ripper fantasy seem too far-fetched. Denise may indeed have been the catalyst for this, the most alarming sculpture Alberto ever made, but, as in every major work he created, its roots lie deeper and wider. Violence was very much in the creative air. The visual shock of *Un Chien andalou* still reverberated, and one need look no further than the brilliant, half-crazed poet and actor Antonin Artaud to find eloquent incitements to violence in the theatre. Artaud, whose path crossed Alberto's often, took up a position as extreme and individualistic as Bataille's, claiming the need for actual, physical violence on stage in any play that was to have a meaningful impact. He elaborated his influential theory in two manifestos, published jointly as *The Theatre of Cruelty* in 1932.

Similarly, Alberto's notebooks of the time contain jottings such as: 'Woman eats son/son suckles woman/man penetrates woman/woman absorbs man/at the same level.'[11] Fantasies of sexual violence stretch back to the very first stirrings of Alberto's erotic life. They permeate not only the sculptures he made throughout his adherence to Surrealism, such as *Point to the Eye* (1931–2),* but the texts that he began to compose while directly under the influence of Breton as well as other writer friends, such as the poets Louis Aragon and Paul Eluard, in what remained a predominantly literary movement. At this time, he became close friends with Crevel, making his first ever engraving for the frontispiece of the Surrealist poet's fantastical 1933 novel, *Les pieds dans le plat*.†

*Since the artist lived principally through his eye, this sadomasochistic imagining that represents a threateningly pointed object about to gouge out an eye carries a particular charge of self-aggression. Violent attacks on the eye figured widely in the avant-garde art of the time, notably in *Un Chien andalou* (as previously discussed) and in Georges Bataille's strange, erotic *Story of the Eye*, evocatively illustrated by André Masson and published in 1928.

†Translated and published in English as *Putting My Foot in It*.

Following Breton's advice, Alberto had also begun reading the Marquis de Sade, whose long-banned libertine writings had gained great favour among the Surrealists, both dissident, like Bataille and Masson, and orthodox, notably Buñuel and Dalí. Seeking to affirm his Surrealist credentials, Alberto no doubt exaggerates his cruel, sexual imaginings by tracing them all the way back to his early adolescence, while he was still at school. Towards the end of an early text, entitled 'Yesterday, Shifting Sands', he writes:

> I remember a similar kind of repetitive requirement my mind made on me during that same period. I could not get to sleep in the evening without first imagining that I had crossed a dense forest at dusk and come to a grey castle which stood in the most hidden, unknown spot. There I killed two men before they could defend themselves. One of them, about seventeen years old, always looked pale and frightened; the other wore a suit of armour with something on its left side that shone like gold. I raped two women once I had ripped off their clothes. One was thirty-two years old and dressed in black with a face like alabaster; then her daughter, who wore loosely floating white veils. The whole forest echoed with their cries and their groans. I killed them too, but very slowly (night had fallen by then) and often beside a stagnant green pond in front of the castle. Then I burnt down the castle and fell contentedly asleep.*

Alarming and fascinating in equal measure as both Alberto's sculptures and writings of this period are, the young artist could be regarded as so swayed by his recent Surrealist affiliation as to be overwhelmed by it and, eventually, half consciously playing up to it. Despite his desire to 'not let myself be influenced by anything',[12] he appears to have been swept up by the potent promises of Surrealism to replace the old, decayed order with a new, liberated world where instinct and dream, creativity and freedom would reign unchecked. He had, moreover, developed an admiration for Breton that at times seems close to the kind of crush a schoolboy might have on an older pupil. Yet, for all his eagerness to absorb new interests

*First published in *Le surréalisme au service de la révolution*, no. 5, 1933. Translated by the author.

and his increasingly tolerant sociability, which allowed him to traverse these agitated, polarised times without losing close friends, there was a steely side to Alberto that left him unbound to anything outside his central, artistic quest, even if that would take another decade to emerge fully fledged. The fact that he never entirely espoused any cause but his own also protected him from compromising his individuality, unlike many of Surrealism's long-term recruits. If *Woman with Her Throat Cut* stands out as a key, indeed arguably *the* key, work of this period, it is because it succeeds in combining many of the movement's major interests with the sculptor's own personality; also, one suspects, a generous dose of Alberto's impish humour which, particularly during these times of revolutionary fervour and invention, infused his work as much as the dialectical bent of his reasoning and his teasing style of conversation.

One other element was Alberto's natural desire (which he would rue) to stand out, to show how far he was prepared to go with his Surrealist aim to shock the eye. There was a definite sense of rivalry among the unruly band of Surrealists, with some of them trying to outdo each other in their slavish adherence to the imperious Breton's latest rulings, while others vied to go to the furthest extremes in challenging convention, both in their work and in their behaviour in public. Salvador Dalí, with whom Alberto enjoyed a cordial, if not close, relationship, had singled himself out by his carefully curated blend of weird, deliquescent imagery and shameless self-exhibitionism, and the young Swiss sculptor, while of a very different cast of mind and temperament, would not have taken kindly to being outshone by the witty but perfidious Catalan. *Woman with Her Throat Cut* had delivered a savage blow to every notion of classical beauty and the female image itself, long enshrined in the great tradition of art as muse and mother, goddess and *femme fatale*. But for some time now a more complete, more dream-like and enigmatic composition had been forming in Alberto's imagination. Towards the end of 1932, the concept had evolved so completely in his mind that it took only a day to construct: *The Palace at 4am*. 'I knew to the nearest millimetre how it ought to be. I didn't retouch a thing,' Alberto commented later.[13] While the process of producing an image that is already fully formed in one's imagination is typical of Surrealist practice, the piece's basic structure in fact derived from a set design, made for the Meyerhold Theatre in Moscow in 1922, which Alberto had seen in reproduction.

The genesis of this key work in Alberto's Surrealist period could equally be described as lengthy and torturous, growing out of the interstices of his anguished, on-off affair with Denise. 'The happiest days with Denise and the ghastliest days because of Denise', as he put it in one of the notebooks he kept for sketches and jottings.[14] Their encounters always took place at night, since Alberto doggedly reserved the daytime for work and any other art-related business. Caught between a fear of commitment to Denise and an equally powerful fear of losing her – to Andy the Grape or another passing, and no doubt more sexually satisfying, lover – Alberto had entered a kind of twilight zone in which whatever move he made might prove disastrous (and the title he devised for his autobiographical text, 'Yesterday, Shifting Sands', may well have been prompted by this long-drawn-out uncertainty). The repetitive swings between ecstatic intimacy and raging jealousy in this *délire à deux* had bred an atmosphere of unreality out of which Alberto had created a kind of equivalent construction. In it, as in a hauntingly confused dream, everything seems charged with significance without ever disclosing an identifiable meaning.

In Alberto's own account, *The Palace at 4am* began as a game in which he and Denise would spend time building fragile little structures out of matchsticks that invariably collapsed at the slightest movement. Eventually this game grew in his imagination into a delicate construction containing an anonymous female figure and, placed at intervals, three spectral forms resembling a bird's skeleton (which had apparently appeared in one of Denise's dreams), a disembodied backbone and a ball housed in a niche. Alberto underlines the almost unconscious and fully surreal evolution of the work in another text, written shortly after completing *The Palace*:

> This object gradually came together at the end of summer 1932, dawning slowly on me as the various parts took on their exact shapes and their precise placements in the whole. Come autumn, it had such presence that actually making it took me no more than a day.
>
> It harks back, for sure, to the period of my life that had come to an end a year earlier, a period of six months spent hour after hour with a woman who embodied the whole of life within her, transforming my every second into a marvel.

> We built a fantastic palace in the night (days and nights had the same colour, as if everything had happened just before early morning; throughout that time I never saw the sun), a very fragile palace made of matchsticks – with the slightest wrong move, a whole bit of the tiny structure would collapse and we would start on it all over again.*

The text continues in the same half-mystical, half-magical vein, and in keeping with the oneiric tone of Breton's *Nadja* Alberto purports not to know how the backbone in its cage or the bird skeleton found their way into this evanescent structure. More tellingly, he does mention that the female figure arose out of a very early memory of his mother, whose long black dress swept along the floor and which, since it seemed to him to be part of her body, had frightened him as a child. (As the dutiful son dared not take his mistress to meet his mother, had he solved the issue by introducing the two women subliminally in this dramatic figment?) These observations, as well as others that Alberto published subsequently, have become crucial texts in Giacometti scholarship. It is worth noting at this point that, alongside his prowess as a sought-after avant-garde sculptor, Alberto's intellectual and linguistic skills won him the distinction of being published regularly in the leading art journals of the day – a feat made all the more remarkable by the fact that he had arrived in Paris a decade earlier with only the broken French of a gauche, mountain-bred foreigner. Another sign of recognition came when *The Palace* was photographed by Man Ray – once purely as a work of art, then with two legendary young women of Montparnasse, Kiki and Lili, posing seductively behind its web of enigmatic spatial connections.†

Coming after a variety of provocative art objects left deliberately open to interpretation, *The Palace* is shrouded in a dream-like enigma reminiscent of the taut, unresolved atmosphere of Giorgio de Chirico's *Squares* (Alberto also made frequent use of the square as a spatial platform in subsequent sculptures). It may be seen best as a stage on

*Published in *Minotaure*, no. 3–4, December 1933. Founded in Paris in 1933 by Albert Skira and the Greek-born publisher Tériade, *Minotaure* was a lavishly illustrated art and literary magazine that ran for thirteen issues before ceasing publication in 1939. The *Minotaure* title had originally been suggested by Bataille and Masson, who would have contributed prominently to the magazine had they not been ousted by the more formidable duo of Picasso and Breton.

†Kiki, Man Ray's mistress, later nicknamed the 'Queen of Montparnasse', and Lili (Emilie Carlu), who later shared her life with the painter Jean Dubuffet, were prominent in avant-garde circles.

which Alberto is acting out not only such key Surrealist themes as the interdependence of sex and death, man and woman, memory and desire, but also his more personal preoccupations of finding himself cast adrift by his destructive liaison with Denise. The unreality and sense of having lost his bearings in existence might not have stemmed solely from the deeply disruptive affair but also from something that touched him as deeply: the direction that his art had taken. Alberto periodically chafed at the constrictions that being a 'party member' imposed, and it is notable that, although he maintained a well-informed position on the left, reading *L'Humanité*, the French Communist Party's newspaper, every day, the young sculptor never signed up to the party like many of his Surrealist colleagues, including Breton and Aragon. He liked both the effervescence and the commitment of the Surrealists, as well as the lively companionship it provided for him after the first long, lonely years as a foreign art student. Fundamentally, Alberto had not changed. However much he enjoyed company and conversation, he remained a loner, an artist who sensed, instinctively if still obscurely, that his future lay not with modern movements and manifestos but with a far more ancient and elusive quest, for a far more ancient and elusive truth.

In his elation at having become fêted as a young star to watch, Alberto had another worry that would gnaw at him increasingly over the next few years. Although France was partially protected by the strength of its agricultural economy, the effects of the Depression had started to seep seriously into the Parisian art world, with even a resourceful dealer like Pierre Loeb obliged to acknowledge that sales of his avant-garde artists' work were drying up. While Alberto lived frugally, he nevertheless needed to pay Diego, and the cost of his materials, to say nothing of occasional forays to the Sphinx or dinners at the Dôme, mounted up. He had promised himself that he would stand on his 'own two feet', both artistically and financially, but the overall economic situation was clearly worsening.

In the Parisian cultural milieu of the early 1930s, where everybody either knew everybody or knew someone who did, Man Ray, the resourceful American photographer, introduced Alberto to interior decorator Jean-Michel Frank. Having become the go-to designer for wealthy Parisians with adventurous tastes like the Noailles, Frank imposed a starkly minimalist, if highly expensive, aesthetic on his clients,* as Coco Chanel had done with her 'casual chic' in fashion, and he chose materials ranging from the simple, such as gypsum or straw, to the exotic, notably shagreen, ebony and parchment. Frank was also intensely interested in all the truly inventive developments in modern art, and the first meeting with Alberto, whose work Frank already knew, led not only to a lengthy series of commissions for lamps, sconces and sculpted mantelpieces, but also to a close friendship. 'We see each other very often,' Alberto wrote to his parents about his new friend, 'and he's one of the people I like most.'[15]

Alberto thoroughly enjoyed the new, part-time work with Frank. It allowed him to draw and create pleasingly pared-down forms that evolved out of a variety of styles ranging from Cycladic art to the sleek forms of Brancusi. To their parents' satisfaction, it also meant fuller employment for Diego who, not always stretched by his tasks in the studio, had already shown a natural talent for making and fixing things. Together, the brothers produced around a hundred different objects and decorative designs. Furnishing the interiors of the rich was hardly something that would go down well when it reached the ears of his Surrealist comrades (even though Breton happily boosted his own income as a part-time art dealer and adviser). But there was another, altogether more disquieting discovery. Alberto soon realised that he was giving as much thought and care to designing a pair of candlesticks or firedogs as he did to his latest sculptures. Hitherto he had always supposed that the sculptures were intrinsically more interesting and important. That notion no longer seemed so unassailable: perhaps they were indeed both no more than objects, one of them fulfilling a specific function and the other not? The question did not offer an easy response, adding to troubled thoughts about the true value of his activities that were to plague the young artist for several years to come.

Even if Alberto had intended *The Palace* as a kind of epitaph on his relations with Denise, the stormy affair showed no signs of abating. If we didn't already know him better, we might be surprised that he had not found a more suitable female companion. Numerous unusual,

*The French writer François Mauriac, who had acquired some lamps by Alberto, neatly summarised Frank's style as an 'aesthetics of renunciation'.

gifted women moved in the same circles as he did – artists, writers, collectors, as well as models and mistresses – and there was a fairly brisk turnover in the relationships as they evolved. If the manipulative Gala had dumped Eluard for Dalí, the lyrical love poet had found the altogether more enticing Nusch, while Aragon had Elsa Triolet as his muse and Breton, having divorced his first wife, would soon marry Jacqueline Lamba. A lively conversationalist, as well as a good listener, sympathetically attuned to women, Alberto might also have found a soulmate in the upper reaches of society among the art collectors and aristocrats that he mingled with during his visits to the Noailles in their palatial residences. On his visits to Hyères he met such various and gifted personalities as the composer Francis Poulenc, the writer Aldous Huxley and, as mentioned, the poet Max Jacob, an old friend of Picasso's[16] – but apparently no women who captivated him.

One encounter with the opposite sex that challenged Alberto's predilection for the whole range of what are politely termed 'demi-mondaines' was with the Countess Madina Visconti, a wealthy Italian art collector who visited Alberto several times in his studio and sat for her portrait in 1932. Executed in a conventional style that brings Balthus's flattering line* to mind more than Alberto's, the drawing reveals the delicate, refined profile of a young woman with a long, slender neck. As he drew the latter, the Countess recalled, Alberto remarked admiringly that her neck cried out to be strangled or cut – not every woman's idea of seduction. But an attraction in some shape or form had clearly taken place, with Alberto giving his alluring visitor two far more significant drawings as a fond souvenir. One is entitled simply *My Studio*: it shows what amounts to an inventory of Alberto's recent work (and hence a kind of self-portrait), including the *Spoon Woman* and *The Palace at 4am*, and it bears an inscription to the Countess thanking her for finding the dingy surroundings 'not too detestable'. The other one, *Bed, Coat and Sculptures in the Studio*, features another of Alberto's highly suggestive pieces, *Woman in the Shape of a Spider*, shown hanging from a thread-like string over his bed, where apparently it stayed, dangling threateningly, for several years. Although they record some of Alberto's major Surrealist works, one might note in passing, the calm, almost

*Alberto may already have seen Balthus's languorous drawings of young women, but the two artists did not become friendly until after Balthus's show at Galerie Pierre in April 1934.

Ingresque line of these topographical studies makes them look as if Surrealism had never existed.

If Alberto was sexually attracted to the Countess, we have no way of knowing whether the feeling was reciprocated. At all events, since womankind was basically divided for him into two categories – 'goddesses' and 'whores' – it is likely that Madina belonged too clearly to the former for any earthly, or indeed earthy, passion to be involved. Thanks to the two factually precise drawings, the winner in this encounter was the studio itself which, from this point on, began to assume a parallel existence, not only as the definitive arena of Alberto's creativity, but also as the most reliable archive of his work and a mirror of his life.* Talented photographers were not slow to see the picturesque possibilities of a cave-like space in which the most challenging modern sculpture was being produced in almost slum-like surroundings before ending up in the refined interiors of wealthy taste-makers such as the Noailles or sophisticated bankers like Pierre David-Weill,† or indeed their decorators – although Jean-Michel Frank himself preferred to exclude any works of art that might disturb the neutral tones of his sparse interiors. 'Such a nice boy,' Cocteau remarked when he saw Frank's own minimalist flat. 'Pity he's been burgled.'

To accompany their publication of Alberto's text on *The Palace*, the influential art magazine *Minotaure* commissioned the affable Hungarian-born photographer Brassaï – who had just made a name for himself with *Paris by Night*, his dramatically lit studies of the city's seamier but undeniably atmospheric side – to do a reportage on Alberto's studio. As a good convert to Surrealist dogma, Alberto made a point of informing Brassaï that he had 'visualised all these forms in almost final form, that he had executed them without any thought about their significance, and that their meaning was revealed to him only later'.[17] Like the drawings given to Donna Madina, Brassaï's photographs record numerous sculptural elements but none of the photogenic chaos that later characterised the studio. Indeed, although dour, the space has been meticulously arranged and swept for the shoot or, unlikely as it seems, perhaps Alberto still

*Diego's activities had become more demanding and essential as Alberto's commissions for decorative objects and elements grew, and a room on the other side of the narrow alleyway outside the studio had been rented for him to work in. Later Diego took over a less exiguous space in the rue Hippolyte complex.

†Grandson of one of the founders of the Lazard Frères bank.

Brassaï, Self-portrait, 1932

adhered to Swiss orderliness and kept his surroundings neat and tidy. The two gregarious men hit it off right away, and Brassaï continued to record Alberto's universe with his camera frequently thereafter. Alberto was delighted when he saw the shots Brassaï had taken, and he was quick to appreciate how useful such documents could be, not only to illustrate articles and reviews, but to circulate in the art world and to promote the kind of aura that artists like Picasso and Matisse had created through being photographed with their work. He was also fully aware that photogenic studios added an extra dimension to the myth that evolves around all artists in the public eye. As Giacometti's renown grew, so did his studio's. Like its inmate, the hovel at 46 rue Hippolyte-Maindron had begun its long, unlikely rise to fame.

Another degree of success attended Alberto on the Paris gallery scene, badly affected though it was by the general economic downturn. Pierre Loeb had shown Alberto's work in his Miró–Arp–Giacometti selection and in a subsequent group exhibition entitled 'Where Are We Going?' in 1931. But the one-year contract that bound them had run out, and Alberto had been chafing under it. 'Pierre is only interested in one-off sales and', he wrote in a letter home, 'I don't want to go on like that. I can handle the odd sale myself, and I want a different context to show my sculpture.'[18] That opportunity had been waiting in the wings in the form of another Pierre, Pierre Colle, who had opened a gallery on the more formal, Right Bank rue Cambacérès and caused a stir by giving Dalí's *The Persistence of Memory* its Paris première. When Alberto accepted Colle's offer of a first solo show in 1932, he was sufficiently aware of its importance to his future career to spend several months fine-tuning the chosen contents, which included a wood-and-steel version of *Suspended Ball*. In the meantime, he remained open – a sign of the worsening economic situation – to any offers for sales from both Loeb and Jeanne Bucher. Since the show went well, Alberto agreed with Colle, a friend of Frank and Max Jacob, to exhibit in a joint Surrealist show at his gallery in July the following year, from which the Noailles bought Alberto's plaster *Table*, with its mysterious, half-veiled head, incongruous polyhedron – a direct reference to Dürer's engraving *Melencolia* – and disembodied hand.* Alongside photographs by Man Ray, Christian Zervos gave the show a positive review, naming Alberto 'the only young sculptor at the moment whose work confirms and prolongs the new directions taken by sculpture'.[19] That autumn, Alberto sent a version in wood of his *Cage* (1930–31) to the Sixth Salon des Surindépendants, where most of the Surrealist artists, from Arp and Dalí to Miró and Man Ray, were exhibiting. Having experimented with it as a device for defining an object in space, Alberto was to use the cage motif frequently during his Surrealist period and on several subsequent occasions (as well as, later, in his paintings). This early example, which frames a clash of aggressively erotic forms, was executed in plaster before

*Alberto's friend the poet René Crevel was close to the Noailles and encouraged them to purchase the *Table*.

being reproduced in wood by a local cabinetmaker. Once the Salon had ended, Alberto left the wooden construction for safekeeping with his friend Max Ernst, who parked it on the balcony of his apartment where, exposed to the wind and rain, it slowly fell apart.

———

What gratified Alberto most about his first one-man show was surely the fact that one of the first visitors was none other than Picasso, at that time still on the prowl to see what was happening on the Paris art scene. The two artists had known each other for a while, but they did not meet properly until Miró brought them together in December 1931. Picasso had just turned fifty and acquired the château at Boisgeloup in Normandy, where he set up a sculpture studio and entertained his lover, Marie-Thérèse Walter, while his wife, Olga, stayed behind in Paris. Twenty years older than Alberto, Picasso could claim world renown and a lifestyle resplendent with grand residences, Hispano-Suiza motor cars and a string of mistresses. More to the point, the younger artist had been following the Spaniard's work closely, along with everyone else in the art world. Einstein, for instance, had published a perceptive analysis of the astonishing 'Bather' pictures that Picasso had painted at Dinard in the first issue of *Documents*, and Zervos had just undertaken to publish the catalogue raisonné of Picasso's entire oeuvre.

Alberto was especially drawn to the inventive fluency with which Picasso took apart and reinvented the female body, since he now also approached the human frame, in a violent and radical way, as an assemblage of limbs and features that could be reconstrued according to the dictates of fantasy or emotion. Alberto had been sufficiently impressed by the major Picasso exhibition he had seen at the Kunsthaus in Zurich in 1932 to copy a number of the works on show into one of his notebooks. Over the next decade their relationship was to deepen considerably until, at the beginning of the war, they were meeting, both alone and with mutual friends, almost daily. Then, in the harsh post-war years, the friendship began to tail off until things grew acrimonious between them. This coincided with the way the art they produced grew more and more distinctly apart, with Alberto concentrating on a single vision in ever more reductive terms, seeking an absolute essence, while Picasso, like the master artificer he was, continued to expand his sources and juggle with an impressive medley of styles.

Of a different order, and of more immediate significance at that particular moment, was Alberto's growing closeness to André Breton who, though only five years older, was becoming almost a father figure to him because of his prominence in the Surrealist movement, his authoritative self-assurance and manifest literary brilliance. It was around this time that Alberto made an idealised, statue-like head of Breton in pencil. 'Seeing Breton every day all winter, when we spent most of our evenings together, was of huge advantage to me. He is by far the most intelligent and sensitive person I know and the only one from whom I learned so much,' Alberto wrote to his father in June 1933.[20] He also turned up at the various Surrealist meetings, many of them provocative and rowdy, that were held at Cyrano's, a working-class café on place Blanche in Montmartre, much favoured by prostitutes and their pimps, or at Breton's apartment, modest yet filled with striking works of art, nearby on rue Fontaine. At one of these meetings, Alberto joined in what were termed 'experimental investigations into irrational knowledge'. Both the questions and the answers in this session admirably capture the Surrealist blend of earnest revolt and witty tomfoolery. One senses that, while confirming the artistic themes he had been exploring, Alberto is also playing for laughs in his replies:

- *Which sex has the crystal ball?* Hermaphrodite.
- *How does it end?* It explodes.
- *On what part of the bed would you put it?* At the height of the heart, when the bed is empty.
- *What crime is associated with it?* Cruelty, violence.
- *On what part of a naked dead woman would you place a piece of pink velvet?* On her chest, over her breast.
- *What disease do you associate with that?* Dementia praecox.
- *In what way would you wrap it?* In two naked arms.
- *What language does it speak?* Ancient Egyptian.
- *How would you kill it?* With a dagger.
- *What perversion was very widespread in the year 409?* They tickled the hips of young girls with a feather as they ran past.
- *How did they pick up girls back then?* You hid yourself at nightfall and when a girl came past you threw yourself on her and raped her.[21]

Man Ray, reproduction of a photograph of the Surrealist group: Man Ray, Hans Arp, Yves Tanguy, André Breton; front: Tristan Tzara, Salvador Dalí, Paul Eluard, Max Ernst, René Crevel [left to right], around 1930

Thanks in large part to Breton's influence, Alberto was growing increasingly interested in exploring his ideas and sensations through writing texts of various kinds, whether for publication or as scraps jotted down pell-mell in his notebooks – partly in his native Italian, but also in French, which he continued to adopt and adapt to his particular needs. He drew on his literary talents throughout his career, and he might have developed them significantly if he had not been so intently focused on art. Although he had several artist friends, particularly during this period in his life, Alberto was clearly most drawn to writers of every kind, from Bataille, Leiris and Artaud to Crevel, Aragon and Breton, and for the rest of his life he continued to gravitate towards literary circles.

Articulate and widely read, Breton took Alberto's literary education deliberately in hand, recommending specific authors for him to discover, such as the poet Achim von Arnim. Alberto was already familiar with the German Romantic writers from his Swiss German schooling, and since one of the attractions of Surrealism was the escape it offered from the Protestant ethic of his upbringing, he was more struck by other authors they admired – Sade, Alfred Jarry, Raymond Roussel – and the writings of the Surrealists themselves. As a mark of his admiration for Breton, Alberto presented him with the portrait he had recently done of the writer. He also made four etchings to be included in *L'Air de l'eau*, Breton's new volume of poems.*

What drew artist and writer even closer was the death of Alberto's father, Giovanni, from a cerebral haemorrhage at the age of sixty-five on 25 June 1933 in a clinic near Montreux. On hearing the news, Alberto and Diego left Paris immediately on the night train, arriving in Switzerland the following day. Having felt so ill that he was unable to attend the funeral, Alberto stayed at the hospital, falling into a deep depression, then returned to Paris without any particular illness having been diagnosed. After this distressing period, the exchange of letters between Alberto and Breton grew unusually confiding, almost as if Breton had taken on Giovanni's role, confirming the paternal nature of the relationship between them. 'I've been thinking a lot about you and never has it been more difficult for me to leave Paris,' Alberto wrote to Breton. 'Every day I would have loved to drop in and see you, to stay in rue Fontaine for a moment, or to go and eat somewhere together.'[22] Breton's replies struck an affectionate note, addressing Alberto as his '*enfant*': 'Very dear child and friend, you well know that you are the person I miss most. When you're not here, there's no youth, no clarity, no play, no intellectual certainty, not to mention that, if it's not you we're waiting for in the evening at the café, it's perhaps because we're waiting for nobody. Quite apart from my pleasure in seeing you again, it is absolutely necessary for you to come back as soon as you can.'[23]

His father's death had affected Alberto so deeply that later in the summer he felt the need to return to the Val Bregaglia, both to recuperate, as he had done after his appendectomy, and to spend time with his mother, still the anchor of the family, until his father's affairs had been settled. During his extended stay, he organised an exhibition of his father's painting in Zurich and designed the headstone for his grave. Still listless, Alberto felt too discouraged to

*The poems were inspired by Breton's encounter with Jacqueline Lamba, who was to become his new wife and the heroine of *L'Amour fou* (1937).

Giovanni and Annetta Giacometti, early 1930s

do any original work, not least because he knew that his father had disliked Surrealism and disapproved of the objects and constructions he had been making. For all his enthusiasm for his new friends and the gratifying wave of recognition he had been riding, Alberto had never come to terms with doubts about the direction his work had taken. The Surrealist pieces came together successfully enough, and some of them even sold, very handily. They were clever, clever enough to amuse and interest most of the very clever people in Paris who decided what was in and what wasn't, what was avant-garde and what was oh-so-boringly *passé*.

His father had not liked the Surrealists for the kind of 'art' they did, and his mother worried that they would end up making a dreadful Communist of her son. Alberto would never have wanted his parents to disapprove of anything he did. But his father was now dead and his mother in another country. In Paris all he had was his poisoned love affair with Denise, one that was going from bad to worse. In the Surrealists, though, he had found a new family, a tribe almost, with its own rules and rituals. Even when he was in disagreement with their latest party line, they stimulated him, taking him out of himself into a wider world where he could talk and debate. They would become all the more important, all the more central to his future now that his father had gone, leaving a void that could never be filled.

4

Convulsive Beauty (1933–37)

After a decade of living and working in the city, Alberto could still not claim to be a Parisian, let alone French. The core of his being remained rooted in the mountains of the Val Bregaglia, the closest thing he could imagine, far beyond Sumerian or Cycladic art, to eternity. Since turning thirty, however, he had at least become a Montparnassian, as familiar with his neighbours – the carpenters, welders and shopkeepers of Alésia – as he was with the cosmopolitan crowd of artists, writers and drifters who turned up at the Dôme or the Coupole, admiring themselves and each other, along with the latest sleek roadsters that wealthier customers parked along either side of the boulevard. At all these brasseries, including the more discreet Closerie des Lilas* further east towards boulevard Saint-Michel, you could find a tableful of Surrealists presided over by Aragon or Breton, another reserved for Man Ray and Kiki, the 'Queen of Montparnasse', groups of rich Americans doing something or other in the arts while downing endless cocktails, and Dalí, dressed outlandishly and making a dramatically planned entrance to further burnish his image as the mad genius in full 'paranoiac-critical' mode.

*The Closerie has been running since the mid-nineteenth century, patronised by Monet and Cézanne, Baudelaire and Zola; Picasso first went there with Apollinaire. It was particularly favoured by Hemingway, who wrote part of *The Sun Also Rises* there, and another habitué, James Joyce, chose it to celebrate the news that Sylvia Beach, owner of the legendary Shakespeare & Company bookshop, had agreed to publish his controversial *Ulysses*. Joyce could also be found at the bar in the Coupole where he liked to have several whiskies lined up so that he could drink one while enjoying the prospect of the second and third tot.

Café du Dôme, around 1935

Outside the odd invitation to a gallery opening or a collector's house, Alberto's social life revolved around these and a handful of smaller cafés. He would knock back a couple of strong black coffees at the smoke-filled local before moving on to one or other of the grand watering holes that stood out in Montparnasse and Saint-Germain like so many glittering palaces offering warmth and companionship. He didn't keep track of his outings, but his loyal friend and obsessive self-chronicler Michel Leiris did. In his diary covering this anxiously gregarious pre-war period, Leiris records one fairly typical, socially hectic evening: 'Drinks at the Deux Magots with Picasso, Shipman, Baron, the American matador Sidney Franklin, Dora Maar, Pancho Picabia. Saw Miró with his wife and daughter, Roux and Pauline, Vitrac, Janine and Raymond, etc. Met Fargue. At dinner met Giacometti, who was dining with Derain and Balthus. Met Al Brown who was dining with Schiaparelli and Cocteau. Dos Passos passed by. After dinner went to Desnos's place.'[1]

Being Montparnassian meant discovering and becoming truly oneself, another good reason why Alberto could never adhere fully to an all-embracing, programmatic movement like Surrealism, especially in its more dogmatic aspects that sometimes seemed to be conjured up at the whim of its leader. Minor signs of non-conformism – Alberto's flouting of Breton's all-green drink rule, for instance – gradually led to more serious differences, such as when he sympathised openly with Aragon at the height of '*l'affaire Aragon*' in the early 1930s, during which Aragon had been threatened with legal proceedings for publishing an inflammatory poem, *Front rouge*, that incited 'comrades' to 'Kill the cops' and 'Shoot Léon Blum' (prime minister of France). Having defended Aragon against prosecution, Breton then declared that creativity should not be subjected to political influence, at which Aragon declared the Surrealists anti-revolutionary and publicly broke with the movement via the pages of *L'Humanité*. Aragon later recanted, saying that he regretted that he had not cut off the hand that had written the incendiary verses, but his break with the Surrealists was final.

As mentioned, Alberto never officially joined the French Communist Party, as many Surrealists did, but, at Aragon's behest, he contributed crudely expressive drawings to various short-lived, far-left publications. If Aragon gladly accepted the drawings as vivid illustrations of the class struggle, he was also cautious enough to recommend that Alberto use a pseudonym ('Ferrache') in case it became known that the illustrator was one and the same as the designer who created lamps and other decorative objects for the *grands bourgeois* in their (and indeed Aragon's own) well-appointed homes.

A certain flexibility, even permeability, characterised much of the literary and political stance-taking of the period. If Breton excommunicated Surrealists for minor peccadilloes, it did not dissuade him from wooing the rejected back into the fold. Dalí was one example. Having been 'tried' and expelled from the movement in 1934 for 'the glorification of Hitlerian fascism', the irrepressible Catalan self-publicist slunk out of sight for a while, but not before reducing his accusers to laughter by his clowning. The expulsion lasted only a few days, however, after which Dalí wrote an apology and was readmitted; he was not in fact definitively banished until 1939, and then, like several other leading Surrealists, he left for America and never rejoined the group.

Alberto had clearly understood the porousness of these constantly evolving predicaments where, in perhaps a more Latin, relaxed way, people were inclined to alter their once most vehemently held convictions as their own thoughts or the temper of the times changed. Certainly Alberto became adept at changing his own stance while keeping former alliances, just as he had done when distancing himself from the dissident Surrealists, including old friends like Bataille and

Leiris, and drawing closer to the orthodox camp. Having made one or two more directly political moves, such as joining the anti-Fascist 'Association des Artistes et Écrivains Révolutionnaires',* Alberto soon realised that such activities absorbed time and energy that would be better devoted to his art. 'As far as politics goes: everything is pretty clear, there is now nothing for me to do,' he noted. 'Get back to the things that matter. Write often, as often as possible. – Take up my work again completely independently, without the slightest control, complete freedom, and only occupy myself with the things that attract me, whatever and however.'[2]

Although Breton might well have resented Alberto for the support he gave Aragon as he broke with Surrealism, the two men appeared, on the contrary, to grow closer. When Breton decided impetuously to remarry, he asked Alberto to act as a 'best man'. It was a joint ceremony with Eluard who (Gala having forsaken him for Dalí) was marrying Maria Benz, better known by her nickname Nusch. If ever there was to be a Surrealist marriage, this was it, placed firmly under the sign of the 'marvellous', even though the actual ceremony appears to have taken place without any high jinks at the very conventional town hall of the 9th *arrondissement*.

From their beginnings the core Surrealists had taken to finding marvels – the enigmatic, the unsuspected, the incongruous – all over Paris. It was not difficult: if you set your mind to it, as you paced and haunted the old streets of the city, so many things revealed themselves as mysterious, filled with unexplained signs and ambiguous portents. What personal tragedy did that severed porcelain arm gathering dust in a forgotten shop's window record? Who was the beautiful woman in long white gloves who walked every day beneath the clock at the Gare d'Orsay as it struck 4 p.m.? Why did the no. 49 bus appear never to carry any passengers? Before becoming more Communist than Surrealist, Aragon had written a whole book about such everyday marvels in his *Paysan de Paris*, focusing on such strange spectacles as the pedestrian warren of small shops built between the late eighteenth and mid-nineteenth century near the old (now demolished) Opéra le Peletier

*The Association, which numerous left-wing intellectuals joined in the 1930s, published *Commune*, one of the journals to which Alberto contributed political drawings.

and known as the *passages de Paris*.* These covered passages created a city within a city allowing you to go as if underground and incognito from one central area of Paris to another; or, better still, to wander in a dream-like state awaiting an unexpected revelation. To compound their mystery, by the time the Surrealists came to explore them, the grimy windows displayed a variety of merchandise that had lost all relevance, with ancient orthopaedic aids, Balkan military medals and outmoded corsetry to the fore; some abandoned-looking boutiques appeared to have no activity whatsoever, hinting at a range of bizarre purposes. Scouring Paris for oddities of this kind became one of the Surrealists' favourite pastimes, with Breton himself regularly on the lookout for incongruous objects (including 'primitive' art) at flea markets.

A group of Surrealists at the opening of *Dada Max Ernst*, 2 May 1921

Everything about Breton's encounter with Jacqueline Lamba had taken place under the star of wonder: how she had heard of him and come

*Massive works were under way on boulevard Haussmann, which did not open until 1926, and Aragon also laments the damage they did to the old city, including the destruction of his cherished Passage de l'Opéra.

especially to a Surrealist meeting, how 'scandalously beautiful' he found her and how their meeting sparked off the writing of *L'Amour fou*, a trilogy that had begun with *Nadja*. If that were not enough, Jacqueline's whole aura took on spectacular proportions since she had performed naked under water in the large aquarium at the Coliseum on rue Rochechouart, not far from Breton's own apartment. However beautiful, Jacqueline would not only participate fully in the Surrealist movement but become an Abstract Expressionist painter in her own right, developing close friendships with Frida Kahlo and Dora Maar. To commemorate the marriage, Alberto made engravings to illustrate a long love poem of Breton's (inspired by Jacqueline's aquatic dance) at the press that the young English printmaker Stanley Hayter had set up on rue Campagne-Première, not far from the studio that Alberto had rented from Archipenko.*

The closer friendship between sculptor and writer no doubt nourished what was to be Alberto's most consummate, and final, Surrealist sculpture, *Hands Holding the Void* (1934), which also became Breton's favourite Giacometti (ironically enough, given the void into which Breton was about to cast his friend). Later entitled *Invisible Object*, this haunting work is both explicit and ambiguous. The smooth, precise contours of head and body, whether in its original plaster or cast in bronze, speak of clear, rational intent, rendering the space between the two delicately elongated hands all the more evident and puzzling. All Alberto's previous work in a Surrealist vein had contained a fair measure of fantasy, theatricality, even playful comedy. This slender, semi-supernatural or at least other-worldly figure is seated on its chair, leaning forward as if in divination of a mystery: the mystery of absence, of nothingness. The sculpture dramatically combines the unsettling ambiguity of Alberto's Surrealist constructions with the totemic quality of the Cycladic idols that he had long admired and which had inspired two stone female figures he carved in 1932.

The void between the figure's hands, evoking the inability to touch, harks back to Giovanni's recent death, which weighed heavily on Alberto,

*Located at 17 rue Campagne-Première, Hayter's printing shop, Atelier 17, became one of the best-known fine art presses in Paris as well as a regular meeting place for artists – including Picasso, Miró, Dalí and Ernst – to meet, discuss techniques and gossip. A copy of the original edition of *L'Air de l'eau*, published by Editions Cahiers d'art and signed by both Breton and Giacometti, now fetches impressive prices at auction.

whose complex feelings towards his father were above all those of love and admiration for a man who had always been on hand to help him towards becoming the artist he knew he was destined to be. Giovanni had been the person who, as much as his mother, had followed every step of his career and proffered carefully considered advice, personally and by letter, not just on technical and aesthetic issues but practical matters like hanging exhibitions and negotiating with art dealers. But he was the father, too, who had always questioned the validity of Surrealist art: how did it compare to the great achievements they both admired, from the Egyptians to Cézanne, and was it not ultimately an offshoot of the nonsense art of Dada which both father and son had once derided?

Forever questing, forever sceptical, Alberto was increasingly plagued by similar doubts. He acknowledged readily that even his best recent work would never stand comparison with a Cézanne, let alone an Old Master, but he saw the problem from a different angle. Had he not made a serious mistake in joining this merry band of intellectual madcaps and misfits? They were innovative and brilliant, and always catching public attention by their antics, slapping adversaries' faces (as Breton had slapped Soviet writer Ilya Ehrenburg's in Montparnasse in retaliation for describing the Surrealists as 'pederasts'*) and regularly distributing incendiary manifestos. They had shaken up the post-war world. But in its constant revolutions, alignments and expulsions that often seemed like change for change's sake, where was the movement heading, and above all how good, how lasting, was the art it produced? There was Dalí, of course, whose skilful, outrageous fantasies and 'paranoiac-critical' stunts grabbed the headlines, as when at a major Surrealist exhibition in London in 1936 he donned a deep-sea diving helmet before giving a lecture that no one could hear (the audience roared with laughter, but Dalí all but literally suffocated). Then there was the more serious-minded Miró and Ernst, Arp and himself. Yet surely his father had been right to look at all their work more sceptically, from a historical perspective. How would it stand up when placed beside a Rembrandt or a Velázquez, or even a Picasso, who had been focusing more and more on sculpture at his château in Normandy?

*Ehrenburg had written that Surrealists, finding sex with women too conventional, preferred 'onanism, pederasty, fetishism, exhibitionism, and even sodomy'.

The doubts would not go away, enjoyable though it had been to invent these pieces. They came quite easily, like little plays, dramas teeming through his highly sensitive and susceptible imagination that he re-enacted by finding them a form. He was good at it, effortlessly inventive, and people were impressed by the results; increasingly, however, they seemed to be a way of sidestepping the real issue, the issue that had been there ever since he first put pencil to paper, that had dogged him throughout the fruitless hours he had spent at the Grande Chaumière. It seemed so simple and yet forever out of reach: the unattainable mystery of reality. All he wished was to be able to transmit things as he saw them. He could go on inventing the playlets, the clever games, until kingdom come, but he could not catch the spark in his brother's eye or the curve of a model's nose. It seemed like nothing – Breton himself had pooh-poohed the idea of trying to recreate a head – and yet in the end it was everything. If you couldn't catch that extraordinary flicker of life that lay in the eye like the sun glinting on the sea – what did your art become? Clever, perhaps, but mechanical, hollow, repetitive – lifeless.

Later on, Alberto saw his predicament of that time calmly and clearly. 'With time I realized I had let myself get involved,' he told the art critic Jean Clay. 'Without wanting to, you let yourself be influenced by superficial things, you want to win, to be successful. You let yourself be challenged. You work to impress people. Or you begin to repeat yourself ... I was on the wrong path, the downward path.'[3] He himself was above all conscious of *Invisible Object*'s shortcomings. 'I was satisfied with her hands and her head because they were just as I intended them,' he recounted in another interview. 'But I wasn't satisfied in the least with the legs, the body or the breast. They seemed too academic, too conventional. That made me want to work from life again.'[4]

In one of life's ironies, all the soul-searching that Alberto underwent did nothing to diminish the success of the sculpture. Breton felt especially involved in its genesis because the two of them had made a visit to the Puces de Saint-Ouen, the flea market where Alberto had come across an iron mask which proved useful in the inception of his ambiguous figure's head, and he wrote about the piece fulsomely in *L'Amour fou*. Photographer and painter Dora Maar, soon to become Picasso's latest flame (an event which the Paris art world greeted with much the same rapture as the court at Versailles when Louis XIV changed mistresses), came to photograph the piece in Alberto's studio, and she later made a fine portrait of him. Man Ray also stopped by to capture other recent works, *Head-Skull* and *Cube*, an irregular polyhedron that ranks as his most abstract sculpture, to illustrate a general essay published in Skira and Tériade's review, *Minotaure*. Just as he was reacting against Surrealism, Alberto was reaping the benefits of his success as a committed party member.

It has been suggested that *Head-Skull* was originally situated between those hands holding the void. For Alberto, death itself – the 'undiscovered country, from whose bourn/No traveller returns' – was the void, and the void was very much on his mind, since not only his father had disappeared into it but also his two paternal uncles, leaving him, at only thirty-three, the oldest male in the whole family. But death did not end there, as Alberto was painfully aware.

His close friend Crevel had, with his Rimbaud-like rebelliousness and youthful good looks, become something of a poster boy for Surrealism, even though he became openly critical of what he called the movement's 'craze for originality at all costs',[5] particularly as the political situation in Europe worsened. Breton frowned conspicuously on homosexuality and let everyone know it. That was one of the problems that the bisexual Crevel* had to contend with, but he was also badly affected by the growing schism between the two causes he espoused: the Surrealists on the one hand and the French Communists, who regarded all bourgeois intellectuals with distrust, on the other. The situation worsened after Breton's spat with Ehrenburg, and Crevel despaired not only of any reconciliation between the two parties but also of recovering from the renal tuberculosis that threatened his life. Having attempted to self-medicate with morphine, he had been treated for the illness in Switzerland, where Alberto had visited him several times. Crevel believed he had been cured, wrongly as it turned out, and the news that the disease was still rampant overwhelmed him. Just before he committed suicide in June 1935, he left a note requesting that his body be cremated and ending in a single word: 'Disgust'.

---

*The Argentinian Countess Tota Cuevas de Vera, who was also close to Buñuel, was his last mistress.

Another close friend of Alberto's, also queer and who also took his own life, was Jean-Michel Frank, now widely acknowledged as the most innovative designer and decorator of the day. Frank, who came from a wealthy Jewish family marked by tragedy (both his brothers were killed in the Great War, and his father hanged himself, as did Crevel's),* had developed adventurous tastes in modern art and literature, especially the writings of Marcel Proust and André Gide, before falling mostly by chance into the profession because Aragon happened to suggest that he might decorate his Paris apartment. This fact in itself sheds an interesting light on the whole period: just as the left-leaning Alberto saw no particular contradiction between his political beliefs and hobnobbing with ultra-wealthy aristocrats, neither did Aragon, whose politics at that time were similar, see anything seriously amiss about living in luxury while being a lifelong member of the French Communist Party and fiercely plotting the downfall of the bourgeoisie, whose material comforts he continued to enjoy. Because of Aragon's enthusiasm for it, nevertheless, Frank's pared-down style took off, rooting out both Art Nouveau remnants and any suspicion of inherited clutter as it revolutionised the chic, minimalist Parisian interior. Less was uniformly more while colours in these new, sparse, airy rooms were toned down to creamy whites and beige. Alberto's objects and wall decorations, conceived mostly in plaster, made for a pleasing white-on-white harmony and, with Diego as an able accomplice, he went on to design many of the most sought-after elements in Frank's immaculate décors. Those who knew Alberto well, such as Aragon, were not unmindful of the irony that he designed items for luxurious interiors in obscure, not to say squalid, quarters.

Among Frank's considerable talents was his ability to choose the right clients, who ranged from the Noailles to the Rockefellers and Cole Porter, as well as Surrealists like poet and muse Lise Deharme, celebrated as the 'Lady of the Glove' in Breton's *Nadja*, who held regular salons for artists and writers at her house.† He also surrounded himself with gifted colleagues, such as the cabinetmaker Adolphe Chanaux, the architect Emilio Terry, who invented what he called, camp tongue in

*Frank and Crevel had been friends since their schooldays at the prestigious Lycée Janson de Sailly in Paris. Frank was deeply distressed by Crevel's suicide.

†Lise Deharme also published an avant-garde review, *Le Phare de Neuilly*, that included work by writers as diverse as Natalie Barney, D. H. Lawrence, James Joyce and Jacques Lacan.

cheek, the 'Louis XVII style', and the decorator and general arbiter of taste Christian Bérard. In 1935, Frank opened his own design shop with Chanaux on the elegant rue du Faubourg Saint-Honoré where his well-heeled clients came to discuss the latest in interior design. Prominently displayed, the Giacomettis' lamps, chandeliers, vases and candlesticks were much in demand, to the point where Frank added a humorous postscript to a letter he sent to Alberto: 'Everyone who comes here swoons over your work. It's the only thing they like. If you make some more models, perhaps I'll be able to buy myself a new suit. Don't forget me – lamps, vases, and when will there be furniture? Tables, chairs, armchairs, beds, sofas, etc?'[6]

The Giacometti brothers found the sophisticated, easy-going company of Frank and his entourage a relief from the intellectual and political intensity of the Surrealists, and they welcomed the varied commissions which not only challenged their abilities as designers but also provided a basic income throughout the financially precarious 1930s. For Diego, it proved particularly fulfilling because it gave him a distinct metier which he was able to develop throughout the rest of his life, even if assisting his brother in all technical matters, and sitting for him whenever needed, always took priority. But, eventually, it allowed him to emerge from his brother's shadow and take on a separate identity as an accomplished furniture designer in his own right.* For Alberto who, like many Renaissance artists, did not look down on the decorative arts as an inferior activity, the designs he made complemented his sculptures, to the extent that he wondered, at times anxiously, where the one ceased and the other began. What at all events interested him as a creator of the 'plastic' arts was how his inventions, whether 'decorative' or 'artistic', played out in a variety of spaces. Designing three-dimensional objects, some of them not dissimilar to his 'Plaques', allowed him to experiment freely with various combinations of forms and stylistic sources in a different register. As mentioned earlier, the similarities between making a Surrealist object and designing a wall sconce came back to haunt their creator. Were they not altogether too similar, too close for comfort? As

*Although he began to sign various pieces with his own first name during the 1930s, Diego became increasingly well known as a furniture designer after his brother's death in 1966. The Musée Picasso in Paris contains some fifty chairs, benches, tables and light fittings that were designed by him for its opening in 1985.

Alberto grew aware of the implications of this problem, he came back frequently to it, ever prompt to pounce on his own contradictions and analyse them:

> The fact that I made decorative objects to earn my living for the best interior decorator of the time, Jean-Michel Frank (whom I liked very much), seemed to the others like a step down. Nevertheless I tried to make a vase, for instance, as good as possible, and I realised then that I worked on a vase just as I would work on a sculpture and that there was obviously no difference between what I called a sculpture and what was just a vase. But I thought that a sculpture should be something different from an object. In other words I had failed with wonder, with mystery. If my work wasn't a creation then it was no different from a carpenter's work when he makes a table. So I had to go back to the source of art and start all over again from the beginning.[7]

The inner conflict did not prevent Alberto from carrying out important decorative commissions until the outbreak of the Second World War and his ill-fated friend Frank, who had taken refuge from the Nazis in New York, was dead. Weakened by ill health and a phenomenal intake of drugs, Frank had succumbed to despair about his future in a world gone mad and killed himself.[†] One project that especially tempted Alberto was the invitation in January 1932 by the Russian-born choreographer Boris Kochno, who had been Sergei Diaghilev's secretary and lover,[*] to design a set for the theatre. Mindful of Picasso's décors for the Ballets Russes, Alberto took on the project, made several sketches, then submitted a detailed proposal. When Kochno suggested making substantial changes to it, Alberto ruled out any further involvement, but he clearly drew on his experience of designing for the theatre in certain subsequent sculptures, especially *The Palace at 4am*, in which figures are placed to deliberate dramatic effect on a stage.

[†]Frank died in 1940, but not by throwing himself from an upper floor of a building in Manhattan, as is generally believed. Recent research has established that he died from an overdose of barbiturates (see Maarten van Buuren, *Leben und Werk von Jean-Michel Frank*, Frankfurt, 2016).

[*]Kochno also conducted celebrated affairs with Cole Porter and Christian Bérard.

Alberto's relationship with Elsa Schiaparelli, the flamboyant couturière known familiarly as 'Schiap' who produced several 'scandalous' garments with Dalí (who else?), such as the suggestive lobster dress and the perky shoe hat, and whose clothes were worn by prominent women from Marlene Dietrich to the (future) Duchess of Windsor, proved more fruitful. With Diego's advice and help, he produced not only pleasingly archaic-looking bracelets and brooches but pillar-shaped standing lamps in plaster and other decorative elements for the fashionable dressmaker when she opened her premises on the ultra-chic place Vendôme.*

Although his bedraggled appearance, in a period that set great store by sartorial elegance, and his heavily accented French tended to belie the fact, Alberto was talented not only in all the plastic arts, from sculpture and painting (which came to the fore in the latter half of his career) to book illustration, providing engravings for over fifty texts, and interior design, but also as a redoubtable dialectician, able to hold his own with the best minds of his generation, and a gifted writer. Preoccupied though he was with his latest creations, both Surrealist and decorative, he eagerly discussed political and philosophical ideas whenever the occasion arose as well as reading – above all, poetry and his friends' books – and writing extensively. In the numerous notebooks he kept from his earliest years in Paris, text and sketch are constantly interwoven. Notes appear, either in Italian or in French, regularly exhorting himself to read, write and generally broaden his culture, which he had already undertaken assiduously to keep pace with the Surrealists' wide range of literary reference. 'Reread: 1. Reverdy. 2. Scève and then Apollinaire, Jarry, Roux, and modern writers above all … write/draw/sculptures', one entry runs,[8] while another note reads: 'An absolutely independent activity: Poetry. Heraclitus. Hegel.'[9]

One might not reasonably expect a sculptor brought up in the Swiss mountains and most conversant with the ways of metal and wood, paint and plaster, to be involved in Hegelian dialectics or indeed the philosophy of Heraclitus of Ephesus. But that would be to miss one of Alberto's central characteristics and a leading reason why he both

*The Maison Schiaparelli still exists with its Giacometti 'pillar' lamps intact at 21 place Vendôme.

absorbed and profoundly marked his times. By now he was not only welcomed in the smartest salons and receptions but in the most adventurous literary circles because he was such lively and intellectually stimulating company. In many ways, he was a natural Hegelian since he thought and talked in a directly dialectical manner, taking one extreme stance in a discussion with persuasive commitment, only to adopt the contrary view with similar conviction. He used this method to clarify his position on numerous ethical, political and aesthetic questions, and it would carry over into his working process, especially later, as he pinched and palped his clay sculptures or wove a head into being through a web of restless, contradictory pencil strokes.

Hegel was very much to the fore in the Parisian intellectual world throughout the 1930s, particularly as a result of the influential seminars given by the intriguing Russian émigré Alexandre Kojève* at the Ecole Pratique des Hautes Etudes.[10] Kojève promulgated a specifically 'French', so-called 'terrorist' Hegel that captivated the attention of the Surrealists as well as Bataille, Leiris, the budding psychoanalyst Jacques Lacan and the young phenomenologist Maurice Merleau-Ponty, who was to become an important, although diffuse, influence on Alberto's post-war development. Kojève's lectures stressed the importance Hegel gave to the forces of negativity and destruction in the dialectical unfolding of history. Admittedly, it is doubtful that Alberto himself attended the lectures, or even focused closely on either Hegel's writings or Kojève's seductive interpretations of them, which followed on the renewed interest in Hegel that Edmund Husserl's *Cartesian Meditations*, published in French in 1929, had stimulated. What is certain is that Alberto heard about them, discussed them and picked up on what might be of use to him in their abstruse arguments, adapting it intuitively to his practice. Hegel gave a theoretical structure to the way Alberto's mind had always worked: take often extreme contrary positions on everything and seek to reconcile them so as to produce an integrated whole that would, well beyond the fleeting grasp of intellectual fashion, stand the test of time. Already, as those fashions briefly dominated and

*Kojève, nephew of Wassily Kandinsky (who was also living in Paris), had studied mainly in Germany, where he came under the influence of Heidegger. This impressive scholar was, moreover, fluent in numerous languages, from classical Greek to Chinese. After his death in 1968, it was revealed that for thirty years he had also been a Soviet agent, spying for the KGB.

died, littering the landscape of the period, his sculptures had begun to take root and survive.

Alberto was also sufficiently taken by Heraclitus's saying 'No man ever steps in the same river twice (for it's not the same river, and he's not the same man)' to jot it down.[11] It is the sort of phrase he would have readily quoted in the rambling conversations he enjoyed with his friends, above all with the two 'dissident' writers he remained close to, Leiris and Bataille. Leiris had returned from a two-year Dakar–Djibouti ethnographical expedition and recently published his account of the trip, *Phantom Africa* (1934), in what was to become his characteristic mixture of meticulous documentation and tortured self-analysis. If Leiris's inner turmoil, which led to a suicide attempt in later life, worried his friends, the degree of self-harm to which Bataille was prepared to go was alarming. Bataille had formed a 'secret society' grouped around a new review entitled *Acéphale* (from the Greek for 'headless'), with a cover illustration by Masson derived from Leonardo's drawing 'Vitruvian Man', but headless, with a skull positioned over its groin, a flaming heart in one outstretched hand and a dagger in the other. The content was no less violent, with Bataille claiming baldly in the first issue: '… we need to change completely or cease to be.' Never one to avoid extreme measures, Bataille actually convened members of his secret society to cloak-and-dagger meetings under oaks he designated as having been struck by lightning in forests around Paris. There he proposed in deadly earnest that he offer himself up as a sacrificial victim, to be beheaded by an executioner chosen from his small but ardent following. In the end, no one stepped up to the task and Bataille survived.* But by putting his life at risk, he had made a very clear point about the ever more anxious times that prevailed. The world was on a crash course, careering inevitably towards a disaster of unimaginable consequences. Only the most far-reaching actions were worth consideration as a warning and potential deterrent to the disaster that was about to unfold.

Alberto felt keenly attuned by his very temperament to catastrophe in all its guises, and the notion of his work as a series of petrified 'crises', as

*In the light of this exploit, Sartre's later taunt in *Saint Genet, Comédien et Martyre* (Paris, 1952, p. 311) – 'Bataille tortures himself "upon occasion"; the rest of the time he is a librarian' – seems less amusing than cheap.

Leiris had perceptively foreseen, was to remain one of the most revealing approaches to his whole oeuvre. The political situation seemed to worsen every day, hovering over Europe like a dark cloud and lurching from one crisis to another. One Alberto had not foreseen, although he had done much, perhaps only half-consciously, to foment it, was his abrupt exclusion from the Surrealist movement, barely six months after having been a best man at Breton's wedding. Alberto appears to have been unaware of the impending expulsion, although he knew that his open avowal to Breton that he wanted to return to direct studies of the human head had stirred up some opposition. Breton had replied contemptuously, 'A head? Everyone knows what a head is.' Alberto had also sided with Aragon a couple of years earlier, it will be remembered, denouncing Breton's tract, *The Poverty of Poetry*,* as 'conservative and reactionary'; at this juncture, he himself seriously considered leaving the Surrealists. And then there was the design work he did for the rich and fashionable which displeased Breton, despite the fact that, as mentioned earlier, both he and Eluard unabashedly supplemented their meagre writer's income by advising collectors and buying major works of contemporary art on their behalf.†

Towards the end of 1934, Alberto had no reason to expect any sudden reversal in his fortunes. On the contrary, his work had begun to receive international recognition, with a dozen works in an exhibition devoted to abstract art at the Kunsthaus in Zurich, and a further dozen Surrealist sculptures (including *No More Play* and *Hands Holding the Void [Invisible Object]*) put on show at the Julien Levy Gallery in New York, where Dalí had also exhibited. These were still very much the days, above all in the US, when Surrealism was regarded as a crazy sideshow put on by European clowns and lunatics, a notion amply confirmed by Dalí's antics in the press.§ Unsurprisingly, Alberto sold nothing, although the

*Here Breton loftily condemns 'all art conditioned by an external necessity'.

†Breton worked as a secretary-cum-adviser for the noted couturier and collector Jacques Doucet, and it was he who convinced Doucet to acquire no less a key modernist masterpiece than Picasso's *Demoiselles d'Avignon*.

§Dalí's numerous exploits in New York included crashing a bathtub through the windows of the Bonwit Teller department store into the street to the delight of huge, applauding crowds. He was jailed for this, and the subsequent publicity helped promote him to international fame.

sculptures had been priced modestly at $150 to $250. The attention was welcome, nonetheless, and it helped pave the way to the enthusiastic reception and respect Alberto's work was to receive later in America.

Meanwhile, the trouble brewing at the Surrealist high command in Paris had come to a head. The dinner to which Breton invited Alberto (also attended by Breton's trusty henchman, Benjamin Péret, a prolific writer, agitator and major Surrealist zealot), began cordially enough but grew heated as the Swiss recruit's failures to toe the party line came up for discussion. The group moved with deadly intent to another member's apartment where several more Surrealist trusties had gathered in the kind of kangaroo court that Breton favoured. Alberto realised that he had been led into a trap. Instead of clowning around and later officially apologising for his wayward behaviour, as Dalí had done unashamedly, Alberto stood his ground. If he had to make his living through decorative work, and if he wished to return to working directly from a model, so be it: he did not accept that such practices stood in contradiction to his artistic or political beliefs. Indeed, he is believed to have announced that all the work he had done in a Surrealist vein had been nothing more than 'masturbation'. Seeing his authority thus flouted, Breton intervened imperiously, but instead of being intimidated Alberto stormed out of the room, saying, 'Don't worry. I'm off!' Thus the die was cast. On a document dated 14 February 1935 and handwritten on a sheet of paper torn from a modest exercise book, Péret formally excluded him from the movement in a short text countersigned by Breton in his trademark green ink.

From having been very much 'in', Alberto found himself abruptly 'out', just as the worst days of winter drained any last hope of brightness from a grey city under a grey sky. In itself, that was hardly likely to affect him, since he had long made drabness and a hard, solitary path his own; now they were to become even more so as he returned to spending whole afternoons and much of the night within the pitted, grey walls of his studio, tirelessly kneading grey clay into grey heads and small grey figures. This emptiness devoid of seduction seemed closer to the search for truth that, he knew clearly now, he had abandoned after having joined the Surrealists. Vainly he had wanted to show that he could be as clever and as inventive as any of them, even out-surrealising the others in storming the barricades of bourgeois taste and taking outrage further, playing with it as he continued to explore not just fantasy and dreams but the most basic themes of sex, violence and death.

Perhaps beauty had to be convulsive if it were to exist – it sounded exciting, even orgasmic – but where did those convulsions lead beyond themselves? Perhaps they were self-consuming, and Surrealism as a whole would end up cannibalised by its own sayings and strictures. In any case, it was not beauty that he sought in his art but an extraordinary, elusive truth. He knew what that truth was. He had seen it, fleetingly, above all in those rare flashes when the veils of appearance fell away and the underlying reality stood revealed. That was the truth, terrifying in its immediacy and its simplicity, that he wanted to capture, even though he knew it was impossible to pin it down, even perhaps because it *was* impossible to pin down.

The road ahead was long and lined with failure, milestones of defeat in a doomed quest, but that was his road, and deep down, amid all his Surrealist successes, he had always known it. No other road was worth travelling. Surrealism was behind him now, even if his former artist comrades would sometimes invite him to join them in certain exhibitions held under the Surrealist banner and he would occasionally accept, for old times' sake. When the leading dealer in 'primitive' art in Paris, Charles Ratton, put on an exhibition of 'Surrealist Objects' in his Right Bank gallery in May 1936, for instance, Alberto agreed to show his *Hour of the Traces* (owned at the time by Breton) alongside objects made by Surrealist writers (notably Eluard and Breton) and ready-mades, including Magritte's *This Is a Piece of Cheese*, and works by Picasso, Dalí and Arp. As already noted, nothing in the small, fluid art and literary world in Paris remained durably hard and fast. People fell out, political and philosophical positions were taken, then changed, publicly and vehemently, movements clashed and their leaders wrote defamatory pamphlets about each other – as demonstrated in the high-flown spats between Breton and Bataille, or later Sartre and Camus, to take the most obvious examples. Then tempers cooled, insults were forgotten and alliances resumed (or not), and the ensuing truce allowed all participants to regroup, reconsider their innermost convictions and reignite the debate.

If anything about his abrupt exclusion from the Surrealists hurt Alberto – and it did hurt him for months to come – it was the loss of friends, a whole family of talented breakaways, oddballs and lost souls. Though divisive and unpredictable, this was a difficult community to be separated from, especially as the sense of the irreconcilable conflicts, both in ideas and between nations, gathered sinister momentum through the 1930s. But an implicit pact had been broken. However well he had known them, most of Alberto's Surrealist companions now cut him, some of them crossing the street to avoid him. A few remained, such as Ernst, Miró and, for a while longer, Aragon[*] as well as his allies, including Bataille and Leiris, in the dissident camp. For a man as gregarious as Alberto (for all his hermit-like propensities) and as loyal in friendship, the sudden isolation weighed heavily. But it was not long before he struck up new acquaintances, above all with other artists. Francis Gruber, a painter of tortured, expressionistic figures who died young, had moved into a studio nearby, as had the self-taught, eccentric Tanguy, and Alberto began seeing more of them. He also drew closer to Derain, a former 'Fauve' whose soberly classical still lifes and nudes he admired and at one point reinterpreted in homage to the older, more established artist.

Partly under Derain's influence and the impact of a major Cézanne exhibition at the Orangerie in 1936, Alberto began to paint again, producing a mesmerising *Apple on a Sideboard* (1937), in which the small, isolated, yellowish fruit vibrates through the picture plane with the intensity of a staring eye. He was already aware, after the profusion of Surrealist motifs, of an overriding need to reduce: 'On my mother's sideboard,' he recounted later, 'there were some objects with which you could paint a very nice still life: a bowl, flowers and three apples. But painting them all at once was just as impossible as modelling a head from life. So I took the bowl away, the plate too, the flowers. Have you ever tried to look at three apples at once from a distance of three metres? I had to take two away. And I had to make the third very small because with that alone there was still plenty to paint.'[12]

At the same time, Alberto also experimented with small-scale portraits of his mother, enclosing her image within the outline of the

[*]'Too literary to be political, and too political to be literary' was Alberto's summing up of the agile Aragon.

wood panelling behind her to accentuate its Cézanne-like solidity.* Although Alberto did not pursue this brief painterly diversion at the time, the simple, frontal format, cage-like motif and intense profusion of thin lines which he deployed in *The Artist's Mother* (1937) would form the backbone of his pictorial style after the war. This particular portrait gives little surface detail and offers no sense of the sitter's psychological state but, rather, focuses on her solidity and isolation within the surrounding space. Cézanne, the so-called 'hermit of Aix', would remain an artistic touchstone for the hermit of rue Hippolyte; even on a superficial level, the two artists showed significant similarities, from the violently erotic imaginings of their youth through their practice of drawing every day and their stubbornly repetitive exploration of a handful of themes.†

An artist who had recently arrived in Paris and who intrigued Alberto as soon as he saw his first show at Galerie Pierre in 1933 was the sexually suggestive painter Balthasar Klossowski, who went by his childhood nickname, Balthus. Although barely thirty years old at this time, Balthus had succeeded in blending an Old Master technique with subtly dream-like, risqué depictions of young girls in various states of abandonment, most provocatively in the *Guitar Lesson* (1934) which shows an adolescent girl arched over the lap of her female teacher whose hand hovers above her clearly delineated sex as if she were about to strum it like a guitar. Polish by birth but already highly cosmopolitan and fluent in several languages, Balthus added further to his ability to charm and fascinate by claiming an illustrious background, some of which was well founded (his mother had indeed had a love affair with the poet Rilke), while other later additions, such as his being descended from Lord Byron§ and having the right to be addressed as the Comte Klossowski de Rola, were not. One might say that Balthus,

*This solid, one might almost say 'stolid', quality also harks back to Alberto's admiration for Giotto, whose figures had so impressed him when he visited the Scrovegni Chapel on an early trip to Padua with his father.

†Alberto repeatedly acknowledged that, because of Cézanne, the whole vision of reality in painting had been brought acutely into question.

§Balthus made this claim persuasively when I interviewed him at the Villa Medici in Rome in 1967 (see *Réalités*, English edition, Paris, October 1967 and Michael Peppiatt, *Interviews with Artists, 1966-2012*, New Haven and London, 2012, pp. 173–177).

talented, handsome and on the make, was fashioning his artist's myth much as Alberto was, but in more patently fictitious ways. If he was demonstrably not a descendant of Byron, he saw himself in the mould of a Byronic hero and longed to be accepted as such.

Alberto admired the skill and daring of Balthus's immaculate, enigmatic paintings – *The Street* (1932) had caused a stir when exhibited at Galerie Pierre – as well as his commitment to being uncompromisingly himself (and his legend), just as Balthus appreciated Alberto's already impressive artistic achievements as well as the implacable logic that had led him to reconsider his entire stylistic development to date. They also shared a growing artistic friendship with Derain* and another figure who haunted the same streets and bistros with his increasingly erratic behaviour and who was to mark indelibly the whole period they lived through in Paris: Antonin Artaud. Poet, dramatist, actor and theatre director, Artaud had also been expelled from the Surrealist movement, shortly after its inception, before creating his own one-man revolution that led to numerous happenings, scandals, internments in psychiatric clinics and vociferations against politics ('I shit on Marxism!' he declared) as well as all authorities, such as God. From these events and the radical theories that accompanied them, the no-holds-barred 'Theatre of Cruelty'† was to emerge. A remarkable draughtsman to boot, Artaud was given a show of his disturbingly expressive, intense portraits at the Galerie Pierre in 1947. As he became increasingly destitute, a fund was set up in his name and, as often when his friends were in need, Alberto contributed readily to it.

Although encounters with such a variety of powerful, unusual personalities made his new isolation more tolerable, Alberto remained focused on the problems posed by his return to working directly from nature, from a flesh-and-blood model, and having to square up once again to the overwhelming difficulties posed by attempting to recreate and record the reality he found wherever his gaze fell, whether on a face, a figure or a simple chair – not so simple when you struggled

*Indeed, for a time the artists (whom, as noted earlier, Leiris found dining together) became a triumvirate united in shared artistic convictions – a theme very ably explored in the exhibition 'Derain, Balthus, Giacometti. Une amitié artistique' at the Musée d'Art moderne de la Ville de Paris in 2017.

†The concept for what Artaud called the 'Theatre of Cruelty' grew out of a series of essays that he published between 1931 and 1936 in the *Nouvelle Revue Française*. They were brought out together as *Le Théâtre et son double* (The Theatre and Its Double) in 1938.

to catch it and its evanescence as a complex structure forever shifting and recreating itself in space. Indeed, the simpler the subject appeared to be, Alberto found, the more unfathomable and elusive it grew. From having invented a whole category of unfathomable objects and delicately ambiguous sculptures, all he wished, as he explained endlessly to himself and anyone who would listen, was to catch 'reality' – the skull behind the face, the pulse beneath the skin or, most fleeting of all, the mystery of another being. Those simple, everyday phenomena turned out, however, to be the most challenging for anyone as benighted as he was for having undertaken the impossible quest of seizing the very flow of life. It was, of course, an impossibility. Everything was an impossibility: even the nose on a face grew into the immensity of a 'pyramid' as you looked closely at it, he said. A nose, a chair, a glass on the table, all unachievable. He was doomed to fail. But – and here we might imagine the artist's already deeply lined face creasing into a smile – that was the whole point. That was why he would devote the rest of his life to it alone. It was worth it precisely *because* it was impossible.

Alberto adopted his new routine without difficulty because he was essentially returning to the way he had always worked before he reinvented himself as a Surrealist. It consisted chiefly of drawing, correcting, destroying, drawing again, drawing endlessly. Like many dedicated artists before him, he saw drawing as the basis of all art, and if he could not achieve what he wanted, what he saw, in a drawing, there was no point in taking an idea, a vision, a snatch of reality further into the realms of painting or sculpture. Accordingly he had the uncomplaining Diego, always conveniently to hand, sit for him in the morning, and a professional model, Rita Gueyfier (whose name has gone down to posterity as a result), in the afternoon, a regular routine that went on with minor interruptions from 1935 until he made his first attempt to leave occupied Paris in 1940. Under Alberto's fluttering hand, making mark after mark in pencil, taking sightings and notations, dozens of portraits were made and discarded in the same day: cobwebs of lines woven tirelessly over appearances that came and went, lived for a second before cancelling themselves out, leaving only the dirty white void of the paper behind.

Head (Skull) had been coaxed into being without too much difficulty, as had *Head of Woman (Rita)*, which was finished in 1935. But the subject he knew best, the head of his brother Diego, was more problematic, precisely no doubt because he had studied it, from every angle and in every light, since childhood. Shortly after beginning to model his brother's head, Alberto wrote reassuringly to their mother: 'What's keeping me busiest is finishing the bust of Diego. You'll see, what I'm doing here is more normal! I might have a long way to go before I'll get to where I want to, but I'm ready to work for years.'[13] In point of fact, *Head of Diego (Mask)* took five years (1935–40) to complete, but it can be regarded as Alberto's most substantial response to Breton's dismissive claim that 'Everyone knows what a head is'. The most searching and resourceful sculptor of the twentieth century would show how misguided the leader of organised intellectual revolution could be.

While the models of Rita's head (pert nose, short, bobbed hair) exhibit a comforting naturalism, with the influence of Cubist analysis still perceptible but mediated by fluid, Rodin-like modelling, Diego's bust is less conventional. There are hints of naturalism in its voluminous nose and well-defined bone structure, but these features are ingrained with the sculpture's general rugged character. Cropped just below the collar, the bust looks like a fossil fallen from a cliff face and worn down to a blunt, ovular shape over many years (which, in a sense, it had been). Diego's stern gaze reaches out through a heavily pitted visage – the result of five years of anxious reworking – as if across geological stretches of time. This surface, particularly the striated forehead and the piece's simplified, slightly elongated form, hint at the iconic, mature style Alberto would develop on his return to Paris after the war.

The loneliness and commitment to failure that marked Alberto's dour, post-Surrealist existence was relieved sporadically by the odd piece of good news. Alfred Barr, the youthful director of the Museum of Modern Art, appeared like an envoy from the New World in the equally young sculptor's dilapidated shack where, for his landmark exhibition – 'Fantastic Art, Dada, Surrealism' – he chose several works, including *The Palace at 4am*, which was bought for the Museum's permanent collection. This sudden upturn in Alberto's fortunes, which was soon to prompt further interest in New York from two influential dealers, Peggy Guggenheim and Pierre Matisse, would be all the more welcome since, without knowing it, he had begun, as the French say, 'crossing the desert' – an arid, isolated period, with no solo exhibitions until well after the end of the war. Alberto remembered the time as a kind of quagmire. While he had extensive experience of working directly from a model, he later complained about how conceptually challenging the return to this practice turned out to be. For one thing, seduced as he had been by Breton's suggestion that 'the eye exists in a wild state', he found on the contrary that his eye demanded, not novelty or revelation, but the assurance that what it saw – in all its amazing reality – could be reproduced. To his growing alarm, a seemingly simple action, flowing from the eye down the arm directly into the hand quivering over the paper or plucking at a mound of clay, grew steadily more uncertain and complex. 'I modelled just as I did when I was a student,' he later told one interviewer. 'The more I looked at the model, the thicker the veil between her reality and mine grew. One begins by seeing the person who is posing but little by little every other imaginable sculpture intervenes. The more one's real vision disappears, the more unknown the head becomes. One is no longer sure of its appearance, its dimensions or anything whatsoever.'[14]

Time and time again, Alberto attempted to define, at least in words, the impossibility that he faced. 'There were too many sculptures between my model and myself,' he remarked in the same interview. 'And when there were no more sculptures, there was something so unfamiliar I no longer knew who I was seeing or what I was seeing.'[15] At the same time, Alberto filled his notebooks with exhortations to renew. 'For my part, I will go on with my new sculptures,' he confides in a slightly desperate, yet defiant tone. 'I will make drawings and etchings. I will write new things that will find a form of their own. Against religion, patriotism and capitalism of course, about politics too, that goes without saying, but I want more, new insights, and I will have them. And then I will soon exhibit my new sculptures, completely new …'[16]

Just as Alberto grew increasingly obsessed with all the insoluble problems that stood between his vision of things and the way they materialised as he attempted doggedly to record them day after day, something altogether unexpected happened – something that could only have happened unexpectedly. Whenever he needed a proper break from the endless, usually unsuccessful round of modelling clay or trying to clarify an image on paper – the lines crisscrossing like a spider's web – he would wash at the communal tap, brush himself down, straighten his tie and head out of the studio towards boulevard du Montparnasse. Most of the time he sat alone, reading *L'Humanité* and doodling in its margins while exchanging wisecracks with the waiters and observing the changing clientele. What he always hoped was that he might see someone with whom he could still share a drink, even though he was now only an *ex*-Surrealist. If not, there was always plenty to look at – as the tables on the terraces filled steadily with artists and writers coming up for air, fashionably dressed Parisiennes in cloche hats and a fair sprinkling of onlookers, many of them new to town.

Tourists often headed for Le Dôme when they arrived in Montparnasse, so much so that the establishment was also known as the 'Anglo-American café'. The price of a drink or even a modest dish of the day, like their Toulouse sausage and mash with white-wine mustard, was still affordable. Once you had ordered, you could stay as long as you liked, observing the comings and goings, carrying on interminable conversations or passionately intense, silent love affairs.* Young people also abounded, using it as a place to meet friends and horse about, often making so much noise that the manager, an awesome figure in a dark, double-breasted suit, would tell them to pipe down or leave. A group of mainly art students from the nearby academies had taken to dropping in every day, Alberto noted, since he himself had begun coming by regularly, making his glass last and staring more and more openly at a young woman whose delicate, exotic looks and high-pitched, metallic laugh fascinated him. Sometimes he managed to get a table close enough to hers to overhear the chatter. She was not French, he knew that, because she spoke with an accent that was as marked as his own. But she joined in the talk without hesitation, her slender, supple body moving to and fro confidently and her slightly slanted eyes bright with amusement and mischief. Gradually she started returning his gaze between snatches of laughter, so directly that he felt intimidated by her. Attractive, confident women always put him on the back foot like this, unless they were on the game and he knew that in the end it was all

*Some clients would go in with no money and have to sit there for hours on end until someone they knew dropped in who could settle their bill and 'release' them, as – the photographer Brassaï recounts in his memoirs – his friend, the impoverished American writer Henry Miller, did regularly.

about payment, not involvement. As she rose to leave, he suddenly felt panicked, as if he were about to lose something that would never come within his reach again, and he got up at the same time and without knowing what he was going to do moved over towards her and blurted out: 'Can we speak?'

5

Reality Unveiled (1937–44)

Her name was Isabel Nicholas, she was twenty-three and she had been making her way in Paris for the past year as a student, a budding painter and artist's model. The daughter of a master mariner and brought up in Liverpool, Isabel had won a scholarship to the Royal Academy in London, where she also modelled for Jacob Epstein, who made three busts of her (as well as fathering a son with her who was then brought up by Epstein's wife*). A sell-out show of Isabel's early watercolours in a London gallery provided her with sufficient funds to make the trip to Paris in 1934. Her striking appearance and lithe self-assurance immediately attracted attention in the streets and cafés of Montparnasse. Epstein had given her some introductions to people he knew in Paris but she hardly had time to follow them up before Pierre Colle, the dealer in whose gallery Alberto had shown two years earlier, noticed her and introduced her to the burly Derain, the former Fauve firebrand who had since ably embraced and enhanced the traditional values of painting. A connoisseur of pretty women and life's pleasures in general,† Derain (whom Isabel described as 'the most French Frenchman I ever met') painted half a dozen portraits of her, including one which he gave her, while making a space available in his own studio for the young English artist to focus on her own painting.

*Jackie Epstein (1934–2009), who became a noted racing car driver.

†A keen motorist, Derain delighted the Surrealists by declaring that his Bugatti was more beautiful than all the artworks in the world.

Isabel had not lost sight of the main reason why she, like scores of other young artists, had made a beeline to Montparnasse. She enrolled at the Académie de la Grande Chaumière, less to follow a specific course, as Alberto had done, than to work freely from the models that were available for a small fee every day. She also liked a good time, with proper French food and any amount of wine, as well as plenty of friends, lovers and admirers to hand. On top of her distinctive looks, it was this animal voraciousness that both attracted and alarmed Alberto, who freely admitted, both in conversation and in his notebooks, to having an 'inferiority complex towards women' (as well as, contradictorily enough, to wanting to have 'a woman again always *and life*').[1] Isabel also kept notes and in her diary confides how important that meeting at the Dôme had been: 'I noticed a man looking at me … From that moment on, we met daily at 5pm. Months went by before he asked me to come to his studio to pose. I already knew that he had changed my life forever.'[2]

Of all Alberto's intimate encounters with women, we know most about his entanglement with Isabel because they were both deeply affected by it and both highly articulate, exchanging numerous letters that have survived. As an artist herself, Isabel would have understood the dilemmas that confronted Alberto more implicitly than any of his other important female companions. She was also as independent and self-willed as he, as their intense but short-lived love affair would prove. While Isabel left accounts of their relationship both in her diaries and in the ample correspondence between them, Alberto referred explicitly to the impact Isabel had on him in several interviews. Above all, he made a body of drawings and several distinctive sculptures of her. The sculptures cover an unusually wide range of reference, going from the regal *Isabel* (c. 1937), with its markedly Egyptian overtones (for a time Isabel herself was nicknamed '*l'Egyptienne*' in Paris), to a more freely expressive, lifelike *Isabel* (c. 1938) – both in bronze – and a *Head of Isabel* (c. 1938–9) with pencil marks that add a tragically haggard look to the plaster cast. Viewed together, the three busts appear to record the trajectory of Alberto's infatuation with this new whirlwind, from unapproachably divine presence through a lusty, dishevelled normality to a pale absence that has been quite literally written off by the pencil marks that the sculptor added like an afterthought.

At the same time, life itself had come coursing back through Alberto's hand in these portraits. What he had sensed as the missing vital element in his Surrealist work, inventive and skilful as it was, now stood plainly revealed. In all its subtle implications, his sculpture had lost contact with reality: it was indeed 'sur-real', leaving the representation of the real behind in an attempt to rise above it and reach new realms of instinctual and imaginative freedom. Sooner and more definitively than most adherents of Surrealism, Alberto's sceptical, probing cast of mind had located flaws and inconsistencies in the movement's constantly shifting dogma. Ironically enough, it had been Breton's own dismissal of Alberto's need to record the fleetingness of everyday visual experience that pinpointed the central divergence between Surrealism's aims and his own. Surrealism sought the unknown, the repressed, the dreamed, the exotic. Alberto had followed that path enthusiastically enough, crafting this enigma, dramatising that trauma, until he had become easily the Surrealist sculptor *par excellence*. Then, slowly, inevitably, it had come to a dead end. What he now sought was the very opposite of what he had achieved: to record the ordinary, the everyday, the mystery that played out before him, for an instant, like a shadow in the sun. This had already proved to be a far more demanding task. In Alberto's eyes, the human face had been revealed as more enigmatic, more elusive than the most far-fetched fantasy. Had he not tried, each and every morning, to set down in pencil on paper what he knew best in the world: the well-defined features of his brother, Diego, which he had been trying, and failing, to capture since childhood? There was the mystery, perhaps the greatest mystery of all, that the Surrealists had not even acknowledged as they charged after their wildest dreams and delved into the deepest unconscious.

It was as plain as the nose on your face, indeed it *was* the nose on your face, yet it had always resisted being fully pinned down and realistically recorded. No one had ever succeeded completely in capturing the pulsations of being. Rembrandt had come close, Velázquez too, in a handful of portraits that had set blood coursing through paint. By some magic they not only captured appearance, as they were supposed to, but the living, breathing reality beneath. But it didn't last, it couldn't be taught, and once again it became an illusion, a mirage. But why, then, would you persist in chasing after made-up worlds of melting clocks and giant insects when you could not even create the single most important human fact: a fully lifelike head? He had made successful paintings and busts of his parents from early on, copied the Old Masters convincingly, paraphrased Sumerian heads and Cycladic figures, experimented with Cubist forms and most recently become the leading proponent of Surrealist sculpture. Nothing appeared to resist him, so that at certain moments his talents seemed so varied he thought he could do anything. And indeed he had, but now, like a punishment, he had been brought up short, face to face with his own facility, his superficiality, his obvious impotence when faced by what seemed the simplest task of all.

If Alberto were to declare a faith, it would be in the steadfast search for his own way, his alone, obscure and hopeless as it might appear to others. He had always been considered something of an oddball, talented certainly, but definitely beyond the norm. He even considered himself a bit of a number, a bit of a joke, and relished sharing his oddity with others, even in conversations that he knew would be published, letting out things that might have been better left unsaid, as in this sober self-analysis: 'it's a rather unusual thing for a person to spend more of his time trying to copy a head than in living life – telling the same person to sit still on a chair every evening for five years and trying to copy him without succeeding, and never stopping. It's really not an activity one would call normal, is it? One has to belong to a certain society for it even to be tolerated. It's an activity that is of no use to the whole of society. It's a purely individual satisfaction. Extremely selfish and thus antisocial.'[3]

The more you thought about the problem, the more complex it became, because everything in life was in flux. Heraclitus had nailed it once and for all when he said you never stepped in the same river twice. Just as human beings altered from second to second, water flowed, contours and substances reshaped, light changed, so you literally never saw the same thing more than once. Even a simple glass on the table shifted because by the time you had looked at it and then gone back to your sheet of drawing paper you were no longer copying it but the residue of your vision of it. And so many other images seemed to intercede between you and that glass, between you and that particular head at that particular moment. If you really thought about it, it was enough to drive you mad. There you were, chasing a chimera that modified its appearance every time you looked at it, every time you attempted to pin it down, and then everything else you saw, all the heads milling past you in the street – all the heads you had ever seen, studied or imagined – began to alter and obscure the head you had before you.

Diego no longer looked like Diego, while Rita could have been any model, any woman, that had sat for him. And as you tried mentally to strip all the memories away, stripping one veil after another off the reality you wanted to record before you, you realised that you no longer recognised the head at all. It had changed now beyond recognition. You never saw the same head twice.

Late one evening in 1937 Alberto walked over to boulevard Saint-Michel to meet Isabel. He had been thinking about her a great deal, troubled by her beauty – by the way her face metamorphosed constantly, recording every shift of emotion, and his desire to capture it and make it his own. Although still barely adult, she seemed so sure of her ability to attract men, women, every passer-by, luring them by sheer magnetism. Her uproarious laughter, with its odd, metallic timbre, could cut through the noise of a crowded café, and it seemed to grow louder every evening he spent with her: he was fascinated by her rowdiness, her love of any fun that was going backed by her ability to put back as much booze as any hard-drinking artist he knew. He was also on edge because almost all the women he had spent time with were either on the game, where you paid and that was that, or they made it clear that sexual intimacy was available only as part of a relationship or, God forbid, marriage. Isabel was different. She respected his position in the art world and clearly appreciated the fact that he seemed to be happy to introduce her to everyone he knew, from Tzara and Bataille to Balthus and Picasso. What took Alberto aback about Isabel was that the usual sexual conventions did not apply. Isabel viewed the whole question more liberally, having affairs freely, even though she had recently married the journalist Sefton Delmer* and moved with him as head of the *Daily Express* Paris bureau into his swanky apartment overlooking the place Vendôme. For all his talk about 'free love', now that he was confronted by it so directly Alberto was alarmed. He felt safer with 'bought love'. And then … he was also falling in love, and that complicated everything, especially since Isabel did not seem to care

*Delmer recalls having been entranced by Isabel's 'pouting, almost negroid mouth, high cheekbones, and those slanting Nefertiti eyes' in his autobiography, *Trail Sinister*, London, 1961, p. 241.

Isabel Rawsthorne arriving for a private viewing of the Royal Academy Summer Show, London, April 28 1933

two hoots about the turmoil she created around her. As repelled as he was attracted, Alberto felt increasingly lost and confused. Where did he stand with her? Was he just an older man with more experience in the world, particularly the art world? What did she feel? Would she take him as her lover – or would she scorn him? He was now completely out of his depth. If life were to go on, he would have to know.

The big apartment buildings loomed up on either side of the boulevard, dark, almost black, against the overarching night sky. It had been raining and the street lamps glinted dully on the wide, tree-lined street as it plunged down from the Luxembourg Gardens towards the Seine. Each time a car passed, its tyres made a slightly threatening hiss. It was almost midnight, and most of the cafés had already pulled their shutters down. Suddenly, Alberto saw Isabel in her winter coat, waiting for him further down. She looked tiny, silhouetted against a big, dark doorway. Alberto stopped. It was as if he were seeing her for the first time, from head to toe, totally present and complete, but reduced to the dimensions of a distant statuette – something minuscule he could pick up and hold, or perhaps even make: an Isabel he could mould and palp out of damp, grey clay. The sight filled him with a strange sense of possession, as if Isabel were suddenly, entirely, his. He possessed her through his eye, as no one else could, not merely by writhing around and coupling with her but absorbing her from head to foot. It was a revelation. This was what he needed to capture her, to make her his own. The vision lodged itself in his mind with lightning clarity, stopping time, holding the transient durably in a single image.

In the days that followed, the vision remained so powerfully in Alberto's imagination that the heads of Diego and Rita he had been so closely focusing on lost all urgency. Standing there, Isabel had looked as if she were outside time, lost in the immensity of space. How could he translate that extraordinary sense of night, of nothingness, like a vast, dark ocean, lapping around such a small figure? In a painting, he might have tried to capture the sensation by introducing a repoussoir element of the kind that classical artists used, or by the way he constructed the picture plane, as he had attempted to do when he captured his little yellow apple, caught between the table and the panelled wall. In sculpture he would have to recreate a portion of the building behind her, but that would introduce the kind of narrative that contradicted everything he was trying to achieve; it would also fail to suggest the boundless space, the emptiness of the universe, that had struck him so strongly. Ridiculous as it might look, the only way to recreate the sensation might be to make a tiny figure and set it on top of a huge base, a clash of volumes that evoked the surrounding void. Well, all he could do was try. Trying, after all, was everything.

That vision was one of a handful of 'epiphanies' that marked Alberto's imagination profoundly and had a decisive effect on his development as a sculptor. Whatever he did, he now knew that he had to translate that poignant sight, both majestic and frail, fragile yet resilient, into an altogether new raid on the real. The Isabel he had glimpsed had been as sovereign as Nefertiti and as vulnerable as a young girl swallowed up by darkness in a big, foreign city. The event was as real as anything he could imagine, more real in fact because it was more dramatic, summing up so many of the contradictions, the persistent longings and the inbred fears, that divided him like a mountain rock split in two. Instinctively he knew that if he ever managed to convey that sensation, even in a drawing, it would help overcome the split he felt inside and make him more whole. But then, perversely, following the argument for and against closely in his head, he also realised that resolving the divide might be the end of all his endeavours, because if he ever achieved that inner resolution, there would be nothing more to strive for and struggle against, no ultimate work forever slipping beyond his grasp and forever providing him with a pressing reason to go on.

What had seemed like a dream of possessing Isabel, the free spirit, the feline, the sexually empowered goddess that looked down on his botched attempts to make love, turned into a nightmare. Here he was, with all the skill in the world – he could effortlessly draw you Velázquez's portrait of Pope Innocent X or a mask of Akhenaten – but he couldn't grasp a small, far-off figure on a pavement sufficiently to convey his sensation of it. He tried and he tried, but the drawings began to tail off and then the sculptures became so small that one too many touches with the penknife in his outsize hands and they were no more. As he whittled the tiny forms down to their ultimate essence, they ended up as just that: blobs of clay, heaps of plaster, that made a mockery of all his cherished ambitions.

Like a practised dialectician, Alberto moved the problem around in his mind, trying to put it into perspective, then take it to a conclusion. Having mastered not only the traditional skills of representational art but a swathe of current styles and idioms, was he now taking aim at the art object itself, as if willing (perhaps unconsciously) its destruction? Had the fact that he no longer believed in its ability to represent either the surface appearance of reality or the depths of the unconscious led him to wield his knife destructively, with the tiny sculptures that remained as witnesses to a near-total annihilation? After all, the destructive, self-sabotaging impulse might already have been at work when he made that earlier plaster cast of Isabel's bust, on which the aggressive pencil marks began to look like knife wounds, attacking the serene form of the face beneath. He closed his eyes and clasped his big, rough hands over them to concentrate more clearly. Nimbly as his mind moved in the strangely luminous darkness, and perceptive as his line of cool reasoning had promised to be, one stubborn fact remained: whatever he touched, crumbled. He felt a surge of rage rise inside him, that old rage that had led him to strangle and eviscerate in his old sculpture, his clever Surrealist sculpture. The rage, the violence, was still in him, and had he turned it now, not on strangled female figures but on himself, on all his deepest longing – on sculpture itself, killing it blow by blow until it was reduced to dust?

The minuscule figures that did survive were 'no bigger than an almond', the Franco-German sculptor François Stahly remarked, or even the 'size of a pea', according to Simone de Beauvoir, who dropped in after she and Sartre had met Alberto by chance in Saint-Germain. In its run-down state, the studio was revealed as the perfect setting for this apparently unending series of failures, of self-inflicted wounds, as the plaster-caked sculptor laboured on, as if he had William Blake's adage 'If the fool would persist in his folly he would become wise' ringing in his ears. Before long, the whole precarious, seemingly futile undertaking would become a joke, one tinged with despair, which made it all the stranger and funnier. Alberto, always prompt to mock his own endeavours, was the first to proclaim its absurdity to anyone who would bend an ear. Years later, he would still be shaking his head over the predicament he had got himself into, as his remarks from two different interviews confirm:

> At that time and until the war the odd thing was that, when I was drawing, I always drew things smaller than I believed I saw them; that is, when I was drawing, I was astonished that the thing became so small; when I wasn't drawing I felt I saw heads the size they really were. And gradually, above all since the war, it has become so much a part of my nature, so ingrained, this kind of vision I have when

> working, that I have it even when I am not working. I mean that now I can never get a figure back to life-size. When I'm outside a café and see people passing on the opposite pavement, I see them very small as tiny little figurines, which I find marvellous, but it's impossible for me to imagine they are life-size. They become no more than appearances at that distance. If the same person comes near, it's another person. But if they get too near, six feet, say, I don't really see them any more; they're not life-size at that point either; they fill your whole visual field, don't they? And you see them out of focus. And if you get a bit closer still, there's no seeing them at all any more. Anyway, it's not done, I mean you would touch each other. Which takes you into another domain.[4]

> To my horror my statues got even smaller after 1940. It was a horrible catastrophe. I remember for instance that I wanted to sculpt a girl I loved from memory as I had seen her on boulevard Saint-Michel. I wanted to make her about eighty centimetres high. To make a long story short: she got so small that I couldn't put any more details on the figure. It was a mystery to me. All my figures stubbornly shrank to one centimetre high. Another touch with the thumb and whoops! – no more figure.
>
> I began to think about it only later. At first I had instinctively made the sculpture so small to indicate the distance from which I had seen the model. From a distance of fifteen metres, that girl was not eighty centimetres tall for me but a little over ten. And then too, in order to give the appearance of the whole and not lose myself in details, I had to choose an even greater distance. But even when I put in details it seemed to contradict the whole … so I moved farther and farther back still, until at last everything disappeared.[5]

News of Alberto's manic quest rapidly made the rounds of the Paris art world until he began to be written off as a once talented, successful artist, now estranged from influential friends and art dealers because of his manic obsession with whittling figures down, down, down until they vanished. The phenomenon of artists losing their mind was not unknown, particularly in France where Balzac's *The Unknown Masterpiece*, a short story about an artist called Frenhofer gone mad in the pursuit of perfection, had made a lasting impression.* Opposition to Alberto's pea-sized figurines arose even in his country of birth. His youngest brother, Bruno, now a budding architect, had invited Alberto to contribute a work on a pedestal in the courtyard of an official exhibition in Zurich. Since he had been experimenting with the problems of scale that arise when a small sculpture is placed on a large base, Alberto went to work with a will, convinced that the exhibition organisers would appreciate the way his work called into question and altered the perception of the huge space around it, thus making a startling statement about the nature and impact of scale. But the small head he proposed, which would have made the courtyard look almost infinite, met with uniform disapproval and derision. The news enraged Alberto, who had seen the possibility of a breakthrough for his new work, but his brother prevailed on him and the less controversial, highly abstract *Cube* (1934) was exhibited instead.

An incident of this nature was never going to deter Alberto in his search for the irreducible essence of what he saw. Any hindrance or opposition would only convince him further that, with the intellectual games of Surrealism consigned to the past, his real quest stood before him: his conviction in this ultimately unattainable goal would remain unshakeable through years of trial and error, frustration and neglect. With characteristic contrariness, Alberto embraced the risk of repeated failure, coming to see failed sculptures as quite as interesting and worthwhile as so-called successful works, since he took the view that all art, indeed all human endeavour, was doomed eventually to failure.

Were Alberto's encounters with Picasso increasingly frequent because of his new independence of any group or movement? Although he remained wary of the mercurial Spanish master, no artist in Paris in the 1930s could be anything but acutely aware of Picasso's extraordinary gifts and overwhelming success. Alberto had already rubbed shoulders with Picasso during his involvement with the Surrealists. Sharply differing in

*Both Cézanne ('*Frenhofer c'est moi!*') and Picasso (who illustrated *The Unknown Masterpiece*) were deeply affected by the plausibility of the story. Moreover, one of the reasons Picasso chose his studio on rue des Grands-Augustins was that Balzac had reputedly set his story in that very building.

temperament and outlook, the two men nevertheless shared numerous characteristics, including an intense, parallel involvement with the political issues of the day about which they saw mostly eye to eye. A more personal relationship began to develop around the period that Picasso was working on *Guernica* in 1937. Already the most famous artist in the world, as well as the richest, while hopeful visitors formed a queue to his studio on the Left Bank, a stone's throw from the Seine on rue des Grands-Augustins, Picasso always welcomed Alberto into its cavernous space because he was intrigued by the latter's new artistic ventures as well as his puzzling indifference to the blandishments of fame. Picasso also turned up periodically at Alberto's much less impressive studio since he was curious about his friend's tireless experimentation, going as far as to comment, spitefully but revealingly: 'Giacometti wants us to regret the masterpieces that he will never make.'[6] At the same time, Alberto was flattered by Picasso's friendship, mentioning it in his letters home and remarking on the fact that Picasso loved to hear his stories of local characters and everyday life back in rural Stampa.[7]

Alberto was already aware that Picasso had a well-earned reputation for treating his friends and mistresses callously, even pitting them against each other and drawing energy and enjoyment from any clashes that ensued. This came memorably to the fore when he allowed his previous mistress, Marie-Thérèse Walter, and his new companion, Dora Maar, to come to blows as he continued to work uninterruptedly on his huge new canvas depicting man's inhumanity to man. Alberto was certainly not without a distinct streak of cruelty, especially with regard to women, as *Woman with Her Throat Cut* (1932) and certain of his writings amply reveal. On the whole those impulses were channelled into his fantasies and his work rather than into his relationships, where his behaviour seems to have been teasing and contradictory but mostly gentle, despite the stormy affair with Denise and the problems that he later incurred as a married man. Alberto criticised Picasso's treatment both of his lovers and his children with an increasing rigour – tinged perhaps by less avowable feelings of envy.

Even so, the two men increasingly appreciated each other's company as the atmosphere in Paris grew tenser and darker with the threat of impending war. Conversation inevitably turned to the changing problems each artist encountered every day in the studio although, as *Guernica* continued to win praise and stir up controversy, Alberto's

Picasso and his Afghan hound Kazbek in his workshop at 7 rue des Grands-Augustins, c.1939–1944

struggle to pin down his fleeting visions came across as hopeless and marginal. Yet Picasso understood his predicament implicitly and, as Isabel's diary of the time relates, the all-conquering Spaniard would often 'sneak round to Giacometti's at 46 rue Hippolyte-Maindron to see what he was up to'.[8] Not all their conversation was devoted to artistic problems. Friends and their pretensions (including Balthus's elaboration of aristocratic Polish forebears) always cropped up along with every aspect of art world gossip, from collectors and dealers to the latest exhibitions. Given both men's obsession with sex, it might come as no surprise that on some of his visits to Alberto's studio Picasso brought pornographic magazines over which the two widely respected artists pored and sniggered like schoolboys.[9]

As the outbreak of hostilities loomed ever nearer, keeping the whole of Europe in a state of suspended anxiety, the two artists began to meet almost daily. At one point, at Picasso's request, Alberto started to sculpt a bust of his famous friend, although his initial enthusiasm waned and the work was never completed, and Picasso gave him a drawing. By this point Picasso had begun his liaison with Dora Maar, of whom he made numerous portraits, including the famous *Weeping Woman*, while he was working on *Guernica*. Alberto's relationship with Isabel, although still unconsummated, had grown more intimate as she visited the studio – which she described in her diary as 'both hypnotic and ordinary' – to sit for him regularly and chat. Later, in the early evening, they would go for drinks at the cafés and bistros in Saint-Germain-des-Prés, which had begun to supplant Montparnasse as the city's fashionable area for artists and writers to meet, plot and gossip, all of which was facilitated by the waiters who acted as go-betweens, passing on messages and sightings of customers who had been 'in'.

One of Alberto's and Isabel's favourite spots was Brasserie Lipp, where they could linger over an aperitif while observing which friends or acquaintances were around that evening and who was with them. Picasso was also an habitué of Lipp, and if he were seated nearby, he took to staring intently at Isabel for long periods, annoying her and Alberto, the latter being fully aware of Picasso's reputation as a womaniser. Having run his famous *mirada fuerte*, or 'hard look', all over Isabel one evening, Picasso got up abruptly and announced: 'Now I know how to do it', returning to his studio to begin the first of three portraits of her.[10]

With his confidence already undermined by the impasse that now confronted his work, Alberto also had to contend with the impasse that threatened his relationship with Isabel. Although he continued to admire Picasso's artistic prowess for a while longer, the Spaniard's competitiveness and boastfulness began to wear the friendship down. Accompanied by

Isabel and Dora, the two men continued to spend evenings together, but Alberto began to notice the way Picasso, who had once stated that 'every act of creation is first of all an act of destruction', succeeded in pulling the people who came into his orbit to pieces, very much as he had pulled apart the human image in his painting. It was only later, once the close relationship had come to an end, that Alberto realised what had happened, as he confessed in an interview: 'One day I had to admit to myself that he was stealing my self-confidence with his insinuations and malicious criticism. I put a distance between myself and him and became my old self again. Picasso is someone who has the tendency to take his models apart, to destroy everything he touches.' Years later, while he was drawing a portrait of Igor Stravinsky, Alberto described Picasso as a 'monster'. When Stravinsky remonstrated with him, Alberto remained unperturbed, adding, 'Picasso himself knows he is a monster'.[11]

Once the Munich Agreement had been signed in September 1938 and a fragile peace came into view, people in Paris did their best to go about their lives as usual. But the underlying tensions affected everyone, and, against a background of jittery ill humour, Alberto sensed a crisis building up in himself that he could no longer contain. It wasn't the drift to war or the banter in the bars as Chamberlain and Daladier were roundly cursed and punters outdid each other in mock Nazi salutes to get a laugh. It wasn't even the wretched work, which began well once he had got himself going, but then got swallowed into a skein of random pencil lines or literally crumbled under his fingers. It was yet more personal, and the sharp, subtle analyst in Alberto knew that the conflict in his inner life cried out for resolution.

For some three years he had been seeing Isabel between her visits back to London and her trips abroad. They had spent innumerable hours together in the studio, in cafés and museums, and on long walks across Paris at night. After her whirlwind relationship with Sefton Delmer, she had begun to lead her life independently again. Crisscrossing Europe with her journalist husband as he interviewed leading political figures (including Adolf Hitler) and reported on major events had seemed glamorous to begin with – not least because Delmer was a dedicated gastronome with a generous expense account. But Isabel had become more rooted in her groups of artist and writer friends in Saint-Germain, and she eventually traded her husband's apartment on place Vendôme (where her rowdy bohemian parties got on his nerves) for a modest hotel room set back from the Tuileries on rue Saint-Roch. Alberto often walked Isabel back to the Hôtel Saint-Roch after a dinner in Saint-Germain rounded out by a *fine à l'eau* – cognac with a shot of Perrier had become a fashionable drink in Paris – along the way. But he always stood around irresolutely in the hotel's lobby, not daring to take the definitive step up to Isabel's bedroom. If he had been in one of his old haunts in Montparnasse or the familiar, pink-lit interior of the Sphinx, he might easily have agreed to a quick transaction with Delphine or Suzy, proper professionals he knew well and could joke with. But Isabel, with her independence and unconstrained sexuality, frightened him. He had killed women like that in his imagination, cut their throats and juggled their limbs, like his friend Picasso, because they were threatening, dangerous. Isabel was a man-eater (and also, it was rumoured, a woman-eater), Alberto thought to himself, taking lovers on a whim, then disposing of them, like the female praying mantises that his old Surrealist friends used to keep. The situation was unendurable: he had no idea where he stood. He had, he told Isabel, completely lost his footing. Either he would become her lover that very evening or he would break off all relations.

Once again, hesitating at the foot of the hotel staircase, Alberto's nerve failed him. After a mumbled farewell he slunk off into the dark, a poor figure of a man, with plaster dust in his halo of wiry hair and clay under his nails; however hard he brushed them, the plaster seemed ingrained. Then as he emerged from the arcades along rue de Rivoli and was about to cross the place des Pyramides, where the gilded equestrian statue of Jeanne d'Arc glinted in the dark, a car careened out of the night and crashed up on the pavement, coming so close that it ran over and crushed his foot before ramming through a shop window. Knocked to the ground, Alberto felt nothing for a moment, but once he had got himself up he noticed that his foot was sticking out at an unusual angle, and it was only when he tried to twist it back into its normal position that the pain began. Shortly afterwards the police arrived on the scene and he was taken to a clinic where the broken bones were reset and his foot put in plaster.

Throughout his hospital stay, Alberto remained unusually cheerful, joking with the nurses bringing him meals or pushing a metal trolley filled with medical paraphernalia that jingled and tinkled as it passed.

This chariot-like contraption intrigued the sculptor so much that, propped up in his bed and jollier than ever, he made several drawings of it. Even better, Isabel – whom he thought had been terminally put off by his seeming lack of ardour – now visited him every day, bringing books and the latest Left Bank gossip. But what really counted for Alberto was that, having told her he had lost his footing because of their unrequited affair, his plaster cast was now there to prove it! The whole episode struck him as suffused with beneficent meaning. He had felt totally conflicted as to whether he should continue the relationship but then, like a bolt out of the blue, a car accident had settled the whole matter, a *deus ex machina* bringing an anxiously affectionate Isabel to his bedside and resolving what had seemed irresolvable. Life itself had made the decision for him.

In reality, nothing had been resolved. But that did not stop Alberto, once released, from swinging himself along triumphantly on his crutches, telling everyone he met what a great lark it was to have extra legs, and later, when he still limped, walking with a cane which he deployed to great effect, drumming the ground with it to underline a point or register agreement. The whole incident felt like a clarification of his bearings in the universe, and he went so far as to describe it enthusiastically in a detailed text that ran to twenty-eight pages. He later destroyed the text, but the importance of the event to him resurfaced with a vengeance much later when Jean-Paul Sartre gave his own interpretation of the episode in his memoir *The Words*, sending Alberto into a paroxysm of disagreement and virtually terminating what had developed by then into a firm friendship.

An injured foot was not going to stop the indefatigable artist from resuming his impossible task. On the contrary, its very impossibility elated him, pitting him against fate: a Sisyphus condemned eternally to roll his fleeting vision up a hill every day, working at all hours in extreme, insalubrious conditions, only to see that vision, that sparsely modelled figure, tumble down again and end in little heaps of plaster. It was failure after failure, but oddly, perversely, Alberto found a growing satisfaction in this. Failure, to his paradoxical cast of mind, was its own success. Every day he would fail again. Eventually, he would find out how to fail better.

Failure of one kind or another seemed in any case in the air everyone breathed as the world stumbled from one crisis to the next. There was not only the failure of nerve at Munich but also a failure of imagination

The Paris exodus, 1940

as the non-events of the 'phoney war' – the '*drôle de guerre*' – slid as smoothly as in a nightmare towards irreparable disaster. Rumours of an imminent German attack on the city had Parisians fleeing en masse, by whatever means – cars with mattresses strapped to the roof, panier-laden bicycles, handcarts piled high. Long, straggling lines of ordinary folk who had become refugees overnight swarmed out of the city, their bare necessities in bundles and knapsacks, intent on reaching some safe haven, a relative's house deep in the provinces or at least a barn they could hide in. The Giacometti brothers were caught up in the same wave of anxiety, and once those tiny sculptures that had survived had been wrapped up in damp rags and buried in a hole that they dug together in one corner of the studio ('If I were true to myself,' the artist once remarked, 'I'd bury all my sculptures so that they wouldn't be found for a thousand years'), they managed to procure bicycles and wend their way precariously out of the city – meeting up with others they knew at the Café de Flore, typically enough – just before the German army marched down the Champs-Elysées and began its occupation of Paris in June 1940. As the fleeing crowds moved south towards Etampes, enemy planes appeared, strafing them indiscriminately. In the horror of maimed and killed bodies, Alberto was particularly struck by a disembodied arm with widely outstretched fingers which he commemorated later in the sculpture *The Hand* (1947). After four days, horrified by what they had seen, the brothers turned their bikes round and by 22 June they were back in Paris. On the same day, a ceasefire was declared.

As German troops patrolled the streets, soon to be plastered with swastika-bedaubed notices and signposts in Gothic script, the city assumed a new normality with soldiers sitting on the café terraces, patronising the shops and attempting to blend into Parisian life. With so many inhabitants having fled in their cars, the city had grown eerily empty and silent, but slowly the new regime took hold and became an everyday reality. Alberto resumed work on his small heads, leaving the studio less and less frequently and never without his cane. He had a few last meetings with Isabel, spending one whole night with her holding hands in the Tuileries Gardens, where the untended grass had grown tall and wild. They promised to meet again after the war and live together: 'Remember, it is decided …', Isabel confirmed in a letter after they parted. Once Isabel was back in London, Alberto began worrying about his mother, making a more concerted effort to obtain the appropriate visa to go to Switzerland to see her. On the last day of 1941, just as the visa he had been given was due to run out, he finally made the break and boarded the night train, thinking he would only be away for a few months or so. In reality, he would become exiled in his own homeland and would not see Paris again for nearly four years.

The moment his eyes locked with hers, he was in a different world. He was ten years old again and had just got back from the damp, dark caves where he had been hiding to the warmth of the wood-panelled living room in Stampa. She was scolding him, saying his father had been waiting for him in the studio all afternoon, and in the same instant he was in another space he loved that smelled of paint and turpentine, of wood and old books. That smell had become the smell of his father, and the smell of his love for him. Giovanni would chide him gently for being late, then show him his new landscape, painted directly from the nature all around them. Then they would pore over illustrations of works by the Egyptians and the great European masters before they began to work, side by side, the old artist and the young,

German soldiers in Paris, July 1940

roughing out a still life, touching in the colour. Then she was there again, bathing him, washing his hair, scolding him again, the silly boy, then, as now, a fully grown man who had made his way in Paris and knew all those famous people but still had clay in his pockets and holes in his socks that she held in her lap to darn. Now, with Giovanni dead and her daughter Ottilia having died in 1937 giving birth, he was more than her first-born, and, somehow, without proper warning, the head of the family. He watched her, with her determined gaze framed by a halo of white hair, drawing her as she mended things by lamplight. She was unchanged, more her matriarchal self than ever: a 'Stampa' by birth, with roots running deep into the Bregaglia, and now in charge of her son-in-law's household in Geneva, with her grandson Silvio, poor Ottilia's boy, to look after. For his part, Alberto was still under her power, loving her, listening to her and fearing her as before. For him, she was never to be replaced, either by man or woman. She reigned supreme, enthroned in that big black dress, even as he struggled to escape and form an independent relationship with another woman.

If Annetta remained indomitable, she was also not at all happy about her son's scruffiness, or the stick that he brandished even though he no longer needed it to walk, and she was quick to tell him so. She had seen a successful career for him, making a good living among the swanky decorators and collectors in Paris while keeping Diego out of trouble. But he was back, looking older than his years, thin, his face prematurely lined, and without two pennies to rub together. Worst of all, his sculpture had grown so small as to be almost non-existent. Alberto joked about it, but Annetta saw nothing funny about the little figurines he had been making and kept producing like a hawker's trinkets. He'd never get a show or earn any money with miniatures. His father had done very well as an artist, painting proper pictures, making a name for himself and bringing up a big family in comfort. Alberto had always wanted to go his own way, of course. He had always been full of fantasies and contradictions. But now, with all this silly scraping his sculpture down into nothing, he had really gone too far.

Irked by his mother's disapproval, Alberto made every attempt to justify what he was doing, discussing it with her on evenings together, and later going out of his way to sum up his situation and how he intended to resolve it in the letters he wrote to her after she left Geneva for the family home in the Val Bregaglia:

> But you know very well, dear Mother, the kind of long and difficult work I have undertaken; you know, having seen me, how much I apply myself and how much patience I must have. This cannot continue without difficulty and taking difficult attitudes to life in general, which displeases me, but which I cannot avoid because I must do things exactly as I do them, it is my very equilibrium and the meaning in my life. I know that I have something to say that others do not say and if I persevere, it is because I have the deep and absolute certainty that I will achieve what I want and that these years have not been lost but gained. But you know, Mother, how impatient I am to satisfy you and to be able to give back to you, in some small measure, what you are and what you do for me, my greatest desire is to see you happy with me, and nothing could satisfy me like your confidence.[12]

Loving his mother and respecting her hardly made his financial situation any easier. He had left Paris virtually broke, having sold less work since his break with Surrealism, and most of the decorative commissions had dried up. So even for his basic expenses he was now dependent on his mother who, apart from being naturally careful with money, was also feeling the pinch since Giovanni's paintings had not been selling well. Alberto felt humiliated having to ask for regular handouts, and he argued that part of the savings Giovanni had kept to one side was his by rights. Even so, Annetta wasn't overly keen to open the family coffers – just enough for Alberto to keep life and limb together, but no more.

Luckily, Alberto could get by on very little. He had found a small room in the run-down Hôtel de Rive in Geneva where, he observed, the local girls on the game took their clients. His room had a narrow bed, a table and chair, with toilet and running water on the landing outside. He could work in front of the one small window as long as he had his sculpture stand and enough plaster to hand. No one seemed to mind the mess, not even the dusty white footsteps he left on the stairs as he humped sacks of plaster up the three flights. People always knew if he was working because they could see him moving about through the gap under the flimsy bedroom door. So the arrangement worked well enough. After all, it was about as close as he could get to the working conditions of rue Hippolyte.

Geneva was, even so, a far cry from Paris. Alberto had never cared much for Switzerland's second largest city, which he had got to know when he had done his early art-school courses there back in 1919, even though it had all kinds of food and American cigarettes that were now rare in occupied Paris. He disliked the smug, prosperous bourgeoisie and the kind of Protestant self-righteousness that he had forgotten about while living abroad. Big, bustling brasseries and intimate bars of the kind that made Montparnasse and Saint-Germain such stimulating areas to live in were limited to a handful of average cafés in the centre. Calvinism had long made its mark on the nightlife and its attendant entertainments. Such naughty activity as there was tended to be concentrated in a couple of cabarets, the Piccadilly strip club and the perky-sounding Perroquet, twin focal points for the nocturnal wanderings now so much part and parcel of Alberto's existence.

More intellectual pursuits were nonetheless available, albeit once again on a reduced scale. To avoid the scourge of the Nazis in Paris, the colourful and enterprising publisher Albert Skira was now back in his native Geneva. Alberto had known him from the time he launched the Surrealist-orientated art magazine *Minotaure*, with Tériade as co-founder, in 1933. It was Skira, too, who had persuaded Picasso to illustrate Ovid's *Metamorphoses*. Soon he and Alberto formed the hub of a small circle of artists and writers, including Balthus, Jean Starobinski, the Swiss writer who sparked Alberto's interest in phenomenology, and the rootless Romanian-born photographer Eli Lotar, later the subject of several of Alberto's most expressive sculptures. Their regular meetings for drinks and discussions in Skira's office eventually led to the publication of a less luxurious but equally inspired arts review entitled *Labyrinthe*. When he was not manically reducing his tiny heads in the tiny hotel room (described by Skira as 'just a bed and plaster'), or indeed roaming around Geneva's scanty red-light district, Alberto was generally to be found in Skira's office, in full flow, arguing both for and against numerous ideas and projects, banging the floor with his walking stick to underline a particular point. Balthus remembered their conversations, which included fierce debates about Konrad Witz and Grünewald,[13] in vivid detail: 'He liked to say the opposite of what I was arguing. We systematically contradicted one another. We would argue all night long, and "come to an agreement" as dawn approached, before going to bed.'[14] Even Skira, used to debating with the best minds in Paris, was impressed, later giving this perceptive summary of their encounters:

> Our conversations were always punctuated by 'Ah, yes! Ah, no!' But if we kept it up then you noticed how much further Giacometti thought than the person he was talking with. When he raised his eyes his look was doubting, sceptical, piercing, and, in a way, ironic. He gave the impression of playing with you, and before you answered his questions he knew what you were going to say. I have never met anyone who could speak on so many different subjects with such authority.[15]

Alberto contributed not only numerous drawings to the pages of *Labyrinthe* but several texts, notably a tribute to the Baroque printmaker Jacques Callot's scenes of war, massacre and rape, and an intimate appreciation of his friend Henri Laurens's sculpture. Later, after the war, Alberto was also to publish 'The Dream, the Sphinx and the Death of T.' – one of his and, indeed, one of all Surrealism's key texts – in *Labyrinthe*, reaffirming his reputation as a writer of rare insight that had prompted the poet Pierre Reverdy to suggest that he give up his 'palette' for the pen. If his literary talents were flourishing, however, his sculpture most certainly was not: not for lack of trying, because Alberto was a prodigious worker, pouncing on his ever-elusive, ever-dissolving vision again and again, always convinced that repeated failure would allow him eventually to make progress. He knew how difficult his task was, and how ridiculous it looked to most people who saw him at work in his bedroom or heard about it on the waves of art gossip that continued to flow back to Paris despite the occupation. Play as he might on the tiny scale of the figure once mounted on a disproportionately large base, or even a double base (as he had done for a small head of his nephew Silvio), they never did more than approximate that vision of Isabel against the vast, dark building on boulevard Saint-Michel. Busts shrank, figurines crumbled, while the heaps of plaster with their scatterings of tiny limbs and heads the size of marbles grew. As he trekked across cold, grey Geneva to the few bright lights of the Café des Négociants, Alberto cut an increasingly sorry figure, bent over his stick, in shabby, soiled clothes* – a kind of outcast, an art tramp, foreshadowing Samuel Beckett's down and outs, an eccentric who had gone too far and begun to annoy by his obstinacy and his clever-clever way of turning other folk's remarks and ideas upside down.

Then, at long last, the miracle occurred. Up in the mountains overlooking their family home in the Val Bregaglia, the Giacomettis owned a summer chalet at Maloja that they used regularly once winter had passed and the meadows began to fill with wildflowers. Alberto had fond memories of holidays spent there at the edge of Lake Sils (like Nietzsche before him), and now he also had full run of his father's summer studio, considerably more spacious and agreeable than his hotel room. In summer 1943, when he found he was making some progress on his small heads, he began work on a larger female figure there. With Isabel's slender silhouette framed by the night on boulevard Saint-Michel burnt into his memory, he painted an almost life-size figure in

*Yet the artist was not unaware of his appearance and, according to an acquaintance of the time, he broke into a rage when someone smoking next to him in the café accidentally burnt a hole in his one and only suit.

white, its arms held tightly to its sides, on one of the studio's wood-panelled walls. For the sculpture itself the artist resorted to a method he had not used before: instead of clay over a wire armature, he applied plaster directly to a core of straw, giving the finished work a curiously rag-doll air with prominent eyebrows and intense, painted eyes. Alberto used a child's toy cart lying about in the studio to move the figure around to get the best light. It reminded him of the medicine cart that had caught his attention while in hospital recovering from his accident, and he decided to use a similar chariot-like structure as the base of the work. A passing friend, the sculptor Mario Negri, left this moving description of seeing the strange, wheeled sculpture for the first time:

> I shall never forget the deserted studio in Maloja, where the light fell vertically into the bare room … Unmoving in the thin air, almost like a vacuum, stood an unfinished statue frozen in plaster (I don't know how many years she had stood there already): naked and delicate in her simple pose, her long arms pressed to her sides – like an antique deity in a deserted temple … She was not standing on a typical pedestal, but on a cube-shaped base with four small wooden wheels, like a child's toy, as if she had to leave this place, as if she were intended for a long, unbelievably long journey.[16]

Remarkably, the slender, elongated form – a prototype for the later, more fully developed and famous *Chariot* of 1950 – survived as the only large, indeed almost life-size, figure to come out of Alberto's Swiss exile. Elevated above ordinary life, both goddess-like and fragile, this figure represented the most eloquent expression to date of the vision that still haunted him of the woman, loved and feared, that he had seen isolated and yet unapproachable under the darkness of the Parisian night.

In Alberto's imagination, Isabel remained fully present, even as his mother reassumed her direct control over him. If Isabel and the self-destructive turmoil she had unleashed in him was the reason why his sculptures had shrunk, she was also the reason they had revived and begun to grow again. The correspondence between them, full of hope and nostalgia, continued its desultory course, with Isabel reminding him of their troth that, once the war was over, they would live together.

Both felt deeply their absence from the intellectual stimulus and allure of Paris where Alberto's new friends, Sartre and Beauvoir, had begun to take centre stage despite the occupation, he because two of his plays, *Les Mouches* (The Flies) and *Huis Clos* (No Exit), had been put on, and she because her first novel, *L'Invitée* (She Came to Stay), had just come out. Parisians appeared to have found a new modus vivendi, some of them all too eagerly, with their German invaders, and harsh though conditions became, with fuel and food strictly rationed for most and the permanent fear of Nazi persecution, life continued.

But while Alberto yearned for the old routine of days working at rue Hippolyte followed by nights at the Flore and the Sphinx, another miracle, another unsuspected shift of fate, was about to take place. On a notably reduced scale, Alberto had resumed his Parisian pattern by ending most working days at Geneva's Café des Négociants or at one of the brasseries where he could be fairly sure of finding a cheerful atmosphere and a few friends for company, even if it was only Eli Lotar, who had photographed him at work in his little hotel room and was always keen for a chat and even keener for a drink. On one evening at the Brasserie de l'Univers, at a meeting organised in support of the Resistance, Alberto noticed a conventional-looking, attractive girl who had been caught up in the general swell of discussion. He always had an eye for a pretty woman, but what was unusual was that she also noticed him, returning his gaze, if only primly at first. Her name was Annette, he found out – a name almost like his mother's – and she had trained as a secretary before finding a job at the local Red Cross. He might have forgotten her if she had not seemed as attracted to him as he was to her youth and looks. To his astonishment, she laughed at all his sly jokes, as if egging him on for more, and listened carefully when he got into a debate over art and reality with Balthus (with whom, more discreetly, he also discussed Isabel) or clarified some finer point of the new craze for phenomenology and its exploration of consciousness with Starobinski.

The atmosphere grew lighter and more convivial at the Brasserie Centrale, with more glasses of Dôle and Fendant knocked back and, clearly less conventional than he had imagined, she didn't seem to mind that he was almost twice her age and couldn't complete any of the bizarre and apparently insoluble tasks he had set himself. She found her job and life with her family in Le Grand-Saconnex – not even Geneva, but a *suburb* of Geneva – boring. Alberto's freewheeling life in Paris, hobnobbing with famous artists, and so far removed from petit bourgeois restrictions, was on the contrary terrifically exciting. And although he knew that she was naïve, that they should leave it there and not go any further, he found himself simply submitting, giving in to what life dished out, just as he'd done when the car had knocked him over, and soon they were seeing each other every evening, and she brought her girlish light and laughter into a life that had gone grey with failure. And gradually the stooped, dusty, Beckettian figure began to straighten up, to respond bit by bit to the charm of having an enthusiastic, fresh-faced young thing on his arm. And for all his infinite doubts and forebodings, for all his distrust of nice girls, Alberto began to fall in love again.

Was it really because Alberto wanted to have more better, bigger sculpture to show – above all, to Isabel – for his years of absence that he clung onto his Geneva existence for a good year after the liberation of Paris in August 1944 (and even, awkwardly enough, after the grand farewell dinner Skira had organised in his honour)? Was it the hope that, having shrunk, the sculptures would shoot back to some kind of normality after the figure on the chariot-like stand that had come to him in Maloja? Or had he simply given in to a romance that should never have happened between a child-like girl and a hardened bachelor who lived like a tramp and could find sexual satisfaction only with a bought woman? It might have been no more than that, and this certainly troubled him, not least because of the pact he had made with Isabel – and, if nothing else, he would always be a man of his word. Then why, when there was already so much confusion in his mind, did he not break off clearly with Annette but, rather, get in deeper by borrowing money from her, rather than from his beloved but close-fisted mother, to pay his return fare from Geneva to Paris? Annette had even bailed him out by buying some of his work with her hard-earned cash.[17] Was that not an indication that he had already accepted that she would follow him and claim the debt? Now he was triply bound to her, emotionally, ethically and financially. It was a clear contradiction, but perhaps he would be able to solve it dialectically, salving his conscience, coming to the correct conclusion once night had fallen and he was on the train in September 1945, unable to sleep, restless and tormented, his life suspended between the two cities …

The train clattered on regardless, transporting him again, this time clutching a box of diminutive figurines,* through the dark mountains and silent forests of eastern France towards the fabled City of Light.

*The story that Alberto had put his entire, surviving oeuvre from the Geneva years into six matchboxes was first told by Albert Skira. It was probably an exaggeration, as many good stories are. Annette claimed it was not true, and the more likely fact is that the figurines were carried in what Georges Sadoul, the French cinema critic (for whom Annette worked briefly as a secretary), described as a 'small cardboard suitcase (of a type carried by Italian masons whom he looks like so much)'.

PART TWO

(1945–55)

6

Post-war Paris (1945–46)

The Gare de Lyon looked much the same that autumn as when Alberto had first seen it nearly a quarter of a century before, a bit rundown but far less changed than he was. Even so, the people milling around him on the platforms came as a shock: pale and worn in their shabby clothes, some of their luggage so old and battered that it was held together with string, and they seemed nothing like the sleek, worldly Parisians flaunting the latest fashions who had so impressed him all those years ago. In comparison the folk he had just left in Geneva seemed well fed and prosperous. Alberto tried not to look too hard at the faces around him because he knew his intense stare got on people's nerves. With a few sweeping glances he took them all in, and as he did so the intervening years began to shrink: he saw them as they had been and as they were now. This one might have been pretty once, but she looked as if she might have lost her husband and would perhaps be going back, with her little boy in short trousers, to live for a while with her parents outside the city. The man in faded blue overalls could have been a policeman, but he was probably on his way to a factory job, or any job he could find if he had been accused of working too enthusiastically for the Germans. The youngish, hollow-eyed couple reminded Alberto of French Communist Party meetings he had attended before the war: decent, simple people, their illusions dented by years of hardship but who had probably done their bit for the Resistance. On the other hand, the cynical-looking one wearing a new overcoat and felt hat over to the right was the same as ever, out for himself only, and now looking unabashedly prosperous, as if he were doing well out of butter, eggs and cheese on the thriving black market.

In the streets outside the station, people were going about their business in a dejected way – the women in faded house dresses, the men in frayed shirts and jackets that had seen better days. What stuck out were the shoes, buckled and creased, so down at heel that often there was no heel at all. Not that things like that worried Alberto. His own shoes were quite as shabby, ingrained with plaster dust and furrowed, just like the deep lines that had crept into his face. Then the shoes put him in mind of Annette, who was always fussing over her carefully preserved best pair of pumps, and also of the way he had not told her clearly enough that he was too old for her, and too poor, and that in any case his life was too devoted to work and too harsh to share with a romantic young girl who was bored with the modest prospects of a life in the outskirts of Geneva.

Diego (who had stayed in Paris throughout the war) had offered to come and meet him at the station, but Alberto missed the train and, in the end, his arrival was considerably delayed. Now that he was in Paris at last, Alberto decided to take his time to get back into the city again. He had always got around on foot in Geneva, and little by little his walking had improved until no distance seemed too great and he stopped using his cane on every occasion. It was not as if he had much to carry: a bag with a few clothes and the box with the figurines, which he had wrapped up carefully, like little mummies, in rags. Apart from the big 'chariot' piece done up at Maloja, they were all he had to show for four years of trial and error, years of relentless creation and destruction. But in his own mind the little figures, sole survivors of all that concentrated effort, were nonetheless not as pathetic as they seemed. They were a stage to be gone through, a stage without hope, like life itself often turned out to be. Only by going through that process could he make any progress. Annette had simply accepted that at its face value, as had a few of his friends, but Isabel might actually understand the necessity they represented.

As he walked along the *quais*, noticing how sparse the *bouquinistes*' offerings had become with their yellowing, dog-eared old novels, Alberto kept the figurine case carefully pressed against his thigh. These little people he had saved from his own mass destruction had not gone through so much only to be shattered by some clumsy passer-by. But that hardly looked likely. The old, self-entitled swagger that he had known Parisians to have in their step, claiming right of way on the pavement as if by ancestral decree, was gone, replaced by an altogether humbler demeanour. People looked wary, furtive, on the defensive, as if all they wanted was to scurry past unchallenged. It was not difficult to see why, when images of the occupation were still so fresh in everyone's memory and signposts in German still rose like barked-out orders over certain streets. This new, humbled people, as Alberto knew from the newspapers he read daily in Geneva, had long been short of food and fuel. How could a Frenchman act proud on iron rations of food, on coffee so laced with chicory it had neither the smell nor the taste of coffee – real, aromatic coffee being, like real nylon stockings, a scarcely imaginable luxury? If there seemed to be fewer people on the streets, it must have been partly because there were such long queues outside every butcher's and baker's, waiting to buy provisions to get them through the day. As for fuel, it was September and pleasantly warm, but the spectre of an unusually cold winter was already on the horizon, and alarmed Parisians had piled their bathtubs high with as much coal and coke as they could lay their hands on.

Paris was still Paris, as people kept reminding themselves, and, as he came opposite Notre-Dame, Alberto reflected that the old city had weathered the occupation as it had so many disasters in the past. The great rose window of the cathedral which had struck him when he first arrived still looked out across the Seine, keeping its eye on the city as it had done since the Middle Ages – a witness to every defeat and conquest. The place was not only beautiful, with its ancient monuments lining either side of the Seine, but tough. A bit of rationing wasn't going to hurt it. He himself could put up with hunger and cold, and he smiled at the anecdote he had heard about Picasso – him again – who had brushed off a German high-up's offer of coal by saying, 'Spaniards are never cold'. Neither were boys from the Val Bregaglia …

Alberto had worried about Diego often while in Geneva. Communication between them had been infrequent, and neither he nor his mother felt confident that the younger man would not go back to his old ways and get mixed up in various scrapes and petty crimes. He still had his Nelly (the less said about mistresses to their mother the better), but Alberto could just see him doing little black market deals with some of his former cronies and, worse still, getting caught. Times had been hard and many people had got up to things they wouldn't have dreamed of doing in peacetime. He would find out soon enough, and the moment he turned off the *quais* and headed up rue de Seine, everything felt so familiar that his feeling of anxiety began to subside. How had the art galleries fared during the occupation, he wondered. Jeanne Bucher had left for New York, but she had not been well since returning to Paris. To escape the Germans, the dealer Pierre Loeb had left with his family for Cuba but on his return to Paris, Alberto had heard, he found his old apartment wrecked, the walls daubed with anti-Semitic slogans. Equally disturbing, he found his gallery had been simply bagged by the man he had left in charge of it – until Picasso took it upon himself to tell the usurper to get out immediately.* So, fortunately, Pierre was now back on rue des Beaux-Arts. There would have been many old scores like this to settle across the city, and news of collaborators – including prominent intellectuals – being tried and executed, or forced to commit suicide, had filtered through to Geneva.

Boulevard Saint-Germain looked almost empty. Of the few people Alberto saw out and about, several looked as though they had suffered some severe damage, with some of them hobbling along on crutches as he himself had done for a while after his accident. Others looked oddly displaced, like vagrants, as if they had not been able to find and take up their old lives, or even their old personalities, again. On the terrace outside the Café de Flore where before the war Alberto might have found whole groups of people he knew, there was now no one he recognised among the few customers taking a last cup of coffee or an aperitif before lunch. There were even fewer clients sitting opposite at Brasserie Lipp, but then only a while ago it had been thronged by German officers in their grey-green uniforms, eager to sample its Baltic herring and sauerkraut, and going back to old Nazi haunts now invited suspicion. The boulevard itself was almost spectral, with bicycle riders sliding by, the silence broken only by the odd bus or taxi. Even the people walking on the opposite side of the broad thoroughfare, the Lipp side, seemed dream-like, tiny and isolated, as if cut off in their own space and estranged from the apartment buildings towering overhead.

*Author in conversation with Pierre Loeb's son, the art dealer Albert Loeb, London, 2019.

In Alésia, the feeling of returning from exile grew more manageable. As he passed over the crossroads, limping more noticeably now, Alberto glimpsed several faces he vaguely recognised around the bar at his regular café-tabac, Le Gaulois. Nothing much had changed: it was as ordinary and shabby as ever, and he was tempted to go in for a quick coffee and a smoke. For a moment he watched the men in their overalls gather around a game of cards or dominoes, drinking their glasses of *Picon bière*, the same shandy they had drunk before the war – but even a quick catch-up with the past would have to wait until he had found out what had happened to the studio. Had Diego looked after it properly, or would he find the doors hanging open and all his sculptures dug up and stolen? Overall, the area looked almost exactly as when he had left it nearly four years earlier – a little drabber, but so familiar that Alberto felt his throat tighten. The children in the local primary school were kicking up their playtime racket, and the wisteria growing up the cracked façades seemed as rampant as ever. This was where his life had been, where it might always be. He felt grateful for the grey ordinariness of its little, low houses, relishing the sound of someone beating metal in a dingy courtyard and the two women laughing as they took their baguettes home. This was a place where a man could work undisturbed, not playing the artist but working like the blacksmith at his forge or even the knife-sharpener trundling his grindstone through the streets, doing a job in an ordinary place where, if you really looked, the most extraordinary things happened. But then, as he turned into the little yard in front of the studio, Alberto almost dropped his precious case of figurines. The door to the studio stood gaping open. What had happened – had he been robbed, had everything been taken away? He strode over in a panic, looked inside, then let out a sudden deep sigh of relief. Everything was exactly as he had left it. Even the muddied little penknife with which he pared the clay was where he had left it, as if waiting for him to get back into the struggle …

Better still, there was Diego, standing by the back wall. His closest and most constant friend. His alter ego. The two men, normally gruff and reserved with each other, hugged each other tightly. As they looked searchingly into each other's eyes, they were reunited within seconds. How could I ever have doubted, Alberto wondered, breathing in the studio's dank, musty air voluptuously.

The priority, then, was to reclaim the past, and the moment he and Diego had caught up on the most urgent news, the latest from Geneva and Paris, their mother and friends, the two of them began unearthing, like dogs searching for buried bones, the sculptures that lay hidden in the earth beneath the studio. One by one, they were eased out of the ground and unwrapped. They were only a few years old but for all the world they might have been pre-Hellenic antiquities. The brothers were both visibly moved as they dug up their own recent past which, if things had gone differently, might have lain unclaimed until they had merged back into the soil. It was these little heads, blobs of plaster and clay made human by their rough but recognisable features, that bound both of them together, giving them their identity and their lives meaning. To cover the emotion that surged up, the two brothers fussed around irritably trying to find the best places to put them in relation to the other figures punctuating the forlorn space. The little heads were like orphans that had just been taken in and now needed the right company to feel at home. Diego would grunt every now and then when he felt his older brother had made an obvious mistake, correcting it while looking at him to see whether he agreed.

That had always been their relationship, with Alberto taking the lead, becoming the artist, and Diego following, becoming the model and, increasingly, the technician, adviser and general helping hand. As in any such close, daily relationship, there was discord and tension. In artistic matters, Diego bowed instinctively to Alberto's superior judgement: he, after all, was the artist. But even Diego could not have suppressed a wave of frustration and disappointment as Alberto unpacked the tiny fruits of his long years in Geneva. They were still so small! And however much Alberto might go on about the one normal-sized figure he had achieved – raising it onto a toy-like base with wheels and calling it *Woman on Chariot* – they would be the laughing stock of all those snide, peripheral characters in the art world who were always waiting for a chance to scoff. And, as it happens, yes, Diego did mind when those sorts of people turned up out of the blue, whether greedy dealers, needy art critics or flashy American collectors, and asked whether he was 'Monsieur Giacometti' and he had to say no, he wasn't Monsieur Giacometti, that the real Monsieur Giacometti, *Alberto* Giacometti, was just over the road in the café.*

The brothers seldom argued, but Alberto was not above being miffed occasionally either. He didn't like it when a new idea took root in his mind or he found a new friend, and Diego was sceptical. Diego never said as much; he didn't have to. Taciturn and with a tendency to keep his own counsel at the best of times, he merely grunted and said nothing. He'd been like that about some of the Surrealist things, about Denise, too, and nothing unnerved Alberto, as he continued to expatiate on a subject, so much as Diego's silence. There was something absolute about it, like the unanswerable silence of the mountains at home where you could scream time after time and nothing changed. The more he babbled on to Diego, the sillier and more meaningless he sounded.

Every now and then, nevertheless, Alberto had to put his foot down, as he did about that terrible smell he began to notice wafting up ever more strongly once his precious figures had been unearthed and installed. While he had been away, Diego had adopted a fox. He had always loved animals, and he allowed the wily little beast, which he called 'Miss Rose', free run of the place, feeding it and playing with it like a pet; often it would pretend to be asleep or dead, then leap at him as he walked past, which never failed to amuse him. That would have been irritating enough in the cramped studio, but the stench was invasive, so that the earth underfoot and even his clay smelled of fox, a feral odour that lodged itself in your nostrils and tainted every breath you took. Diego would not hear of letting the little creature go and continually admonished Alberto to make sure he shut the door when he went out. Still, everybody knew how absent-minded Alberto could be. He was always forgetting his cigarettes or his keys. He even hid some of the meagre sums of money that came in from a random sale, then forgot where he'd stashed the notes. So if, on a certain evening, he went out for a drink and, in his usual careless way, left the door open and Miss Rose escaped, it would hardly come as a surprise …

But it did come as a surprise to Diego, and a painful wrench for which he did not forgive Alberto for quite some time. After the earlier

*The distinction extended to some of the decorative objects that Diego made for Jean-Michel Frank, which were signed simply 'Diego'.

effusions, a hostile silence fell momentarily over rue Hippolyte. Then the two of them had a better than usual dinner at a bistro Diego had found and which, he reckoned, produced the best *pot au feu* in Paris. Mollified by a couple of bottles of Beaune, then pressed by the patron to sample his *marc*, distilled in his own family's little vineyard, they clinked glasses and agreed that it must have been an accident. In the end, the brothers would always agree, and they would always stick together.

Other urgent business called. Before he left Paris, Alberto and Isabel had made a pact, like wartime lovers all over the world, that if they both survived the cataclysm they would reunite and live together. Neither had forgotten, as their correspondence reveals, with Isabel even spelling it out in one letter: 'Don't forget it is decided even if there is a delay of several years (I don't think so), I am coming to live with you.'[1] She had divorced Delmer and had already returned to Paris from London, both because she preferred living there and, presumably, to keep to their agreement. More ambiguous, Alberto had not hurried back after the liberation but continued his makeshift life in exile, ostensibly because he felt on the cusp of a breakthrough in his sculpture. Earlier in the year he had written to Isabel:

> I've been paralysed here since I came in 1942 (infinitely regretting leaving Paris even for a short time) fully intending to return after five months at the latest but with the sculpture the way I wanted it; after that time I found myself with a sculpture that was all wrong so I was incapable of moving and put off my departure from day to day until now, working as much as I could. I started the same thing over and over again, never getting it right. My figure ended up so minuscule every time and the work was becoming so imponderable and yet it was nearly what I wanted only I had the idea of a certain size that I wanted to achieve and it's only during the last year that I've managed it but not to the point I want, the size, yes, yet I know that I shan't give up the one I've been working on since September and that I shall finish it in spite of everything unless I'm completely deluding myself which I find hard to believe since I make a little progress every day ...[2]

Then, a couple of months later, on 30 July 1945, he had returned to the same theme, reassuring her:

> I shall see you soon, it isn't the lack of a visa that's stopping me coming back, I can come back when I like, yes it's my sculpture that's stopped me coming back for the last three years, it's been keeping me here in Geneva my life stagnating cut off from everything and I'm doing my utmost to get out of it as quickly as possible so as to be able to leave, I shall have to spend a fortnight in Maloja for various things and then I'll come back. Bring all my sculptures, Isabel? If only I can manage to bring one back I shall be more than happy. There are some very small ones, four or five but they're not right and then one I'm working on at the moment to make a cast, always the same one, destroyed 20 times since I've been here – 20 sculptures really destroyed – I'm not going to destroy it any more but get as far as I can with it and not start it again but if I manage to have a cast that is just a little bit all right that'll satisfy me, it'll give me endless work just to go on with it without ever starting the whole thing again. But it could also be that I went about it the wrong way and have wasted a lot of time, no I don't think so, the time hasn't been wasted, that work had to be done first quite apart from the result but anyway there will be a result …[3]

If these were hardly the passionate letters of a lover pining to be reunited with his beloved, it had already been established between them that their work came first. Even if Isabel, more easily taken off course by her amours and omnivorous appetite for larks, had not shown the same degree of commitment as Alberto to her art, she was unusually talented and ambitious. She was also sufficiently impressed by his work and by the recognition he had achieved to see beyond whatever deficiencies he might have as a lover. She admired his unusual intelligence and his extraordinary artistic versatility, as well as the constant tests to which he subjected that versatility. She knew that he had set out to catch the very pulse of life in whatever medium – drawing, painting, sculpting or even writing – that he chose. But that was not a question of making a bunch of grapes so real, like the ancient Greek painter, that the birds came down to peck them. It was about capturing human existence as it palpitated in time and space, with all its shifts and ambiguities, its defiance of fate and its essential vulnerability. In the shattered world they had inherited, his attempts to catch everything that could not be caught, the very fleetingness of being, were more important than ever. Isabel often looked at the drawings

Alberto had given her. Somehow out of the flux of lines that invaded the pale sheets of Rives paper, a new truth was breaking through: a continuity in the net of fragile outlines, a persistence of consciousness in a void, of human awareness in the vast expanse of space. Sometimes that space, the smudged and slightly yellowing sheet of paper, looked corrosive, a faint acid, as if bathed in an uneasy conscience that was eating away at the sharp but fragile pencil lines …

To a relationship with a man of this quality, how much importance did one give to his performance in bed? It was key to an intimate relationship, and, along with good food and wine, it was what perhaps in the end pleased her most, as she took advantage of every overture to pleasure. But there was also something rarer here than a satisfying tumble between the sheets. Having grown up as the eldest child in a matriarchy, Alberto was conflicted, both attracted by women, and repulsed, even terrified, by them. His mother, Annetta, who was née Stampa of Stampa and didn't care who knew it, had ruled unchallenged, least of all by her husband, the gentle, accommodating Giovanni. Alberto loved and feared her in equal measure, and in the end his most devout wish, seasoned Parisian intellectual though he had become, was to gain her approval. Nothing else, including the flattering interest shown by his more recent friends, Jean-Paul Sartre and Simone de Beauvoir, really mattered. Since she, as a strict Protestant, would not have approved of sex outside marriage, Alberto obeyed her as closely as he could – once his rocky relationship with Denise was over – by avoiding 'nice' girls and consorting only with prostitutes, mostly at the Sphinx and other, less upmarket bars nearby like Chez Adrien on rue Vavin. Now, abruptly, life had changed course, putting not only one but potentially two very desirable and different female partners in his path.

With Annette, Alberto had tried in his admittedly conflicted fashion to be clear. An extended relationship between them was out of the question. Yet she continued to make contact, confirming her decision to leave narrow-minded Geneva behind and join him in the bright lights of artistic Paris. He repeated how little suited, even hostile, he and his brother's hard, uncomfortable existence was to female companionship – but to no avail. He also had the far thornier problem of life with Isabel to resolve. He loved her unusual beauty and animal grace – he could hardly imagine a more exciting model, and he had already drawn her before she even began sitting for him. But Isabel presented an unusual

John Deakin, Isabel Rawsthorne in London, around 1953

challenge. To begin with, she was the most independent woman he had ever been involved with: she showed both real promise as a painter and a readiness to engage with him at any intellectual level. As he had already sensed, she was fluent in sexual matters, confident and adventurous, as ready to explore a lesbian relationship as one with a confirmed homosexual, making him all the more aware of his own shortcomings. In that regard, he had often wondered, as one tiny image after another had crumbled under his figures, whether it was not her, who now held such sway over him, that he was trying to destroy.

A pact made was a pact to be kept. When they met again, it was in a suitably dark bar, so dark indeed, Isabel remembered, that they could barely see one another, although it was clear that through the intervening years both had aged noticeably, with Isabel's own beauty showing the first, puffy ravages of drink. Perhaps neither was convinced that living together would be as desirable as it had seemed before the war, but both believed that they owed it to the pledge they had made in 1940, sitting hand in hand in the Tuileries at night ... The long grass would have been trimmed back by now, perhaps even the fountains were playing again. For all its failures and humiliations, Paris seemed to be rising swiftly from its ashes and making an unexpected claim to a new freedom, both physical and intellectual. Even though residual signs of the occupation persisted, the need for release and renewal was in the air, almost tangibly, and it was underlined by the challenging new plays and books coming out and the new songs, full of promise, floating off the radio. Jazz cellars and start-up clubs were opening all over the Latin Quarter and little, chic touches to the way Parisians dressed were making a comeback.

One of the watchwords currently being bandied about was the responsibility of the individual, and that was certainly not the exclusive domain of Jean-Paul Sartre (or 'Jean-Sol Partre', as one wit* humorously labelled him), but clearly an issue to be debated by any intellectual worthy of the name. As individuals aware of their own responsibilities, Alberto and Isabel lived together for the following couple of months. Almost no records of that crucial period have survived, but at all events it was not to last long. Some sources say that Alberto took on a couple of extra rooms, with the unlikely luxury of a bathroom, in the warren of tiny dwellings behind his studio, while others suggest he rented a bedroom at the nearby Hôtel Primavera, to which he often repaired when it was too cold or damp at rue Hippolyte. The new couple took up Alberto's old life, with him working most of the day, and her often posing for him, doing her own work insofar as circumstances allowed and seeing friends. Being gregarious and already aware of who was who in Parisian cultural circles, Isabel would have been quick to appreciate that she had moved to the very centre of Parisian intellectual life, dining with Picasso and Dora Maar at the Spaniard's local 'canteen', Le Catalan, or meeting Sartre and Beauvoir in the Flore for drinks and rambling conversations about art and politics. At any time of day, Isabel was

*Boris Vian, a poet and trumpet player who came to symbolise Existentialist irreverence.

delighted to find, she could walk out of Alésia towards Saint-Germain and be sure to find either old or new acquaintances, such as Michel and Zette Leiris, or Balthus and his wife, Antoinette de Watteville (with whom Isabel had a brief affair). There was also Tristan Tzara and Georges Bataille accompanied by his flamboyantly titled spouse, Princess Diane Kotchoubey de Beauharnais, as well as a fair sprinkling of American expatriates longing for the glory days and cheap booze of pre-war Paris.

For a brief period, these privileged contacts appeared to hold the couple together, she strikingly vivacious with a laugh recognisable at a hundred metres, and he already a local celebrity, misleadingly shabby and dusty, who had just reinvigorated his strange myth by making sculptures so small that they disintegrated into dust. But whatever their intimate circumstances had become, a daily routine must have quickly shown up the inconsistencies of a shared life. Having left both a child (with Epstein) and a marriage (to Delmer) behind, Isabel would have had little compunction about dumping an unsatisfactory lover. Alberto, for his part, was no doubt soon missing the strict bachelor existence he had just re-established with Diego and the occasional embrace of a streetwalker in a rented room. Being by far the more decisive of the two, Isabel took the lead in ending the failed experiment. At a Christmas party they both attended in 1946, she came across a young musician, René Leibowitz, whom she knew already and liked for his involvement in the latest musical trends. Here was another artist, younger, full of admiration for Schoenberg and apparently less inhibited than poor, complicated Alberto. To the latter's astonishment, she broke with him there and then amid the Yuletide celebrations and left with the young musician firmly hooked on her arm. The new couple then fled Paris altogether to live out their amours far from prying eyes.

Although this sudden turn of events certainly took Alberto aback, he seems never to have held the abrupt dismissal against Isabel or, perhaps more accurately, never to have shown that he did – vigorously proclaiming, at least later in life as a married man, his innate scorn for any form of sexual possessiveness. After a while, he and Isabel renewed cordial if infrequent relations, and Alberto rapidly resumed his role as a sympathetic regular at the Sphinx who never failed to pay for the girls' drinks and generally conduct himself as a gentleman. But the artist was about to be overtaken by other, unforeseen events that would, more deeply than his dalliances with different ladies, transform the very basis of his vision and work.

One of Alberto's passions was politics, and he followed every twist and turn of world events from a committed left-wing position, reading *L'Humanité* daily and following the trials and tribulations of the French Communist Party assiduously. He had also remained an avid cinemagoer, in a city that since before the recent war had catered to every taste. During this post-war period, Parisian cinemas devoted the first part of their programme to the latest news and particularly to reports on the atrocities revealed in the Nazi death camps.* Alberto had gone one evening to the Actualités Montparnasse, a cinema on boulevard du Montparnasse that specialised in current events. The artist fumbled his way to a seat in the dark and prepared himself for a treat: a bombardment of images from the silver screen, a wealth of material from across space and time that he could never obtain so easily elsewhere, even in one of the great museums he loved, such as the Louvre or the Museum of Antiquities in Saint-Germain-en-Laye. The cinema was an Aladdin's cave, a treasure trove of the familiar and the unexpected, a hoard of visual surprises.

Something that evening did not click into place, or it might have been more that Alberto, still obsessively focused on the ever-shrinking figure he had left in the studio, did not click into the experience unfolding before his eyes. Instead of being riveted by the newsreel, as he usually was, his eyes no longer registered the succession of events before him but wandered around the darkened temple in which his fellow spectators were held spellbound. But the moment Alberto took in the massive head of the man seated next to him, looming through the gloom with a presence that dominated the surrounding space with unquestionable authority, the cinema screen was reduced to a mere jumble of black and white blobs: he had eyes only for the head. As the newsreel faded into the background, Alberto found to his astonishment that things stood revealed as never before and that, as he re-emerged onto boulevard du Montparnasse, this new way of looking persisted, with the buildings, the trees and the passers-by all assuming a vividness he had never noticed;

*There was also an exhibition at the Grand Palais in Paris in 1945 entitled 'Hitler's Crimes'.

it was, in his own words, as if 'boulevard Montparnasse was dipped in the beauty of the Thousand and One Nights, fabulous, absolutely strange ...'[4]

This abrupt 'scission in reality', as Alberto called it, affected him deeply, and in his obsessive way he began to analyse it from every angle, discuss it with friends, and eventually in several key interviews he gave thereafter, turned it into a major epiphany that had changed his entire course as an artist. The scales had fallen from his eyes and from this point on he was convinced he saw reality anew, with the clarity of a sudden, transformative vision. His description of the event differed on every occasion, but each time it was couched in dramatic terms, re-enforcing the capital importance it assumed for him (as had the accident to his foot and his sighting of Isabel), while demonstrating how intuitively he wove myth into his life and art:

> Suddenly I no longer knew just what it was that I saw on the screen. Instead of figures moving in three-dimensional space I saw only black and white specks shifting on a flat surface. They had lost all meaning. I looked at the people beside me, and all at once *by contrast* I saw a spectacle completely unknown. It was fantastic. The unknown was the reality all around me, and no longer what was happening on the screen! When I came out onto the boulevard Montparnasse, it was as if I'd never seen it before, a complete transformation of reality, marvellous, totally strange ...
>
> I began to see heads in the void, in the space which surrounds them. When for the first time I clearly perceived how a head I was looking at could become fixed, immobilized definitively in time, I trembled with terror as never before in my life and a cold sweat ran down my back. It was no longer a living head, but an object I was looking at like any other object, but no, differently, not like any other object but like something simultaneously living and dead. I gave a cry of terror, as if I had just crossed a threshold, as if I was entering a world never seen before. All the living were dead, and that vision was often repeated, in the Métro, in the street, in a restaurant, in front of my friends. The waiter at the Brasserie Lipp became immobile, leaning towards me, with his mouth open, without any relation to the preceding moment, to the moment following, with his mouth open, his eyes fixed in an absolute immobility. And not only people but

> objects at the same time underwent a transformation: tables, chairs, clothes, the street, even the trees and the landscapes.[5]

The 'scission' allowed Alberto to establish a 'before' and 'after' in his existence. Where he had seen reality under a kind of photographic screen before, it now stood revealed in a new, naked intensity. This shuddering revelation sounds akin to an experience under drugs, if not an actual psychotic event, but although the use of substances such as amphetamines, opium and mescaline was widespread among the intelligentsia at the time, with Cocteau and Sartre to the fore, there is no evidence, apart from the incident surrounding Robert Jourdan's death, that Alberto himself experimented much with stimulants beyond his abundant daily intake of tobacco and coffee, with a few cognacs or whiskies thrown in. At the same time, it can be reasonably assumed that years of doubt, failure and deprivation had taken their toll and that he longed to break through the long, self-imposed tyranny of reducing his sculpture to little heaps of rubble. At certain points, the Damascene 'scission' brought a sense of liberation and joy to the wonder he felt at the world, while at others it made him, by his own account, tremble with fear: the towel hanging over the chair or the chair itself seemed suddenly weightless, emptied of all substance and sense, just as the waiter in the familiar surroundings of Brasserie Lipp appeared to freeze as he leant over to take the order, his eyes dead in a face devoid of all expression.

Though rooted in an authentic experience, this would not have been the first time that Alberto had given free rein to his literary flair. Before the war, he had absorbed the range of Surrealist subjects and techniques so well as to have become a minor Surrealist writer while keeping a unique personal voice. While in Geneva, Alberto would have already picked up on the new wave of Existentialist writing and read Sartre's *Nausea* (1938), and his own texts, notably for Skira's *Labyrinthe*, were to take on a distinctly Sartrean tinge. The famous passage in which Roquentin, the protagonist of Sartre's novel, stares at the root of the chestnut tree which suddenly appears – like a philosophical annunciation – stripped back to the 'nothingness' of its existence reverberates through Alberto's various retellings of his 'scission'. Alberto's intense focus on the way in which he experiences the appearances of the world is also inflected by the philosophical investigations of Maurice Merleau-Ponty, whose much admired and

Maurice Merleau-Ponty, around 1950

debated *Phenomenology of Perception* was published in 1945. What drew Alberto's interest immediately was Merleau-Ponty's conviction, which echoed his own, that the perception of objects in space, being both physiological and psychological, was inherently subjective.* But,

*To quote one instance, Merleau-Ponty argued that through his painting Cézanne discovered that 'the lived perspective, that which we actually perceive, is not a geometric or photographic one'. Maurice Merleau-Ponty, 'Cézanne's Doubt [1954]', in *Sense and Non-Sense*, translated by H. and P. Dreyfus (Evanston: Northwestern University Press, 1964), p. 114.

whatever theoretical sources influenced it, the experience that night on boulevard du Montparnasse appears to have jolted the artist out of his impasse, heralding a radical change in his reductive practice and representing a watershed moment in his career.

If Alberto continued working on small busts of his friends, such as his early supporter Marie-Laure de Noailles and his new confidante Simone de Beauvoir, he also began experimenting with bigger pieces. A frail plaster silhouette with little highlights of colour began to form under his fingers and, although still small (barely eight inches), it would have towered over his other works, some of them barely an inch high, had these not been mounted on huge bases – thus amply demonstrating that scale, rather than size, is key to the effect of sculpture in space. Called *Night*, it was described by Alberto as 'a frail young girl feeling her way in the dark',[6] whose figure he cut closer and closer to the bone, removing every last, tiny fragment of plaster until she looked barely more substantial than the wire armature at her core. She was, in her maker's words, quite literally as 'tall and as thin as a thread'. The shift from what were jocularly called the 'pin' people to the 'beanpole' women was graphically recorded in a series of photographs of them sited side by side by Marc Vaux and published over no fewer than sixteen pages (a sign of Alberto's growing recognition) in the first post-war issue of Christian Zervos's journal *Cahiers d'art*. The dramatically lit shots showed clumps of heads, busts and figures of varying dimensions on plinths of varying size and mass, establishing a complex overview that finally gave the lie to the popular notion that Alberto had spent years producing the same tiny blob of plaster over and over again. At long last, after years in literal and artistic exile, a sense of fruitful direction and productive experimentation had returned to his practice. This figurine's striding legs, breaking from the static pose of his recent work, represent his own newfound freedom to move forward once more.

Thus, the next few years were to witness a flourishing of creativity for Alberto that would generate his mature style and many of his most famous works.

Although Alberto's sculptures now started to grow in height, they nevertheless shrank in volume to the bone, as if the ambient air had conspired with some unseen force to compress them to an irreducible essence. Once again, the sculptor protested that he himself should not be held accountable for this new race of taller but distinctly skeletal figures. 'The more I tried to make them broader,' he would say, almost apologetically, 'the narrower they got.' He returned to this in later life, joking that he would have far preferred to create voluptuous women like Marilyn Monroe, if only he had been able. If they came about that way, he continued, it was simply in the process of attempting to recreate what he had seen and thus beyond his conscious control. It was frequently suggested at the time that the sculptor must have been affected by the shocking images that had filtered through of the prisoners in the German death camps; indeed, some of the emaciated survivors had returned to Paris and were visible on the streets. But Alberto emphatically rejected any such influence, reiterating his conviction that there was no such rational or objective explanation for their scrawny silhouettes. Since the figures were to continue to grow in height without taking on more volume, and the slender style became Alberto's signature idiom, the questions persisted, with the artist providing ever more ingenious reasoning by bringing the new phenomenological theories of perception to his aid. As his sculptures had once been infinitesimal, they were now tall and shrunk to their skeleton so that at first sight, particularly in that early post-war period, they came across as barely more than rapid scribbles on space.

It comes as no surprise that during this period Alberto had been drawing ceaselessly, using the medium as he always did as a testing board for ideas and impressions; indeed, his figures had first begun to grow in sketches of that time. Although the drawings could be anything from the most summary jotting to a fully fledged study, they always formed the essential first phase, like a litmus test for the validity of any new thought. If the idea did not work in pencil on paper, it would be abandoned, without further experimentation as sculpture or painting (to which, prompted by his more buoyant mood, the artist had recently returned). In his desire to find solutions through drawing, Alberto was making frequent use of an eraser, rubbing out parts and drawing over them, increasing their spectral look, which in turn appeared to be incorporated in the plasters that he had under way. The three media in which he worked informed each other; his frenetic yet controlled use of the eraser found its three-dimensional equivalent in the sharp edge of his sculptor's knife, both being deployed to strip an image down to its core.

Certainly, the artist stayed true to his old working methods, building up rapidly and skilfully one plaster figment after another, then destroying almost as many in order to begin all over again. One of Alberto's friends, the writer Georges Limbour, who was also close to Masson, Leiris and Bataille, visited him during this period and described what he found:

> When one enters Giacometti's little studio, it is not immediately clear where to go: one is afraid to overturn the slender and fragile (or so they seem) figures rising from the floorboards, or to tumble over an enormous pile of plaster leaning against the wall and spreading under a table, rising so much it lifts it from beneath. From this perspective, Giacometti's studio more resembles a wrecking field than a building site. Wrecking what palaces, what dreams? All this plaster was once statues, but Alberto, dissatisfied with his works, destroys them, scrapes away at them, amputates them, redoes them … It is a poignant, plaster mass-grave that speaks to Alberto Giacometti's patient and astonishing dedication.[7]

Alberto's work also continued to attract the attention of Pierre Matisse, the New York art dealer, who visited Paris frequently to view the galleries and to spend time with his famous father. With one-man shows devoted to Miró and Balthus, his gallery in the Fuller Building on 57th Street had already established itself as a hub for contemporary European art, and during his frequent contacts with Alberto, Matisse had already outlined his interest in organising a major new exhibition to open in January 1948. Alberto responded favourably, although he did not hide the problems he had encountered during the war with the scale of his figures. 'To my terror,' he admitted in a letter to Matisse, 'the sculptures became smaller and smaller. Only when they were very small did they have a likeness. Yet their dimensions disgusted me. Tirelessly I began again, only to end up again several months later at the same point.'[8]

In a subsequent letter, after Matisse had visited him at the studio, Alberto hastened to reassure him, almost as if he were talking about anaemic children now on the road to recovery: 'Don't be too worried about the sculptures you saw! Their appearance was misleading. I've been working in the studio since you left, until the day before yesterday. When you saw the sculptures they were only beginnings. Now they're quite different. I can finish them quite soon, but I have to take a short holiday first. The largest of them is about forty-eight inches high, without its plinth. That's twice as much as before, but I think it's really coming on very well.'[9]

Thus Alberto's first exhibition in fourteen years began gradually to come into perspective.

Picking up on a pre-war habit, Picasso once again became a regular visitor to the studio (causing something of a stir in modest Alésia as he arrived in his chauffeur-driven limousine) just as in turn Alberto came and went to rue des Grands-Augustins. The relationship between the younger and older artist was to remain cordial for some time to come, with the two of them discussing each other's work freely, and Alberto even beginning work on the (ultimately abandoned) bust of Picasso. Picasso had remained in Paris throughout the war but did not exhibit during the occupation. Deemed 'degenerate' by the Nazis, in July 1942 paintings of his were burned in the gardens behind the Galerie du Jeu de Paume along with works by Miró and Fernand Léger. He had managed nevertheless to live in more comfort than most. In 1944, he even put on a read-through of his own play, *Desire Caught by the Tail*, in Michel and Zette Leiris's apartment on the Quai des Grands-Augustins which was filled with his paintings (Zette being the stepdaughter of Kahnweiler, an early advocate of Cubism*). Had Alberto been back in Paris by then, he might well have been ascribed a role in this rambling farce, written three years earlier, since the participants that evening included Sartre and Beauvoir as well as Leiris himself and Raymond Queneau, with Albert Camus directing the play. Meanwhile, Picasso had to deal with the odd visit from the Gestapo. On one notable occasion, a German officer picked up a photograph of *Guernica* lying around the studio and asked Picasso menacingly: 'Did you do that?', to which Picasso coolly replied: 'No. You did.'

*Zette Leiris ran Kahnweiler's gallery during the war and hid him throughout the occupation in the spacious apartment she shared with Leiris.

The occupation had clearly not been without its lighter moments, with Sartre famously reflecting that 'never had we been so free', since the loss of freedom under the occupation threw freedom's very nature and value into such stark relief. This kind of provocative statement that cut through superficial and conventional thinking had turned Sartre from a relatively obscure schoolteacher formed by the prestigious Ecole normale supérieure into a rising literary and philosophical star, whose first novel, *Nausea*, had garnered significant acclaim. The author's gift for both abstract thought and vivid, sometimes almost journalistic expression coalesced in such a timely way as to make his ideas about freedom and existence dominate the period. Some remarked tartly that this rise had been much facilitated by the relative absence of competition from other writers and thinkers during the war years, and others noted that Sartre had avoided active, political commitment throughout; he was, as his friend at the time Camus put it, a writer who acted politically rather than a political activist who wrote.

Given that the Wehrmacht had been relatively tolerant of publications deemed too obscure to have much political impact, Sartre had been able to bring out his first major philosophical work, *Being and Nothingness*,* as well as two plays already mentioned, *The Flies* and *No Exit*. He also contributed frequently to clandestine publications such as *Combat*, the newspaper founded and edited by Camus. By the time Alberto arrived back in Paris, Sartre's name was on everybody's lips in the tightly connected intellectual circles around Saint-Germain-des-Prés. The talk entitled 'Existentialism is a Humanism' which Sartre gave at the Club Maintenant in October 1945 was so tense with expectation and so jam-packed that women fainted. Sartre himself turned up considerably the worse for wear since he had spent the night before drinking with Arthur Koestler, whose *Darkness at Noon* had also generated debate across Europe.† Short in stature and barely visible to the crowd, Sartre overcame not only the 'night before' but a prodigious, daily intake of

***Being and Nothingness* sold comparatively well for a very long philosophical tract. It weighed almost exactly one kilo, and it has been claimed that many Parisian housewives purchased it as a handy substitute for the weights they would normally use on their kitchen scales.

†Having become a bestseller in English, *Darkness at Noon* did even better in French, selling some 500,000 copies. Simone de Beauvoir recounts finding Alberto and Tzara in an animated discussion of the book at the Café de Flore, adding that Alberto was the only one who had an intelligent point of view on it.

hard liquor and amphetamines* to give a long, complex talk that then reverberated across the city. The key phrase (or superficial catchword) of Existentialism was 'existence precedes essence'; essence is made up of all the shallow and false ways in which humanity classifies and gives meaning to the world, while existence is the mere and meaningless fact that things exist. The statement that 'existence precedes essence' is a liberating one because it proclaims that the meaning of the world is not fixed to the existence of things, which is in itself meaningless. So each individual is tasked with finding their own meaning, defining his or her own life. This heady intellectual revolt against rationality, religious doctrine and conventional meaning found enthusiastic support on café terraces and in basement jazz clubs where a newly freed, younger generation met in black polo necks and dark glasses to discuss their uncertain futures while having as much fun as they could.

Soon all heads would turn whenever Sartre and the equally gifted Simone de Beauvoir made their way to the Café de Flore on whose quieter upper floor they and a few chosen allies, such as Camus and the philosophers Raymond Aron and Merleau-Ponty, wrote their books by day, since it was better heated and more agreeable than their own digs. At first the manager was peeved to see how long they occupied the tables while spending so little, but as Sartre's reputation grew, bringing new customers to the Flore, he had a telephone especially installed so that people could get in touch with the celebrated writer. After writing bouts of some six hours, Sartre and Beauvoir would dine with a few others at local bistros like Le Petit Saint-Benoît, then end the evening at a new club, such as Le Tabou, which Boris Vian had just opened on rue Dauphine. The pair hardly looked like the leading lights of the most exciting and intellectually challenging square mile in the world, but dumpy, wall-eyed, pipe-smoking Sartre and handsome, but severe, almost schoolmarmish-looking Beauvoir – whom Sartre had nicknamed the 'beaver' for her unrelenting industriousness – reigned supreme, commenting on topics of the day, adhering to numerous causes and indulging tirelessly in a sexual promiscuity that somehow allowed their lifelong commitment to each other to flourish.

*Amphetamines had been doled out liberally to the German troops to redouble their efforts as they made their phenomenal entry and conquest of France. Meanwhile, much of the art and literature of the period was achieved with the aid of a wide variety of stimulants.

Simone de Beauvoir and Jean-Paul Sartre in Paris, 1970

This fascinating couple, whose every move was followed by a growing tribe of lovers, disciples and lost souls known as the 'Sartre family', started seeing Alberto in 1939, after an earlier chance encounter at the Dôme, and they responded instinctively to his unusual appearance, charm and intelligence. Alberto was first drawn to Sartre as not only a leading thinker and writer but as a conversationalist with as broad, unusual and contradictory a cast of mind as his own with whom he could engage in Homeric discussion. But he was even more receptive and eventually closer to Beauvoir, who had been immediately impressed by his presence, describing him as 'a man with a craggy face, wild hair, avid eyes, who was out every night wandering the pavement, alone or with a very pretty woman; he looked both as solid as a rock and freer than an elf …'[10] While Beauvoir wrote about him on several occasions, Alberto drew and made a small, sensitive bust of her (as he did of several women he knew well, including Marie-Laure de Noailles and Diane Bataille). The two became fast friends, confiding in each other, with Alberto talking about Isabel and meeting Annette, and Beauvoir describing her drawn-out, passionate affair with the American writer Nelson Algren.[11]

Sartre and above all Beauvoir's friendship also extended to Annette, whom they met in 1946 on a trip to Geneva, and they actively encouraged her liaison with Alberto, later lending the pair money to survive the months of post-war penury (Sartre was unusually open-handed, carrying wads of cash on him to give large tips and share with those in need). When Annette arrived in Paris, without a proper winter coat or adequate shoes, Beauvoir made sure she was provided for by giving her hand-me-downs. The war might be over but, as Beauvoir put it, 'it remained on our hands like a great, unwanted corpse, and there was no place on earth to bury it'.[12]

If Alberto still felt somewhat orphaned by his expulsion from the Surrealists, he now had friends united by what Beauvoir called 'a deep bond of understanding'. With them and the group that had formed around them, he had at last rediscovered the kind of intellectual camaraderie that he had enjoyed within Breton's circle. Everything could be discussed, from the latest jazz club to the finer points of a new philosophical system, but without the diktats and constraints that Breton had imposed: politics, for instance, was approached, as Beauvoir put it, as 'a family affair' in which everyone took sides, squabbled frequently and generally made up. The famous couple had just joined forces with the increasingly influential Merleau-Ponty to found *Les Temps modernes*, a political and literary review established in the autumn of 1945 that filled the gap left by the prestigious *Nouvelle revue française*, banned for 'collaborationism'. In the second issue of the new publication (which took its title from the popular Charlie Chaplin film *Modern Times*), Beauvoir wrote a positive review of Merleau-Ponty's *Phenomenology of Perception*. She shared her enthusiasm for the young philosopher's revealingly inventive approach with Alberto, who was sufficiently impressed to familiarise himself with the text.

Although Alberto himself never engaged whole-heartedly with either phenomenology or Existentialism, this development turned out to be crucial to the interpretation of his work and the future of his career. By the time Breton had returned to Paris from exile in New York in October 1946, Surrealism was increasingly regarded as a spent force (despite a new generation of 'revolutionary' Surrealists) as well as being discredited for its poor Resistance record and the defection of several of its leading lights to the Communist Party. Breton was nevertheless a name still to be reckoned with and Alberto might perhaps have considered him briefly as a potential writer for the catalogue preface of his forthcoming show at the Pierre Matisse Gallery. But by now his loyalty was firmly with the '*famille Sartre*', and even though he remained partly sceptical of Existentialism's claims, Alberto sensed they were far more attuned both to the times and to his own visionary art. In retrospect, it seems almost inevitable that he would go on to ask Sartre to write the preface to his all-important New York show. At the time, it was an inspired choice. The conjunction of Sartre's persuasive brilliance and a notable success at a prestigious gallery in the New World was to lift Alberto's career out of its slough of doubt and despair into a context that transformed both the interpretation and the impact of his achievement across every phase of its development. That would not happen overnight, however. Alberto would first have to define his bearings in an unexpectedly effervescent post-war Parisian art world and undergo several more radically transformative experiences, before all the stars in his firmament were aligned to extend and confirm his reputation.

7

The Dream, the Sphinx and the Death of T. (1946–47)

Even casual contact with Alberto left no one indifferent. As he turned forty-five, his craggy face, already deeply lined and set beneath a crown of wiry, greying hair, gravelly voice and probing yet compassionate gaze made an immediate impression. So did his shambling gait and wrinkled clothes, which made him appear like a tramp who had seen better days but still never forgot to adjust his stained tie and button his jacket, as if on his way to some formal occasion. Then came the impact of his conversation. He was unassuming at first – as if to allay the shock of the strange originality to come – but would then come out with an unexpected or controversial remark and pursue it with implacable logic. With the dexterity of a practised barrister, Alberto then liked to take up the exact contrary notion and argue the new position until it collapsed amid general laughter under the weight of its contradictions.

This nimble performance was his delight, and he once admitted to Leiris that he would do anything for an in-depth conversation of this kind. He would even sacrifice both his arms and his legs if he could be propped up as a trunk on a mantelpiece and talk to his heart's content to a roomful of friends.[1] Such extraordinary dialectics, which Alberto practised on another register in his artistic practice – adding and subtracting, constantly changing tack – did not fail to impress and amuse regulars at the local café-tabac or the girls that clustered round him at the Sphinx, giggling at this strange character who kept the drinks coming as he developed his weird ideas, then flatly contradicted them with equal aplomb. Conundrums of all kinds fascinated him and he never tired of posing them with what Leiris called his 'gentle cannibal grin'. If your house were on fire, Alberto would ask, what would you save: your rare Rembrandt painting or the cat? Then he might raise the stakes, insisting that he, personally, would sacrifice the entire contents of the Louvre to save a cat.

Le Sphinx, 1946

At a moment when Paris still held sway over the creative fortunes of the century, the subtle perversities of Alberto's conversation also won over the city's movers and shakers. Although his Surrealist days were well behind him, and he was now intellectually closer to Sartre and Beauvoir, he still fraternised with many of his illustrious friends from the pre-war years. In 1947, he even undertook a series of spectral engravings to illustrate Bataille's *Histoire de rats* – which launched such haunting assertions as: 'Nakedness is only death and the tenderest kisses have an aftertaste of rat.'[2]

Not so surprising, then, that a girl from a conventional, modest background but with a rebellious streak should have been entranced by this unusual character from the glamorous, subversive Parisian intelligentsia and should even have sought to throw her lot in with him, even if he appeared to have failed on most fronts – as well as being twice her age and about the most unmarriageable proposition in sight. When Alberto returned to Switzerland to visit his mother at Easter 1946, Annette, still convinced that she had found the man of her dreams, was waiting for him; she even went a crucial step further and modelled for him. He was still dead set against the idea that she would join him in his bachelor lair, but the fiasco into which his long-awaited reunion with Isabel had descended still rankled and Annette's youthful good looks and unbounded admiration for him could hardly fail to seduce. When she asked him point blank whether he would take her in if she arrived in Paris, his iron will and total devotion to art first faltered, then melted altogether.

True to his word, Alberto was waiting in the cavernous Gare de Lyon as the Geneva night train came rumbling in on a fine morning in July 1946. Like most folk in that needy period, Annette was travelling light, with a few schoolgirlish clothes neatly folded into a cheap suitcase. She had a wide-eyed eagerness for life – Aragon described her as always looking 'startled' – and Alberto enjoyed showing off the city's sights to her, taking her over the Seine and across the enchanted Ile Saint-Louis to the soaring splendour of Notre-Dame. There could be few better consorts to guide an eager newcomer through the medieval Latin Quarter, still resonant with student knife fights and Villon's lewd slang, before crossing into the stately Luxembourg Gardens and on to the beating heart of Saint-Germain-des-Prés. And if this were not enough to turn a young girl's head, there was Picasso and Balthus to gossip about the art world with at the Deux Magots, Michel and Zette Leiris for an intimate dinner in the comfort of their art-lined apartment overlooking the Seine, then brandy and water with Sartre and Beauvoir, hiding from the adulation that followed them all over the Left Bank in their panelled recess upstairs at the Flore. Once the famous literary couple had warmed to Annette they would occasionally protect her from Alberto's gruffness and neglect that sometimes left her supperless while he went out to dine with the intellectual royalty of the day.

Still buoyed on that wave of enthusiasm, however, Annette hardly missed a beat as Alberto opened the door onto his crummy abode and introduced her to Diego, silent keeper of the flame, who always looked askance at any new arrival in their lugubrious domain with its jealously protected, skeletal figures. Yet within days Annette's laughter was ringing loud and clear through the shabby, plaster-littered barracks,

Café des Deux-Magots, late 1930s

as she slipped with feline grace between the thickets of old and new sculptures, admiring the dramatic difference of scale that existed between them as they lent the space the pathos of a cemetery. After a few weeks, once Annette had settled in and made a few improvements to the rude surroundings, the brothers exchanged a rare, complicit smile. What they had both dreaded – a 'woman's touch' to their fiercely preserved male mess – had not turned out to be so bad after all. The three of them were by now shaking down quite nicely, and for once, thanks to Annette's boiling and mending, they had clean shirts and neatly repaired socks to wear. If Alberto worked late and slept late into the morning, Annette would go out to buy provisions or pick up various studio materials; once the weather turned, she would fire up the stove before Alberto got down to work. They in turn made few demands on her, and she seldom had to cook, since the three of them always went out locally, even for coffee, although as money became increasingly scarce, supper was rarely more than bread and Camembert washed down with rough red wine in litre bottles. Since she had time on her hands and needed money beyond the loans Sartre and the publisher Tériade had given them, Annette picked up a temporary job as secretary to the film critic Georges Sadoul, one of Alberto's many friends from the now rapidly receding Surrealist era.

Annette did not really come into her own in the Giacometti lair, even so, until she began modelling every day for Alberto, who had tapped into a new confidence in his work, not only in the scale of the figures he was bringing into being – they, too, seemed more confident and were beginning to grow – but in his desire to focus more on painting, which he had virtually abandoned over the previous twenty years. While Diego continued to sit stolidly for the sculpture, Annette *became* his painting. Like a wraith or a spirit, she materialised and disappeared, waxed and waned in the greyish indeterminate space of the canvas. Now that she had fully entered his world, he could both capture her and set her free in his cobwebs of black and grey, white and ochre, celebrating her within a skein of lines that softened over that first year of concubinage into a dirtyish yellow halo that has come over the years to look like the colour of his affection. Primly seated and dressed in her kinkily Calvinistic white blouse and navy skirt, Annette grew into whatever Alberto wished her to be, child and woman, all women, all figures, all life suspended between being and nothingness.

Not given to effusions of personal emotion, Alberto could nevertheless not deny a sense of resurgence, of things going well after they had gone so badly. There was a new spring in his step, and even the dandyish Aragon remarked on how much younger his dishevelled friend suddenly looked. As a grudging concession to Annette's moving in, Alberto started renting the room behind the studio and, after considerable grumbling, eventually had its earthen floor covered in red tiles so that it better resembled a bedroom. Here Annette was allowed partial sway, cleaning and even decking it out with a flower or two in a jar. On one of the walls Alberto painted a still life with an apple that would not have looked out of place in a crumbling Pompeian villa. This loving gesture can be seen to symbolise the change that was happening in his art: after years of barren failure, a new fruitfulness had emerged.

Close friends and passing visitors noted the change. Alex Liberman, the American magazine editor who had come to photograph the Giacometti trio for his book about artists' studios, recorded the following, fleeting impression of the two of them together:

> [Annette] is about five feet four, like a slender girl of fourteen. She is not fourteen, she is much older, but her youth, her beauty, a poetic quality of mood are a contrast to Giacometti's somber brooding. She has the naïve and innocent expression of a child and

> laughs often with a girl's laughter. This girl-wife seems made to be the companion who does not distract the artist from his work … She always says the formal '*vous*' to Giacometti. He sometimes teases her; with her child's face she breaks into large laughter. Then the wrinkles, the two deep furrows in Giacometti's face crease even deeper, and he beams like a mountaineer enjoying a good joke.[3]

Simone de Beauvoir, now a firm friend of both, went one better, and in a letter to Nelson Algren she left (in fluent, picturesque English) an unusually telling portrait of life during that time at rue Hippolyte:

> I don't think I happened to speak about a very good friend of us who is a sculptor, though we see him often and he is maybe the only one we always see with pleasure. I tried to describe him partly in *Le sang des autres*.[4] I admire him as an artist immensely. First because he does the best modern sculpture I know; then because he works with so much purity and patience and strength. He is called Giacometti, and will have a big exhibition of his works in New York next month. Twenty years ago he was very successful and made much money with a kind of surrealistic sculpture. Rich snobs payed expensive prices, as for a Picasso. But then he felt he was going nowhere, and wasting something of himself, and he turned his back on snobs; he began to work all alone, nearly not selling anything but just what was wanted to live. So he lives quite poorly; he is very dirty in his clothes. I must say he seems to like dirt: to have a bath is a problem for him.
>
> Yesterday I saw his house and it is dreadful. In a nice little forgotten garden, he has an atelier full of plaster where he works, and next door is a kind of hangar, big and cold, without furniture nor store, just walls and roof. There are holes in the roof so the rain falls on the floor, and there are lots of pots and pans to receive it, but there are holes in them too! He works 15 hours a day, chiefly at night, and when you see him he has always plaster on his clothes, his hands and his rich dirty hair; he works in cold with hands freezing, he does not care. He lives with a very young girl whom I admire much for accepting his life; she works as a secretary the whole day, and coming back just finds this hopeless room. She has no coat

> in winter and shoes with holes in them. She left her family and everything to come to Paris and live with him; she is very nice. He cares much for her but he is not of the sweet kind at all, and she has some hard moments to get through. What I like in Giacometti chiefly is how he could one day break into pieces all that he had done during two years: he just broke it and his friends thought it dreadful. He has his idea about sculpture, and for years he just tried and tried, like a maniac, not show anything, breaking and beginning again and again. And he could easily have got money and praises and a good name. He has very peculiar, interesting ideas about sculpture. Well, I think that now he really achieved something; I was deeply moved by what I saw yesterday.[5]

Any relationship would have been sorely tested by the living conditions at rue Hippolyte, and as the unusually bitter winter of 1946 set in, they were to grow more dire. Both the water pipes and the one toilet in the courtyard froze, while the temperature in the studio plummeted to -5°C. The roof leaked so much that Pierre Matisse was prevailed on to send a special tar paper from New York to patch the worst gaps. Food was already rationed and becoming scarcer, especially if you could not afford black market prices, and fuel so hard to find that Parisians still found it necessary to pile it high into their baths in the hope that it would help them last out the winter; there being no bathtub at rue Hippolyte, heating depended on what was on sale at the local *café-bougnat*. If Annette accepted these privations stoically (and all the more remarkably since she had no experience of such hardships in the relatively comfortable neutrality of her native Switzerland), Alberto appeared to exult in them. If the snow lay all about, the inner freeze that had kept him for ten years in its vice had started to thaw. He had reduced so much to so little that his figures, if they were to come about at all, could only grow. Miraculously, like the tiny plant that had sprung up through the studio floor and was now thriving, the figures rose between Alberto's fingers with the vigour of severely pruned and reinvigorated saplings.

A glut of new sculptures began to invade the already crowded space of the studio. Deprived of his little fox, Diego had taken to keeping a cat, and both he and Alberto marvelled at the way it managed, even more nimbly than Annette, to slink between the thickets of emaciated sculptures without ever disturbing them. Along with the renewed confidence in his powers that having an attractive young partner had given him, Alberto drew growing satisfaction from Pierre Matisse's proposal that he hold a retrospective show in New York. As well as being the son of an artist he admired immensely, he knew that Matisse's gallery was now the main gateway for European artists wanting to gain recognition in America, and that there was a hunger there for art with an Old World imprimatur. Alberto was also much encouraged by Matisse's decision to have several sculptures cast in bronze for the exhibition, thus adding to the considerable investment the dealer was already making by insuring and shipping a large number of his works across the ocean.

The run-up to the show was bound to create a new sense of urgency, and Alberto began to go out less in the evening and work later into the night. Although he might not have acknowledged it in so many words, Annette's presence had softened the harshness of his daily existence and lessened the urge to break the daily studio routine. While Alberto saw no reason to cease his nocturnal prowling, the new domesticity provided a pleasant alternative and above all emotional security that would continue to support the extraordinary burst of productivity in his work during these post-war years.

As always, the first ideas for a new sculpture were born and tried out in numerous drawings that were remarkable works of art in themselves. As the artist repeated frequently, describing his martyr's path down to the last detail, he could only paint or model once he had achieved a certain level of accuracy in the drawings he made of his subject – although, of course, that was no indication whatsoever of eventual success. In some instances, such as the heads he was to draw of Sartre, the sheets would grow blacker and blacker with repeated strokes of the pencil that seemed to be plucking an image miraculously out of the blankness of the page, like a magnet drawing it up to the surface; at other times, above all when he began to erase marks constantly, the drawings retained an ethereal quality as though they floated over the paper like gossamer. Alberto regularly made light of these achievements, although they were already increasingly appreciated in their own right, and he dropped even the most highly worked of them carelessly to the floor. Notable examples of the time include a portrait of Sartre (1946), his bespectacled face scored with talismanic insistence against a lightly outlined background, and a *Standing Woman* of the same year, elongated and skeletally thin, whose entire silhouette is so shadowed with faint, half-erased pencil marks that she takes on a commandingly sculptural presence. She was no doubt inspired, not only by Annette, but also by the half-naked girls Alberto enjoyed chatting to and possessing, at least visually, at the Sphinx.

Out of a decade of reduction, a mature style began to evolve as if in response to a change of gravity. In 1946, Alberto gradually advanced towards a larger format with a selection of standing female plaster models which have not survived. The following year, he would develop upon the striding form of the small figure in *Night* to create his first life-size *Walking Man*. Slowly there emerged the cast of 'characters', or figural types, for which he was to become famous, and which would populate his studio for the rest of his life.

Sprung out of their own creator's deep-rooted, destructive instincts, these emaciated figures were as indestructible as any human phenomenon pared back to the bone could be, and they stood or strode there now, ready to withstand a brave new post-war world. Small wonder that they would be seized on by observers as the very embodiment of both existential man and death-camp survivor. News of their emergence soon did the rounds of the Paris art world, with reverberations in New York as the studio's contents were repeatedly photographed and Alberto's new exhibition, having been delayed, was confirmed for January 1948. The female figures, it was soon noted, all stayed stock still, both offering themselves and waiting, like statues in a pagan temple, demanding worship and devotion. The men could not keep still, however, as if they had ants in their shrunken pants, and progressed doggedly, at some points even comically, towards an unidentified destination. In Alberto's sculpted world, men did, women were. Bone-white and ethereal in plaster, they became more ominous once cast in bronze, with the varied patinas – shades of green, gold, brown – applied by Diego, catching the light or absorbing it, emphasising the tactility of the surface on which Alberto's restless fingers still seemed to be racing. No sculpture could have been further removed from the smooth, soaring modernity of Alberto's major rival, Brancusi.

Although these figures drew so evocatively on contemporary sources and resonated so specifically with recent history, they also looked as old as statues from ancient Egypt and Greece, or even the stick men painted on the walls of prehistoric caves. In the 1940s, Alberto continued to make drawings after Egyptian sculpture from books of illustrations, as he had with his father decades ago in the studio at Stampa. The influence of Egyptian art is clear in the hieratic, iconic simplicity of his famous skeletal figures. The pose of the walking men is derived in part from statues of ancient Greek kouroi, which have one foot placed ahead of the other, but they also recall Rodin's bronze *Walking Man*. Alberto used these sources to create work both transhistorical and contemporary – figures burdened with the suffering of their century yet appearing as if from elsewhere.

If the new figures looked both forward and to the past it was because they had acceded to another realm, another state: timelessness.

Annette slept. As Alberto came into the bedroom after one more late night spent labouring on a new sculpture of a man pointing into the distance – a man for all time – he was pleased to find the light still burning. Annette had laughed at first when he told her that he could not sleep unless the light was on, protecting him from the darkness enveloping the world outside. Fortunately, she was used to that now and rarely forgot. Having undressed and placed his shoes and socks in the exact order he wanted, Alberto lowered his exhausted frame into bed and eventually dropped off into a deep, uneasy sleep. Even though the light burned, it would never ward off the spectre of death. In the room next door to them, as Alberto had been painfully aware over the past few days, a neighbour, Tonio Pototschnig, lay dying. Swiss or possibly Italian by birth, Pototschnig (whose name has been consistently misspelled in Giacometti literature) was in charge of the complex of studios that ran from rue Hippolyte through to rue du Moulin-Vert, but was also an artist who for a time shared a large studio space with Alberto.[6] It was rumoured that, having collaborated with the Germans during the war, he had disappeared after the liberation, like so many others, to avoid any unpleasant denunciations, not to say savage or fatal retributions; several summary executions by Resistance fighters had taken place in the area. By the time he did return to his previous lodgings, with his live-in girlfriend, Pototschnig had become very sick. Having few options, he threw himself on the Giacometti brothers' mercy and took to his bed, while complaining bitterly to anyone who would listen.

The following evening, chain-smoking and muttering to himself, Alberto fell into a kind of trance over the figure he was moulding. The images crowding his mind came from having watched from a café the ceaseless progress of the little figures moving to and fro on the pavement opposite. It was marvellous to watch them: all life seemed concentrated in the way they mingled and separated, then mingled again. Yet essentially they were all alone, and if you could catch one of them and copy that one person perfectly you would have caught them all and, somehow, caught life itself, in all its magnificent meaninglessness – a constant commotion, signifying nothing. But it was his obsession, it was what kept him going. His fingers continued to run up and down the mound of dark clay, kneading it like dough, like a little, fat, wet bun; then the penknife came up to lop off a bit, a ribbon of extraneous flesh, then several bits more, paring it further and further down to its essence, to the irreducible skeleton that lay waiting to emerge from the dank mass. As they dried, the figures looked increasingly ethereal, as if they had come together not out of their original material but out of the dust that floated eternally on the void around them.

The Giacomettis' lights had long been the only ones burning in the building. Outside, the whole area with its exhausted artisans and careworn housewives was plunged into sleep. This was when Alberto worked best now, in the absolute silence of the hours before dawn, confident he would not be disturbed from the task at hand. Then without warning the silence was shattered by a rap at the door that opened to reveal Tonio's long-suffering mistress saying, 'Monsieur Alberto, I'm sorry, you're the only one awake. It's Tonio, Monsieur Alberto. I think he's dead.'*

It was everything Alberto had come to fear most, the dread he had tried at all costs to keep at bay, but once again he was confronted by a corpse, far worse than anything he had experienced. Tonio lay there, inert in the gloom, with distended limbs and a swollen belly. As Alberto watched the face in terror, its cheeks seemed slowly to cave in and its nose grow longer, as if it had taken on a life of its own. It might have been comical if it had not travestied the last moments of life before death took over for ever; Alberto would later exorcise its memory in a similarly grotesque, caged sculpture of a head with a Pinocchio-like

*According to his death certificate, Pototschnig died on 25 July 1946 at 3 a.m., his death having been declared by the 'gardienne' of the building, Renée Alexis.

nose. Then, as the sculptor stood there paralysed beside the body, a fly landed on the dead man's face, crawling slowly over it before it disappeared into the darkness of the open mouth.

The next night, when he came back to his own bedroom, it was pitch black because Annette had forgotten to leave the light on. The terror Alberto had tried to contain welled up. Tonio was still next door, stretched out and now fully dressed in jacket and tie, as if for a wedding. But his presence extended beyond the room, invading the whole building and the darkness of the night. Now Tonio was everywhere. Death was everywhere. At one point, half out of his senses, Alberto sensed Tonio's arm reaching through their adjoining wall, as if to seize him and take him too.

Alberto clawed his way to the bed and turned the light back on. He was trembling, and as he lay there, trying to master his fear, sleep did not come. Instead, he lived once more through the trauma of Van Meurs's death twenty-five years ago: the sight of the Dutchman's rigid body, lying open-mouthed up there in the freezing mountains. Then Jourdan's death from an overdose, the handsome young artist laid out next to him as he came groggily to in the morning after an opium binge. But now, here, Tonio was the worst of all, even more pitiful, even more meaningless in death than he had been in life. He lay there, like a dead animal waiting to be thrown into a hole in the earth. He lay there, like death itself, on the other side of the wall.

With Tonio's life ending just as the new figures came into being, Alberto, forever seeking patterns and portents in his life, grew aware of the irony of the situation. But there was no time to analyse it and tease out its meaning properly before another event overtook him. The Sphinx had by this time established itself firmly as one of the poles of his existence, the place above all others where he could go after a day's hard work to relax and enjoy himself in his own particular way – a home from home, a club that catered to his special tastes. Accordingly, he was alarmed, even outraged, to hear that, along with about two hundred other Parisian brothels, the Sphinx (favoured by German officers during the occupation) was to be closed down thanks to a campaign led by Marthe Richard, herself a former prostitute.*

*Richard was an intriguing character, having been also a spy, a pilot and a politician.

A wave of puritanism was washing over the city, he quickly realised, threatening to make it as joyless as Calvinist Geneva. Alberto hurried over to boulevard Edgar Quinet and found the girls were quite as aghast at the news. The clients at the Sphinx were on the whole civilised, liberal people. Some of them, like Sartre and Beauvoir, would come as couples on a night out, to have a drink, chat with friends and simply enjoy the atmosphere of sexual licence and general contentment. The Sphinx was indeed, as Alberto himself had called it, 'a marvel above all others'. It had been tolerant of human desire and human frailty, a civilised refuge against hypocrisy. All that was about to vanish, and the girls – several of whom were now good friends of Alberto's – would be forced out and doomed to ply their trade unsupervised and unprotected on the streets.

The more he thought about it, the more dismayed and troubled Alberto became. It was not only because he loved the Sphinx for its mix of easy sociability and the thrill of being surrounded by naked women; above all, it was because its heroines and the gauzy, glitzy atmosphere they inhabited had become the focus of his art. The women who were growing under his febrile fingers had first been glimpsed across an expanse of polished wooden floor at the Sphinx, waiting in a line-up for clients to appreciate their charms, then be chosen and come forward. Here, in that singular, dizzying perspective of the shiny floorboards, they took on a mesmerising aura: tall, distant presences, wrapped in inviolable mystery and unattainable to mere mortals. He returned to the theme and recorded it, in memoriam as it were, in two paintings from around 1950. The artist, who went there mainly to worship them across the gleaming divide, would hark back to the effect they had on him. 'When I'm walking in the street and see a whore from a distance with her clothes on, I see a whore,' he admitted. 'When she's in the room and naked in front of me, I see a goddess.'[7] These figures whom he went to observe and draw were about to lose their magic and vanish like cats to street corners.

If they were the Standing Women, then he – and by extension the many males making their way, alertly, urgently, from all over the city towards these goddesses – were the Walking Men. The inner dynamic that brought his new race of sculptures into being was in the end as simple and as basic as that: the elemental attraction between the sexes, a force that undercut and outstripped all the Surrealism, Existentialism and phenomenology in the world. In Alberto's case, that had taken on an extreme, personal cast, but there could be no doubting that, from a childhood ruled by his mother – that figure in a long black dress still dominating *The Palace at 4am* – he had been completely in thrall to women, to the extent that he feared and loathed as much as he adored them. What else could have driven him from the voluptuous cruelty of *Woman with Her Throat Cut* to the unquestioning worship of hookers? Men were powerless in front of them, drawn by an uncontrollable urge that only they could fully allay. As Marlene Dietrich, with whom Alberto was to have a close rapport, sang so memorably in *The Blue Angel*:

> Men cluster to me like moths around a flame
> And if their wings burn, I know I'm not to blame …

The manageress of the Sphinx invited Alberto to the brothel's farewell party and on this final, valedictory visit he participated sufficiently in the services on offer to catch the clap. From the start, he had made no secret to Annette that nothing in his sexual modus operandi would change after her arrival, and although she can hardly have enthused about it, she appeared to condone his visits to the cathouse – to the extent, Alberto later recalled, that they inspected the evidence of his gonorrhoea together, laughing it off light-heartedly as if it were just another of his funny little ways. A course of drugs recommended by Théodore Fraenkel, Alberto's doctor from the Surrealist years who had remained a good friend, eventually cleared up the infection. But the two recent incidents, Tonio's demise and the closure of the Sphinx, continued to play on Alberto's mind.

Both events affected him deeply and he wondered whether there might not be an important, hidden connection between the two. But this significance remained shrouded and obscure, nagging at him as he kept turning it over in his mind. Then one night he had a dream about a spider so vivid that he could think of nothing else, not least because spiders fascinated him and had already played a role in his work.* A few

*Quite apart from the spider-like *Woman with Her Throat Cut*, there exists a spider-woman drawing at the Fondation Alberto Giacometti in Paris, and a spider-woman sculpture represented hanging from a web-like cord in one of the drawings (now at the Kunstmuseum Basel) that the sculptor did of his studio in 1932.

days before, Albert Skira had asked him to write a new text for his review *Labyrinthe*. Alberto, who thought only of his art now that a breakthrough had come about, barely responded, but now, sitting in a café in the ill-famed Barbès-Rochechouart area – where the prostitutes, he could not help remarking, had unusually long, tapering legs – he realised that the best way of understanding his dream would be to write about it.

The penetrating, self-reflective text he produced, 'The Dream, the Sphinx and the Death of T.', is the most substantial of all Alberto's many, varied writings.* The piece follows a cryptic sequence of anxiety-inducing events, taking on the frenetic tone of a conspiracy theorist to trace coincidences and document paranoias. Equal parts schizophrenic's diary and philosopher's manifesto, it represents a unique key to the workings of Alberto's imagination. It begins with a graphic recollection of the spider, 'covered by smooth, yellow scales', which appears at the end of his bed before being crushed by an anonymous figure 'with heavy, violent blows'. Alberto awakes to find the dream has unsettled the fabric of his existence. It opens the flood gates of his psyche and unleashes a stream of heightened consciousness. The rest of the text flits between Tonio's death, the closing of the Sphinx, lunch with Roger Montandon (a Swiss painter and one of Alberto's companions in Geneva), the death of Van Meurs, and 'the ivory yellow traces of pus' on his bedsheets which signal his sexually contracted illness – hopping restlessly from distant memories to unfolding events, undeniable facts to opaque philosophical statements, concrete observations to aesthetic revelations. For Alberto, Tonio's death takes on as much meaning as his major epiphany during the newsreel in the *Actualités* cinema a few months before.

In the cinema in Montparnasse, he explains, he 'had begun to see heads in the void, in the space that surrounded them'. He suddenly perceived the vibrating power of the human head, its uniquely important place in relation to the space around it. This affirmed the belief in humanity's exceptional subjectivity which is foundational to so much figurative art – the hierarchy between man and matter, figure and ground, statue and pavement. Looking at Tonio's corpse though, as

*The full text appears, translated by the author, as an appendix in Michael Peppiatt, *In Giacometti's Studio* (New Haven and London, 2010).

'worthless rubbish to be thrown out like a dead cat into the gutter', he experiences the opposite sensation.

> This was no longer a living head, but an object which I looked at as I would look at any other object; yet not quite, not like any other object, differently, like something that was dead and alive at the same time. I let out a cry of terror as if I had just crossed over a threshold, as if I had gone into a world that nobody had seen before. All the living were dead, and this vision came back often, in the metro, in the street, in restaurants or with friends.

This disturbing realisation of Tonio's return to inert matter, which seems to infect, even kill, the world around him, is in striking contrast with the joy Alberto felt immediately after his breakthrough in the cinema – when the streets were 'dipped in the beauty of the Thousand and One Nights'. After seeing Tonio, he says, 'I looked at my room in terror and a cold sweat ran down my back'. He looks at the lifeless world around him, noting that all objects now seem to be 'separated by immeasurable chasms of emptiness'.

Alberto accepted the offer to have the (suitably labyrinthine) text published in *Labyrinthe* – despite fretting at the idea of his mother coming across it in the Swiss review – so he clearly believed in its relevance to his work and reputation. 'The Dream' opens up endless possibilities for Freudian analysis, beginning with the 'enormous, furry, brown' spider in his bed as a symbolic representation of the female sex, and several detailed accounts of its implications have already been advanced.[8]

What is also interesting is the care with which he composed the piece, drawing not only on his earlier Surrealist writing but also on more recent Sartrean literature (with its penchant for the definitive epiphany) as well as on the vogue for autobiography, used to reveal dark psychological depths in the case of Leiris and to provoke readers with scandalous sexual detail in the case of Dalí's 1935 memoir, *The Secret Life of Salvador Dalí*. The self-revelation was, of course, also a form of self-publicity (Dalí being a past master). 'The Dream' gives the lie to the legend that Alberto persistently turned his back on self-promotion.

The truth is stranger and more nuanced. In this, as in every other domain, Alberto would handle things his way, less flauntingly than

Dalí, less flamboyantly than Picasso, yet with uncompromising intent. He had already experienced a moment of fame in 1929 when he exhibited his 'Plaques' at Galerie Jeanne Bucher but had turned his back on this fast success to achieve his long-term ambition. Alberto had gone through his fill of 'styles' but now he had to go further. The only thing that counted was to find and develop *his* way of seeing.

He appeared to be closing in on this, and now, with a prominent New York gallery waiting in the wings to give him his first exhibition in fourteen years, he was only too ready to unveil his discoveries, accompanying them by publishing what amounts to a manifesto about his inner conflicts and preoccupations. Just as Alberto had worked with *Cahiers d'art* to announce his new work after the war, so he would provide a detailed introduction, illustrated by hand, to the whole evolution of his oeuvre for the catalogue of his forthcoming show. The pressure to produce was on as never before, with Alberto caught up in the effort so intensely that exhaustion took over, condemning him, with overtaxed limbs and chapped, cracked hands, to bed for ten days. 'My studio has become impossible,' he complained to Matisse. 'There are mountains of plaster everywhere with little paths between them, and I have no time to see anyone anymore.'[9]

Nevertheless, the new work was coming together with a hitherto unknown urgency because Alberto had to apply an extra degree of self-control to stop himself from destroying work after work. Rather than focus on a single theme – a single head or figure – he now struck out into a variety of subjects. From watching over Van Meurs as he died years ago in the Alps and now Tonio's bloating features, he reproduced the strangely elongated nose, a comic if terrifying proboscis poking beyond its open-mouthed face and the cage-like structure from which he hung it on a piece of noose-like cord. This was an Alberto nobody had ever seen before, combining a strain of Surrealism with the grotesque disguises of *Fasnacht* (the carnival parade that takes place in Switzerland before Ash Wednesday) as well as apotropaic tribal masks to record and come to terms with his latest brush with death. Other fragmented representations of the human body, also attempts to ward off the 'evil eye', were to accompany *The Nose* to New York: the *Head on a Rod*, its open-mouthed scream suspended in a halo of silence encircling it, and *The Hand*, outstretched on its meagre arm like a warning. The sight of scattered body parts that Alberto had seen years earlier as he attempted to flee Paris with thousands of other refugees as the Luftwaffe flew over strafing the ground had resurfaced with all the insistence of a nightmare.

To underline the urgency of the exhibition's opening date, Matisse asked Patricia Kane (wife of the Chilean artist Roberto Matta) to take photographs of the studio as it filled up with the new work. The images she captured were spectacular, recording the plaster models as they came into being, then, over the following years, the entire studio, enshrining its stark poverty and naked grandeur more surely than the many, more famous photographers before and after her. Once these were dispatched along with the last works to New York, and even Sartre's overdue catalogue text had been delivered, the die was cast. Emptied and still exhausted by the strain, Alberto decided not to make the extra effort of crossing the Atlantic to be present at the opening. A summary of his entire oeuvre, in reality the very first retrospective of his work, was about to be shown in the New World. Its unforeseen success and the lasting reverberations it created around his achievement would alter the whole course of Alberto's subsequent career.

8

Cutting the Fat Off Space (1947–50)

The afternoon light was fading quickly. Outside, the scraggy courtyard looked darker and danker than at any time Alberto could remember, even though winter had only just begun. It was barely warmer or lighter inside the studio, but the pockmarked walls and the ghostly plaster figures combined to give off a kind of greyish glow, like a graveyard at twilight. Some of the figures had indeed been buried, wrapped in rags and hidden in the soil beneath his feet. There they had been released from time, going back beyond the earliest tomb sculptures of Sumer and Egypt to the earth itself. Exhumed like ancient artefacts communing with the past, they had touched everything else in the studio with timelessness. Elongated or reduced almost to extinction, in clay or plaster or bronze, all the heads and figures, the disembodied limbs and gaping mouths, now appeared to belong more to death than to life in the fast-fading light.

Why was death so present, so pervasive, in Alberto's work? His childhood in the Val Bregaglia had been relatively idyllic. The occasional dramas – getting lost in the snow, vendettas at school, Diego deliberately maiming his hand in a threshing machine – had not affected him so deeply. But even then, it was true, he had been attracted mostly to pain and suffering, violence and death. In his father's studio, it was the most distressing images that had fascinated him: Snow White lying in her crystal coffin (his copy of it was the very first drawing he could remember doing), Dürer's *Knight, Death and the Devil*, torture and battle scenes. Was it simply a morbid cast of mind, or did it run deeper? It was the pulse of life – the vein throbbing beneath the skin, the breath on the mirror – that he wanted to capture; but perhaps it was life made more poignant by the halo of death, life in death, death in life.

Death had erupted in his life frequently, and recently he had reacted to it more violently. Apart from Van Meurs, Jourdan and Pototschnig, there had been the deaths of his father, then of his sister Ottilia, of numerous friends like Crevel and Frank, but no more than many other artists who did not seem to dwell on death so intimately. And now, here he was in the last light of day, surrounded by his pale, skeletal figures, silent and motionless, waiting to be swallowed by the dark, as if they had all been preserved in a morgue of his own making.

At this time of day – that twilight hour when the French say you cannot tell a dog from a wolf – Alberto would usually be bent over a clay figure, intently palping it this way and that, removing a damp shard here and there with his knife, squinting at it anew, then letting his fingers run up and down its whole meagre frame. It was like a guitarist practising chords or a physiotherapist massaging a spine, in a single unbroken motion that flowed from his intense stare down through his arm into the instinctive reaction of his hands. Wreathed in cigarette smoke and grunting with dissatisfaction, he would continue the process until he, or more often his model, could go on no longer. Then there would be a break for more cigarettes and louder outbursts – *Merde! Merde! Merde!* – unless things were going so badly that sculptor and subject would call a halt for the day and go out to get a change of scenery and a shot of coffee.

But today was not quite like most days. With a bit of the money that Pierre Matisse had wired from New York, Diego had gone out to replenish their stock of plaster and Annette to see where she could get her only decent pair of shoes mended. For once, Alberto was alone, unobserved, sitting on the edge of his bed as night fell, idle. Idle! He suddenly buried his face in his hands, the way he did whenever he sensed he had reached exhaustion point, now a semi-permanent state. For weeks the pressure had not let up, with everything for the New York show suddenly urgent and needing immediate attention. One sculpture after another had been taken to be cast at Rudier's,* before he was even sure they were ready for

*The Alexis Rudier foundry, originally situated in the Marais and then at Malakoff, had worked with Auguste Rodin and Aristide Maillol. Alberto liked the quality of their casting

casting; he just hoped Matisse would not baulk at how much the whole thing was costing. Of course, nothing would ever be really ready because nothing was ever really finished. He knew that all life, and sculpture in particular, was always suspended in a state of becoming. But he had forced himself to give in, knowing he could come back to them, once all the hullabaloo in New York had died down, and go on tweaking other versions for as long as he liked. Luckily Diego was always on hand to liaise with Rudier and try out various patinas – or even a simple varnish – on the bronzes, always on hand to make the armatures, to sit for him and give him his gruff opinion about how well or badly a work was going or what he thought of the latest offer or telegram from Matisse. And even Annette, much less fragile than she looked, had been pulling her weight, correcting his written French, typing lists for the shipping and export formalities, sitting for him whenever he wanted. She was the only person now who could get that damned stove firing up so that they didn't freeze to death in the morning.

He was the problem, of course. It was always him. He could never finish anything, and if he had half a chance he would destroy whatever was under way and start all over again, making far more work for everyone and for himself most of all, especially just before an exhibition. Even Matisse was running out of patience, with the telegrams that arrived via the Radio Corps of America growing more frequent (the postman's special deliveries impressed the neighbours) and curtly anxious. But didn't he already have enough to do, filling a floor in a skyscraper in New York with sculpture, without having to find titles and dates for this and that, ensure the works were ready to be photographed and catalogued before they were shipped across the ocean, and all the rest of it? Perhaps the final straw was when Pierre barked at him across the Atlantic: 'URGENT SEND SARTRE PREFACE'. Was he also meant to trail the great philosopher around his regular haunts in Saint-Germain and chivvy him to put pen to paper right away? Wasn't it enough that over the past few months more sculpture had been made in the studio and sent out into the world than over the past fourteen years?

but found it expensive. In the 1950s the Giacometti brothers changed foundries and began working with Susse Frères.

Now those works had been shipped, despite all Alberto's last-minute misgivings, and Sartre's text sent and translated into English. The sculpture had left, the problems had gone away, just like the light that slipped further into darkness outside the grimy studio window. He had done everything he could to complete the work, and now it was sitting over there, at what seemed like the other end of the universe – the New World. Perhaps it would have been better to bury it all, Alberto thought, with a melancholy pleasure rising through his fatigue. If I were true to myself, I would bury it all, so that it could be discovered centuries from now, like a Viking hoard or an Etruscan burial mound. That would be by far the best solution, he thought, levering himself up and beginning to brush some of the plaster off his clothes. Yes, bury the lot. That would be a good one. He'd tell his brother when he got back. Diego would see the funny side of that. For a moment he felt almost elated, as though he could already hear Annette's bright laughter as she joined in the joke.

On the other side of the Atlantic, Pierre Matisse had just walked through the door of his gallery in the Fuller Building at 57th Street and Madison Avenue. The differences between the two men could not have been more marked. Where Alberto was stooped and perennially dusty, Matisse bore himself like a ship's captain on deck (he was an avid sailor with a yacht moored on the Mediterranean at Cap Ferrat) and was always impeccably turned out in bespoke suits or navy blazers. If Alberto tended to be warm and loquacious in social situations, Matisse came across as reserved, downbeat, even dour. The interiors where each man worked obsessively stood in even starker contrast. From the seventeenth floor of an iconic Art Deco skyscraper, Matisse enjoyed a panoramic view over a city in constant evolution. As he looked down, the human figures milling across the geometric, Midtown grid appeared even tinier than the smallest Giacometti sculpture. Inside, the plain white cube was exactly that, conceived as many of the floors in the building, for the sole purpose of displaying works of art, with large windows and no distracting decorative elements of its own. This space (and another larger one that Matisse came to occupy lower down in the building) had already become synonymous with expertly chosen, sensitively hung exhibitions with outstanding catalogues, but it was also a place where numerous European artists and intellectuals who had fled the recent war liked to gather. Meanwhile, not a speck of plaster, let alone a damp rag or empty turps bottle, marred its pristine, clear-cut volumes.

Dissimilar as they were, Alberto and Matisse were to form a close, mutually beneficial bond, particularly remarkable given how fraught the artist–dealer relationship can be. For Matisse, the sculptor was to become, alongside Balthus, Chagall, Dubuffet and Miró, one of the mainstays of his gallery, as well as a lifelong friend whom he saw regularly on his visits to Europe and with whom he maintained an illuminating correspondence. As his gallery grew in reputation, so did Alberto's career. For Alberto, no other art dealer would play as central a role as Matisse in his overall development. Before Matisse, his fortunes had sunk so low that he was generally regarded as a gifted Surrealist has-been now mired in obsessive and fruitless figuration. Before Matisse, few people understood that the real Giacometti had not yet emerged; after Matisse, this would become self-evident and, as New York replaced Paris as the centre of the art world, an awareness of his true worth would spread internationally. At another level, Matisse was the aesthetically perceptive son of an artist Alberto admired, and slowly he became an ideal sounding board. The artist remained modest in his demands on Matisse and highly appreciative of their relationship, frequently offering his works as gifts. 'You cannot know how much all this has helped me in my work,' he wrote in simple sincerity to Matisse. 'I have made great progress since we began to work together.'[1]

As he paced the gallery floor, Matisse wondered how he might reconcile the suggestions Alberto had sent him about the layout of the show with the puzzlement in which his visitors would be plunged as they encountered, first the enigmatic Surrealist pieces of a relatively unknown artist; then the tiny wartime statuettes; and finally the gaunt, elongated figures that had formed most recently under Alberto's restless fingertips. New York at this time rolled easily enough with the aesthetic punches, Duchamp's urinal having eventually made it through, partly because most citizens' driving interests lay a million miles away in mass production and the stock market. The Surrealists, at least in the spectacularly clownish persona of Dalí and his well-organised japes, had been accepted genially enough, and esteem for Europe's culture, taste and artistic achievement still ran high. Nevertheless, as he tentatively placed a group of Surrealist pieces here, and a *Standing Woman* there, Matisse realised that this show would put him more than ever on his mettle. Between a disembodied *Hand* and an apparently comic *Nose*, how could he give the strangely mythical, unarguably majestic *Man Pointing* the pride of place it deserved? And could he mix plasters and bronzes without confusing visitors who would already be bemused by this new, strangely starved vision of mankind, ranging from the brutality of *Woman with Her Throat Cut* abandoned on the ground, to the delicacy of the little heads on their ancient-looking plinths?

If Pierre Matisse would at times denigrate his profession in private,* he took endless pains to ensure that every aspect of his exhibitions and catalogues met the highest standards. Since Alberto was virtually unknown in New York, having last exhibited there at Julien Levy's gallery in 1934, he asked Alberto (as he had in previous shows with Calder and Miró) to write a letter outlining the genesis of the works on show. No less meticulous over both the making and the presentation of his art, Alberto went to work with a will, even though his first reaction in his notebook to drawing up a list of all the pieces was: 'List. List of what? List of shit, the Surrealist period is a long time ago …' In the end, he drew up an inventory of his key works, accompanied by little sketches of them and, running alongside, a résumé of his life and career (gallantly typed up by Annette, then altered with additions in longhand by Alberto). Written in the revelatory, self-confessional mode he had adopted during his Surrealist days, the letter eventually ran to eight pages and was reproduced in facsimile in the catalogue. For many years thereafter, this concise, tightly edited text served as holy writ, the *fons et origo* of what was to become the vast and ever-growing edifice of Giacometti scholarship.

Accompanying it in the landmark catalogue to the show, with its 'long, narrow vaginal slit on the cover' allowing 'a tantalizing peek at the naked figure of a young woman inside',† was Sartre's preface. One

*'I don't belong to the great family of artists. I'm just a ghastly dealer [*un sale marchand*]', Matisse once remarked to the author, who was visiting him at his home, with its amazing collection of European and tribal art, in New York in the late 1970s.

†John Russell, *Father and Son*, p. 156. The cover design was apparently suggested by the mischievous Roberto Matta, whose wife, the talented photographer Patricia Kane who had photographed Alberto's studio, was shortly to become Mrs Pierre Matisse II, after Matisse separated from Teeny (who then married Marcel Duchamp).

famed Parisian intellectual* was presenting another, somewhat lesser-known cultural icon to the New York art world, which had recently taken on a new resonance with the advent of the wild, spontaneous practice and future financial bonanza of Abstract Expressionism. It is difficult to know how canny Alberto had been in asking Sartre to take the introduction on; having told Matisse that he did not want to include the bust of Picasso he was working on because it might look like an attempt at self-promotion, he would not have wanted to risk the same charge by choosing such a literary and philosophical star. There were after all several other prominent writers he might have turned to, such as Leiris, with whom he was already closely associated. Artists and writers forming close relationships was a long-established practice in France, and never more so than in post-war Paris, with the writer and publisher Jean Paulhan championing Jean Fautrier and Jean Dubuffet, for instance, and the poet Francis Ponge endorsing the sculptor Germaine Richier and the painter Jean Hélion.

To make this strategic choice, Alberto might even have turned to Breton, with whom the rift had never been as definitive as his expulsion from the Surrealists suggested. Having returned to Paris in 1946, Breton had set about re-establishing his authority, opening up old quarrels and curating an international exhibition of Surrealism (which Alberto declined to join) at the newly opened Galerie Maeght. Although the show proved less provocative than he had hoped, the former 'pope' jovially remarked 'how wonderful it is to be reviled at our age' while dismissing Existentialism as 'academic quarrels' – to which Sartre replied, acidly, that Surrealism belonged to the period after the First World War, 'like the Charleston and the yoyo'. Even though the leading lights were constantly reassessing their positions in Parisian intellectual life, Alberto appears to have gone out of his way to put his Surrealist past firmly behind him (while nevertheless allowing his work to be included occasionally in subsequent Surrealist exhibitions). He certainly made the point to Breton himself by sending him a copy of the New York catalogue

*Sartre was certainly not unknown in the US. He worked for a spell as the New York correspondent for *Combat* (then edited by Camus) from January 1945, and he gave several well-attended talks in and around the city. His play *Huis Clos* (No Exit) was put on in a Broadway production directed by John Huston in 1946. Huston also invited him to write the screenplay for a film on Freud, but Sartre pulled out of the project when he was told that the long text he had handed in would require severe pruning.

with the inscription: 'Do not forget, I do not compromise.' At all events, the choice proved inspired. In America, Sartre's status was still far from the one he had begun to acquire in Europe, but the combination of his prophetic text with Alberto's vision of gaunt, post-war humanity was irresistible. By peering through the keyhole on the cover, the New York art world was about to be introduced to far more than naked ladies.

'The Search for the Absolute', as Sartre called his essay (borrowing the title of Balzac's novel about the lure of alchemy), continues to fascinate by its brilliance and audacity. Sartre was nothing if not ambitious, and unlike his friend Merleau-Ponty, whose analysis of Cézanne remains more focused and ultimately more revealing, he takes the whole sweep of art history and classical philosophy, as well as the main tenets of his own theoretical thinking, as the perspective from which to view Giacometti's achievement. Rereading it today, one can sense the excitement that the text must once have generated, mainly because Sartre's approach is so boldly original when compared to most writing on art. Its actual content, on the other hand, is overly long and diffuse, exploring so many different directions and flights of fancy at once, that it could hardly be said to lead to a deeper or more complete understanding of Giacometti's work. Where it triumphs and becomes memorable is in a handful of oft-quoted phrases that strike the reader like an electric shock. In such moments, Sartre is incomparable:

> After three thousand years, the task of Giacometti and of contemporary sculptors is not to enrich the galleries with new works but to prove that sculpture itself is possible.
>
> Thoughts of stone haunt Giacometti. Once he had a terror of emptiness; for months he came and went with an abyss at his side; space had come to know through him its desolate sterility.
>
> Giacometti knows that there is nothing redundant in a living man, because everything there is functional; he knows that space is a cancer on being and eats everything; to sculpt, for him, is to cut the fat off space; he compresses space, so as to drain off its exteriority …

But, in the main, this extraordinarily gifted and prolific writer appears to have lost himself to his own imaginative and metaphorical facility, and also, conceivably, to the effects of relentless overstimulation from drink, drugs and unceasing intellectual acrobatics. In his fecundity, it should be remembered, Sartre had produced another high-flown essay not long before on a very different artist, Alexander Calder, for a show of his work at the Galerie Louis Carré in Paris. Alberto, who had made a few edits on Sartre's text, was not unaware of its faults – just as later he would take issue with the whole Existentialist argument – but he knew that it would turn a unique spotlight on his arduous, solitary path, even if, in an important sense, his work was the diametric opposite of Sartre's: strictly disciplined, based on a single, repetitive theme and pared down to the bone.

The short-term effect of the preface was, as Sartre had intended, that Alberto would now be regarded as an 'Existentialist' artist. In re-establishing himself after his break with the Surrealists, and during his lengthy, virtual withdrawal from the world, Alberto had come to the inescapable conclusion that, existence preceding essence, he had to assume his freedom and reinvent himself. This was indeed very much the case, but if Sartre had not intervened Alberto himself would have explained the situation quite differently. What had happened is that he had been diverted by the seductive experiments of Surrealism and, subsequently, been obliged to fight his way back to his original quest of attempting, by whatever means, to capture the mystery of life. Parrying Breton's contemptuous dismissal, 'Everyone knows what a head is', Alberto claimed not only that no one knew, but that no artist had ever satisfactorily recreated a head in all its complexity. Similarly, he was not engaged in illustrating the precepts of Existentialism but, rather, retrograde as it might sound to both Surrealist and Existentialist ears, engaged in a continuous and desperate struggle to convey the wings of his model's nose as he saw them, with all the 'distances of the Sahara', as he put it, that intervened between them.

That this did not fit into the Existentialist position any more than it had into the Surrealist one did not bother Sartre any more than it had Breton. All the so-called *misérabiliste* post-war artists might have been roped in under the existential banner, but none of the others, such as Francis Gruber (a close friend of Alberto's who died prematurely in 1948), had forged such a singular line through the proliferation of contemporary styles while preserving so clear a resonance with the past. Alberto had been Surrealism's sculptor par excellence. He would now play the same role for seductively liberating, sexily anguished Existentialism – at least for a while.

The joint impact of Alberto's skeletal sculpture and Sartre's startling words reached a broad segment of what was still a small, comparatively conservative New York art world, focused around a few score artists, collectors, art writers, museum directors, art dealers and other general cultural aficionados. Since Matisse had started out in the business in 1924 (opening his own gallery in 1931), he was by this time in contact with all the main players, having already put on a landmark exhibition of 'Artists in Exile' in New York (mainly Surrealists, alongside Chagall, Léger and Mondrian) and a legendary show of Miró's masterly *Constellations* series, while continuing to promote his own father's sought-after paintings and drawings. If what Matisse called Sartre's 'brand of mental agility' tended to antagonise both public and press, Alberto's figures were praised by the more discerning critics. Thomas Hess, arguably the brightest, came out immediately in favour, commenting in *ARTnews*, 'This is one of the newest, most exciting shows of modern sculpture that this reviewer has ever seen', and he was followed by the feisty Dore Ashton, who wrote: 'As far as the interest of artists [in New York] goes, nobody, I think, has provoked more discussion than Giacometti. For us Giacometti is the bridge to the artistic thought of post-war France. The unmistakable Existentialist milieu of his work has attracted the attention of the most serious artists and writers and enriched the local art scene with an element that was completely unknown to it.'

Inevitably, some reviewers were less enthusiastic overall, with Clement Greenberg at *The Nation* going out of his way to praise the earlier work from 1925 to 1934 ('the audacious inventiveness that shocked the spectator's vision'), only to find in the recent sculpture 'a sad falling-off'. The artist Barnett Newman described them memorably as being 'made out of spit [illegible] new things with no form, no texture, but somehow filled; I took my hat off to him'.[2] More predictably, in its February 1948 issue, *Art Digest* likened the new sculpture to 'the fleshless martyrs of Buchenwald', a comparison that would be made frequently throughout the post-war period. The popular women's fashion magazine *Harper's Bazaar* devoted a full review to the show with photographs by Brassaï (who had also photographed Picasso's recent work).

Matisse himself had good reason to be happy with the results, and not only in the press, since he quickly recouped his investment in the casting and shipping of the work by selling seven of the bronzes, including *Man Pointing* and *Tall Figure*; he also managed to place some of the brothers' decorative work in apartments around the city. Moreover, under its far-sighted director Alfred Barr, already a valuable ally, MoMA acquired *Woman with Her Throat Cut, The Chariot* and *Man Pointing*.

Unsurprisingly, Alberto himself was overjoyed, both by the general success of the show and the sales, which would go some way to keeping the wolf from his studio door and, as he joked, allow him to go on smoking the American cigarettes he preferred. At this point, he was staying with his mother in Stampa, being cajoled into regular meals and ablutions while recuperating more completely in the flowering mountain valleys from his recent stress and labour. Nevertheless, he longed to be back in Paris and at work on his sculpture, he told Matisse, adding: 'Everything I have done so far is just a beginning.'[3] On this optimistic note, Alberto's key exhibition in New York came to an end, although it continued to influence the perception of his work for years to come.

Back in war-ravaged Europe, the atmosphere was notably less buoyant than in boom-time America, but it was beginning to show some signs of optimism, and nowhere more visibly than in Paris. Although traces of the occupation still abounded, most restrictions had been lifted and what had been considered as luxury items a short while ago, from real butter to fuel and shoes, began to creep back onto the open market. Parisians dressed better, ate better and breathed the heady air of a new-found freedom. Released after more than four years of Nazi subjugation, they no longer had to look over their shoulder continually to make sure they were not being overheard or followed, unless they had been identified as *collaborateurs* and now lived in fear of the often random or personally motivated reprisals that swept through Paris. Nevertheless, the shame and rancour of defeat and 'sleeping with the enemy' in one form or another, lived on, slipping underground, festering at every level in society, and bursting out in spates of revenge and denunciation against a background of political instability with twenty-four cabinets formed under sixteen prime ministers during the Fourth Republic's relatively brief history from 1946 to 1958.

In this edgy but liberating climate that allowed issues long bottled up to be aired, a new, specifically Left Bank culture was breaking through more noisily and enthusiastically. Where the press had been severely muzzled, it sprouted Hydra-like into dozens of hard-line newspapers, experimental reviews, militant pamphlets and radical publishers. Thanks to the emergence of a handful of writers like Sartre, Beauvoir, Camus and Merleau-Ponty, traditional forms of thinking appeared to have been swept aside, leaving life to be reinvented from its fundamental meaning, or lack thereof, down to the details and decisions of everyday existence. The end of the occupation had ushered in a dizzying freedom in which individuals were totally responsible for every move and decision they took. In order to give sense to lives without purpose, the new philosophy seemed to be saying, humans were henceforth obliged to reinvent themselves constantly and tirelessly from scratch.

From having had no voice, Parisians, and in particular Parisian intellectuals nurtured on a popular, explosive mix of neo-Hegelianism and amphetamines, were suddenly all voice, talking, endlessly talking and fiercely taking sides in every political and philosophical debate, then changing their positions abruptly and justifying these volte-faces in yards of prose that came out in everything from weighty tomes of phenomenological speculation to ephemeral pamphlets or extreme situations acted out on stage. Where political meetings, indeed meetings of any kind, had been discouraged or banned, they now mushroomed, not only among the elite but also those who in normal times had no strong political convictions or affiliations. It was a period when not only could no one be apolitical but politics coloured every aspect of life.

Towards evening in Saint-Germain, jazz riffs took over from the most partisan arguments, and neither politics nor philosophy found their way onto the heaving Left Bank dance floors. What might have sounded too silly to say, as the adage went, could always be sung, most memorably in the case of Juliette Gréco, for whom Sartre found poems to put to music and who went on to spellbind audiences in smoky bars and jazz cellars around Saint-Germain-des-Prés with 'Si tu t'imagines' by Raymond Queneau and 'Rue des Blancs Manteaux', Sartre's one and only song (originally written for his play *No Exit*, then cut). If Gréco, who numbered phenomenologist Merleau-Ponty and jazz musician Miles Davis among her conquests, went on to become the Existentialist muse with her husky voice and smouldering, sexy looks, the main '*animateur*' at the epicentre of the new philosophical craze was Boris Vian, the lanky multi-talented oddball who for a few years put his manic energy into promoting jazz and helping to create

Juliette Gréco, 1950

venues where the new generation could jive until dawn in their black turtlenecks and dark glasses. Alongside a few new watering holes like the Bar Napoléon or the Bar Vert, Saint-Germain erupted with basement jazz clubs where the new wave of black American performers took to the stage and seemingly only those who had the committed existential look were admitted. Gréco herself embodied both the look and the attitude at the Tabou club which Vian, nicknamed the 'white negro' for his love of black music, had opened. Other similar clubs included the Caveau de la Huchette and the Caveau des Lorientals. The latter, in the ancient and normally tranquil rue des Carmes, has gone down in the annals of the Latin Quarter because of a party for Simone de Beauvoir held there at which Vian mixed such lethal cocktails that Alberto, by now Beauvoir's close confidant, fell asleep on the floor and the other guests could remember nothing the following day except for the disturbing presence of a glass eye, parked on the top of the piano, that had observed them throughout.

If the high jinks in Saint-Germain were short-lived and mainly fuelled by the new generation's urge to stay out late and search for love, all the leading cultural lights of the time joined in the fun enthusiastically. Merleau-Ponty left no one in doubt about his prowess on the dance floor and Sartre, the unlikely life and soul of the party and always the first to pay for more drinks, would burst at the drop of a hat into a soulful 'Old Man River' or do a very passable Donald Duck impersonation. Wild horses would not drag Alberto into a freestyle jive in a jazz-filled cellar, but he loved watching other people enjoy themselves as he took close note of the prettiest, sexiest girls in Paris being whirled round with their skirts ballooning up to their waists. It was a good way to wind down after a hard day, especially, as he mentioned earlier in one of his letters to Matisse, when it had been spent standing ankle-deep in rainwater let in by his leaky roof. Alberto was nevertheless still buoyed by his success in New York as well as the news that the Tate Gallery in London was considering buying two of his paintings and a version of *Pointing Man*. (They did so the following year, in 1949, becoming the first museum in Europe to acquire his work.) The Paris art world had not been slow to pick up on Alberto's recent triumph in the United States, whose films and novels they devoured and whose styles they had begun to imitate, not least because Sartre had republished his New York catalogue essay in *Les Temps modernes*, the review published by Gallimard that Sartre had founded with Beauvoir and a group of close writer friends and allies.*

*The editorial board included Raymond Aron, Michel Leiris, Maurice Merleau-Ponty, Albert Olivier and Jean Paulhan. Sartre appears light-fingered when it comes to titles: first, Balzac's 'The Search for the Absolute', then Chaplin's 'Modern Times'.

Café de Flore, 1946

The Sartre–Beauvoir tandem was becoming ever more famous, being followed around not only by a French press avid for scandalous details about their unconventional love lives but by foreign tourists (encouraged by the recent devaluation of the franc) eager to see where they sat, worked, smoked and held court at the Café de Flore. This omnivorous attention became so intrusive that the pair began meeting their friends at the more discreet bar in the nearby Hôtel Montalambert's elegant basement. The couple's prolific output of books and reviews, as well as their pronouncements on current affairs, also kept their names in the headlines, with Sartre bringing out his latest play, *Les Mains sales* (and not failing to invite Alberto to accompany him on the opening night), and Beauvoir creating a scandal with *The Second Sex*, which could be deemed today to have had a greater influence than all her companion's publications put together. Alberto's ties with the couple had grown ever closer since his New York show, and they met regularly for lunch at La Palette, a café favoured by the art world on the gallery-lined rue de Seine. The conversation during these convivial weekly encounters would have kept all present on their mettle, while doubtless including plenty of insider gossip, and later Beauvoir reminisced tantalisingly that the exchanges between sculptor and philosopher on every subject were of such a high order that they should have been recorded word for word. For a long moment, there seemed to be nowhere as stimulating to be, even as one debated what 'being' itself meant, than Saint-Germain-des-Prés, the unexpected cynosure of the Western artistic and intellectual world. Gratifyingly, its movers and shakers were not above poking fun at all the fashionable fuss being made of it, as the popular poet Jacques Prévert proved when he remarked with deflating cynicism: 'Perhaps one needs a war to launch a *quartier*.'*

While Alberto's art rarely reflected his surroundings outside the studio in Paris, he did incorporate city environments into his work around this time. Sculptures like *City Square II* (1948) and *Woman Walking Between Two Houses* (1950) show figures within implicitly urban situations, suggesting his concern with the place of the human in social, architectural space. This unavoidably recalls Sartre's own focus in books such as *Nausea* on the place of the individual within the city, but it also acts as a kind of celebration of urban space, which Alberto himself adored despite his need for regular refuge in the Swiss mountains.

Everything was to hand. That was what struck him as so marvellous, even while he was still waking up. He could truthfully say he lacked for nothing. However overcast the light, however flooded the floor, however badly he had slept, racked by his hacking cough, everything he could want was there, gathered around him, as soon as he awoke: the new figure he had been working on late the night before, carefully wrapped in her damp shroud, all his tools and drawing materials, and then, cramming in on every side, like a gathering of ghosts, so many of the works he had made over the years. At any instant, he could take in the whole plaster and bronze crowd of them, his life's work, in a single, sweeping glance. All the marvellous failures, all the things he should have destroyed and begun again, pressing round him. People protested when he said they were failures, but that much was obvious. How could

*For Prévert, see page 43. Another spontaneous wit, Raymond Queneau, author of *Zazie dans le Métro*, commented that Surrealism had above all given him 'the impression of having been young'.

you not fail when you were pretentious enough, presumptuous enough, stubborn enough, to want to capture life in all its fleeting immediacy and complexity with a few pinches of clay or a few scratchy lines? Even drawing as apparently ordinary a thing as a glass on a table was impossible, because as soon as you put pencil to paper it was no longer the glass you were copying but the residue of your vision of it, and God knows how unreliable that was in the first place.

But seeing them all here was like the most astounding vision of what he had *wanted* to do – to transfer the whole, everything you could see in a single glimpse of the eye and could never relay. That was also the reason why he had to go on, the only reason for all this obsessive, and arguably even anti-social, activity. What could be odder than spending your whole life trying to draw, and failing to draw, a nose? No. He was an oddball, possibly even a danger to society. Yes, that much was beyond doubt.

Sartre had been right enough when he talked about 'cutting the fat off space' – a catchy phrase if you could accept the notion that space had any fat on it in the first instance. When he first read it, Alberto had laughed out loud because it made him think of the sandwich he had every day at the café round the corner – that slice of ham in a half-baguette with its fatty white rind hanging out. Nobody bothered to cut it off, but of course that was what most sculptors, most artists, wanted: the ham without the fat, reducing, intensifying the image, making it so condensed within its own contours that it would go on down through the centuries like the Egyptian figures (which seemed so alive when they were first seen in Greece, went one of Alberto's stories, that at night the Greeks tied them up to ensure they did not escape). And that was only the beginning of it. What you really wanted was your figures to be so vivid, so alive, that they created their own space, like anything strange or beautiful – a beautiful naked woman, or an apple sitting like a tiny orb of light on the table. In itself, space didn't exist; it had to contain something in order to come into being. And that's what you asked above all of your figures. You wanted them to absorb everything around them so that even the ambient air was theirs, so that even when they were removed and returned to the collector's house or to a crate in the ship's hold, they took that air with them, leaving only a cut-out space behind.

Nowadays he always kept one of those new-fangled ballpoint pens on him, using it to cover any scrap of paper, including the margins of books, that came his way. The scribbled mass of lines still looked like Surrealist automatism, he realised wryly. But he was no longer trying to unleash the unconscious onto the page. Quite the opposite: he wanted a specific subject to shine through the mass of random-looking lines. That was his real aim, to generate a figure out of nothing, out of the blankness of the page, with the inevitability of a truth. His hand had been moving across the sheet of paper from the moment he sat down on the edge of the old bed, racing, erasing, with such a will of its own that he hardly knew what he was doing – recording whatever met his eye, the studio, like a play within a play, the studio wall, then the studio with sculptures, what he knew best, his world, the refuge, the childhood cave where he was safe. And even that he couldn't get, the drawing was too flat, too indistinct, it didn't look like that at all.

'Merde! Espèce de pauvre con!' he shouted out loud. You don't even know what you don't know. Talk about phenomenology, but at least Merleau-Ponty got it. Reality remains ambiguous, enigmatic. Rub it out. Start again. Start better. All very well talking to yourself, you old fool, nothing's changed, it's all as hopeless as ever. Keep trying, open it up, put less in, try to get the totality, the overall picture, quickly, with a minimum of technique. With any luck, Diego or Annette will be in soon and you can start drawing them and fuck all that up as well. Always been good at failing at one thing, moving on, and failing at that, too. Jack of all trades: a bit of drawing here, a bit of modelling there, a few design ideas for someone's fancy apartment, a handful of etchings (Loeb kept asking for more when he was here for his portrait). Master of none, even when you're copying, copying not just the old studio but the Old Masters, from the beginning of time, from Sumer to Byzantium, Dürer to Cézanne. Then all those tens of thousands of things you scribbled, over lunch round the corner and late at night, whiling away the time in bars and bistros, on newspapers, even on the cover of the latest issue of *Les Temps modernes* ... all useless, all worse than useless.

There was also the whole other world of painting, which had always opened wide up for him at times, then drifted away, just as mysteriously, as if he had taken things as far as he could there, at least for a while, and had been called back to sculpture and, as always, to drawing, but drawing-towards-sculpture rather than drawing-towards-painting, because at that point even his drawings changed their focus subtly. His passion for painting never weakened, and even if for long periods it led a subterranean existence, his interest was immediately rekindled at the sight of a Cézanne, or recently by the Van Gogh exhibition at the Orangerie and about which poor Artaud had written so movingly.* Quite clearly, in painting you entered a parallel but entirely different universe – less tactile than modelling at first, then increasingly demanding as one touch of the brush led to another: a distinct medium with its own illusions and enigmas, its own mysteries and laws as well, where space did not exist at all until you invented it. He could see each picture quite clearly, in the blink of eye, just waiting to be slapped down in a single seance, with the entire pictorial space and everything it contained interlocked, just as it was as you gazed at it, with all its uncertainties and changes from one glance to the next. How else to catch the primordial fact that we and the world around us are in a constant state of flux? The pulse beats, the eyelid flutters, through a skein of lines and colours that the brush presumes to record.

It only presumes, naturally, and more often than not the lofty endeavour ends in a muddle, a puddle, of random strokes and dejected, lifeless colour. Ah colour! If only he could make a big, bold statement like those guys who were popping up in New York with their huge canvases and rainbow hues. That was real painting, and it wasn't hard to understand why people would prefer that to his own miserable-looking efforts – even though he and Matisse had been agreeably surprised when Teeny Duchamp had managed to sell the two pictures that had been in the show. What's more, he was known as a sculptor, not a painter, over there, if he was known at all. Perhaps someone in America liked grey, because that was about the only colour he seemed able to use, various shades of grey, indeed the whole palette of grey, with the odd touch of sienna or fleck of red. Other painters told him he should use more colour, but he felt he had no choice. He seemed to see everything in grey. Grey was all colours. Only grey made sense.

*Inspired by this exhibition – and outraged by the psychiatrist François-Joachim Beer's book, *Du démon de Van Gogh* – Artaud had written *Van Gogh: The Man Suicided by Society*, published shortly before his death in 1948. Alberto, who admired both Artaud's writing and his drawings, compared the writer and dramatist's tragic life to Van Gogh's and attended his funeral. Not unlike Alberto, Artaud saw everything as a *beginning*: 'We are not yet born, we are not yet in the world, things have not yet been made, the reason for being has not yet been found.' (Quoted in Frances Morris, introduction to *Paris Post War: Art and Existentialism 1945–55*, exhib. cat., London, 1993, p. 16.)

The morning was nearly over. He should stop drawing and get back to the bust. Or begin a new painting of Annette. He reached for another cigarette, noting that the new pack was already half empty and the floor around his feet was covered with extinguished stubs. Then he noticed another cigarette, smouldering on the sculpture stand, and went to retrieve it. He'd been trying to do a picture of her in the studio for some time, but it never seemed to come together, always stayed on the verge, often too flat, then too distant, so that he was always changing the positions where they sat. The distance was primordial, it regulated the whole picture plane, and he couldn't start a picture of Annette without having her in front of him, situated at an exact position as he leaned into the blank canvas on the easel. She was probably still tidying the bedroom. He called out, and within a minute she came through the studio door, neat as a pin in her white cardigan and pleated tartan skirt.

The chairs were shuffled around until they were squarely covering the little red marks Alberto had made on the floor. Then the work began, slowly at first, with Alberto staking out the contour of the nose and the eyebrows in a few deft strokes of black paint. It was noticeably silent in the studio, only distant voices in the street and the rumble of a car on cobblestones. Alberto stared at Annette, stared at his canvas, made a few strokes, stared at Annette again. It went on for hours, the most exacting visual cross-examination imaginable. Occasionally they took a break. Once they crossed the road to get a coffee. Then the ordeal got worse, with Alberto cursing, cursing the impossibility, cursing life, cursing himself. He had lost it, lost everything, could do nothing, not even a nose let alone an eye, he was worthless, a down-and-out, old before his time. Another vehicle rumbled past. The silence returned. Annette had become anyone, any human being, plucked out of the crowd and pinned with her anonymous reality against the grey shadow of the canvas. Annette was no one and everyone in the hallucinated space that had evolved between them. Alberto dabbed at the canvas as if in desperation, fretting, then slowly calmed down. Things were not quite as bad as they seemed, he admitted, almost mollified. The work went on, the artist focusing on his canvas like a surgeon, making an incision here, an ablation there, all with absolute concentration. Mercifully the light began to fade, but Alberto did not appear to notice it until the darkness had almost swallowed up the whole interior, with just the whiteness of the plasters and the whiteness of the half-painted canvas still visible. They were both exhausted.

Then they realised that neither of them had eaten all day. Alberto brightened up at the thought that they had endured an extra privation. In his contrary way, he looked almost pleased and began to tease Annette, who managed a wan smile. The work had gone better than might have been expected, and for once money had arrived from New York. Alberto rarely asked for more than a minimum, enough to pay for materials and keep body and soul together, but Matisse, meticulously prompt in most matters, was known to be a slow payer. Luckily Patricia, who had taken all those marvellous photographs of his works, had come to his rescue and ensured that her future husband settled without further delay.

As Annette tried to get some of the paint stains out of Alberto's trousers and brush the dandruff off his shoulders, he became almost expansive. It had been a good day, why didn't they take a taxi over to the Coupole and treat themselves to dinner there? Annette was always happy to escape the dingy studio so they set off, greeting a few friends and waiters when they arrived before claiming Alberto's regular table. He had a glass of his favourite vermouth, then ordered a better wine than the usual carafe of house red. It had been a good day, he repeated to himself, just a pity that Diego hadn't come back to share the evening with them. He continued to stare at Annette, sitting primly and prettily on the banquette opposite him but beginning to laugh again as the wine and Alberto's fond teasing began to soothe her. Then she noticed he was still staring at her as though with his eyes alone he was starting to penetrate deeper and deeper into the kernel of her being, the marrow of her existence. Although she had grown used to it after the long day of interrogation in the studio now it began to bother her and make her feel uneasy. She looked away, over the sea of heads, all eating their oysters and their cutlets and chatting across the brasserie's vast space. But when she looked back, he was still staring.

'What are you looking at me for like that?' she demanded suddenly.

'Because,' Alberto said, without taking his eyes off hers, 'I haven't seen you all day.'[4]

A woman of lesser determination than Annette would have been worn down after so many months of near-poverty and extreme physical discomfort. To the contrary, she had not only survived, making the best of hovel-like conditions, but triumphed, turning the gruff Diego into a loyal, even gallant, ally, and providing Alberto not only with a new, main model but an admiration and emotional security he had never experienced before outside his tightly knit family circle. Observant friends, like Balthus and Beauvoir, Brassaï and Tériade, were already surprised at how seamlessly the little Genevoise had managed to fit into the brothers' spartan world, making it slightly less dour and scruffy. What astonished them even more was when Alberto announced in a matter-of-fact way that the two of them would be getting married. Alberto – the lone wolf, the cave-dweller, the brothel regular – married! A rumour circulated that poor Annette, although signing up for a life of apparent privation and squalor, had threatened suicide if Alberto would not make an 'honest woman' of her.[5] Well, the tongues wagged on knowingly, there was nothing to stop them, but at least there would be no children because of the mumps and subsequent orchitis Alberto had suffered in adolescence.

Michel Sima, Alberto and Annette in front of the studio, 1953

The most likely explanation was that having thrown in her lot so completely with Alberto's, Annette had sought some kind of security, if not reciprocity, while Alberto knew that it was only as his wife that he could take Annette home to introduce her to his mother, and thus get the approval he so craved from her. He wrote to his mother to let her know of his decision, reassuring her by saying not only that Diego liked her but, more importantly, Annette was the only woman he could live with, since she allowed him to focus entirely on his work. It was a logical development, he now told himself, perfectly logical and even inevitable. So, on 19 July 1949, Annette Arm and Alberto Giacometti were married according to French law in the 14th *arrondissement*'s town hall, with Diego in his sharpest suit and the rue Hippolyte concierge, replacing Pototschnig, as the two mandatory witnesses. The wedding feast was little more than an ordinary midday meal at a local restaurant. Then Alberto returned to the studio to rest, having got up earlier than usual, before going back to the work at hand.

Annette ascribed far greater importance to the event. She had entered the *mairie*'s awesome halls as a 'concubine' and emerged, after a brief ceremony conducted by a bored-looking official wearing a tricolour sash, as a lawful, wedded wife, not just some live-in girlfriend, a *copine*, who washed and darned for the brothers, regularly sweeping huge mounds of plaster away and running errands before sitting for hours on that horribly uncomfortable straw-bottomed chair. She would stare out into space, trying not to move while Alberto cursed and groaned. She felt sure that Patricia Matisse, who had given her several hand-me-down dresses, would never have put up with a beaten-earth floor, either before or after her marriage (a state which Patricia referred to, intriguingly as a '*corrida*', a bullfight). She herself was a married woman now, with rights and a position. She was part of the family, a wife and a daughter-in-law, dutiful and respectful, but with a mind of her own. She would see eye-to-eye with her mother-in-law, Madame Giacometti, even over small things that she quarrelled about with Alberto, such as getting those cheap tiles put down on the beaten-earth floor in the dreadful little, sweet little, bedroom they now shared, for richer or poorer, for better or worse.

9

All the Power of a Head (1950–55)

When Alberto visited Venice in 1950 to prepare his work for the French Pavilion at the Biennale, it had been almost thirty years since he last set foot in the floating city. Year after year, he had made his regular pilgrimage to his mother's house in the Val Bregaglia, spending the better part of the summer soaking up the silence and the mountain air until he felt fully reinvigorated. Otherwise, he almost never ventured beyond the confines of his Parisian world, the '*chez moi*' of his own deliberate and obsessive making. For three decades he had crisscrossed that small section of the city leading from the humble backstreets of Alésia down through the bright lights of Montparnasse and Saint-Germain to the Seine. He knew every stone of it, every shopfront and café awning, the carriage porches and the hidden courtyards, the grand townhouses and the concierges' *loges*. He loved the lines of horse chestnut and plane trees and the way they seemed to lead at times out of the city to the grey sky on the horizon. Even blindfolded,* he could find his way from the Dôme to the Flore, from the Petit Saint-Benoît to the terrace of Chez Lipp, and then to Picasso's cavernous studio on rue des Grands-Augustins where the Spaniard's handsome Afghan hound, Kasbek, stood guard. If he closed his eyes, it became a film running round his mind, and he moved on just around the corner, mounting floor by carpeted floor up to Michel and Zette Leiris's plush apartment,

*The notion of blindness recurs in Alberto's writings, most memorably in a poem beginning 'Un aveugle avance la main dans la nuit. Les jours passent et je m'illusionne d'attraper, d'arrêter ce qui fuit'. (A blind man puts out his hand into the night. The days go by and I delude myself that I am recording, retaining, what is in flux'.)

St Mark's Basilica, Venice, 1956

with its serene view over the *quais* and the grey-green river on whose banks the ancient city had emerged.

Venice, on the other hand, remained relatively uncharted territory. He had come here first with his father in 1920, feasting his eyes not only on the palace-lined canals and the glittering waterways, but on the unique collections of Tintoretto (Sartre's 'favourite' painter*) at the Accademia, the Scuola Grande di San Rocco and the great churches across the city. The subsequent visit, just over a year later, was the one he was to describe memorably in 'The Dream, the Sphinx and the Death of T.' – and very different. Venice turned into the city to which he had fled to escape the trauma of watching Van Meurs die. By his own account, walking across the city, between murky canal and slimy black wall, that stay had on the contrary intensified the terror and confused guilt he had brought with him. Even now, the least whiff of stagnant water as he crossed a bridge brought back memories of how the shadow of that death followed him round, all these years later.

Otherwise, Alberto was in an unusually positive mood. Contrary to all predictions, marriage had put a spring in his step. He felt freer, rather than hemmed in as some of his friends seemed to fear he would. Freer to stay in, to go out less at night and so work more. Annette had, like Diego, become a pillar of his everyday life, not just keeping everything in order in the studio and buying his materials but sometimes even choosing the best prints he had been making to include in smaller gallery shows. He was freer to travel as well, since Annette loved the trips and all the glamour and comforts of hotels, while he enjoyed her enthusiasm and company. Not only was there talk of a long overdue exhibition in Paris, but old school friends had helped organise an overview of his work in all three media at the Kunsthalle in Basel. He had shared the honours with André Masson, who had been like a mentor to him in the early Paris days, and the city's august Kunstmuseum actually bought one of his new multi-figure pieces, *City Square*. That his own country was taking an interest in him soothed his earlier feelings of being slighted by the Swiss authorities.

*Sartre devoted a major essay to the painter entitled 'Le Séquestré de Venise' and published in *Situations IV*, Paris, 1964. Once Alberto had moved on to Padua, he was even more spellbound by the Giotto frescoes in the Scrovegni Chapel.

Then there was the pleasure of sauntering through Venice, listening to the Venetian dialects, drinking real espresso by the Rialto Bridge and savouring the smell of freshly caught fish, while catching up here and there with goings-on at the Biennale. He'd heard that Peggy Guggenheim, who had been following his work since the 1930s and exhibited it at her Art of This Century gallery in New York, had bought the Palazzo Venier dei Leoni on the Grand Canal and was thinking of putting her own private collection on show there. It amused him that such a flamboyant figure, famous not just for her extravagant dresses (who could forget the impact of those colourful costumes twinned with her signature batwing sunglasses?) but her numerous lovers, should be spicing up the Venetian scene. He was even more pleased when he visited the palazzo and found both his *Woman with Her Throat Cut* (1932) and the original plaster version of *Walking Woman* (1933) on show. Alberto would later make a cast of *Standing Woman* (1947), generally referred to thenceforth as the *Leoni Woman*, especially for the collection. Was there a better place in the world for your work to be seen than La Serenissima?

Alberto's main business in Venice, though, lay in the collection of individually designed pavilions in the Giardini della Biennale where countries from all over the world sent works for exhibition by their most distinguished or promising artists. The director of the French pavilion there had invited him to show his figures alongside several sculptors, including Henri Laurens, whose work he had long revered and even written about, describing it as a 'veritable projection of Laurens himself in space, a little like a three-dimensional shadow'.[1] But the moment he stepped inside and saw the layout of the show, he was horrified: Zadkine, whom he had long considered second-rate, had been given pride of place, while Laurens's work had been shoved to the back, half out of sight. In one of his rare but characteristic rages, Alberto protested against what he perceived as a gross injustice to Laurens, and as a gesture of solidarity he withdrew his own small figures, bundling them into a kind of military kitbag, and stormed out.[2]

More harmonious was Alberto and Annette's visit to Alberto's mother, Annetta, later in the year. Mother and daughter-in-law bonded, even though Annetta thought Alberto treated Annette like a daughter rather than a wife. As mentioned, she backed Annette – whom she called 'Annettina' – over such modest requests as a proper

Henri Cartier-Bresson, Tériade in the dining room of Villa Natacha, 1953

floor in the rue Hippolyte bedroom; knowing how her son could backslide on such promises, she advised Annette to keep nagging him until he complied. During this stay Alberto painted portraits of both his mother and his new bride in precisely the same pose and place in the house, as if the two women now occupied the same position in his psyche. His paintings at this time give almost as much attention to the setting as the sitter, both being formed out of a dense network of black, white, red and blue brushstrokes, with the spatial constructions often distorted around a disturbingly small head, staring out from the centre of the picture.

After that successful sojourn in their shared homeland – Annetta approved of Annette's Swissness, even though she spoke French rather than Bregagliot – the couple moved on to Saint-Jean-Cap-Ferrat, a peninsula dotted with exclusive villas jutting out into the Mediterranean, where Alberto's friend and ally, the publisher Tériade, had invited them to visit him at Villa Natacha, his summer home. Tériade, who maintained contact with all the major artists in France, arranged for the couple to pay their respects to the ageing Henri Matisse, who lived nearby in Cimiez, in the hills above Nice. Alberto was moved by meeting the man who was both the father of his New York dealer and an artist he had long admired. He would return to Cimiez several times to make drawings of Matisse, who impressed him by his ability to recall entire conversations that had marked him in his early youth. Matisse remained remarkably lucid, even lyrical, to the end. When asked shortly before he died whether there was anything he wanted, he replied: 'A bicycle and a patch of blue sky.'

In what almost amounted to a honeymoon, the couple then made their way towards Antibes to call on Picasso in Vallauris, where the much-fêted Spaniard had withdrawn, ostensibly to devote himself to the abundant production of ceramics. Unsurprisingly, perhaps, the visit did not go well. Alberto was already critical of what he considered Picasso's increasing vainglory and inability to identify and destroy his least successful works, in whatever medium. Alberto had also openly derided the *Dove* lithograph Picasso had produced as a symbol of world peace for the Communist Party, which the Spaniard had joined at the end of the war. Nor had he got over the fact that Picasso had actively intrigued to keep him out of Kahnweiler's gallery (then managed by Zette Leiris) as he searched for a new, prestigious dealership to represent him in Paris. Picasso himself was grappling with problems in his private life, with the result that in the end neither man felt inclined to rekindle what had been a significant friendship. After Picasso broke up with Françoise Giroux in 1953, Alberto gave up trying to foster cordial relations. Thereafter, he frequently disparaged Picasso's paintings in public, likening one he saw in a mixed exhibition at the Galerie Charpentier in Paris in 1956 to 'a poster, a very nice, well-made poster'.[3]

It was also on the Côte d'Azur that Aimé Maeght had begun his irresistible rise in the art world. Ambitious and backed by his commercially astute wife, Marguerite (later known throughout the Paris art world as 'Guiguite'), Maeght made a point while living in Cannes during the war of acquiring work by prominent, often needy, artists living nearby, such as Bonnard and Matisse. Having opened impressive premises in Paris, the Maeghts were bold enough to host Breton's comeback, post-war Surrealist exhibition (in which Alberto had declined to participate). Although Madame Maeght reportedly wailed, 'We're ruined!', the moment she saw what the Surrealists had done to render their space more surreal, the show and the resultant press brouhaha sufficed to put the new gallery firmly on the map. As one of the artists included, Miró agreed to let Maeght handle his career in Europe, an arrangement which Pierre Matisse, having launched him in America, viewed with icy suspicion. Conscious of Matisse's prestige in New York, Maeght would have been well aware of the recent uptick in Alberto's fortunes; and, like any artist struggling to cover even the cost of his materials, Alberto would not have been indifferent to the rumour that Maeght had big money to burn. The French dealer had another card up his sleeve, having recently taken on Louis Clayeux as his *directeur artistique*, whose responsibilities included liaising with artists and ensuring they felt appreciated. Clayeux's knowledge of art, literature and the Parisian art world had grown out of his own intellectual passions as well as practical experience working at the well-regarded Galerie Louis Carré, which had premises nearby and was reassuringly close to such prestigious institutions as the Musée Jacquemart-André and the Musée Camondo.

Discreet and cultivated,* Clayeux had already got to know Alberto and had visited him in his studio, so there could hardly have been a better envoy to convince the sculptor that he should agree to a solo show of his work, for the first time in Paris since 1932. Maeght's exhibition space, just off boulevard Haussmann on rue de Téhéran, was certainly attractive, resembling a vast drawing room more than a commercial gallery.†

Over in Manhattan, Pierre Matisse was able to follow these proceedings blow by blow thanks to the letters Alberto wrote to him, sometimes twice a day. He distrusted what he considered Maeght's brash, flashy style and he would have preferred a more established dealer (indeed, like the Galerie Louis Carré) to be boosting Alberto's reputation in Europe, even though he had taken note of Maeght's financial commitment in having so many of Alberto's sculptures cast in bronze, as well as his commercial cheek in pricing them up. Nevertheless, it was he who had rescued Alberto from obscurity, and he was damned if he was going to let some newcomer in before he himself had put his stamp more clearly on Alberto's career. A second New York exhibition of the most recent work came urgently into focus.

From Alberto's point of view, Matisse would remain his primary dealer, not only because they knew and trusted each other and already had a successful exhibition to show for it, but also because he sensed how powerful the New York art world, with its MoMA and rich collector base, would continue to be. At the same time, he was thoroughly European and deeply rooted in Paris, where recognition meant more to him than anywhere outside its capricious, back-biting but undeniably stimulating centre consisting of a couple of hundred people who met and talked in a handful of cafés and bistros in Saint-Germain. This was his world, whenever he emerged from his troglodytic existence and joined the brilliantly opinionated throng discussing politics and art as well as their turbulent love lives. Alberto was not a vain man in any ordinary sense. He did not crave the kind of adulation that Picasso

*Clayeux was also a passionate bibliophile, specialising in classical and modern French literature and amassing such a rare collection of books and manuscripts that scholars regularly consulted him in the course of their research.

†Like other Maeght artists, Alberto particularly liked the grand but human scale of the gallery space, praising it in a letter to Pierre Matisse.

required but nor did he care to be written off as a has-been, a crank who had shown a moment's flair as a Surrealist and then vanished into thin air.

Alberto also liked the emphasis Maeght had placed, under Clayeux's expert guidance, on the quality publications the gallery produced. In fact, he had already agreed to contribute lithographs to his own catalogue, destined to come out in an outsize format as part of a series entitled *Derrière le miroir.*[*] Maeght himself had trained as a lithographer, and Alberto, who had illustrated several books for writer friends, came up with a range of prints for the gallery to sell. The most enticing prospect, nevertheless, remained that Maeght would cover the considerable bill for having all his sculpture cast by Rudier. In the gardens around the foundry, the Rudier family kept a copy of *The Burghers of Calais* (1884–9) they had cast for Rodin. Alberto's playful sense of humour is captured in a photograph by Patricia Matisse in which he stands among the bronze burghers, impishly holding their hands.

Having several dealers beat a path to his door (Loeb in Paris and Sidney Janis in New York had also expressed interest) appears to have spurred Alberto's inventiveness and productivity, making the period between 1949 and 1952 one of the most fertile of his career. Once again, he had to provide a representative selection of work at short notice, but whereas his first show at Matisse had taken the form of a retrospective, here all the works were recent and so varied that his decade-long battle to refrain from whittling his figures down into nothingness now seemed a faint, bad memory. The sixteen sculptures, six paintings and one drawing brought together in the new show constitute an extraordinary triumph, not only because most of them are masterpieces but also because together they herald an artist who has come fully into his own. Up until this point, and especially during the Surrealist period, the work exuded an aura of searching and experimenting – of always being in progress. In this brief interlude that runs from the commanding *Three Tall Figures* (1949) through the revised version of *The Chariot* (1950) to the *Composition with Seven Figures and Head [The Forest]* (1950),

[*]Accompanying each of the Galerie Maeght's exhibitions from 1946 to 1982, *Derrière le miroir* (Behind the Looking-Glass) ran to some two hundred issues. Part of its success and longevity might be attributed to the fact that Maeght attracted better writers, as well as printers, by offering higher fees than other art magazines.

Alberto's figures are no longer striving to become: they simply and definitively *are*, existing entirely in their own element, imposing their own rules. In terms of purely sculptural achievement, this exhibition, which ran through November and December 1950,* marks a decisive climax.

Where his sculpture had never previously shed its tentativeness, it now stood resolved, allowing the spectator an altogether different, purely visual experience. If the overriding impact of the first Matisse show had been (with Sartre's adroit prompting) a kind of embodiment of Existentialist principles, here the figures occupy and hold the space as highly individual, subtle and *realistic* reflections of everyday experience. They are nude figures, still shrunk to their essence, yet recognisable as part, not of philosophical investigations, but of daily reflection and the intimate narrative of their own making. Through them, the artist invites us to see directly through his eyes (an achievement that brings Rodin to mind) and to measure how the perception of a figure in space changes constantly as the observer inches further towards it or views it from another angle. In this way the figures come alive, waxing and waning, beckoning and rebuffing, until they absorb all the light playing on their craggy surface, transcending their own materiality and demanding nothing less than absolute attention.

Having tested various patinas on these works with Diego and found none to his satisfaction, Alberto came up with an entirely different solution: to paint his bronzes. He had regularly worked this way on plaster, ever since *Woman with Chariot* in Maloja. He shared his idea in a letter to Matisse: 'Difficulty with some of the patinas up until yesterday morning, especially for the two constructions. None of them satisfy me, not untreated, nor stripped, nor green, nor black, nor anything. They were never what I wanted them to be. Did some tests on old sculptures in the studio, but of what I have always wanted to do, which is paint them. It was so obviously what needed to be done that this morning I painted the two constructions, they were immediately finished, complete just as I had imagined them before starting, much better than what they had been in plaster, no comparison.'[4]

*The exhibition had been planned originally to open in May 1950, but the works chosen were not completed until later in the year.

But the paint on the examples he sent over to New York got so badly chipped in transport that the brave new venture petered out, although he continued to apply touches of colour to some of his plasters.

It may have been easier, or wiser, to explain to the public – and *a fortiori* polite society in mid-century Manhattan – that Alberto's groups of female figures served, among other arcane purposes, to 'cut the fat off space' than to admit that they had been above all inspired by a few startling experiences in Parisian brothels. The crucial scene, which continued to resonate in Alberto's imagination, had taken place at the Sphinx, where clients were confronted by a line of semi-naked women waiting on the other side of the highly polished parquet floor. Similar brothel scenes had powerfully inspired other artists from Toulouse-Lautrec and Degas to Picasso, but now, here, the figures stood truly naked, and truly visual, speaking to the eye alone.

Reviewing this exhibition some seventy years later, it is much easier to understand why Alberto came later to repudiate Sartre so violently and terminally over what might otherwise have seemed a minor fault.* As Alberto was still struggling to achieve his own vision, and had come so close, a prominent philosopher had welded the artist's work to his own arresting theories, defining the skeletal sculptures as being 'mid-way between being and nothingness'. After all those years in the wilderness, just as he was establishing a language and vision of his own, it had been wrapped up as the by-product of someone else's, with Existentialism thenceforth colouring, at times even defining, the perception of his art. No one had yet really put their finger on it, but his work had been subtly appropriated. Sartre was brilliant and famous, and in many respects an admirable, fascinating human being, but for an artist who had just fought his way through thickets of doubt and confusion, he was also the kiss of death, as Alberto, who had encouraged Sartre's participation in the first place, was slowly beginning to realise.

For the new catalogue, Matisse avoided an introduction altogether by reprinting instead facsimile excerpts from a new 'Letter' Alberto had sent him describing the origins of the works selected and observations about the titles he had given them. In this way, at least, the public – and by now Alberto had a distinct following in New York – heard the artist's voice directly. The most recent works had not only gained dramatically

*See the account of their definitive falling-out on p. 297.

in height, with one of the *Three Tall Figures* only a whisker beneath six feet, but they had multiplied into several groups, as Alberto explains:

> I began by making a composition with three figures and a head. I made it almost in spite of myself (or, rather, it made itself before I thought of it). Almost immediately, I wanted to do something less rigid with them. But what? I couldn't decide.
>
> A few days later, I cleared the table and laid the figures down on the floor, at random. They formed two groups that seemed to correspond to what I was looking for. I set up the two groups on platforms, leaving them just as they were, and I worked on them, leaving both their positions and their dimensions unchanged.
>
> To my amazement, the one with nine figures reminded me of a clearing – like a meadow grown wild, with trees and shrubs on the edge of a forest – which had always fascinated me.
>
> As for the group with seven figures and a head, it reminded me of a corner of a forest that I knew well in my childhood. The trees were tall, with slender, high-reaching trunks that had no branches until almost at the top. Behind them blocks of granite could be glimpsed. They always seemed to me like people who were out for a walk and had stopped to talk among themselves.[5]

Rising above and dominating the whole exhibition, unsurprisingly, was the new version of *The Chariot*, now a far cry from the plaster original on toy wheels that Alberto had made during the war in Maloja. It had been prompted, improbably enough, by a commission to create a public statue to replace another in bronze (melted down by the German invaders) that had stood outside the town hall in the 19th *arrondissement*. Now, instead of a nursery plaything, or indeed a hospital trolley glimpsed while laid up, it was endowed like a fully fledged, ancient war machine with each wheel mounted on a base, and the central female figure elevated on a small platform above the axle. Alberto claimed that he had foreseen the work down to the last detail before making it, and that what drove it forward was his desire to see a figure thus raised up in space, almost like an acrobat. Although his idea was rejected by the town hall, the sculpture fascinated visitors in New York by its imperious majesty. It was destined to remain in the popular imagination as perhaps Alberto's most iconic single work.

Given his love of flamboyance and readiness to fling money at projects, one might have more easily imagined a dealer like Maeght emerging in New York than in the discreet, tradition-bound French capital. If it had not been so starved in the war, the flighty Paris art world might well have given him a thumbs down, citing vulgar, provincial opportunism, then feeling terribly pleased at its own, seignorial superiority. As it happened, it crumbled before him, lapping up the lavish parties and dinners he put on and goggling at the prices being achieved for modern art. Maeght continued on this path, enticing the most promising artists into his stable and making the news by flying his entire staff with him when he paid his extravagant, state-like visits to New York. Having secured Braque, Chagall and Miró, it was not long before he successfully courted Alberto with the promise of substantial financial investment and the odd munificence such as whisking him away to visit Braque at his coastal retreat in Normandy.

Not needing to be reminded that his last one-man show in Paris dated back nearly twenty years to 1932, Alberto went to work with a will. Thanks to Annette's comforting presence, he now spent his evenings in the studio, working as relentlessly into the night as his considerable reserves of energy would allow. But the combined effort of creating new work for two big, ambitious galleries – to say nothing of other projects, such as illustrating new volumes of poetry and continuing to work with Diego on decorative commissions – had begun to take its toll. It was not so much that the dealers were breathing down his neck to finish the work in time, but that his own insatiable drive – which kept him drawing or modelling even when half asleep – and his manic quest for perfection had begun to wear him out. Smoking more and caring less about his health, Alberto had gone far beyond feeling simply tired. He was now in a state of permanent exhaustion. Prompted by her mother-in-law, Annette tried to coax her husband out of his nightly vigils, but the light in the studio, as in the bedroom, burned on.

Maeght had good reason to be pleased with the show, in which he had already invested heavily. Some fifty works had been expertly arranged around his immaculate, salon-like gallery, creating an ideal combination for future clients of intellectually daring vision and reassuringly wealthy interior. The works comprised an overview of Alberto's post-war development, presented on white, stele-like bases rather than the usual plinths. Another new departure was the inclusion of a skeletal bronze horse (seventeen centimetres tall, but less than a centimetre in depth) as well as an equally skinny *Cat* and *Dog*. *Cat* had been modelled on the one that Diego had kept, while *Dog*, he conceded, was more of a self-portrait that came to him as he mooched along a Parisian pavement in the rain, feeling dejected.

Mindful of the ambivalent reaction to Sartre's preface in the New York art world, and to avoid being serially pigeonholed as Existentialist, Alberto chose Michel Leiris, a safer pair of hands, to write the preface of the Maeght catalogue. Conceived of as a series of allusive notes, weaving snatches of the author's memories and dreams with factual information gleaned from his conversations, the text had in fact been originally published (in a translation by the Cubist collector Douglas Cooper) in *Horizon*, the English literary magazine edited by Cyril Connolly.* One arresting remark by Leiris certainly merits reflection: 'Given the kind of destruction that Giacometti goes in for, I have sometimes wondered whether sculpture, for him, did not mean creating something that could then be annihilated.' Yet Alberto never lost sight of the fact that he was not only creating his sculptures as (in Genet's phrase) 'guardians of the dead' but for posterity as a whole. A visit to the prehistoric caves of Lascaux, a rare treat with Annette in 1953, had brought that home to him with a vitalising jolt.

Not long after the new show had been dismantled, dissected and discussed by those in intellectual and fashionable society, thus re-establishing the sculptor's reputation on his own turf, a young American writer called James Lord dropped into Les Deux Magots one evening and began talking to Alberto. In the early 1950s, one of the charms of Saint-Germain café life was that, in theory at least, everyone talked to everyone else. Sartre and Beauvoir (who had just won the Prix Goncourt for her *roman à clef*, *The Mandarins*) might have withdrawn to the more secluded bar downstairs at the Hôtel Montalambert, but, whenever they were not working, most writers and artists were easily approachable, with some even positioning themselves prominently on café terraces in the hope of making useful contacts or at least mopping

**Horizon*, which ran between 1939 and 1950, was a London literary review funded by Peter Watson, a friend and collector of Giacometti. One of its editorial assistants was the Francophile Sonia Brownell (later Orwell), who conducted a doomed love affair with the married phenomenologist Maurice Merleau-Ponty.

up the odd compliment on their recent efforts. Curious, well off and above all American when American culture, from jazz and movies to cool clothes, held sway over Paris, Lord had already managed to get to know Picasso and Dora Maar, as well as to hobnob with Cocteau and Gertrude Stein (whose physical presence he once described memorably as 'a burlap bag filled with cement and left to harden').

This first, chance contact with the scruffy-looking artist proved definitive. Although the two men could not have been more opposite in their tastes and their outlook on life, Lord fell under Alberto's spell to the extent that the experience gave a specific direction to a life spent thus far chiefly as a dilettante with literary ambitions.* He began visiting Alberto in his studio, getting to know him, his inner circle and his daily round at close quarters, without ever, as he openly acknowledged, becoming a close friend or confidant. But Lord did begin to sit for a portrait, and the concise volume that he wrote about that experience, *A Giacometti Portrait*, remains a key text because it provides such a direct description of the various phases and complexities that the arduous process (for both) went through over a period of eighteen days. While Alberto is creating a study of Lord in oil, Lord takes the opportunity to put together a portrait of the artist, drawn from the notes he jotted down at the time. Lord went on to take many more notes and carry out extensive research, including a formidable number of interviews with people who knew Alberto, in order to write a lengthy biography of the artist. Discursive, opinionated and frequently tendentious, this study of the man and the life took fifteen years to complete and was not published until 1985, almost twenty years after the artist's death. Although it met with a hostile reception – what the French call 'a raising of shields' – namely from Annette and certain close friends of Alberto's, including Leiris, the book remains a unique record of the period by virtue of its author having been there with an eye for ambiguous detail and a nose for the slightest whiff of scandal.

A sure sign that Alberto had arrived at a new plateau of appreciation was that Lord was by no means the only talented foreign writer to devote himself to the artist's achievements. Across the Channel, David

*Lord had already achieved the distinction of having a story, 'The Boy Who Wrote NO', published in *Horizon* in 1949.

Sylvester, a heavyweight young critic beginning to make his mark on the less active and glamorous London art world, had come across a copy of the issue that *Cahiers d'art* brought out on Alberto's sculptures and drawings in 1946 and then devoured a much-thumbed catalogue of the 1948 New York show. Shortly thereafter, while visiting Kahnweiler in the apartment he shared with the Leirises, Sylvester met Alberto and, like Lord, came under his spell,[6] going to the studio where he also sat for his portrait over twenty sittings each lasting several hours. Again like Lord, Sylvester embarked on a major study of the artist, although the text originated as an introduction to a small retrospective exhibition he had organised at the Arts Council Gallery in 1955 and focused much more directly on a revealing, if somewhat dogged, perception of the work rather than the life.* Over the years this monograph took on a mythical dimension because Sylvester, like Alberto himself, constantly questioned the validity of what he was writing and subjected the book to endless restructurings and revisions, in a quest that might have inspired Jorge Luis Borges. Having curated the major Giacometti retrospective at the Tate Gallery that opened in 1965, Sylvester announced to the comparatively starveling London art world (fixated on Paris, then gradually on New York) that his monograph was still in progress; in fact it was not until 1994, forty years after its inception, that his *Looking at Giacometti* was finally published.

While adding to the reputation of the two writers as serious, committed commentators and critics of contemporary art, this kind of homage fed into a Giacometti legend that was growing in leaps and bounds. Unlike Picasso's exuberant myth, fuelled by his superhuman productivity, notorious womanising and fondness for posing for the camera, Giacometti's had grown imperceptibly, as if seeping out of the damp clay he moulded, the despair of repeated failure and the primitive conditions of his daily existence. Indeed, Picasso himself remarked to the photographer David Douglas Duncan that Alberto was the only artist who had been able to conjure up a legend that could vie with his. As the Cold War cast its shadow over life in the 1950s, making way for a Beckett as it had for a Giacometti, the paradox of a supremely talented artist showing success the back of his hand in favour of repeated failure

*Sylvester organised two influential symposia on Giacometti's work at the ICA in London.

struck a deeper chord. Weren't artists meant to suffer so as to plumb the depths of human experience and confront us with a reality that our own shallow lives attempted to evade?

Surrealism and Existentialism had certainly nurtured the Giacometti myth, but as the anxious decade grew progressively attuned to the horrors of the H-bomb and the atrocities of wars in both Korea and Algeria, accompanied by a disorienting sense of the Absurd, the legend surrounding the obsessive sculptor began to thrive on its own terms, needing no infusions of meaning from other intellectual systems even as it appeared to absorb them. If spectators could accept the validity of a Vladimir and an Estragon confirming their pointlessness as they waited endlessly for Godot, they certainly understood the stick-like figures of Giacometti stuck in space with their disproportionately large feet and no apparent purpose beyond presenting an impassive frontality and painful fragility to the eye. How strange, and how apposite, that the creators of these parallel visions, near-contemporaries and both foreigners, should be living almost side by side in Paris.

Beckett and Giacometti were by now a familiar sight, above all together and especially at night, as they moved, not always steadily, along the boulevards and down the side streets of their home ground of bustling brasseries and furtive pick-up bars in Montparnasse. They could be spotted from afar. One was tall and lean, with an eagle-like profile and piercing blue eyes. Comfortably but elegantly dressed, he leaned forward as he paced through the *quartier* for all the world like one of Alberto's striding figures. The other was stooped, with a deeply lined, compassionate face and wiry, grey hair filled with bits of plaster that also clung to his scruffy clothes. They had known each other since the 1930s when Beckett was employed as James Joyce's assistant until Lucia, Joyce's schizophrenic daughter, fell unhappily in love with him. As with many artists and writers in Paris at the time, the friendship between sculptor and playwright had slowly matured through shared acquaintances and chance encounters. They had also both experienced similarly sudden, physical accidents. In 1938, when Alberto had suffered the serious foot injury that left him with a limp, Beckett had been stabbed in the lung for no apparent reason by a passing vagrant in the street. Although reclusive, Beckett had translated Eluard's poetry into

Germaine de France and Georges Adet in the première of Beckett's *Endgame*, April 1957

English, been published in various small magazines, such as the avant-garde, English-language *transition*, and played chess with Duchamp (unavailingly, of course, given Duchamp's mastery of the game), while for long periods the equally reclusive Giacometti had emerged often enough from his studio to become a fixture around Montparnasse at night. At the time, seeing the curious pair together aroused little attention, to the extent that, when they were sitting together at one of the well-known Montparnasse cafés, another client went to the trouble of informing the manager that he had 'two of the most remarkable men of our age' sitting on his terrace and that he 'should know it'. According to the Greek painter Constantin Byzantios, who arrived in Paris just after the war, it was Alberto who appeared to make the running in the relationship: '… one evening, or one night rather,' he relates, 'Giacometti came to sit next to Samuel Beckett in the Coupole. And

Brassaï, Avenue de l'Observatoire, Paris, 1934

he whom one normally listened to, around whom people gathered – he made an unprecedented effort to enter into his neighbour's thoughts, to surround him with an ever-tighter net of questions, as if driven by unbounded curiosity – which Beckett, however, seemed not to notice.'[7]

What drew the two men together, apart from a shared taste for nocturnal wanderings, brothels and drinking whiskey (Jameson or Bushmills, whenever available, for Beckett) in dark, after-hours bars like the Falstaff or the Rosebud, was an acknowledgement of each other's artistic predicament and their determination to grapple with it. Not for nothing had Beckett written: 'Ever tried. Ever failed. No matter. Try again. Fail again. Fail better',[8] to which one might append one of Alberto's last written notes, when he was close to dying: 'Trying is everything. How marvellous!'[9] Although they were too caught up in their work and their own times to be able to realise it clearly, they distilled between them the essential mood and outlook of a Europe that had 'survived into peacetime'. If Sartre had come up with a brilliant theory and an influential movement (dismissed by Beckett as 'all their balls about being and existing'), they were engaged in an obscure struggle to define a bitter, unacknowledged truth. To escape Joyce's overarching influence, Beckett had abandoned writing in English, the mother tongue in which he had shown exceptional mastery, for French. As a result, the two writers attained the two opposite summits of language, Joyce in allusive inclusion, Beckett in such sparseness that he seemed to reveal the very sinews of French and English. An equally talented virtuoso, Alberto had renounced his inventive fluency as a Surrealist sculptor to confront the more stringent, and more evasive, demands of reality. Even Beckett's gifts were challenged to the limit by a 'foreign' language (although he was already a formidable linguist), as Alberto's were when faced with nothing more than a human head. 'I shall never succeed in putting into a portrait all the power a head contains,' the artist said around this time. 'The very fact of living already requires so much will-power and energy ...'[10] What both artists capture so poignantly is the fragility of life, and the strength required simply to exist.

Although their Sisyphean task grew slightly less desolate and daunting as they both attained a certain celebrity, there was no capitulation to success; if anything, it threw their essential isolation into starker relief. At the same time, the similarities in their vision, in their clear-sighted pessimism, pared-down materiality and dark humour – two haunting voices in the wilderness – became more defined. Some of Beckett's utterances read like a manifesto for Giacometti's despairing attitudes towards his art, notably: 'To be an artist is to fail, as no other dares fail.'[11] Or (commenting on the painter Tal-Coat): 'There is nothing to express, nothing with which to express, nothing from which to express, no power to express, no desire to express, together with the obligation to express.'[12] And what could come closer to a Giacometti bust than a Beckett head buried up to its neck in the ground (as in *Happy Days*), or even bottled up in a kind of canopic jar (like Mahood in *The Unnameable*)? Or more evocative of Beckett's *The Lost Ones* or *A Piece of Monologue*[*] with their sorry tales ('Birth was the death of him') than Alberto's stock-still figures, particularly when raised on a plinth as if on a stage, their ravaged features caught in an unwavering beam of light.

At times, the similarities are uncanny. Beckett could almost be looking at one of Alberto's colourless pictures when he describes

[*]Especially in the magnificent performances of these pieces by one of Beckett's favourite actors, David Warrilow (1934–95).

the air circulating around Mahood: 'Close to me it is grey, dimly transparent, and beyond that charmed circle it deepens and spreads in fine impenetrable veils … This grey, first murky, then frankly opaque, is luminous none the less …'[13] Another striking parallel occurs at the end of *The Unnameable*, when Beckett writes, 'I don't know, I'll never know, in the silence you don't know, you must go on, I can't go on, I'll go on', where Alberto, close to the end in October 1965, sums himself up: 'I don't know, am I an actor, a scoundrel, an idiot, or a scrupulous character? I only know that I've got to keep trying to draw a nose from nature.'[14] And one famous line from *Waiting for Godot* could stand as an emblem for Giacometti's whole race of funerary figures: 'They give birth astride a grave, the light gleams an instant, then it's night once more.'

At the end of a long night, as dawn broke over Montparnasse Cemetery, the two men would walk home, with Alberto usually accompanying Beckett to his door on boulevard Saint-Jacques to avoid finding himself alone again. Although one imagines that their conversation might have been the most penetrating and illuminating anywhere in the world at that moment, the time they spent together, as Beckett remembered, was made up mostly of 'pleasant silences' – even though, as was his wont, Alberto had taken every opportunity to explain at length the 'impossibility' of what he was trying to achieve.* Beckett later described him as being not so much 'obsessed' as 'possessed'. On one occasion, Beckett broke his silence as they passed under a line of trees, crying out: 'I can't look at the trees any longer!', to which Alberto responded gently: 'That's because you love them so much, Sam.'

Interest from a widening circle of writers and critics was just one of the signs of the recognition that Alberto's work was attracting across the world. From this point on, most exhibitions of contemporary art, whether at the Musée d'art moderne in Paris,† the Kunsthaus in Zurich, the Art Institute in Chicago, the Philadelphia Museum of Art or MoMA in New York, acknowledged his growing reputation by including works

*Beckett likened Alberto's way of working to the game in which one hand tries to catch the other, adding 'but that kept him going'.

†Somewhat behind its American counterparts, the Musée d'art moderne was the first museum in France to acquire a work by Giacometti when Charles de Noailles donated his *La Table* (1933) to its collection in 1951.

by him. More significantly, in 1953, the Art Club in Chicago put on a one-man show, and by 1955 retrospective exhibitions were being organised at the Arts Council in London and (with James Johnson Sweeney[15] as director) at the Guggenheim Museum in New York, while another in Germany travelled from Krefeld to Düsseldorf before ending in Stuttgart. Judged by such external events at least, the obscurity in which Alberto had lingered was now firmly in the past, even though budding international fame, as we shall see, did nothing to allay his frustrations and doubts, never far from the surface, about the quality of his work.

Not only museum directors and art dealers but private collectors began beating a path to the humble studio in Alésia. A wealthy English couple, Lisa and Robert Sainsbury, had been forming a Giacometti collection via Pierre Loeb since 1949 when they bought a painting of *Diego Seated* (1948) and a *Self Portrait* drawing (1935) for £123 and £6 respectively (the latter sum being about what the couple would have paid for a good dinner in Paris at the time).* Other enthusiastic cross-Channel collectors included Peter Watson, who funded *Horizon* magazine, and the ICA (Institute of Contemporary Arts) in London. But the largest collection of all was amassed by an American steel magnate from Pittsburgh called G. David Thompson, whose collection already included Matisse, Picasso, Léger and Miró, as well as numerous works by Paul Klee. Thompson's interest in Alberto's early work prompted Pierre Matisse to have whatever plaster models remained in the studio cast in bronze at Susse Frères, the foundry that Alberto was now using. Unsurprisingly, the ambitious new collector went to Paris and sought out the brothers in the hope that he could purchase large numbers of works directly from them, thus replacing any need he imagined they might have for art dealers.† Thompson was the collector who, on his first visit to the studio, bumped straight into Diego and asked him whether he was Mr Giacometti – to which Diego, motioning towards Alberto, replied: 'No, Mr Giacometti is over there.'

*Sir Robert and Lady Sainsbury founded the Sainsbury Centre for Visual Arts, a museum designed by Norman Foster, at the University of East Anglia, just outside Norwich, in 1974. Their huge, diverse collection spans many cultures and includes a substantial number of sculptures, paintings and drawings by Giacometti.

†Thompson also encouraged Alberto (fruitlessly) to paint a self-portrait with Annette that he might have as a memento of the time he had spent with the couple.

Perennially modest (apart from the very infrequent outburst of resentment), Diego was now fundamental to Alberto's life and work. Over and above his usual studio duties, his time was taken up by a steady stream of commissions for decorative objects, which had become more and more his sole responsibility. Beyond making one drawing after another of his brother, Alberto also began a series of magnificently assured paintings of him and of Annette, as well as, for the first time, others outside his inner circle, including his collectors Thompson,* Watson, and two of the Sainsburys' children as well as Sylvester, and Jean Genet, whom he had recently met and who was to play an important role in his life and art over the following years. By now Diego had come to represent not only such powerfully frontal presences as *Diego in a Plaid Shirt* (1954) but all humanity to Alberto, to the extent that he paid him the ambiguous compliment of remarking: 'He has sat 10,000 times for me, and when he sits I don't recognise him … Whenever I do a head from memory, people say "That's Diego", but that comes as news to me.'

Diego also provided, if not the 'inspiration', then certainly the patiently forbearing presence for an impressive series of busts known as the *Heads of Diego* between 1951 and 1954, which drew not only on Alberto's recent pictorial explorations but also on such other sources as ancient Etruscan portraits on terracotta. As he focused on the Diego heads, his restless experiments ranged from naturalistic to knife-edge, from creating a sharply differentiated front and profile view, as in the *Large Head of Diego* of 1954 (now in the Zurich Kunsthaus), to the vast torsos, with their surfaces as cleft as the mountainsides of the Val Bregaglia, ending in distant pin heads. These imposing creations, which record instant by instant Alberto's continuously changing perception of his subject, could almost be compared to stills in a film, harking back to preceding images while suggesting new ones, since Alberto worked in an unending flux, making and unmaking at lightning speed, so that he might make dozens of major variations within a single day. From this endless remaking, the craggy mounds rear up, radiating a primal threat, as if they were volcanic matter still half-liquid. Alberto appeared to have this in mind when he stated: 'It's sculpture that's like a contained violence that touches me most. Violence touches me in sculpture.'[16] The

*In his portrait of Thompson, Alberto emphasised the size of the magnate's hands, made, the artist commented, 'to scoop up the money'.

torsos are inventive in another sense as well, in that their massive, apex-shaped bulk does away with the necessity of the traditional kind of base that had hitherto been used.

Such a new departure had not gone unnoticed by the formidable Maeght/Clayeux duo that had already begun to dominate the Paris art world by the spectacular exhibitions, catalogues and promotional fanfare that they accorded to many of the foremost contemporary artists, from Braque and Chagall to Miró and Léger. Having already made its mark with Giacometti, the Galerie Maeght held its second one-man show of his work in May 1954. This time, however, the pair concentrated on revealing a lesser-known aspect: Alberto as a painter and draughtsman as visionary and exciting as he was a sculptor. Already alerted by his success in America, European collectors were wooed during extravagant private views and lavish receptions to the point where they accepted the mark-up Maeght had made on the works for sale, a move which Pierre Matisse, after grumbling about 'parvenus in Paris', was not slow to follow. Both collectors and the general public also had the benefit of an introduction by Sartre which, less existentially partisan than his 1948 text, focused on the paintings' spatial implications as voids ensnaring the indeterminate, elusive human presence.* Once the fortunate collectors had installed their new Giacometti in interiors resplendent with marble mantelpieces and Art Deco furniture, they could look forward to an extra frisson as they felt ever more acutely and meaningfully suspended, at the cutting edge of the avant-garde, between being and nothingness.

Between 1952 and 1954, after a period of varied output and international success, Alberto's work grew more sharply focused. In his sculpture, he omitted architectural elements and dynamic, multi-figure compositions to concentrate exclusively on busts and simplified standing nudes. Increasingly, he also used a knife to inscribe surface details on his subjects, which took on more naturalistic and less skeletal forms. Much of his recent work had emerged from a blur of post-war productivity,

*Sartre actually quotes Alberto, having read the artist's second letter to Pierre Matisse and discussed it with him in preparation for the essay.

but now individual pieces would be heavily reworked over extended periods. A similar transition occurred within Alberto's painting. Having painted a wide range of subjects, including landscapes and still lifes, he now focused on simple, frontal portraits of Annette and Diego, eliminating surrounding details to capture their gazes more intensely. The frenzied web of paint strokes he had used to model his subjects and their surroundings gave way to a more painterly style, with the subjects in these new pictures emerging from and disappearing back into an ambiguous, blurred cloud of grey.

Shortly after the success, both commercial and critical, of his second Maeght exhibition, Alberto left Paris to make the first of two further visits to Henri Matisse at his home in Cimiez. He had been commissioned to make drawings of the ageing painter, who was by now mostly bedridden but still mentally acute, for an official medal (which was never struck). Matisse proved to be a difficult model, posing for only very short periods and commenting that neither he nor Alberto really knew how to draw, a view with which the latter readily concurred. Relations between the two artists were cordial and led to Alberto giving a sculpture and a painting to the older man. The handful of drawings that survive are nevertheless strikingly evocative of a great artist with his strong personality intact during the last months of his life. Matisse himself knew he was close to death, much to his regret since he claimed that he needed another twenty years to complete his life's work. He died later that year, a loss made more melancholic for Alberto since several artists and writers he admired, including Derain and Eluard, Bonnard and Laurens, had also died recently.

The nagging financial problems that had dogged Alberto and Annette since they had been living together started little by little to recede, with the loans from Tériade and Sartre, and the hand-me-downs from Beauvoir, merging into a grim, post-war memory. A new era of prosperous Parisians and art-loving American millionaires had begun. Alberto had overreacted to such novelties as the length of sumptuous brocade G. David Thompson had given Annette to have made into a gown by nailing it, once and for all, to their bedroom wall (a sculptor's wife had to be decently, but not extravagantly, dressed), and living conditions at rue Hippolyte had barely improved even though money was trickling in from sales around the world. Outwardly, little changed. There were more festive dinners, both locally and at La Coupole, as well as greater ease in taking taxis to ferry him from restaurant to bar, and from bar back home. But such suggestions as came from his mother that he should now buy Annette a proper wedding ring fell on deaf ears. Outside the evening sorties and the drinks he bought at Chez Adrien or the more upmarket La Villa, he spent next to nothing on himself beyond the very occasional visit to Old England, a posh gentleman's outfitter near the Opéra, where he would enter with dust-ridden tweed coat and stained, baggy trousers and re-emerge wearing an almost identical, albeit new, outfit, right down to the essential midnight-blue necktie.

It would have been ridiculous, nevertheless, to put up with the same monotonous supper of Camembert and baguette as the envelopes of cash from Matisse and Maeght grew thicker and more frequent, but Alberto persisted in working through the day on his usual late lunch of hard-boiled eggs with ham and bread, washed down with wine and coffee at Le Gaulois round the corner. True, he had taken on one more ramshackle room, adjoining the bedroom; a much-coveted telephone, still a rarity at the time, had been installed, and the space served mostly for making regular calls to his mother. But very few other changes were allowed at home, and Annette's dream of having proper, modern heating and an inside bathroom complete with toilet would never become a reality. The studio was for working, and all ablutions remained strictly an outside activity performed at the communal pump. If Annette had imagined that, after sharing the lean years, she would now benefit from the new cashflow – even if it never included the 'New Look' Dior dress that she saw other women wearing – she was sorely disappointed. Occasional wads of notes were handed to Diego, who promptly salted them away with his own meagre savings, and others ended up in Stampa, giving Alberto the satisfaction at least that he had repaid earlier debts to his mother many times over. The girls in the bars were also well looked after, with extra notes slipped roguishly to them late at night, but by some logic best known to himself Alberto kept Annette on the same short financial leash, as if she, like the studio and anything else that affected his work, should not change a jot.

Like his mother, Alberto did not like spending money. If he were content to live on next to nothing, he might well have reasoned, then his wife should do the same, both of them martyrs to a life of unceasing toil and unwavering frugality. Yet he was a deeply compassionate man, and he is known to have given generous handouts to a variety of people in need, as well as occasionally splurging on the best champagne in nightclubs, not unlike Sartre, suggesting a relationship with money that was as contradictory as other aspects of his nature.*

Given that he appeared to set such little store by his drawings, letting them languish in the mess on the floor, one might imagine that he would have been very prompt to distribute them freely to acquaintances who showed interest. It is perhaps surprising, then, that he was upset on the rare occasions when he suspected visitors had stolen drawings. But his reaction even to supposed theft was far from simple, as this anecdote told by the Belgian writer and film-director François Weyergans shows:

> One day, I had a meeting with him and I arrived a little ahead of time, and the studio was open. So, I enter, I wait, I look around a bit, I wait. I wait an hour there and then suddenly he walks in, he looks at me and says, 'Did you steal anything?' I say, no, of course not, and he replies, 'Shame, because if you had, you would have something of mine, because I have a hard time giving things away, and I do not think I will give you anything, but if you had stolen it, I would have been happy knowing you had something of mine.'[17]

The wads of cash, and later the gold bars with which certain collectors paid Alberto, presented him with an insolvable quandary. He was not the kind to go out and squander it on gambling and luxury living but he also, like a good, old-fashioned peasant, disliked and distrusted banks. So, contrary to the last, he stashed his loot in shoe boxes and hid them in the very first place that any self-respecting burglar would look: under his bed.

*The poet and gallerist Jacques Dupin, who spent long periods with Alberto, remembered him as being parsimonious with money although less so with gifts of his work.

PART THREE

(1956–66)

10

The Secret Wound (1955–59)

No one could say, as they might easily have said of certain other artists, that Alberto chased success. If anything, he deliberately shunned it, cutting short a brilliant career as the foremost Surrealist sculptor to spend a decade being written off as a deluded has-been. He stacked the odds against himself in a continuous, self-defeating frenzy that led to crises in which the very impossibility of what he was striving to achieve paralysed him.

Alberto was tough-minded enough to keep to the martyr's path, accepting defeat after defeat. Highly sceptical, what he found perhaps more difficult to accept was success. He had shown remarkable fortitude during his years in the wilderness, relishing his failures and embracing an ever more sparse, comfortless existence. He had never set much store by earning large sums for his work, even discouraging it by trampling over his own drawings in front of collectors and giving them and his dealers terms that put him at an obvious disadvantage. His apparent masochism added fuel to his myth, and in the long run it boosted his sales because art dealers and other art-market handlers were predictably inspired by the wider margins they could achieve.

Once the wealth began to materialise in bank notes and gold at rue Hippolyte, Alberto was initially at a loss to know what to do with it – until a new woman with a marked talent for splashing the cash made a spectacular and potentially catastrophic entry into his life. Alongside the money came the other more subtle blandishments of fame. From the outset, leading writers of the day, from Leiris and Breton to Sartre and soon the shady, controversial Genet, had been paying homage to Alberto's work, personality and studio. He himself had already published a wide range of texts that gave way during the 1950s to frequent interviews, some of them recorded and, in the 1960s, even filmed; in these, as he talked to art critics and journalists, the artist was able to discuss and reflect on his work more directly and revealingly than in his own allusive writings. Each of his new exhibitions also spawned a variety of reviews in newspapers and magazines, with the result that Giacometti's name and achievements grew commonplace in the French and, increasingly, international press. But what catapulted him to a kind of star status was not so much the written word as the extraordinary eloquence of the photographs that were taken of him – in the street, at work in the studio, in a café talking to Annette – in increasing numbers by scores of famous, obscure and anonymous photographers.

Monastic in his devotion to his art and in his discipline, Alberto was also aware that artists need public recognition in order to thrive. Having been brought up in a studio filled with books, catalogues and magazines, he knew just how vital photographs had been for artists to publicise themselves and get their work more widely known from the late nineteenth century on. That was essentially why Toulouse-Lautrec agreed to have himself immortalised, propped up on a stool as he recreated a scene from the Folies-Bergère, and why Monet posed, brush and palette in hand and puffing on a cigarette, while working on one of his luminous late pictures of water lilies. Even Matisse in his reclusive old age had allowed himself to be portrayed at work and at rest, while Picasso had made a fine art of playing up to the camera in swimming shorts or Native American headdress, allowing his soulful *mirada fuerte* to further mesmerise an adoring public.

Although Alberto was to project a very different image of himself as a manic, reclusive failure, he appears to have lost few opportunities to benefit from being extensively photographed from his art student days onwards, so that even before he moved to rue Hippolyte, he can be seen in a photograph dated 1926 posing beside his Koto reliquary statue in the rue Froidevaux studio. In the early 1930s, the Surrealist photographer Jacques-André Boiffard, formerly Man Ray's assistant, realised how photogenic the young man was in a series of portraits, and Brassaï, Robert Doisneau, Denise Colomb (Pierre Loeb's sister) and Man Ray himself all quickly followed suit. After the war, Patricia

Matisse made her remarkable reportage of Alberto's latest sculpture just prior to its being presented in the landmark show that took place in her husband's New York gallery, and, with those admirable gritty, grainy shots, one might have thought that Alberto had by this time had all the photographic coverage that he could need.

This was the tip of the iceberg. Henri Cartier-Bresson, who thought Giacometti one of the two most remarkable people he ever photographed (the other, since you ask, being Francis Bacon),* captured Alberto at different intervals throughout his career, taking one of the most memorable shots of him ever: holding his raincoat over his head as he crossed rue d'Alésia during a downpour. Most devoted to the artist of all was his fellow Swiss admirer Ernst Scheidegger, who moved to Paris for a couple of years specifically to take photographs of Alberto in every mood and at every period of the day, eventually compiling a whole volume of his shots entitled *Traces of a Friendship* (published first by the photographer himself, then in a French edition by Maeght). Once Gordon Parks had made Alberto the subject of a reportage, several other American photographers, from Loomis Dean and Arnold Newman to Irving Penn, made a beeline to the studio door. Often the most telling photographs were taken on the spur of the moment, such as Alex Liberman's chance grouping of Alberto, Annette and Diego in a complicit trio, or by amateurs like Pierre Matisse, who snapped Alberto between Pierre's new wife, Patricia, chic in a Prince of Wales *tailleur*, and Annette, looking cheerful but dowdy in a baggy, well-worn man's overcoat.

Beginning as a few portraits but multiplying over the years into many hundreds, these images bolstered Alberto's legend significantly. As they were dispersed through newspapers and magazines, then through lengthy critical essays and monographs, Alberto's already numerous followers could feel that they knew not only the work but the man. There was the applied Alberto, entirely focused on moulding his new figure or painting his model; the sombre Alberto, his deep, dark brown gaze fixed on some distant, ultimate masterpiece; the skittish Alberto caught flirting with Annette; the garrulous Alberto holding forth over coffee and cigarettes in the local bistro; the accomplished Alberto surrounded by his progeny of

*Henri Cartier-Bresson in conversation with the author in Paris, 1987.

Henri Cartier-Bresson, Alberto on rue d'Alésia, 1961

skeletal figures; and so on. It helped that the artist, although no pin-up with the deepening furrows in his face and his shabby attire, was physically sympathetic, even attractive and, above all, human. Seen shambling along rue d'Alésia or standing vulnerably beside a tall clay figure wrapped in damp cloths, he also looked very ordinary, a skilled artisan in a tie, perhaps, or a minor, middle-aged civil servant who needed to press his trousers and pull up his socks. It struck a chord, at least in the minds of the already converted, that the man who had given post-war humanity its most accurate and memorable reflection lived in penury and looked like everybody else – a *Monsieur tout-le-monde*.

As the photographers had an increasingly free run of Alberto's inner sanctum, it turned out that the real hero of the countless images taken of every inch of every nook and cranny, from the balcony downwards or the door inwards, was not so much the artist but his studio. As Alberto became sought-after and famous, his studio grew in stature and significance, like a lengthening, deepening shadow of the man or a hinterland that contained the history and all the clues to his life and work. Vivid and powerful as Alberto's presence was, it did not provide the extraordinary archive that the studio harboured. Here the days and years had left their silt, not only in the retrospective of sculptures looming up through the decades, the paintings stacked under the bed and the drawings littering the filthy floor, but on the paint-caked table with its paint-encrusted tubes, the graffiti-laden walls and even the books and crumpled newspapers filling any other available void.

Through the variety of photographs that were published, the studio grew and grew. From its real dimensions of a small, spare room with a large, grubby window and high, rickety ceiling, Alberto's refuge, the centre and circumference of his existence, also became an essential focus for his admirers, almost overshadowing the artist himself. As Alberto said, when he originally took it on it seemed far too small (at barely twenty-four square metres) for him to work satisfactorily, but over the years it appeared to expand magically to fulfil whatever requirements his creativity imposed. One would be hard put to name another space, grand or dingy, that has claimed greater interest and attention in the history of art since the caves of Altamira and Lascaux, which in certain ways it resembles. Meanwhile, the spindly tree that had broken through the studio's beaten-earth floor was now thriving, its fresh green leaves adding the accent of nature to the assembled sculptures that seemed, by contrast to this spontaneous eruption, to hark back to the dawn of mankind.

The person least impressed by the studio was no doubt Alberto himself, since he was as used to it and as tacitly dependent on it as a snail to its shell – the cave he had longed to hide in as a child, the locus and refuge of his dreams. For all Annette's attempts to sweep it clean of plaster shards and other detritus, Alberto's very particular style of chaos continued to reign over the tiny territory now saturated with his activities and presence for three decades. Only he knew what lay under each amorphous mound of literary magazines, many of them filled with his drawings over the texts, or from what period certain works originated – although, since everything was in any case in a permanently shifting state, he did not care much if he were a year or two out. If the neat bedroom with its red tiles and little flower vase had become Annette's domain, no one doubted Alberto's right to rule the studio, where he now realised he would work until the end, and which, he often claimed, he would like to have been even more austere and comfortless than it already was.

For several months the little grey space had become the arena in which Alberto was battling to produce a demanding new series of figures that would become famous collectively as *The Women of Venice*. The work on this impressive group had begun as a result of an invitation to exhibit his work in the French pavilion at the 1956 Venice Biennale, one that gave him special pleasure because it allowed him to acknowledge publicly how important his adopted country had been to his entire career (even though at the time, and for years to come, all his museum exhibitions had taken place outside France). If there is such a close kinship in this key series, which gives it an unusually haunting presence, it came about for a very simple reason: they are all variations on a single, original clay model. Conscious of the strict deadline the Biennale imposed as well as his habit of regularly destroying everything that had begun to take form under his anxious fingers, Alberto resolved that whenever a version of the figure he was modelling seemed better than most he would get Diego to make a plaster cast of it, ensuring its survival in that particular state. Out of the endless palping of clay and the numerous different versions created in any given day, a dozen were thus preserved in plaster, of which nine were eventually cast in bronze.

With their outsize feet set on deliberately slanting bases, which have the effect of precipitating the figures towards the viewer, the *Women* now constitute a highlight of any Giacometti show. Seen separately, they represent 'Woman'; together, they are 'All Women' who have ever been and who will ever be, half of humanity enclosed in their own mystery and majesty. Given half a chance, any curator of a Giacometti exhibition will make the *Women* a central, dramatic feature, choosing how to site them, in close, awesome conjunction or with each carving out her own space, under lighting that accentuates and plays with their near-infinite shadows, cast on the floor or climbing vertiginously up the walls. While these figures are slender and powerful, even goddess-like, they are also deeply ambiguous, referring back to the archetypal thrill the artist felt watching the naked divinities in anticipation of a brief clinch. While the *Women* might have stood between the columns of the Parthenon radiating authority, they might also, with their shrunken, fissured flesh, have watched over Montparnasse Cemetery, rooted to the spot by their earthbound feet. Here Alberto created a series of women for all seasons, set to rule the world from the brothel to the Acropolis, as well as the graveyard.

As soon as he had installed the *Women* in the main gallery of the French pavilion to his satisfaction – in two groups of six and four, surrounded by six other sculptures he had selected – Alberto left Venice before the Biennale opened, but not before stating that he did not wish to be considered for the Golden Lion, the prize regularly awarded with full Venetian ceremony by an international jury. This appears to be a rare instance of the artist actively intervening in his career, and it was prompted by the fact that, since he had another exhibition opening at the Bern Kunsthalle at the same time with far more works, he did not want to be judged on the strength of a mere sixteen sculptures. The Bern event, curated by Franz Meyer, who had married Marc Chagall's daughter, Ida, and who went on to write a book about Giacometti, amounted to a sizeable retrospective with forty-six sculptures, twenty-three paintings (including four portraits of Alberto's mother) and sixteen drawings. The opening in Bern turned into a lively affair with the artist, accompanied by his wife, greeting all and sundry exuberantly, and at one point planting a kiss on a pretty female admirer's cheek. At this, according to a contemporary report, Annette let out a howl of dismay and stormed off.[1] After a promising start, the unorthodox marriage was showing signs of strain.

Back in Paris, Alberto had become fascinated by a man whom he noticed seated in a café in Montparnasse and wanted to draw immediately because his domed, bald head revealed the structure of his skull so vividly. Hair, the artist liked to argue, was a 'lie' hiding the far more important reality lurking beneath (at one point he is believed to have demanded that Annette shave her head – but she never did). Alberto's interest was quickened by the fact that, like every Paris intellectual, he knew who the man was: a writer and ex-convict with a well-earned reputation for scandalous behaviour and treachery called Jean Genet. By this time, Genet, abandoned at birth, brought up in state institutions, accused of theft and repeatedly incarcerated, had made his name by producing subversive novels and plays, including *The Thief's Journal* and *The Maids*. His career on the wrong side of the law had also flourished, to the extent that he would have been condemned to a sentence of life imprisonment had Cocteau and Sartre not interceded vigorously on his behalf at the top, presidential level. Genet claimed that, since he had been charged with theft and then initiated into homosexuality in jail, those pursuits had turned, as in an epiphany, into the twin goals of his existence. It is hardly surprising that a life as bristling with such promising existential features as Genet's should, along with his unusual literary gift, have fascinated Sartre, who went on to devote a book to him entitled *Saint Genet: Actor and Martyr*. This mammoth study in itself established Genet's literary fame, although Sartre's probing analysis reputedly prevented Genet from writing anything thereafter for five years.

Introduced by Sartre at Alberto's request, the two men took to one another instantly, with the artist inviting Genet to the studio and setting up a date for him to begin posing for him, an ordeal rendered all the worse, Genet recalled, by the discomfort of the straw-bottomed chair he was obliged to sit on for hours on end day after day. One reason why sculptor and writer bonded so quickly was that Alberto admired Genet's writing. He had read *Our Lady of the Flowers* and noted the advance extracts of Sartre's mammoth essay on Genet in *Les Temps modernes*. In the same way Genet, who was surrounded by the *Women of Venice* dominating the tiny working space, recognised much in Alberto's vision of humankind that mirrored his own, beginning with most crucially the essential solitude of all human existence, as well as the wonder and fear which it provokes.

The two also shared a deep sympathy for and fascination with people who lived outside the norms of society: prostitutes and their lowlife associates in Alberto's case, criminals and homosexuals in Genet's. Both considered that people living 'close to the edge' remained more in touch with the unvarnished 'reality' of life. Alberto was interested in all forms of sexual 'deviancy' since he thought it made for more unusual human beings, and through Genet he welcomed the opportunity to get closer to the homosexual world (which he also explored avidly later in London with Francis Bacon).[2] The new friends came up with a game in which they would sit together on a café terrace and Alberto would proceed to pick out whichever male passers-by he thought Genet would fancy most, deriving considerable pride from the fact that Genet told him he was almost always right. Moved by Genet's unusual early sufferings and innate difference, Alberto also jotted down a revealing, if strangely staccato and elliptical, verbal portrait of the writer:

> Sharply faceted, concentrated, violent crystal, but above all head obstinately and violently straining forward with features of pain, sadness (regret) at the corners of the mouth, disillusioned as if with regret that life is nothing more than an abyss, as if denying the facts about the idea or feeling he had about life and what he imagined it could be, bitterly denied the belief he had in life but arising from within and not at all provoked by what people or facts could have inflicted upon him, or rather than bitterness, a disillusioned acceptance of the abyss that is life or the universe, with at the same time immense gentleness and kindness and understanding toward beings and things.[3]

The most significant exchange between the two men took place, naturally enough, in their respective areas of expertise. Alberto began by making several unusually sensitive, almost discursive drawings of the writer as if floating through space (compared, say, to the heavily scored, deliberately anchored pencil portraits of Sartre), as he always did before venturing into the more ambitious, consequential realms of painting or modelling. Executed between 1954 and 1957, the three canvases of Genet resemble other portraits of the time in that their posture invariably recalls the famous Egyptian *Seated Scribe* (c. 2500 BC), with its 'compelling gaze', that had struck Alberto so indelibly on his early visits to the Louvre.

As the eye travels up their massive frontality, big widespread legs and dwindling heads, it is summoned and repulsed in rapid alternation. The *Portrait of Jean Genet* (1954–5), currently in the Centre Pompidou collection in Paris, is a masterly composition in which the writer is presented with a larger-than-life body topped by a small, round skull that commands attention as unerringly as a bull's eye at the centre of a target. Genet floats no more, looming out of the muddy shadows and dominating the foreground, then puncturing the canvas with his tiny head: a knob of anguish and vulnerability in an uncertain world.

Genet was as passionately involved in the process as the artist, and he rose fully to the challenge when invited to write the introduction to Alberto's next exhibition at Galerie Maeght.[4] Entitled *The Studio of Alberto Giacometti* and written in a fragmentary, confessional style that remains far removed from any other writing on the artist before and since, the essay goes straight to the heart of Genet's conviction that Giacometti's art is uniquely, pitilessly concerned with the truth, showing humankind what it looks like when surface and superfluity have been stripped away. In one of the opening, lyrical passages, Genet notes:

> Beauty has no other origin than the wound (unique, different in each person, hidden or visible) that we carry within us, that we preserve and to which we withdraw whenever we wish to leave the world for a temporary but profound solitude … I think Giacometti's art seeks to uncover that secret wound in each being, in each thing, so that the wound illuminates them.[5]

The essay, much admired by Picasso and Giacometti's own favourite piece of writing on his work, moves fluidly from subtle aesthetic and philosophical inquiry to down-to-earth factual description and snatches of conversation between the two men. When Genet was released from his duties as a motionless sitter, he took the opportunity to run his hands over a finished figure in bronze while closing his eyes. This was his reward for so much silent concentration. 'I cannot describe,' Genet wrote, 'how happy my fingers were.' Elsewhere he praised Giacometti as 'a sculptor for the blind'.

Towards the end of his essay, Genet takes leave of Giacometti with a description that seems to capture him feverishly at work for ever:

… his fingers rise and fall like a gardener's pruning or grafting a climbing rose. His fingers play up and down the statue, and the whole studio vibrates and comes to life. I get the strange impression that, with him there, without even touching them, the older, already completed statues change and are transformed because he is working on one of their sisters. This ground-floor studio, at all events, is going to cave in at any moment now. It is made of worm-eaten wood and grey powder. The statues are in plaster, with the rope, the fibres or a piece of wire sticking out. The canvases painted in grey have long lost the tranquillity they had at the art supply store. Everything is stained and ready for the bin, everything is precarious

Jean Genet, 1957

> and about to collapse, everything is about to dissolve, everything is floating: and yet it all appears to be captured in an absolute reality. When I leave the studio, when I am outside on the street, then nothing that surrounds me is true. Shall I say it? In that studio a man is dying slowly, being consumed and metamorphosing into goddesses beneath our very eyes.[6]

The coda to this intense relationship adds another baser, but no less revealing, truth. As previously mentioned, Alberto paid little attention to the drawings he kept scattered around the studio, with a few exceptions such as the largest portrait he had drawn of Henri Matisse. Understandably, he was dismayed when he discovered that this particular study had disappeared. The only two people outside the family to have had unsupervised access to the studio were Genet and James Lord. When Alberto confronted Lord, the writer said: 'You'd better ask Genet,' to which Alberto, chagrined, replied, 'I wouldn't dare, given his past as a thief.'[7] The matter was never satisfactorily resolved. When, after Alberto's death, the drawing reappeared for sale and Diego bought it on behalf of Pierre Matisse, Genet firmly insisted that it was not he but Lord who had stolen it.[8]

Hunched and exhausted already from the first few hours of work, Alberto stood, drooping a little over the counter at the café-tabac. They were so used to seeing him that he'd become almost invisible. He was 'Alberto' to the owner behind the bar and 'Monsieur Alberto' to the waiter. He'd get coffee first, then order his lunch, even though they knew he ate the same spartan meal every day. An old woman looking at him pityingly from the other end of the bar seemed to know him. Did he know her? He started coughing, lighting another cigarette to try to hide the lung-hacking sounds. *Did* he know her – come to that, did he know anyone? Had he ever known anyone truly?

He saw them all in a kind of grey mist, occasionally tinged with ochre: figures and faces advancing and receding, merging and separating as he tried hour after hour to capture them, in that split second between looking and recording. It was hopeless. Hopeless! Nothing had ever been more hopeless since fools had first believed they could stop and trap the flow of life. They'd be there one moment, just an instant, then they'd disappear.

Alberto relaxing in a local café

Gone with the flow. With Annette this morning, he hadn't even really got started, and with Diego the day before things began well enough before his brother started vanishing too, swallowed into a black fog. Diego said it was because he'd gone on painting in the dark, without putting the lights on.

But the paintings disappeared whether the lights were on or not, and whatever images remained were called 'Grey Figure' or 'Black Head'. Annette, Diego, still lifes of bottles and brushes in the studio, came and went in their heavy, earthen colours, as though they had been found embedded in the paint like corpses in the ground, like the Fayoum mummy portraits still half-covered with dirt. Why didn't he use a bit of colour, people kept asking him, why were his pictures so gloomy? It wasn't his fault, he'd say. That was the way he saw it, so that was the way it was, he could only follow what he saw. And even then, even there, the more he tried to fix the fleeting semblances, the more he failed.

Who was that old woman at the other end of the bar who kept looking at him? He didn't know her, but he liked her old face so perhaps he could try and draw her one day. Or perhaps he did know her because he met so many people now that he had started going out again, getting away from Annette, drifting along the pavements, drifting into the bars, then mooching home, brushing the walls, under the rain. All the waiters and taxi drivers knew him by name, and after a while you knew everyone who preferred living at night. His mother always told him that, as a child, he had always preferred the dark, even in the summer when he would hide away in his favourite caves. She was right. He did prefer the night and all the creatures of the night. They were more real, they did not hide themselves like people did during the day, hiding in plain daylight. They were there because they needed the night. They longed for the darkness, and then they talked about what really mattered to them, which was always ten times more interesting than all the wit and theory of the writers and intellectuals. And he had met plenty of them as well, by day and by night, even though he had started seeing less of Sartre and Beauvoir, who were now so famous that they always seemed to have a posse of journalists following them. As Simone had said the other day, Sartre only associates with people who associate with Sartre. That was about it now …

'Hey,' the woman at the other end of the bar shouted out suddenly. 'I want to buy that poor old thing that's been standing there a coffee. He looks like he needs a coffee.'

'But, Madame,' the waiter said. 'That's Monsieur Alberto. He's a famous artist. He can buy his own coffee.'

'I don't care who he is,' the old woman said. 'I want to buy the poor old bum a coffee.'

'Thank you very much, Madame,' Alberto said, coming round from his thoughts. 'You are very kind. I appreciate that very much.'[9]

The waiter took the coffee over to the table where the artist usually sat. Alberto thanked the woman humbly again and sat down at the table, lighting another cigarette and lining the ashtray up beside his cup precisely.

She's right, of course, he thought. I am a poor old thing. I'm just a dirty old down-and-out. He felt a sense of relief, as if he'd been burying his face in his hands then raised it up again. At least she'd seen through him, seen him for what he really was. He glanced round the café again and gratefully finished his coffee. There would be no time for lunch today. He had to get back to his other life, his 'famous' life, even though it felt less real now. In less than an hour he was expected to be at the hotel where the composer Igor Stravinsky was staying. Would he become like Sartre soon, he wondered, gathering up his cigarettes and newspaper – only associating with people who associate with the great Giacometti, and fail to understand he is really just an old tramp.

Having followed Alberto's work from early on[10] and seen it in several American collections, Stravinsky had wondered out loud whether the sculptor might make some drawings of him, as several fine draughtsmen, notably Picasso, had done during his long, eventful career. The suggestion was relayed to Alberto, who approved the idea right away. The two artists made a point thereafter of meeting every time the composer came to Paris, and if Stravinsky was conducting anywhere in France, Alberto was sure to receive an invitation. Several incisive portraits came out of the drawing sessions with Stravinsky, who later wrote a lucid account of the experience:

> He had done five or six drawings from photographs before he saw me, and he didn't like them. Then, sitting a few feet from me, he did a whole series, working very fast with only a few minutes of actual drawing for each one. He says that in sculpture, too, he

> achieves the final product very quickly, but does the sometimes hundreds of discarded preparatory ones slowly over long periods of time. He drew with a very hard lead smudging the lines with erasers from time to time. He was forever mumbling: '*Non – impossible – je ne peux pas – une tête violente – je ne peux pas.*'*
>
> He surprised me the first time he came, for I expected Giacometti to be tall and thin. He said he had just escaped from an automobile manufacturer who had been offering him a considerable sum to say that automobiles and sculptures are the same things, i.e., beautiful objects.† In fact, almost Giacometti's favourite topic was the difference between a sculpture and an object. 'Men in the street walking in different directions are not objects in space.' … For him, Canova was not really a sculptor, while Rodin was 'the last great sculptor and in the same line as Donatello.' … Brancusi wasn't a sculptor at all, he said, but a 'maker of objects'.[11]

Stravinsky was a generation older than Alberto, who had always shown instinctive deference to his seniors, especially if they were also artists he admired. As well as gaining new friends, Alberto had also lost several old ones over the past few years. One of his earliest companions and supporters, Michel Leiris, had almost added to the toll by attempting suicide. Alberto made a point of visiting the writer regularly during his lengthy convalescence at home and creating a series of no fewer than fifty-two illustrations for his new book of poems, *Vivantes Cendres, innommées* (Living Ashes, Unnamed), in which Leiris confronts his near-death experience – what he called 'the only major risk I ever dared take' – and its consequences. In fact, Leiris was fixated by what he considered to be his lack of personal courage, even though he had put himself at considerable physical risk in the early Surrealist days, as previously mentioned, and continued to militate for far-left causes despite his own wealthy, ultra-bourgeois lifestyle. Leiris continued to dissect but hardly resolve these deep-seated contradictions in self-excoriating memoirs for the remainder of his long life.

*'No – impossible – I can't – a violent head – I can't.'

†Alberto was sufficiently stimulated by the subject to write a challenging text on it entitled 'La voiture démystifiée', published in the magazine *Arts*, Paris, October 1957.

Alberto enjoyed contemplating and discussing the notion of suicide, sharing with Camus the belief that it was 'the one truly serious philosophical problem', but his unwavering obsession with his own creative problems appears to have dominated all else. Throughout his career, and hardly less during his frequent moments of undisputed success, Alberto remained convinced that he had 'missed the mark'. The refrain was repeated ceaselessly, like a challenge to himself to go ever further, and on the rare occasions when he felt some satisfaction with his work it was rapidly dispelled by more doom and gloom about his capacities and achievements. Although such crises occurred regularly, setting up a kind of leitmotiv, they differed in intensity, with the 1950s (coming after his notable post-war triumph) ranging regularly between moderate setbacks and periods of near-total paralysis, when he destroyed every work he began or, worse, could not even begin. *Cris de coeur* describing the latter abound in his often voluminous letters to Matisse in New York, with random outbursts such as: 'For me, it is no longer so much about an exhibition but to see if I can still put together a sculpture and a painting. I am terribly stuck, I have done everything to end up here, but no I must be done with it, I doubt each grain of plaster, I cannot fall any further, at least that is settled!'[12]

Life changed, but it still carried everything before it, heedless in its serene power to plunge the sculptor into deep despair or jolt him temporarily at least out of his obsession with failure. For all that he seemed as condemned to his studio cell as a hermit, creating and destroying without respite while railing against the world and his own limitations, Alberto's mood was constantly changing. While he might curse the day he had ever tried to draw anything at all, he would suddenly stop in wonder at a plane tree forcing its way out of the pavement towards the sky (murmuring, as he sometimes did: 'We would all be better off as trees') or become fixated by a ray of light glancing brilliantly off a glass on the table. Events overtook him constantly, and several were about to unfold that would challenge him in different ways, all of them unexpected. One was a project that originated among skyscrapers on the other side of the Atlantic, promising the challenging but intensely exciting realisation of a long-cherished dream. The other was the arrival of an enigmatic Japanese scholar who, although remaining mostly impassive and aloof, surpassed the artist's professional expectations as a model while turning his conjugal life upside down. The third development, meanwhile, involved him with a flesh-and-blood goddess who stepped out of the silver screen straight into his grey world.

Prominent and constantly surprising in Alberto's range of gifts was a capacity for friendship, which was rooted in his wide-ranging interest in and sympathy towards other people, coupled with a rare tolerance for human foibles. Despite his solitary, austere working routine, he made and maintained relationships throughout his life, beginning with his own family, notably his mother (whom he wrote to or, now that he owned a telephone, talked to nearly every day) and, of course, his 'other pair of hands', Diego. But they extended to every walk of life, from collectors like the aristocratic Noailles and the leading artists and intellectuals of the day to prostitutes, small-time villains and local down-and-outs. Impressively, many of the friends that he kept in touch with were not only highly talented but temperamental, demanding and difficult not to fall out with; Bataille, Artaud and Genet would each have tried the patience of a saint. Intriguingly, although it is difficult to ascertain why, when Alberto did fall out with people they tended to be the most famous, like Breton, Picasso and (as we shall see) Sartre, who themselves were constantly quarrelling with or abruptly abandoning companions and allies. This was far from Alberto's case: friendships formed a vital part of his everyday existence, unlikely as the link with certain people seemed to be. At the core of his being, there lay a conviction, a basic humility, about himself and other people that Sartre was to sum up admirably (describing himself): 'A whole man, made of all men, worth all of them, and any one of them worth him.'[13] And surely no commitment could have been more unforeseen than the one that came to bind him devotedly to a Japanese philosopher called Isaku Yanaihara who in the mid-1950s had left his teaching post at Osaka University – at the opposite end of the earth – to take up a research scholarship in Paris.

Passionately involved with French literature and Existentialism in particular, Yanaihara had translated Camus' *The Myth of Sisyphus*[14] into Japanese, then taken on and eventually abandoned the more daunting task of translating Sartre's *Being and Nothingness*. Knowing Sartre's writing on Giacometti, Yanaihara was particularly keen to get to know the sculptor who had so impressed France's pre-eminent thinkers. Alberto, always open to new, and especially exotic-sounding, contacts, agreed to meet him at Les Deux Magots and was sufficiently intrigued by the Japanese professor's aura of self-containment to invite him to the studio for the first time in September 1956. Although Yanaihara was secretly appalled by the dilapidation of Alberto's lair, he was struck by the row of phantom-like plaster figures 'frozen' in the dingy space, and soon came under the spell of the sculptor's work, life and analytical, self-probing way of talking. For his part, Alberto found he could open up more and more to his new friend, whose intellectual resourcefulness fascinated him almost as much as his inscrutable features and distant, almost imperial bearing. Meanwhile, Yanaihara had started making notes (which were eventually gathered into a memoir[15]), describing Alberto's physical appearance, above all his large head and outsize hands, as well as details about his punishing daily routine and worsening physical condition, especially his pallor, bloodshot eyes and smoker's cough.

With Yanaihara's visits growing more frequent, the conversations deepened, above all in discussions about painting and sculpture. The philosopher acted as an ideal interviewer, not putting over so much his own views as prompting Alberto to clarify and expand his. Various refrains that the artist had refined over the years, including his inability to draw, paint or sculpt the simplest subject, and his quest only to convey exactly what he saw, return ad infinitum. But they are interspersed by analyses of his contemporaries ('Picasso has unrivalled talent, doesn't he, but he never makes anything but objects … He can't develop and deepen his painting … he always has to change'), as well as admissions of his debts to ancient art, where he describes how, after an intense admiration for Tintoretto, Byzantine mosaics and Rembrandt, he always came back to Egyptian (and Mesopotamian) art as the greatest of all.

When Giacometti began to draw Yanaihara with a view to painting his portrait, neither artist nor model had an idea of how long, arduous and all-consuming the process would become. At the time, in fact, the Japanese professor was due to return shortly to his young family and university post. But Alberto had seen innumerable possibilities in his new, ideal model, who sat 'as immobile as a statue' for hours, moulding himself to the sculptor's tyrannical needs through whole afternoons and late into the night. Proving more patient than a professional model, the stoical Yanaihara even accepted the fact that version after version of his portrait would be scraped off or abandoned with the promise from Alberto that during their next session he would achieve an altogether better result, coming far closer to capturing Yanaihara's head, which seemed to swim continuously in and out of focus as he attempted to trap it with dozens of delicate dabs of his specially fine-haired paint brush;* but more often than not, the hard-won head was reduced to a blob of inert grey. 'As I paint you,' the artist admitted to his sitter, 'I no longer recognise you. You become a complete unknown.' Like Genet, Yanaihara found himself as involved in this singular game of hide-and-seek as the artist, who claimed he was making real progress one moment only to announce that an eye, a nose or an entire face had disappeared irrecoverably. Selflessly, participating to the full in Alberto's struggle, the model accepted every battle lost on the canvas, even encouraging Alberto at the end of each failed session to start all over again. While the artist, who had already encountered mounting problems in his recent paintings, vented his rage and sense of impotence freely, shouting and cursing, the Japanese sitter maintained his impassivity despite struggling with extreme fatigue, hunger and frustration. At certain moments, Alberto broke down, with his arm paralysed, unable to apply the next delicate touch of paint, or (much to his sitter's alarm) weeping uncontrollably as another image filled with great promise vanished into a little pool of muddied colour. For the artist, always close to despair about his work, a full-blown crisis had occurred.

While Alberto had never become fully confident in his ability to achieve his artistic goals, he had at least managed to produce a consistent body of work since his return from Geneva, without any major crises. From 1954, however, he started to agonise over individual paintings, now no longer created out of a rapidly executed mesh of lines but built up incrementally over time to depict frontal figures that emerge like ghosts from a painterly grey haze. This new process meant that the subject might at any point disappear into the background fog, leaving little more than a vague smear behind. That constant danger provoked the crisis which, although it had its

*As Yanaihara notes in his memoir, the unusually fine paint brushes (and most of the other painting materials) that Alberto used were made especially by Lefebvre-Foinet, one of the most reputable suppliers in Paris, long established at the corner of rue Vavin and rue Bréa, beside the Luxembourg Gardens.

precedents, occurred during the painting of the first portrait of Yanaihara. Suddenly the artist was unable to fight off the impending, meaningless grey smudge: a losing battle which his new subject, a committed Existentialist, almost encouraged by admitting that he considered failure inevitable. Significantly, Alberto's paintings only regain a degree of confidence and clarity in 1958, the year Yanaihara did not return to Paris.

During these fraught seances, Alberto repeatedly confessed to feeling terrified: terrified by the impossibility of the task he had set himself, terrified of his inadequacy, even terrified of Yanaihara's head, which he imagined could explode like 'a bomb' at any moment. But what terrified him most was losing his new model whose departure from Paris was looming ever closer. Moved by the artist's entreaties that without him he could no longer take their 'adventure' further or indeed make any progress whatsoever in his art, but also attached to his role of irreplaceable model, Yanaihara changed his flight home to a later date. This turned out to be only the first of several cancellations, as the Japanese risked the mounting ire both of his family and his employers by prolonging his Parisian sojourn. Similarly, the relationship between the two men took on an intensity in which each came to depend on the other for their very identity.

In order to be closer to Alberto's studio, Yanaihara moved from his digs in Montmartre to a modest room on an upper floor at the Hôtel Vavin. But there was no time to enjoy the sweeping view it afforded over Montparnasse because his schedule now revolved entirely around the ever longer, ever more involving studio sittings. The inscrutable model had by now been taken completely into the artist's inner circle, witnessing the squabbles that broke out between the artist and his wife, and regularly dining with them at their local bistro, Les Tamaris, a useful but mediocre eatery in which the major feature was a large mirror pitted with bullet holes from a shoot-out that had occurred there between Nazis and *résistants*. If the sittings went on too late, the trio would pile into a taxi and go either to the Coupole, where Alberto's table awaited them, or to Brasserie Lipp for choucroute or cassoulet. Occasionally Yanaihara took the couple to the only Japanese restaurant in Paris at that time, introducing them to exotic dishes which made a welcome change from their usual bistro fare. Sometimes, once Annette had gone home, Alberto would plunge further into the night, taking Yanaihara to his favourite haunts, such as Chez Adrien, where he knew many of the girls who hung out there, chatting up potential customers and gossiping with their colleagues between tricks.

Yanaihara felt particularly privileged to meet some of the famous writers in Alberto's orbit, notably Genet, who would visit the studio frequently with Abdallah Bentaga, his highwire acrobat boyfriend, and Sartre, who invited Yanaihara to visit him at the apartment he shared with his mother and her Alsatian maidservant on rue Bonaparte, at the heart of Saint-Germain. Most of all, he got to know and like Annette, who would play opera and classical music, above all Mozart, loudly on the gramophone in their bedroom as the two men worked in the studio. (Alberto, who particularly liked Gregorian chant and Handel, as well as jazz, would sometimes yell out, asking her to put on a particular record.) The growing affection between the wife and the younger man never seemed to bother Alberto, who frequently left the two of them alone. One night, however, returning from a concert, Annette followed Yanaihara up to his hotel room, and the inevitable happened. The following day, the Japanese visitor turned up at the studio, fretting about how to tell Alberto, since their close contact precluded any dissemblance. But Annette had already said as much, and Alberto, who seemed in an unusually good mood, went out of his way to stress how well and happy Annette looked that morning. Whether Alberto was pleased that his wife had acted so independently, as he continued to profess, or whether he considered sexual jealousy (from which he had suffered acutely during his affair with Denise) to be beneath him, we will never know. But the observant and sensitive Yanaihara may well have wondered whether their compound infidelity (both of them were trusted implicitly by Alberto) had not added to the artist's burden as he continued at times to burst into tears. One nearby witness of the whole affair, Diego, never commented on it, but he had not taken to Yanaihara and, particularly after overhearing an unambiguous tryst between the newcomer and Annette in the Giacomettis' bedroom, stomped around the little warren of rooms at rue Hippolyte with a face like thunder.

Despite any underlying tensions, the work sessions continued unchanged until Yanaihara left Paris, only to return the following year and on several subsequent occasions. The relationship between the two men altered the lives of each, with Yanaihara acknowledging that the experience had been 'fundamental' for him, and Alberto repeating how much further he had been able to go thanks to his Japanese model, not only in painting and sculpture but in his whole conception of what he could achieve in art. In all, according to Yanaihara's calculation, only six portraits, two sculptures and, as ever, numerous drawings resulted from some 230 lengthy, demanding, at times even excruciating sittings. But the artist went on to paint his model even in his absence, and in the end the number of paintings rose to twenty-two. Yanaihara comes across as a powerful presence in these breakthrough studies, with a small, concentrated head atop a pyramidal body rooting him in the cloudy, greyish-yellowish fluidity of the background, which functions as an inner frame, whereas in the sculpture he appears monumental and indomitable. In terms of Alberto's own progress, the Yanaihara period had taken him deeper into, then beyond, his crises of doubt, leading him from his 'mature' to his 'late', more self-confident, emphatic style. The two men corresponded, with Alberto underlining how much 'progress' he had made with his ideal model, whom he continued to paint 'from memory', and Yanaihara admitting that he pretended at times to be sitting for Alberto, completely motionless, in his bedroom back in Japan. Annette, who felt Yanaihara's absence keenly, would add the odd, homely note to these letters, remarking on the fact that so much plaster had stuck to the soles of Alberto's shoes that 'you could follow his footsteps' all the way down rue Hippolyte.

Across the Atlantic, another person who had followed the whole Yanaihara 'affair' with grave misgivings was Pierre Matisse. Members of the French artistic community in New York were regularly in touch with their counterparts in Paris, with Matisse remaining at the hub of both worlds; and anything concerning Alberto, whose reputation and prices had been steadily gaining ground, immediately focused his attention. Moreover, Alberto wrote to Matisse regularly (more than two hundred letters to him have been preserved*) often beginning with 'Just a line' or 'A quick note', then rambling on, mainly about work in progress but also with regular asides about friends

*At the Morgan Library and Museum in New York, which has become a key destination for all Giacometti scholars.

and everyday life, for half a dozen pages. Mindful of Matisse's anxiety about the various crises he had been undergoing while working with Yanaihara, and how that might affect his artistic output, Alberto hastened to reassure him. 'Don't worry about the Japanese,' he advised him breezily. 'If I get his portrait, and I think I will, you'll have Diegos and Annettes and apples and trees and some better sculpture as well.'[16]

Matisse had in any case recently steered a major project Alberto's way. In downtown Manhattan, the monumental new headquarters of Chase Manhattan Bank overlooked a spacious plaza. Its principal architect, Gordon Bunshaft, whose own art collection included Giacomettis, had put forward Alberto and Alexander Calder as the two sculptors most suited to creating work for the site. Scale fascinated Alberto, and although he was still remembered for creating figures so tiny that they dwindled into dust, he had also gone to another extreme of fashioning taller and taller, bone-thin silhouettes in the wake of the Standing Women he had exhibited at the Venice Biennale in 1956. He was equally fascinated by the idea of making sculpture expressly for outdoor sites and, notably, city squares, and he had already experimented with various possibilities in earlier works, such as *Model for a Square* (1930–31), commissioned by Charles and Marie-Laure de Noailles, *Piazza* (1947–8) and *City Square* (1948). Just after the war, Alberto had told Aragon that if a medium-size figure of his were set on the place Maubert, just off boulevard Saint-Germain, the thronged little market square would look as big as the place de la Concorde. At last, the artist had the chance to position his work in a public, urban setting – to realise in life size the dynamics he explored in those earlier models. As a result, he devoted almost all of 1959 and the first months of 1960 to the execution of pieces for the project.

Unlike most Parisian squares, with their six-storey houses and ground-floor shops and cafés, the Chase Manhattan skyscraper towers some sixty aluminium- and glass-clad floors above an entirely different metropolis laid out on a grid and geared not to the past but a jolting, up-to-the-minute future. Knowing that Alberto had never set foot in New York, Bunshaft sent him a small-scale cardboard model of the site, blithely suggesting that Alberto simply need magnify existing sculptures thirty times to do the job. Alberto was keenly aware that scale was a much more sensitive issue, and he specifically did not want to overpower passers-by with statues of mere magnitude. In the end, he decided to choose three familiar themes: a gigantic standing female figure, a large walking man and a monumental head (based, naturally enough, on the heads he had done of Diego) set on the ground and arranged in a relationship to each other that he had tried and tested outside the studio where these behemoths had been engendered. His small and increasingly cluttered atelier was not set up for the creation of such large-scale works and their size preoccupied him increasingly.

Since he was so firmly against the mechanical enlargement of smaller models (which Bunshaft had suggested), he went to great lengths to make his sculptures as large as he possibly could by hand, deploying a ladder to reach their upper heights and regularly wheeling them outside to get a clearer sense of how they looked in the round. The size and bulky modelling of the walking men and busts he produced for the plaza were particularly influenced by memories of Roman sculpture from a trip Alberto had taken to the Eternal City as a young man.

Worries about whether he could rise to the challenge of the commitment and achieve the right scale without having seen the huge square in question continued to plague him. Well into 1960, after more than a year of angst-ridden trial and error and even having had four sculptures cast in bronze ready to be sent across the Atlantic, he gave up on the project, much to the irritation of both the architect and his New York dealer. Alberto, as was his wont, nevertheless remained upbeat about the failed project, claiming that it had helped him significantly in his ongoing 'adventure' towards the perfect work. The sculptures were eventually cast in bronze, with one being exhibited at the 1962 Venice Biennale, and another installed in the courtyard at the Fondation Maeght in the South of France when it was inaugurated with great pomp by André Malraux in 1964. And indeed, along with the figures from 1947, these were the only larger-than-life sculptures he produced across his career – with the exception of the very different figure Alberto and Diego produced for the garden of the Villa Noailles in 1931 which was hewn from a block of white stone almost eight feet tall.

Alberto made his only visit to New York years later in 1965 and paced round Chase Manhattan Plaza whenever there was a spare moment. He was finally able to gauge the whole space and try out in situ where his sculptures would have been best placed. Back in Paris, he asked Diego to prepare an armature for a figure larger than any he had conceived before. By that time, nevertheless, failing health prevented him from realising his ambitious vision.

Alongside the long-lasting relationships that filled Alberto's life there were, as in any life, a fair number of intermezzos. Most were chance encounters of no lasting consequence – shadows in the night, strangers at a bar, the *clocharde* living in a doorway with whom he used to joke and who, one day, was suddenly no longer there. He did strike up unusual acquaintances with people from every level of society but even so no one would have predicted that he would have a brief liaison with one of the most famous actresses of the day: Marlene Dietrich. Having admired Alberto's *Dog*, with its melancholy mien and prominent ribcage, at the Museum of Modern Art in New York, Dietrich decided she wanted to meet its maker. Accordingly, she asked Alex Liberman (the magazine editor whose description of Annette was quoted earlier) to make the introduction while she was in Paris in November 1959. As an enthusiastic cinemagoer, Giacometti was fully aware of Dietrich's career and reputation, not least since she performed regularly in Paris and had even been awarded the Légion d'honneur. Hollywood star and sculptor met first in a discreet bistro before retreating to rue Hippolyte, but let's listen to the story of that day told by 'Lola-Lola' herself:

> Both of us avoided publicity so we met in a bistro, well out of sight of all those annoying photographers. As usual I couldn't get a word out and just sat silently there; Giacometti took my face in his hands and said, 'You are not at all hungry, are you? Come on, let's go and talk in my studio.'
>
> At the time he was working on figures of women that were so big he had to climb up a ladder to get to the head. The studio was cold and bare. He stood up on his ladder and I crouched down below, watched him and waited for him to come down to say something. In the end he spoke. But what he said was so sad that I would have felt like crying if I could have cried at the right moment. When he was on the same level as me again we embraced each other.
>
> We went into cafés in Montmartre and to restaurants, he watched while I ate. His heart and his body were ill. He gave me a wonderful

> figure of a girl – that was what he called it. He wrapped it in newspaper. 'Take it with you to America and give it to your daughter,' he said. I followed his instructions to the letter. With the little figure on my lap I flew across the Atlantic, knowing that I would never see Giacometti again. He died far too early from an awful illness. Like all artists he was a sad man. He seemed touched by my admiration, but much as I would have wanted to I could not help him in his misfortune.
>
> Now I am sorry that I didn't take all the treasures that he offered me. As usual, I was too well brought-up to accept so many presents. But I never rejected his love – and the 'professors' here can keep out of that! I could not say that he enriched me. I tried to enrich him. But I had too little time. Too little time.[17]

One wonders what might have happened if the relationship had evolved (Dietrich was known to be promiscuous with both men and women), but at least Alberto could allow himself a smile when he saw the photographs of Picasso horsing around with Gary Cooper and wearing his ten-gallon hat for the camera. He had gone one further and had a definite *amitié amoureuse*, and possibly more, with the 'lovely, legendary Marlene' (as Noël Coward called her). What nipped that particular *amitié* in the bud was not lack of time or interest on either side, but the eruption into Alberto's life of a new mistress from the very opposite end of the social spectrum. This young dominatrix with close ties to the Parisian underworld ordered him in no uncertain terms *not* to keep his next date with Marlene – indeed to end the liaison by pointedly standing her up. Or else …

11

A Longing for Darkness (1959–63)

The new 'she who must be obeyed' to burst into Alberto's life was called 'Caroline', although the name, like much else about her, was assumed, since she had been born Yvonne-Marguerite Poiraudeau near the Atlantic coast in the Vendée and brought up by a mother whom she described as having 'gentleman friends'. Alberto had met her, like many another lady of the night, at Chez Adrien where he went often – usually with little in mind beyond relaxing over a few drinks and joining in the bawdy banter that ricocheted around the zinc-topped counter. He fitted in nicely because he knew Abel the barman and several of the girls well and he was never slow to buy a round of whatever anybody was having. Sometimes he just sat at a little table to one side with pen and paper and caught up on his correspondence: letters to his mother, to Pierre Matisse, or even the odd note to himself. Chez Adrien had become Alberto's club, and if there was no one he felt like talking to, he could sit by himself and read the newspaper he kept in his jacket pocket or, with one of the ballpoint pens he always carried around, scribble little drawings of the heads and figures that teemed continuously through his mind.

On one evening in October 1959, Dany and Ginette, two of the girls he had known for years, are chatting with a young, unusually attractive newcomer whom Alberto noticed right away. She looks back at him directly with golden-green eyes set wide apart that give her gaze a strange intensity – 'like a bird's cry', Alberto said later. After a few drinks, the four of them move on to get something to eat at a neon-lit café nearby where they have oysters and chips. Once Alberto slips them a bit of cash, Dany and Ginette melt back into the night, leaving their pert, wide-eyed colleague alone with 'Monsieur Alberto', a tramp-like old josser who they know has plenty of money to spend while never getting out of line.

Another bottle of sourish white wine arrives, and under the yellowish light the two of them, looking from afar like a young woman with her grandfather, begin to open up to each other. She looks into that deeply furrowed face with its sad brown eyes and realises instinctively that she is with someone out of the ordinary, unlike any of the many other *types* she has known in her short life. He looks back at her delicate features, so like Annette's when they first met, and already he is sketching her face in his mind, savouring the contrast it makes with her abrupt gestures and her coarse but affecting way of talking. They agree to meet again at Chez Adrien, and later they agree to meet directly at the more anonymous Dupont-Montparnasse, part of a chain of late-night eateries which advertises itself with the jingle, 'chez Dupont tout est bon'. She starts out saying things that she thinks will shock him, then she sees he absorbs everything, intently, uncritically, and she begins to tell him things she has never told anybody, that she has hardly told herself. He talks to her about whatever he has on his mind, simply and directly, without ever feeling that she does not understand or that he needs to explain. Barriers seem to fall, they talk late into the night, holding less and less back. Neither of them has experienced this before, even if now they each experience it differently. He has held back all his life and he realises the opportunity to pour himself out like this, like a river rushing into the sea, will not come again. She realises the way they are talking is different, far from the usual transaction. But if he is not like the others he is also weird, as well as shabby. She is younger, harder, and she expects to be paid for her time as usual. He pays, a wad of notes under the table. They meet again, the menu has not changed, the wine gets no better, but they don't notice. They go on talking, warmly, affectionately now, drawing closer to each other in a way that seems mysterious, as if preordained. There are moments, even early on, of extraordinary intimacy, like a confession, like a cleansing. The oyster platters come and go as part of a larger ritual over which they sense they have little control. As part of the ritual she regularly puts in her bill, regularly demanding more than the full rate, knowing that her pimps will be pleased. He gives her more, enthusiastically.

Encouraged by the frankness with which Alberto discusses his sexual fantasies and the growing rift in his marriage, Caroline reciprocates, sketching in the strangest, most dramatic details of her life in sex and in crime. Emboldened, she exaggerates the nastiest heists and extortions, embroiders on the lowest and least believable desires. If he does not believe her, she says, she can arrange for him to come and watch, discreetly of course. The more sordid the details, the more beautiful, even angelic, she seems. He just listens now, taking everything into that sad, dark gaze. He listens and looks, entranced.

No human being is free of vanity, but Alberto does come across as freer of that treacherous flaw than many people and most artists. One might argue that, despite being aware of how gifted he was, his habit of endlessly decrying and destroying his work was a mammoth, inverted form of vanity: not only was he a supremely talented artist but, supremely self-critical, he was greater than his achievements, forever insisting that he could do better, and so could destroy the merely 'good'. He had such control of his materials, of his techniques, and such unbounded virtuosity, surely he could push things further and further still. 'It's not enough that I do what I can do,' as he once exclaimed to Yanaihara. 'I must also do what I cannot do,' condemning himself, masochistically and not without intense, secret pleasure, to a life of Sisyphean frustration.

Outside his art, and especially down in the competitive arena of sexuality, he was notably unassuming, going so far as to parade his uncertainties and insufficiencies before anyone who showed interest. Even so, the most modest of lovers could hardly have been expected not to react when a glamorous film star chose him as her new leading man. Alberto might not have doused himself in Chanel No. 5 or even attempted more vigorously to brush the plaster off his person – now that he was rich, he told friends, having holes in his socks or well-worn trousers didn't bother him[1] – but he was undoubtedly proud of his contact with Hollywood stardom, mentioning his new 'friend' Marlene shyly by name to his inner circle, including his mother in distant Stampa.

So how had Caroline, whom many would have found no more than a 'scheming little whore' hoping to break into the big time with her small-time, underworld cronies, bewitched him? Was it a *Blue*

Angel scenario all over again: ageing sculptor – and, as he approached sixty, Alberto looked as old as the mountains he came from – meets wily young hooker, a Parisian 'Naughty Lola', and becomes besotted? He had never made a secret of his preference for prostitutes, but there the guiding principle had been that no emotional attachments were involved, only business as usual. Now he was falling headlong in love, more deeply and powerfully than ever before. He thought of himself as ancient and ugly, and for a time he could not get over the fact that, even if she had come to him at first for the money, she came back to spend time with him of her own free choice. Clearly she knew how to cater to his fantasies and special needs better than any woman he had ever encountered, but Alberto had found something even more important. He had found his ultimate, dominating, dangerous muse.

For a while the household at rue Hippolyte remained unchanged, its inner rhythms still interdependent and unaffected by the bombshell ticking away at the core of Alberto's existence. Things had been less and less harmonious of late, with Annette's frustrated attempts at greater independence being soothed only by Yanaihara's infrequent visits to Paris. Caroline was even invited to the studio and introduced to the artist's long-suffering spouse. Annette found her no greater a threat than Alberto's other unsavoury, night-time acquaintances, and she returned to her search for an apartment of her own with proper plumbing. Diego did not like what he saw. Pulling down the brim of his trademark fedora, he went about his tasks as before but fell more than usually silent.

It was the calm before the storm. As suddenly as she had arrived in Alberto's life, Caroline disappeared. Evening after evening, she had come closer and closer, then she was no longer there. Gone, no trace of her anywhere. Her latest and greatest conquest went berserk, forsaking his studio to trail round any place he thought might yield a clue to her whereabouts, ducking and weaving around Montparnasse. The barman and Dany, Ginette and the other girls at Chez Adrien were keen to help the panicked lover but they had not seen her either; nor had anyone at the other regular rendezvous the two of them used. Soon Alberto was at his wits' end, scrutinising the café terraces like a demented private eye, dodging behind trees, peering into parked cars …

Then, once the word had been passed on to the right quarters, Alberto got a tip-off. Caroline had been apprehended in the course of an armed robbery, tried, then jailed at the Prison de la Petite Roquette, just opposite the Père Lachaise Cemetery. The lover was soon seen pacing up and down outside the penitentiary (where Genet had served an early sentence) with his characteristic limp, dreaming up hare-brained schemes to have her sprung. Fortunately, he could call on a wide circle of friends for help and he turned for advice to the adroit Clayeux, his adviser at the Galerie Maeght whose long arm reached into the political as well as the art world. Wheels began to turn and Alberto found himself pleading Caroline's case to a sympathetic magistrate who eventually agreed to arrange for her release. Once Caroline was safely out, the lovers felt more closely bound than ever, and Alberto went a definitive step further in the relationship by buying her the flashy sports car she had long coveted.

The sight of Caroline in chic Prince of Wales blazer and silk foulard at the wheel of an open-top red MG was all it took to set the cat definitively among the pigeons at rue Hippolyte. Annette's displeasure at the marital status quo had been evident before, as husband and wife frequently bickered, but now it burst out in streams of abuse and recriminations that echoed alarmingly around the scruffy premises. While she put up with an insanitary hovel that she slaved to keep clean, that '*pute*' of his was flaunting herself round Paris in a sports car he had bought her with *their* money. What had this 'Caroline' done for him beyond listen to his sad-sack stories and fleece him mercilessly? All the privations of the past years flooded back to mock her, and as he flinched under her righteousness, all Alberto could do was reference without much conviction her dalliance with Yanaihara and dismiss her, shame-facedly enough, with the nickname 'the sound and the fury', after the title of the Faulkner novel that had become popular in France.

Naturally, the question of alternative accommodation now topped all exchanges between outraged wife and hangdog husband. To some extent, Annette was mollified by the idea that she might at last lay claim to basic domestic comfort, and in less fraught moments, she would even refer to herself, touchingly, as 'the s. & f.'.[2] In short order, the cash in the shoe boxes was supplemented with enough extra from funds that Maeght held in escrow to buy Annette a nondescript apartment on rue Léopold-Robert, off boulevard Raspail. Never managing to settle in there, Annette cast further afield in Saint-Germain until she found another flat more to her liking above a small restaurant on rue Mazarine. She brought her

Wolfgang Kühn, Alberto and Annette in the studio courtyard, 1962

favourite records and some other belongings with her, then consulted better-off friends as to how she should furnish her new home. Having imagined he was off the hook, Alberto promptly aggravated the situation once more by buying Caroline a superior love nest closer to the studio on avenue de Maine. Unsurprisingly, the 's. & f.' redoubled her rage and made frequent scenes, although she continued to turn up at the studio loyally every day to sit for Alberto and take care of the place, ensuring it never grew as ankle-deep in plaster shards and other junk as before.

Diego, who had broken his silence to warn Alberto against Caroline and her milieu, was not left out of this sudden real-estate bonanza. He had been living a stone's throw away on rue du Moulin-Vert, a street of similarly modest dwellings, and in the end he plumped for a ground-floor flat-cum-studio two doors away that Alberto bought for him in 1961, promptly cluttering it up with his table frames, chairs and a menagerie of little animals in wrought iron. Alésia was to remain Diego's home for the rest of his life, the ideal location – a 'paradise', he said later – in which to source the artisanship and materials he needed to produce his own inspired furniture, which was increasingly gaining recognition. Like Annette, Diego had been deeply disturbed by Caroline's irruption into their closely knit inner circle. Like Annette again, Diego's world was entirely centred around Alberto, and even though his designs and objects had begun taking up more of his time, he always put his brother's interests first. Whenever the need for a new armature, a change of patina or simply some advice about a work under way, a transport problem or an appropriate sale price arose, his furniture, with its lovingly moulded little animal details, was put to one side. It is a measure of Alberto's obsession with Caroline that he did not even heed the dour premonitions of his trusty brother, who had got close enough to the Paris underworld to know its ways all too well.

Worming her way closer into her lover's intimacy, Caroline turned her hypnotic gaze on the artist with sufficient intensity for him to do what he had always intended to do: invite her to sit for him so that he could turn his voyeuristic passion into what he loved, more than her, more than anything: his ever alluring, ever failing attempts to capture the flow of life. Here was an opportunity that surpassed all others. Both artist and sitter had rolled in the gutter, drawn in their different ways (like Bataille, like Genet) by the belief, in the wake of a world war which had smashed every article of faith, that the only way to any kind of salvation lay through abasement. Since idealism had led to such chaos, surely one should embrace the base, the putrid, the ignoble.

Alberto had instinctively subscribed to the notion that the long tradition of idealism stretching back to classical times had given way to a nationalism that was ultimately responsible for the bloodbath of war. He had absorbed it, along with Dada, Surrealism, Communism and every other radical argument, from the moment he arrived in Paris. It was now as ingrained in him as plaster, and to a large extent it dictated not only his politics but his aesthetic and his everyday way of living. He could afford a very comfortable, even luxurious lifestyle, as did Picasso in his châteaux and his chauffeured Hispano-Suiza, or Braque with his seaside retreat and Rolls-Royce. His cashflow had grown so plentiful as to be an embarrassment (however much it reassured his watchful mother), and now that he had a few comforts, like the telephone and frequent taxi trips, he found no purpose for it beyond spoiling Caroline with jewellery and other treats. If the studio and his living conditions could be made barer, harsher, he told Genet, he would welcome it; it would help him work better. As for Annette, now that he had bought her a place of her own, that was about it. She would find it even harder than before to prise the least *sou*, penny or red cent out of him.

The harshness is amply captured in the paintings – above all, portraits – on which Alberto was now focusing in the wake of Yanaihara. He could not have asked for more pertinent and challenging subjects, with Annette, the outraged spouse, sitting for him in the earlier part of his truncated day, and Caroline, the inveigling mistress, turning up in the evening, the force of nature whom he nicknamed '*la grisaille*' (the greyness) after scrutinising her for so long through the darkness of his studio at night. Yet both women radiate a similar intensity on canvas. If Caroline had captivated him, Annette remained a mainstay in his life (and it is to her lasting credit that, when recording Alberto's work photographically, she included his progress on the Caroline portraits). In these new portraits, the Yanaihara imagery – obscured by clouds of existential insubstantiality – has been replaced by a strong frontality and firm outline. From receding into uncertain spatial depths, the figures leap forward: they are closer to the spectator, boldly delineated and set against backgrounds that are now no more than dirty haloes of yellowish brown. The colour is almost as muted, even miserabilist, as it has ever been in Alberto's painting, so that even when there are traces of red (as in *Caroline II*, of 1962), they assume all the decorative value of dried blood.

Alberto's painted portraits from the 1960s unleash a latent expressionist tendency in his work, sacrificing surface detail and spatial surroundings to focus fully on the startling intensity of each subject's gaze, to evoke their 'pure presence' (in Sartre's words).* Alberto stresses the openness and frontality of the face, emphasising the lines around his sitters' eyes and thus generating a more dramatic, emotional encounter between subject and viewer. This new development first appeared in his paintings but then influenced his sculptures from around 1962 onwards. In his series of eight busts of Annette from that year, for example, her head appears disproportionately large, hovering slightly in front of her body in a way that projects her gaze forward intently, even alarmingly. One senses, in fact, that 'accurate' representation is no longer Alberto's sole aim. It has been displaced by a compulsion to portray humanity's emotional core,

*Sartre in his 'The Quest for the Absolute' essay for Giacometti's exhibition at the Matisse Gallery in New York in 1948.

expressed through the eyes, which he always looked at first, whether in a person or a portrait. Having spent so many thousands of hours looking so closely at the world, the artist now turned to depict the look itself.

If Alberto's life was changing apace as the 1960s got under way, so was the world around him. Under the Fifth Republic and Charles de Gaulle, France would emerge fully from the aftermath of the war to reclaim its position as a great power, while the long, drawn-out Algerian War limped towards its blood-soaked conclusion. Even Paris, so little changed during the forty years Alberto had known it, was showing signs of modernisation with new highways and its first skyscraper. André Malraux, de Gaulle's minister for culture, decreed a huge clean-up of the city's soot-blackened façades from the historic Marais area outwards. The major poles of Alberto's existence beyond the studio, from La Coupole to Café de Flore and Brasserie Lipp, remained serenely enshrined in Parisian life, but locals were shocked by the emergence of 'Le Drugstore', a streamlined emporium serving all-American hamburgers, first on the Champs-Elysées and then in the heart of Saint-Germain, that would become part of an everyday life in which blue jeans and rock and roll were already well ensconced. While Brigitte Bardot and Jeanne Moreau, Johnny Hallyday and Yves Saint Laurent incarnated a new France, Existentialism barely loosened its grip over philosophical fashion, and Parisian youth still flocked to the smoke-filled jazz cellars in black polo necks and dark glasses to discuss the futility of their fates, then bebop their cosmic purposelessness away.

In Alberto's wider circle of friends and allies, two had died: Camus in a car driven by his publisher, Michel Gallimard, that had skidded out of control and crashed into a tree, and Merleau-Ponty from a heart attack while preparing a lecture on Descartes. Picasso was now rarely seen in Paris, having established himself in the South of France and married Jacqueline Roque (his junior by some fifty years). Alberto's relationship with him had in any case petered out, as it had with Breton, who now looked more like a distinguished elder statesman than a scourge of the bourgeoisie. Sartre and Beauvoir had, on the contrary, grown ever more famous, to the point that they were routinely mobbed when they appeared in public. Sartre had stirred up a media storm when

Noël le Boyer, terrace of Brasserie Lipp

he declined the Nobel Prize. Once his memoir *The Words* came out (just after Beauvoir had published her own autobiographical *Force of Circumstance*), its wit and frankness – based on the claim that 'words' had always been more real to him than the things they describe – turned it into an overnight bestseller. In one notable instance, the 'words' proved to be a double-edged sword, ending (to Sartre's consternation) his valued friendship with Alberto, who took umbrage at the way the writer interpreted the pre-war accident when a car had knocked him down and fractured his ankle. This, for Sartre, represented a classic example of man abruptly confronted by his Existentialist fate, revealing that 'he was not made to be a sculptor … not made for anything at all'. Alberto, who picked the quarrel deliberately, and perhaps not for purely intellectual reasons, claimed that he was outraged by Sartre's tendentious interpretation of what had been a key event in his life (and, one might add, his 'mythology'), thereafter avoiding all contact with the venerated author. Just as he had distanced himself from Surrealism, Alberto had grown increasingly sceptical of the whole Existentialist phenomenon, occasionally going out of his way to deride it* and now publicly breaking with it. Meanwhile, Leiris who, like Alberto himself, managed to maintain most of his many friendships with artists and writers, remained a staunch ally. Alberto made an eloquent drawing of him in 1961 (subsequently bequeathed to the Centre Georges Pompidou), and Leiris was to write several posthumous tributes to Alberto, notably in *L'Ephémère*,† which featured the same engraving of a slender female figure by Giacometti like a tutelary spirit on the cover of each of its twenty issues.

Another prominent writer who by this time counted as an old ally was Samuel Beckett, whose vision and improbable, late success seemed to have taken an almost parallel course to Alberto's. From its modest beginnings as a cult play put on by Roger Blin in the pocket-sized Théâtre de Babylone on boulevard Raspail, *Waiting for Godot* became famous as the starkest, most telling representation of post-war man and the absurdity of his situation to have been put on stage. It is likely that both dramatist and artist would have rejected comparisons between their work out of hand, but what one had achieved in drama seemed to echo more and more significantly what the other had created in sculpture. Even the tall, ascetic-looking Beckett himself recalled one of Alberto's *Walking Men*, a point not lost on the Moroccan writer Tahar ben Jelloun:

*Alberto once said: 'People talk so much about the discontent in the world and about existential anxiety as if it were something new! Everyone at every period in history felt it. You only have to read the Greek and Latin authors!' Quoted in Hohl, *Giacometti: A Biography in Pictures*, p. 176.

†*L'Ephémère*, one of the finest post-war literary reviews, was published in Paris from 1967 to 1972, largely thanks to the efforts of two poets, Jacques Dupin and Yves Bonnefoy, both of whom devoted admirably discerning texts to Giacometti. Cyril Connolly's *Horizon*, perhaps the closest equivalent to it in London, was the first to publish Leiris's *Pierres pour un Alberto Giacometti*, in an English translation by Douglas Cooper, in 1949; these texts were later published in the original French in *Derrière le miroir*. Leiris also wrote a moving essay about Giacometti's studio when its walls and contents were removed for conservation.

> The first time I saw Samuel Beckett was on a winter's day in Tangiers. The sky was gray, Giacometti's preferred colour, and Beckett walked with great big steps along the deserted beach by the town, his hands behind his back. I crossed his path and it seemed to me he must be a vision. The man all on his own striding across the damp sand of Tangiers, his head in the grey clouds, silent and serene. Was it one of his own characters? Or was it one of Giacometti's own sculptures that had made off? Beckett always made me imagine a Giacometti sculpture rebelling against its maker, escaping and now living far from the studio or any museum.[3]

Sculptor and playwright continued to meet, mostly by chance at the Coupole or one of their favourite bars in Montparnasse, and to follow each other's work as a matter of course. Beckett saw Alberto's shows at Galerie Maeght, where his close artist friend Bram van Velde exhibited regularly, and Alberto sat in on rehearsals of Beckett's plays, being so moved by *Krapp's Last Tape* (written first in English, then translated by the author into French) that he had to leave the theatre before the play ended. Alberto remembered the original production of *Godot* in which at the time the bare tree on stage had been run up out of foam rubber, twisted wire coat hangers and tissue paper. For the new production that Jean-Louis Barrault was putting on at the Théâtre de l'Odéon, Beckett had something less makeshift but equally frail in mind and turned to Alberto (in a letter beginning 'We would all be very pleased …') to ask him to design the set. Alberto shared Beckett's love of trees and began to come up with versions of a slender plaster structure that the two of them then debated when Beckett came to see him in the studio. 'We spent the whole night in the studio with a plaster tree, trying to make it smaller, sparser, the branches thinner,' Alberto told the Italian art writer Giorgio Soavi. 'It never looked any good and neither he nor I liked it. And we kept saying to each other: perhaps like this …'[4]

In the event, both performance and set were a resounding success. Although Beckett characteristically criticised the play, he approved of the set, calling it 'Superb. The only good part of what has been up to now a gloomy exhumation' in a letter to his mistress, the gifted translator Barbara Bray.[5] Alberto's tree remained in the bowels of the building until the Théâtre de l'Odéon was occupied during the May 1968 student

Jean-Marie Serreau, Beckett and Giacometti at a rehearsal of *Waiting for Godot* at the Théâtre de l'Odéon, 1961

uprising and transformed into a theatre of impassioned, political debate, in the course of which the much-discussed prop disappeared.

Alberto's relationships with other old friends did not always take on a new lease of life as they had with Beckett. Balthus was one of the few artists (including their late mutual friend Derain, and Picasso) with whom Alberto enjoyed talking about art. They had seen less and less of each other since Balthus had forsaken Paris to nurture his aristocratic fantasies in the half-ruined Château de Chassy. A new opportunity to gild his social status occurred when Malraux appointed him director of the Villa Medici, the seat of the French Academy in Rome. Balthus, now firmly if spuriously established as the Comte Klossowski de Rola (to the extent of disregarding any letter not addressed to him by his full 'title'), took up his functions with gusto, restoring both the sumptuous palace and its garden (which Velázquez had painted while in Rome) and becoming fast friends with such high-fliers as Federico Fellini and the painter Renato Guttuso. Both down-to-earth and generally downwardly mobile, Alberto regarded his old comrade's ascent with scepticism, regretting that he appeared to set greater store by the Eternal City's upper social stratum than by his painting. If certain friends fell away, new ones did not fail to materialise. Having always been drawn more towards writers than fellow artists, Alberto, who kept abreast of all the main literary reviews, began to take an interest in the new generation of poets. The one who came closest to him was Jacques Dupin, whose literary career had been encouraged by René Char, already established as one of the major French poets of the century.*

Dupin first came into contact with Alberto through the art journal *Cahiers d'art*, which sent him to interview the artist and write an in-depth essay about his work. Their relationship developed further once Dupin began working at Galerie Maeght, where his responsibilities centred on looking after some of the artists, notably Miró and Alberto. Gradually the young poet began putting together a book about the sculptor, with photographs by Scheidegger. (The Swiss photographer and Dupin also made a short, revealing film of Alberto at work in the studio.) Although Alberto had given numerous interviews over the years and been the subject of countless articles and reviews, no substantial publication appeared until Dupin's monograph came out in 1962. The book confirmed the unique fascination not only of the work but also of the artist's personality and way of life. Alberto did not fail to repay the compliment by portraying Dupin, for whom he had already illustrated a recent volume of poems, *L'Epervier* (The Sparrowhawk). While these projects were under way, Dupin spent considerable periods of time with the artist, talking to him in his photogenic lair and accompanying him on his regular beat around Paris. There were the regular conversations

*Char had been invited to travel in the car that was to crash and kill his friend Camus but, being a very big man (and former rugby player), declined because the car was already quite full.

about Alberto's obsessive relationship with his own creativity and with art in general, which Dupin recorded and interpreted with admirable, poetic flair. But their evenings together were by no means limited to aesthetic discussion, as Dupin's account of one particularly eventful occasion illustrates:

> One evening, after we'd had dinner, we went on for drinks at Chez Adrien. I'd been carrying a folder of drawings by Alberto around all evening, about thirty of them, and suddenly I realized I'd left everything at the restaurant. And Caroline, who luckily knew the people at the restaurant, went back there and managed to retrieve them. Then another time, late at night, we were sitting in Chez Adrien, and suddenly these men came in and started shooting at the mirror over the bar. There was some kind of gang war going on. So Alberto, Caroline and I got under the table until it was all over. When we got up, there was a lot of glass all over the place and most people had disappeared. We were a bit shaken up so we went to another bar for a drink, and while we were sitting there the same lot of gangsters came in, but they had calmed down by then, and they simply stood there and had a drink too… Alberto loved that. He thought that was really something![6]

Following his romantic conviction that the crooks, pimps and prostitutes of the underworld were more real, and demonstrably less hypocritical, than the bourgeois he rubbed shoulders with in the art world, Alberto continued to indulge his taste for low life, and in particular his passion for Caroline. Quick to spot a weakness she could exploit, Caroline began making ever greater demands on her besotted admirer, while her 'friends' took to bursting into the studio, roughing him up and extorting cash. This was undoubtedly 'real', and Alberto went along with it, using his curious logic to justify the whole process of being systematically dunned. Since Caroline was now sitting for him regularly (usually in the evening, once Annette had finished her modelling session in the afternoon), and since her time was unarguably as valuable as his, there could be no reason not to share the wealth he had accumulated with her and her threatening colleagues. Caroline was now essential to his art, as he doggedly stated whenever Annette resumed her furious attacks on him: therefore, as in all his past dealings with prostitutes, he was ready and willing to pay the requisite price.

'I know everyone says I'm just a silly old man in love with a young woman, but that's far from being the case,' Alberto remarked to his American admirer Herbert Lust. 'She's an explosion of nature, that's what. You know how I feel about night people. I also am of the night, and so is Caroline – a real night creature. Sure, she's beautiful, but you'll see, she can keep up a conversation as well as anyone. She has a real mind. She has real courage … she knows fear, but still she takes enormous risks, the biggest risks.'[7] Certainly, his infatuation had manic aspects, and Caroline appears to have exploited these by continuing to disappear periodically without warning or explanation, leaving Alberto beside himself with anxiety. In those periods, friends reported seeing him haunt the bars and cafés in search of her or dodging into doorways as he followed her to find out where she was going and with whom. As with Marlene Dietrich (although for very different reasons), it is unlikely that Alberto had conventional sexual relations with Caroline, not only because of the difficulties he frequently experienced, but because what he wanted above all was to adore her as a creature beyond defilement, a goddess. One instance of this consecration is the fetishistic pact he made with her to 'purchase' and thus own a small section of her right foot, just above the heel. In their perverse but inescapably human transactions, she shared with him every intimate secret of her 'work', and there is a strong suggestion that Alberto accepted her offer to watch certain acts she performed with clients.[8]

Among Caroline's many passions (alongside sports cars, pearls and the pet toads and other animals she kept at home) was gambling. Like all true gamblers, she loved it whether she won or lost, convinced that 'you always win because you always have the sensation'. Alberto appeared to encourage her every fantasy. The occasional exchange of letters between the two lovers gives fleeting insights into what remains a highly unusual, hermetic relationship in which nothing can be taken at face value. 'I don't understand you anymore, you're just too weird,' went one of her letters to him. 'I don't know what to think. I'm really sad despite it all. You're too complicated. I don't know what you want. You're just a dirty brute. Caroline.'[9] These comments, coming ostensibly after a falling-out, suggest feelings that are more than plain venal, with Alberto taking on a conciliatory tone: 'It is absurd, Caroline, to be jealous of me, no one can be jealous on my account. You know, Caroline, that for me love is very different from the usual idea of love, therefore no one should be unhappy because of it.'[10]

However definitively he had distanced himself from Sartre, Picasso and Balthus, Alberto never sought to cut his ties with Annette even though he was adamant about Caroline remaining at the centre of his life; one might surmise that he also dreaded the reaction that his aged mother would have if he and Annette formally separated. His love was indeed 'very different from the usual idea of love' since he not only appeared to accept Annette's affair with Yanaihara (while professing he would welcome other, similar dalliances for her), but also tried to persuade Annette to accept Caroline. To some extent, he succeeded, to judge from a photograph of all three of them sharing a bottle of Pommery champagne at the Villa Borghese, a fashionable restaurant in Montparnasse. It shows Annette grinning heroically, Alberto staring gloomily at the camera and Caroline fixing her gaze primly elsewhere. As a threesome, it was never going to work, but Alberto was still deeply attached to Annette who was, after all, 'family' and who remained the central pillar of his domestic and working routine. Fond of her as he remained, he felt that she would never be able to understand him in the way he believed Caroline did, as this reported dialogue with Herbert Lust implies:

AG: I've tried explaining myself to Annette because I love her so much. She isn't capable, for whatever reason, of understanding what I'm saying. She seems to understand sometimes but it's more like a kneeling to fear, or something like that. You keep on babbling that we argue all the time, but it's not true that we argue. I'm just trying to make her understand who I am, and she doesn't, or rather, dear thing that she is, just can't.

HL: Caroline can?

AG: Yes, she understands me in everything, just everything … I can say things to her that I never thought about saying to anyone and she so knows what I mean that it amazes me … I've always been afraid that I would die before I ever lived in a full way, now at last I've lived, and lived to the hilt, before my death.[11]

From early on Alberto had experienced intimations of mortality but as he approached his sixtieth birthday in October 1961, he grew more acutely aware of the passing of time and his increasingly apparent decrepitude. 'I'm an old man. Don't you think I've aged terribly? I just can't work. I'm a little old man,' he quipped frequently to Yanaihara as their portrait sessions, now in their fourth year, drew to a close.[12] Overwork, incessant fatigue, excessive smoking and a poor diet had taken a visible toll on a man whose sturdy, mountain-bred physique should have allowed him to survive to a venerable old age, like his brothers: Diego would live to eighty-four and Bruno to 104. Friends noted how deeply lined and sallow his face now looked and how stooped his frame, racked by a deep, bronchial cough, had grown, while people meeting him for the first time, taken aback by his bloodshot eyes and neglected appearance, thought he looked a good ten years older than he actually was. None of this caused Alberto to change his gruelling routine one jot, however. He continued to work at all hours and fret over the results achieved while smoking pack after pack of his favourite American cigarettes, never resting properly and preferring aperitifs like Rossi and slugs of whisky to regular meals. Many of Alberto's contemporaries were similarly negligent of their health; on top of a daily intake of amphetamines and every other stimulant, Sartre, for instance, worked manically, slept little and ate almost nothing but sausages.

Yet even at his busiest and most exhausted, Alberto was always ready to talk, often while continuing the work in hand, as if both processes were so familiar, so instinctive, that they could be performed in tandem. Dupin claims the artist needed to be talking constantly, to the extent that, as he approached the studio, he often used to hear Alberto chatting animatedly to himself.* When his sixtieth birthday did come round, Alberto could think of no better way of commemorating it than to speak, at length, in a reflective but upbeat manner, to a tried and trusted interlocutor, the Swiss art historian Gotthard Jedlicka. Yet, as always when giving an interview, Alberto was following his own intuition that he wanted to explore and record, so that it could become part of the already considerable archive of statements he had made:

*Dupin, in conversation with the author, Paris, 2010.

> I find it harder and harder to finish my work. The older I become, the lonelier I become. I can see that in the end I will be completely on my own. Even if everything I have made so far counts for absolutely nothing (counts for nothing compared to what I would like to make), and even knowing that I have failed and having found everything I set out to do evaporates in my very hands, I now feel more like working than ever. Can you understand that? I don't understand it but that's how it is. I see my sculptures before me: each one a fragment, even the apparently finished ones, each one a failure. Yes, I mean it, a failure! But in each one there is also something of what I want to create one day. In one there is this, in another there is that, in a third there is something that is lacking in the first two, but the sculpture that I have in mind has all those elements which only appear in isolation and fragmented in other sculptures. That fills me with desire, unbounded desire, to go on with my work – and one day maybe I will reach my goal after all.[13]

Alberto gave several interviews to Jedlicka as well as to a variety of art critics and journalists in his mid- to late career. In retrospect, this appears to have been a semi-conscious decision. From the early 1930s through to the early 1950s, he had written and published his own texts, the most notable being the Surrealist-influenced, autobiographical 'Yesterday, Shifting Sands' and 'The Dream, the Sphinx and the Death of T.' as well as his 'Tentative catalogue of early works' and 'Letter to Pierre Matisse' published in the catalogue of the breakthrough New York exhibition of 1948. As his own writings grew rarer, the interviews became more frequent, as if he had decided that they provided a better (and less time-consuming) means of analysing, as well as publicising, his artistic dilemmas while formulating occasional, hesitant conclusions. In the course of a score of such interviews, Alberto created a full, parallel 'guide' and glossary to his work, especially to its origins and his own thought processes as he created it. Although some of the texts verge on repetitive, returning incessantly to a handful of well-defined themes, they remain an extraordinary resource for understanding both the work and the man.

Since Alberto was an especially engaging talker, with a love of paradox and dialectical reasoning, the interviews are often entertaining in themselves, particularly since, by this time, his command of

French, honed by Homeric discussions with the most intelligent and fluent French speakers of the age, was impressive yet markedly individualistic: over the years, he had created a French that served his needs specifically. Of the interviews readily available in English, perhaps the most complete are those conducted in 1964 by David Sylvester, in which one extract captures the artist's manic, reductive approach to art admirably:

> In 1950 I painted a whole series of sculptures. But as you paint them you see what's wrong with the form. And there's no point in painting something you don't believe in. I tried again, only a month ago. Painting brings out the deficiency in the form. Well, I can't waste time fooling myself that I've achieved something by painting it if there's nothing underneath. So I have to sacrifice the painting and try and do the form. In the same way as I have to sacrifice the whole figure to try and do the head. And as I have to sacrifice the whole landscape to try and do one leaf. And as I have to sacrifice all objects to do a glass. You can only get to do anything by limiting yourself to an extremely small field. Up to only a year ago I believed it was much easier to draw a tablecloth than a head. I still think so, in theory. But a few months ago, I spent three or four days simply trying to draw the cloth on a round table, and it seemed to me totally impossible to draw it as I saw it. I should really not have given up on the tablecloth until I had got a better idea of whether I could do it or not. But in that case I would have had to sacrifice painting, sculpture, heads and everything else, confine myself to a single room and reduce my entire activity to sitting in front of the same table, the same cloth and the same chair. And it's easy to foresee that the more I tried, the more difficult it would become. So I'd be reducing my life to practically nothing. That would be a bit worrying, though, because one doesn't want to sacrifice everything! Yet it's the only thing one ought to do. Perhaps. I don't know.
>
> At any rate, since I've become much more responsive to the distance between a table and a chair – fifty centimetres – a room, any room, has become infinitely larger than before. In a way it's become as

> vast as the world. So it's all I need to live in. So that has gradually put an end to going for walks. That's why I don't go for walks any more. When I go out, it's to go to the café, which is necessary, and then I prefer to go by car rather than on foot, since it's no longer for the pleasure of taking a walk. The pleasure of an outing to the forest has completely disappeared for me, because one tree on a Paris pavement is already enough. One tree is enough for me; the thought of seeing two is frightening.[14]

Apart from being a lucid autobiographical fragment, the passage makes it sound as if it had been taken for granted that art in the post-war world had to be reinvented and redefined, root and branch. The piece is also so suggestive of the Absurd that the voice of Molloy* echoes in every phrase; rather than Alberto and Sylvester, it could be Vladimir and Estragon, or indeed any of Beckett's disillusioned, disinherited tribe talking about their ever-shrinking existence. For anyone who still doubts the uncanny way in which Swiss artist and Irish writer blend, the proof that they do is surely confirmed here.

What reading the range of interviews Alberto gave throughout his career also confirms is his ability to dissect the contradictions in his own work and life more persistently and passionately than anyone, as if he were perpetually engaged in a complicated game of his own devising. Some of his convictions – such as the necessity of failing – were unshakeable, as if they were the tenets of a new faith. These return time and again in his statements, as if, like the writer he also was, he sought to make them more pithy and telling over the years. Occasionally this comes through in a single phrase, like a decisive line or brushstroke, summing up a whole page of woollier thought. It would take an entire book to evaluate the interviews in depth, but it is worth quoting a few of these instances here:

> The object of art is not to reproduce reality, but to create a reality of the same intensity.

*First written in French, then translated into English by Beckett and Patrick Bowles, *Molloy* was published by the Editions de Minuit in Paris in 1951. Beckett had wanted Alberto to produce an image for the cover, but the project did not materialise.

> [Art is] the residue of vision.
>
> The form is always the measure of the obsession.
>
> The more you fail, the more you succeed. It is only when everything is lost and – instead of giving up – you go on, that you experience the momentary prospect of some slight progress.
>
> Failure is my best friend. If I succeeded, it would be like dying. Maybe worse.
>
> When I make my drawings … the path traced by my pencil on the sheet of paper to some extent resembles the gesture of a man groping his way in the darkness.
>
> The head is what matters. The rest of the body plays the part of antennae making life possible for people and life itself is inside the skull.
>
> All the sculptures of today, like those of the past, will end one day in pieces … So it is important to fashion one's work carefully in its smallest recess and charge every particle of matter with life.
>
> The real adventure is to watch something unknown emerge each day on the same face – that's worth more than any journey around the world.
>
> I paint and sculpt to get a grip on reality … to protect myself.
>
> All the art of the past rises up before me, the art of all ages and all civilisations, everything becomes simultaneous, as if space had replaced time.

As his sixtieth birthday came and went, Alberto was so rushed off his feet by a spate of awards and new exhibitions that even he could hardly find time to indulge in lengthy conversations. In June 1962 his fourth and, as it turned out, last show at Galerie Maeght took place with twenty-two sculptures, including Standing Women, Walking Men and the huge Head that he had made for Chase Manhattan Plaza, and twenty-four paintings. Most of the paintings were portraits, six of them of Yanaihara, who had paid his last visit to the Giacomettis the previous summer. Among pictures of Annette, Diego and Madame Maeght were six unusually 'visionary' portraits of an unknown model, some of them very large, entitled simply 'Seated Woman'. Where the previous portraits waved and waned, advanced and receded as visitors watched, these abruptly frontal images dominate their grey-ochre space implacably. If ever Alberto managed to achieve Sartre's 'pure presence' again, it was in these painterly incarnations of the woman who had taken on such a central – and manifestly immoveable – importance in his life. As usual, the artist was still gnawed by dissatisfaction, complaining both to Maeght, then to Pierre Matisse (who showed much the same exhibition later that year), that if he had been given more time the work would have been far better. Both events were highly successful, with Alberto's reputation in America becoming more officially established in 1961 when he was awarded the Carnegie Prize for Sculpture (which, Alberto remarked, pleased him because he knew it would particularly please his mother).

While working on both shows up until the last minute took up plenty of time, even greater things were in the offing. In 1962, the Venice Biennale suggested a retrospective for which an ample space had been earmarked. Barely had Alberto visited the city to see his exhibition pavilion than the Kunsthaus in Zurich announced their decision to hold an even larger exhibition of his work – indeed, the largest to date. Gratified as he was, Alberto focused first and foremost on Venice, because he had known the city for years and loved it, but also because he knew that a success at the Biennale would be a well-publicised, international success, boding well for future shows. Conscious, for all his long-practised, unassuming demeanour, of his growing fame abroad, the artist had set his heart on being awarded not only the Biennale's prize for sculpture (which was almost a foregone conclusion) but also, since he was exhibiting numerous pictures as well, for painting. In an all-out effort to gather up the very best of his work, Alberto involved Clayeux and both his dealers in the selection process, choosing about fifty sculptures from the *Spoon Woman* (1926–7) onwards, with as many paintings and drawings, too. He intended to oversee the hanging of the show to the last detail, and he took both Diego and Clayeux along to help him. Having decided to place the work not chronologically but in related groups, adjusting the height of their stands (above all on the Chase Manhattan pieces), Alberto wove to and fro through the designated pavilions, trying out numerous combinations until he felt as sure as he was ever going to feel that he had found the least bad combinations.

After exhausting sessions of trial and error, with his assistants kept mainly commenting on the sidelines, Alberto would continue to develop his curatorial strategy once ensconced in the congenial interior of Harry's Bar, where the famous Bellini cocktail was invented. It may have been there that, emboldened by a drink or two, he first thought of applying dashes of colour to certain sculptures, despite the fact that they had long left the studio and now belonged to a variety of collections. Having warmed to the idea, Alberto swept aside any objections about owners' rights, insisting that this was the *ultima mano* he would apply. Grudgingly he did, however, accept the advice from his friends, Pierre and Patricia Matisse as well as Michel and Zette Leiris, not to refuse the sculpture prize if he were not awarded the painting prize as well. Usually the last to seek recognition, the artist had felt that winning a prize for only one of the two arts he practised with equal intensity would devalue the other. In the end, Alberto was nominated for the Grand Prix for sculpture only. Mollified perhaps by the summer light as it glanced off the water and played over the ancient, patrician façades lining the Grand Canal, unchanged since Tintoretto saw them on his way to decorate the Scuola Grande, he accepted the honour and the celebrations that followed with good grace.

Once those sumptuous festivities had been rounded off with a farewell grappa, Alberto was back on the road, heading for Zurich where the Kunsthaus had brought together some three hundred pieces, a few of them dating all the way back to Alberto's childhood – no doubt to underline the innate Swissness of his artistic stirrings. In the Kunsthaus's modernist spaces, the selection provided a complete overview of the artist's achievement to date and won instant acclaim from cognoscenti and well-wishers alike, many of whom had travelled from abroad to attend the event. Among the many honours conferred, the distinguished Swiss art magazine *Du* devoted an entire issue to the show. Less expected was the controversy that Alberto's figures, with their gaunt frames and intense stares, stirred up among local visitors, who came in droves to the well-publicised exhibition. Having next to no experience of the artist's unsparing vision, they were quickly discomfited, then appalled, by the violence of the Surrealist constructions that led without explanation to thickets of hallucinatory, fleshless figures that reminded them inescapably of the photographs they had seen of concentration camp survivors. The disquiet provoked a drawn-out debate in the local press, adding to the number of journalists craving an interview with the now internationally famous artist. Despite the exhibition's success, this contretemps also caused the Zurich city council to draw in its horns and vote against the recent proposal to establish an Alberto Giacometti Foundation. In his contrary fashion, and as a former Surrealist, Alberto may well have relished a bit of opposition, remembering Breton's pleasure in antagonising the public ('How wonderful to be reviled at our age!'). But Zurich had done him proud and, given the dearth of famous sons to celebrate in Switzerland, the Foundation would come about in its own time if it was going to come about at all; no one knew better than Alberto that the best way to court fame was by showing it the back of your hand. The most urgent thing, now that the hue and cry had died down, was to get back to work and try to make an image at last that corresponded to what he actually saw.

Zurich's cavernous Hauptbahnhof was as crowded as the exhibition openings and receptions had been, but here people seemed driven by a specific purpose, running down platforms, hugging each other, boarding a train with bags, a sandwich clenched in their jaws. Children were crying, lovers parting, old men eyeing the station clock anxiously. Alberto limped past them all, enjoying his sudden anonymity. But perhaps the people – people like these, rushing to get home, to get away – were right. They had basically declared that he had no talent, had no right to go messing people's appearance about to the extent that their own mothers would not recognise them. They said he couldn't draw a figure or a face, couldn't draw a nose, come to that. And they were right. He'd said it himself more than once. It was all very well for the art officials and the dealers and the collectors to crowd round and congratulate him and say how marvellous, but were they looking at the work itself – like Genet did, like Dupin did – or were they looking at all the collections it was in now, how well known it was becoming, with all the prices going up a treat?

He found his carriage and clambered up the steps with his suitcase, only a little bigger and of slightly better quality than the one with which he had arrived in Paris all those years ago. He settled back into his window

Alberto, December 1962

seat. It was padded and much more comfortable than the wooden seats they'd had then, but he had been young and eager and now he was sixty and exhausted, beyond exhausted, with a tiredness that had crept into his bones years ago and lodged there. It seemed to have brought all kind of ailments into his body – aches, worsening coughing fits, and now a persistent pain that flared up almost unbearably in his stomach. He could not go on, he simply could not go on; but he would go on, he would go on until he dropped, not least because there was nothing else to do. Perhaps he could drift into a long sleep, a rejuvenating sleep, in this compartment, where he was huddled by the window and the only other passenger was sitting over by the corridor. It was an ideal place to forget about everything, to dream, to escape, perhaps even to be reunited with Caroline. With Caroline he could forget about art; she thought the whole thing was just a load of old junk, and in many ways of course she was not wrong. The people in Zurich had seen through the whole thing, too. They knew he was an impostor, a sly character on the make, palming off some complicated, highfalutin rubbish. What difference did it make, all the heads in the world staring out at the world, questioning the world, uncomprehending? Why would you go on asking the same questions, in this fancy or that convoluted way, when you knew all the time that you would never get an answer? It was a pointless thing to do. But then life itself was pointless, the whole thing was pointless. The people knew that, too. They didn't have to ask Sartre. They had always known.

The train rumbled on. Perhaps they were crossing the Vosges mountains and the forests now. Night had fallen a while ago and from the train everything looked very dark. The darkness of the trees in the darkness of the night, in the darkness in his mind. The pain stabbed at him again. His ribcage hurt. He peered through the window. It was pitch black now. As he looked hard into the night, it seemed to grow darker still.

12

Paris Without End (1963–66)

Two shows at leading galleries in Paris and New York, a couple of key museum retrospectives with a Venice Grand Prix thrown in, formal tributes and rave reviews in the press. Then this searing pain in his belly that doubled him up, reducing in a trice all the hectic success, the toasts and sparkling wine, the flash photography and admiring crowds to nothing.

The pains seemed to come out of the blue but tracing them back he knew they had been there, building up, for years. He'd almost encouraged them, smoking more, sleeping less and ignoring all the unpleasant warning signs. It was nerves, he had told himself, simply nerves, when his stomach clenched into a tight ball or suddenly flooded with acid like the bad white wine you get in Montparnasse clipjoints late at night. By now his appetite had almost gone. Having your own table at the Coupole sounded all very fine, but what good was it if you didn't even know what to order, what would do you the least harm, then barely picked at the dishes the waiters brought over? Even the hard-boiled eggs he used to crack and gobble down off the local café counter made him feel queasy. He was a shadow of himself, half dead, half alive – like one of the sculptures he had spent his life trying to get right.

Looking at himself in the mirror, Alberto saw one of his busts staring back at him. Its head was as lifeless as the clay he kneaded, its eyes bruised with the strain of trying to understand what they saw. That had always been his defence against life: to capture what he saw before it captured him. It was also his defence against death. That was what art was for. The cavemen and Egyptians had known it, the tribal sculptors still knew it, summoning ancestors through the masks and objects they carved. So what an irony (he would have croaked with laughter if his gut didn't hurt so much) that it was 'art' that had made him ill. The frenzied search, the endless revision, the vanity of it all … If only he could succeed, just the once, he wouldn't have to go through the whole thing again. He could leave it all behind, get away from it and eat and sleep like everyone else. He could have a life.

Ida Kar, Alberto outside his studio, 1954

It took only a few days back at rue Hippolyte in the winter of 1963 for the glitter of Venice and Zurich to sink and disappear into the grey dust of the studio, the dust that was in the air and everywhere. Dust was the only certainty, the one eternity we could be sure of. That was where all life was heading, dust to dust. As soon as he got back into work his fear of death would recede: the two seemed to hold each other in check. His hand had already started tracing lines over a grubby sheet of Rives paper, then his stomach rose again, filling with acid. He lit another Lucky Strike. Chain-smoking the delicious little white tubes calmed the pain at first, then a coughing fit racked his body and he began to vomit bile. His whole instinct went against admitting that he was ill, that he couldn't go on – he would go on, he could only go on – but the pain was so constant and so acute now that there was no chance he could get back into his gruelling studio routine.

A creature of habit in everything he did, Alberto could only think of hobbling back to Dr Fraenkel, whom he had consulted ever since their days as fellow Surrealists and the literature-loving doctor's near-fatal misdiagnosis of his appendicitis. Fraenkel began by assuring him once again that nothing was seriously amiss, but faced with Alberto's increasingly alarming appearance he referred him to their mutual friend Dr Leibovici, the surgeon who had set his fractured ankle a quarter of a century earlier. After taking X-rays, Leibovici acted promptly, suspecting that what might have begun as a gastric ulcer had developed into a full-blown malignant tumour. He told Alberto he would have to remove a large part of his stomach, never mentioning the word cancer for fear of alarming his patient. There he got things quite wrong. Alberto had frequently declared to his friends that, if he were to have a serious illness, he would choose cancer as the most challenging and therefore most interesting illness one could have, and subsequently he asked Fraenkel point blank whether he had it. Solemnly sworn to secrecy by Leibovici, Fraenkel protested that he did not – an equivocation that Alberto later condemned as a treacherous lie, vowing to cut all further contact with the unfortunate physician (who would die less than a year later).

True to his word, Alberto took a keen interest in his condition once he had discovered that he did indeed have cancer, even writing a short account of how he had bellowed with fear during his gastroscopy.[1] The operation, which removed four-fifths of his stomach, was brutal but successful, and during the two weeks he stayed at the Remy-de-Gourmont clinic, next to the Buttes-Chaumont park in northern Paris, he felt well enough to get out of bed, walk around and even start modelling a few clay figures. Ever the contrarian, Alberto appears to have drawn considerable satisfaction from the whole gruelling experience, making optimistic plans for the future and jotting them down in a notebook. 'Start everything from scratch, people and things as I see them, particularly people and heads, their eyes on the horizon, the curve of their eyes …' he notes, only to conclude: 'I no longer understand anything about life, about death, about anything.'[2] Later, as he was convalescing, Alberto expanded on his thoughts in hospital, saying that he had been in a kind of 'morbid exaltation' at the thought that he might die at any moment, and that he was still attracted to the idea of being told that he had only two months left to live: 'To live two months knowing that one was about to die, that would be worth twenty years of unawareness.'[3]

Not surprisingly, life and death, age and youth, remained very much on Alberto's mind. Whereas he had frequently complained, particularly to Yanaihara, about how old he had grown, now that he had survived his radical operation he began to proclaim the very reverse: how young he felt. Having returned to convalesce more fully in Stampa, where he could be cared for by his ageing mother, he remarked with characteristic contrariness, 'I'm still young, whereas all my contemporaries in Stampa are old men, because they've accepted old age. Their lives are already in the past. But mine is still in the future. It's only now that I can envisage the possibility of trying to start on my life's work. But if one could ever really begin, if one could have made a start, then it would be unnecessary to go any further, because the end is implicitly in the realization of the beginning.'[4]

Once he had returned to Paris, restored by the mountain air and regular, home-cooked meals, he sounded even more buoyant, writing to Pierre Matisse that he had now resumed his old routine completely, apart from having cut out both aperitifs and whisky (although there were exceptions: he found it impossible to resist a Campari, and a grappa was welcome at the end of a meal, however little he had managed to eat). While Alberto continued to remain upbeat, resuming his nightly escapades with Caroline around Montparnasse, close friends and other visitors to rue Hippolyte voiced their concerns. Even Brassaï, nicknamed (by Henry Miller) the 'eye of Paris' and used to its seamier sights, was alarmed to find Alberto so thin and haggard, yet still bound to his punishing routine, when he met up with him: 'At the café-tabac, Alberto, who was ravenous, downed a sandwich and some hard-boiled eggs that were set out on the bar. He lit one cigarette after another. I was upset to see that he wasn't taking better care of himself. The life he led, filled as it was with feverish, disorderly and obsessive work, was ridiculous, and I was afraid he wouldn't be able to keep up his present pace for long.'[5]

Alberto's only concession to his wellbeing was to take a room at the Hôtel Aiglon, close by on boulevard Raspail, so as to sleep more comfortably than in the cold, damp studio. Often he lingered in the bedroom, feeling the need to situate himself in the unfamiliar space; as he had once said, 'Space does not exist. You have to create it.' He explored that concept throughout, and not least in that hotel room in a memorable series of drawings where the pencil lines representing a small table and a tall window are partly erased, fracturing the outlines as if they had not yet fully coalesced in his own mind.[6] If Alberto were diminished physically, his graphic gifts were unimpaired, even heightened, since these studies rival even Cézanne's watercolours in the revealing way in which they suggest how light both structures and dislocates space.

Another change to Alberto's routine, after decades punctuated almost exclusively by visits to Stampa, was his sudden wanderlust. Perhaps he was less tied to Paris now that so many of his friends had left or died. Or maybe he was relieved occasionally to escape the extortionate demands of Caroline's thuggish crew. At all events, Jan Krugier, the flamboyant Polish-born art dealer close to Picasso, had recently opened a gallery in Geneva's old town and dedicated one of his first exhibitions to Alberto's work. To show his appreciation, the artist made a special trip in summer 1963. He then travelled on to meet another dealer, Ernst Beyeler, whose gallery, formerly an antiquarian bookshop, was already well established in Basel. Beyeler had been in contact with the American collector G. David Thompson, who had by now put together the largest holding of works by Giacometti in the world, destined for the private museum that the magnate had planned. Thompson's project fell through, however, and Beyeler had moved in to negotiate the purchase of the entire collection. From this the Swiss dealer put on a select, curated show which delighted Alberto because it enabled him to revisit work that he had not seen in decades. To the numerous sculptures, paintings and drawings which were eventually acquired with the support of local patrons and collectors, Alberto added a few more recent pieces, and in 1965 this selection furnished the wherewithal for an Alberto Giacometti Foundation, consisting of around one hundred works divided between the museums of Zurich, Basel and Winterthur.

Long so reluctant to be prised out of his studio shell, Alberto would now indulge this new-found taste for travel by going as far afield as London, New York and Copenhagen. Before leaving Switzerland, he also took advantage of the comfortable night train to Milan to see Michelangelo's final sculpture, the *Rondanini Pietà*, in the Castello Sforzesco. It was surely no coincidence that, having walked so recently in the shadow of death, Alberto went deliberately out of his way to look at the very last work of a sculptor whom he had admired since childhood, and whose tomb figures in the Medici Chapel in Florence he had copied as a very young man. What would surely have moved him most in the *Pietà*, on which Michelangelo was still working days before he died, was the torso of Christ struggling to emerge from the stone.* It was the ultimate sculpture, half frozen in its own white marble, perfect in its arrested state between real, breathing life and inert matter, and more evocative than it would ever have been if completed.

On his return to Paris, Alberto renewed his conscious effort to fully restore the studio routine that had been evolving infinitesimally for nearly forty years. He knew the space so well that he once said he carried it in miniature, with all its tiny objects, around with him in his head. It was both inside him and outside him, and constantly in flux as his paintbrush pecked at an ear or rounded an eyebrow, as a drawing fluttered forgotten to the floor, as the sculptures rose and fell, like disintegrating soldiers, phantoms from another age. If he had absorbed the studio, the apparently derelict space had also absorbed him.

He had been modelling from memory all night, through all those marvellous hours of dark stillness when there was just enough noise – a dog barking, a drunk cursing – to know that it was not the silence of

*It is interesting to think that the *non finito*, which appealed to Michelangelo and Rodin, could be said to characterise *all* Alberto's post-Surrealist work. No Giacometti, whether sculpture, painting or drawing, as the artist himself insisted, was ever 'complete', thus undermining the whole concept. Once everything is *non finito*, it becomes *finito*.

Michelangelo's *Pietà Rondanini*, 1956

the grave and that life still surrounded him as his fingers moved up and down the column of dark grey flesh, seeking the likeness, the 'residue of a vision', that lay like a sediment in the mysterious flickering in his mind. Exhaustion came and went in waves as the air turned into pure cigarette smoke and the sky lightened into a thunderous grey dawn.

By morning he was in bed, but now he was too tired to sleep. The sculptures kept reappearing under his closed eyes. The tribe of gaunt spectres he had been plucking out of the night would be his guardians, accompanying him to the grave. They were all there, a Praetorian Guard reduced to the bone. The clay ones he had just been working on, safely under damp wraps for the moment, blind, invisible, but there, breathing faintly beneath their rags. Then the plasters, held in an intermediate existence, ghostly in their whiteness, as if dressed for an operation in hospital, cold, static, less alive than they had been in their original earthy version. Then the bronzes, massive, confrontational, yet delicately imprinted with a thousand finger marks, enduring, their patinas catching the changing light of day, then the muted glint of night.

The coughing fits began again, then slowly they subsided into a wheezy rattling in his lungs. Exhaustion started releasing him from its grip. It was late, it was light, the day was grey, the bulb was still burning. His breathing was growing easier, he was drifting mercifully into sleep. '*A demain*,' he whispered to himself. 'I'll see you tomorrow, won't I, Caroline? You'll wear that pretty red dress … Caroline?'

She had come into his life at a moment when he was already resigned to growing older and lonelier, emerging as sharply and decisively as his cancer, except he would fight tooth and nail to keep her and let her burrow into every crevice of his existence. He had felt attraction often and every now and then real affection. Annette had helped lift him out of a dead end and made him happy for several years before he realised, once and for all, that they were too different, wanting such contrary things from life, ever to grow closer. What had happened with Caroline had never happened before – a closeness that had no barriers, an obsession, a need that had become part of him and of his art. Perhaps, having gone further in his work, he needed to go further in his love, needed to push his love to endless, questing extremes. Annette still came, she had only half moved out, and once she had tidied things up, she sat for him, in her neat cardigan and pleated skirt, almost as if nothing had changed. From time to time, when the jealous fits and rows died down, it did seem as if nothing had changed. She disappeared into the picture, as she had always done, as Diego had done, becoming everyone and no one, and often he no longer knew who was sitting there a couple of feet away. Only when the long dialogue between sitter and image had ended did they even begin to be themselves again, real people rather than immobile models.

When Caroline arrived well into the evening, Annette had left for her other life, and the hubbub of the day was slowly dying down. The light had faded, too, although it was still summer, and together they eased into the darkness, creatures of the night. Under the electric bulb burning overhead, they might have been at a bar, opening up to each other over the first few drinks, basking in the whisky warmth, but now, as a new sitting got under way, the concentration was total, with his eyes probing her green-gold eyes, she as motionless as if she were tied to the chair, in bondage, under strict interrogation, as he wielded his brush over her and her reality. The limping old man with all his infirmities and deficiencies was now the master, in total command of who she would be. Neither life nor work had ever given him so much. Their eyes locked, the brush jabbed feverishly, spurting marks, making and unmaking, creating her and destroying her at will for hours on end. Never had Alberto maintained such a frenzy of pure energy, with all his inner longing and excessiveness let loose. When he painted Caroline he was painting his own madness.

Alberto's fame seemed to have found a momentum of its own. He might still hamper its progress by announcing, disingenuously enough, that his art was worthless and his talents nil, that all his efforts had only barely begun, but by now he was caught up in the whole momentum, with one success avalanching into others. 'I resisted the intrusion of success and recognition as long as I could,' he remarked at the time. 'But maybe the best way to obtain success is to run away from it. Anyway, since the Biennale it's been much harder to resist. I've refused a lot of exhibitions, but one can't go on refusing for ever. That wouldn't make any sense.'[7]

With the Zurich exhibition barely over, another was about to open at the Phillips Collection in Washington, and that was to mushroom into ever larger retrospectives at two of the world's major modern art museums, the Tate in London and MoMA in New York (the latter then travelled across the US to Chicago, Los Angeles and San Francisco). In his new guise as world traveller, Alberto even made the journey to Denmark, where his work was presented at the Louisiana Museum of Modern Art, set in its own landscaped sculpture garden overlooking the sea. All these events would in turn spawn reviews and essays, photographs in newspapers and on the covers of magazines, further Grands Prix and memberships of such august institutions as the American Academy, as well as an honorary doctorate from the University of Bern.

While juggling constant overwork with an overwrought private life, Alberto remained available to a growing spectrum of art world eminences and admirers. He even allowed himself to be interviewed for a film for the first time in 1963, talking freely to its director, Jean-Marie Drot, while at work at rue Hippolyte and during a visit to his exhibition in Zurich. By this time, Alberto had developed a 'line' – as many artists do – that he had been fine-tuning over decades of discussion. (This tendency in artists caused Beckett to reflect caustically: 'It's not always easy to say which of both, the painting or the artist's talk about it, is the egg and which is the hen.'[8]) By this stage, the artist had taken to lamenting not only the impossible demands of his artistic aims, but the impossible demands they in turn made on his life. Drot's film, *Un homme parmi les hommes* (A Man Among Men), thus opens with a fluent résumé from the artist of his daily round:

> I work all the time. It's not an act of will, it's because I can't turn myself off. My brother sits from midday to half past one, then I putter about, then I spend an hour next door for a bite to eat, and then my wife poses from four to nightfall, then I start again on the same things, I'll go drink a coffee, and then at nine I begin again till midnight. I don't go out on the town at all. Then I'll go out for dinner, I'm half dead, I've no appetite, I hang around a bit, I down a few whiskies and go home. I have to get to bed by three in the morning to be more or less up the next day. It's like being in a chain gang.[9]

Although much of what Alberto goes on to say in the film is familiar from earlier, almost formulaic statements he made, the effect is brought to life vividly by his voice and his physical presence. Watching and listening to him, one becomes more aware of the essentially philosophical basis of his approach to art, to the extent that he reviews the works filmed at the Kunsthaus as little more than the by-products of his overriding search solely to define and record the outside world as he perceives it. He reduces his whole body of work – consecrated in the museum's sleek, modernist interior – to 'essays' or 'sketches', mere traces of a far more demanding undertaking that has barely begun, and so comes across more deeply involved in the theoretical rationale for his work than in the making of it. Although he does not say it here, Alberto had already declared that, if an artisan could actually produce the work for him as he himself saw it, he would be delighted. There is a strange charm to hearing this famous, and strikingly photogenic, artist dismiss his own achievement with such implacable logic, and no less so since the argument is delivered with engaging warmth and a sense of humour.

Given the range of his activity in and outside the studio, as well as his diminished state of health, one might have imagined that Alberto had given up making prints regularly for Maeght to publish. Its graphic sales having grown very nicely, however, the gallery was now keen to take as many lithographs as Alberto could produce. The number of poet friends with new books in need of illustration had grown to include Olivier Larronde (one of Genet's former lovers) who, with his equally charismatic partner Jean-Pierre Lacloche, had grown close to both Alberto and Annette. Another was the intriguing Ilia Zdanevich (known as 'Iliazd'), a Georgian-born avant-garde poet and publisher close to many of the leading artists in Paris, whom Alberto portrayed in a remarkable series of etchings. As he went further into print-making, Alberto studied the various techniques that he might adopt, making frequent visits to the Mourlot atelier, not far away on the Butte-aux-Cailles,* where many leading artists (including Braque, Léger and Picasso) went to work directly on the lithographic stone or oversee and correct their prints. The particular challenge that Alberto faced was to recreate his characteristic spectrum of subtle greys in a medium more suited to bold contrasts and linear designs, and his success here is directly linked to his technical sensitivity and prowess. When Tériade, who printed his magazine *Verve* at Mourlot's, saw how involved Alberto had become with print techniques, he suggested that he start working on a book about Paris, a project that advanced slowly over several years before being published, posthumously, as *Paris Without End.*

A manic, relentless routine that would have exhausted a much younger man did not keep death at bay, any more than the light that burned at rue Hippolyte through the night. In 1963 alone, Alberto lost several old friends and long-standing allies, including Braque, Cocteau and Tzara, all of whom he had known since his early days in Paris. He felt the loss of Braque most keenly, paying his respects in a series of poignant drawings of the artist on his deathbed. One of them records the finality

*A neighbourhood in the 13th *arrondissement* that translates as 'Quail Hill'. Atelier Mourlot had started out printing wallpaper in the mid-nineteenth century, then posters, then fine art prints.

of death in an unflinching perspective that shows Braque laid out from his bony hands up to the sagging flesh under his chin. Alberto was also moved to write one of his last texts, an homage to Braque in which he describes the artist's late paintings as more daring and modern than the more famous Cubist works on which his reputation had been founded.[10]

Ernst Scheidegger, Alberto and his mother Annetta outside the house in Stampa, 1960

Far more significantly, in January the following year, Annetta Giacometti died at the age of ninety-three. Being more anxious about his mother's health than his own, Alberto had been in close contact with her, both by returning to Stampa to stay with her as often as he could, and by letter and regular phone calls. Annetta had been the anchor of the family for longer than anyone could remember, with a life that stretched back far into the Val Bregaglia's ancestral past. The whole family assembled and waited as the old lady moved in and out of consciousness at the end. Alberto himself, who found the very fact of his mother's death difficult to take in for some time, described her last moments:

> Over the last week the house started to shrink around her. In the end, she only had the room where she was lying around her, then the bedroom itself was reduced to the size of her bed, and finally

> to the even smaller space in which she lay. When at last she passed, I couldn't take it in, so much so that in the days that followed I said to myself: 'I must go into my mother's bedroom to see how she is.' When I went out of the house, I would look up at her window as I came back to make sure her light was still on until I remembered, hey, I'd forgotten mother was dead.[11]

Once Annetta had been laid to rest with her husband, Giovanni, who had died thirty years earlier, the family dispersed, relieved at how 'gently' their mother had passed away. Alberto, with his bony profile and halo of hair, had come to resemble his mother noticeably in recent years, just as his lifelong attachment to her had grown as she aged. The only way he knew of managing the grief he felt would be to throw himself back into work and his usual debilitating regime, without the respite of long stays under his mother's care in Stampa. From now on his mind went back often to childhood memories of running free through the Val Bregaglia and crawling into dark caves at the foot of the mountains where no one could find him. Then being scolded by his mother, who terrified him when she was angry, towering above him in her long black dress, before comforting him as she fed him, washed him and put him to bed. Later there had been the long summer evenings in the years after his father's death, when she still scrubbed him and fed him, and they would sit together, while she knitted by lamplight, reminiscing about the old days and the old timers in Stampa as he drew her.

All that was gone now, and so was any caution about his own health as he got back into working at all hours, smoking several packs of Camels or Luckies every day and beginning again to knock back the whiskies with Caroline egging him on as they did their round of the bars. Neither Annette nor Diego liked what they saw as Alberto appeared more on edge and exhausted than ever. This was far worse than what they usually dismissed as his '*bizarreries*'; but they had learned that to chide him about such things only made matters worse. Besides, Alberto was more preoccupied than ever, keeping up with the increasing demands of a runaway successful career.

Ably assisted by his wife, Aimé Maeght had also prospered in his field and now represented an unbeatable roster of artists in Paris that included Matisse, Bonnard and Braque, Chagall, Miró and Léger, as well as the American sculptor Alexander Calder, who worked for part of the year in his studio in the Loire Valley. Having become the premier contemporary art dealer in Paris, Maeght had been looking further afield to establish an art foundation that would embellish both his and his artists' reputations. After acquiring a choice plot of land at Saint-Paul-de-Vence, in the pine-covered hills behind Nice, he and his team, including Clayeux and Dupin, worked to create the first such institution in France. Alberto, who had been involved in these preparations from the outset, was offered two permanent exhibition spaces at the Maeght Foundation: a courtyard and a room in the building designed by the Catalan architect Josep Lluís Sert. He had decided that, in return for the cost of having them cast in bronze, he would gift the sculptures he had designated for Chase Manhattan Plaza, nine *Women of Venice* and a group of works from his Surrealist period, as well as paintings and drawings to be hung in the interior space. Enthusiastic about being able to present this large selection of his work in such a setting, Alberto made several trips to Provence as the building and its terraced, pine-scented gardens came into being.

When the new Foundation was inaugurated in mid-summer 1964, the guest list read like a *Who's Who* of the Western art world. Even more glittering were the works of many of the most admired living artists, integrated into one of the most stunning Mediterranean landscapes. After a sumptuous banquet, as the stars filled the night sky and the cicadas hushed their strident song, Maeght stood up, coiffed and impeccable in black tie, to outline his ambitions for the Foundation and to thank the large cast who had helped to create it. He was followed by André Malraux, not only cultural minister but a celebrated writer, adventurer and art historian as well.* When Malraux sat down, having invoked numerous grand instances of the world's cultural heritage that he deemed worthy of comparison with the magical moment they were experiencing that evening, a few of the guests were aware that one of the key participants in the entire venture had been passed over without mention: Louis Clayeux. It was because of Clayeux that Alberto had entered the Maeght 'stable' in the first place, and his trust in Clayeux's character and judgement had deepened over time. So when Clayeux,

*Malraux had a plan to erect a monumental version of Alberto's painted bronze, *Large Head* (1960), which derived from Alberto's group of works for Chase Manhattan Plaza, at the eastern tip of the Ile de la Cité. Unfortunately, the project stalled and was forgotten.

normally the soul of discretion, exploded and took his grievance angrily, but inconsequentially, to Maeght himself, Alberto stood firmly behind him, saying that if Clayeux left the gallery he would leave with him. Clayeux did in fact hand in his notice, and despite numerous pleas from Maeght and his wife, Alberto followed suit, not unmindful that Maeght had frequently irritated him (and his New York dealer, Matisse) by casting sculptures without prior agreement, on top of being heard boasting that he had 'made' Giacometti. Eventually Dupin intervened and cobbled together a compromise whereby Maeght would continue to publish and sell the prints only. In every other respect, Alberto had broken once and for all with his wily French dealer.

James Lord had become one of Alberto's most assiduous admirers, and since he was also in regular contact with Picasso, Balthus and leading literary figures such as Cocteau, and had chosen to spend his life in Paris, he could reasonably claim to be better placed than any other English-language writer to comment on the Parisian arts scene. He was indeed later to compose a series of intriguing portraits of the outstanding men and women he had known as well as his voluminous biography of Alberto. Although the biography was widely criticised, both for factual errors and tendentious interpretations, no one contests that Lord's earlier *A Giacometti Portrait*, written from notes taken while sitting for eighteen lengthy portrait sessions in 1964, is a model of direct, informative reporting. Moreover, as a brief living likeness of Alberto, it may never be bettered. An added bonus was that Lord took snapshots of the various states through which his portrait passed. Several of them vie with each other and with the 'final' portrait as remarkable works in their own right, underlining Alberto's deeply held conviction about the relativity of success and failure in art. The ultimate version could perhaps be gauged as less anecdotal and more impersonal than its predecessors, but the others have distinct qualities and sometimes equal claim to survival. On this evidence alone, artists are not necessarily the best judges of their own work. In Alberto's case, it is safe to say, such matters remain a close-run affair of individual taste and judgement, in which he always had the last word.

Of the frequent visitors of every stripe to Alberto's studio, from art world potentates to Caroline's racketeering henchmen, Eli Lotar was in a class all of his own. Having appeared first as the author of the notorious abattoir shots published in *Documents* in 1929, then as a refugee in Geneva during the war (where he photographed Alberto in his dingy hotel room for Skira), Lotar had resurfaced, down on his luck and basically living on handouts. Alberto, who identified instinctively with the underdog, found him a few odd jobs and errands, then, as Diego grew more focused on his own work and less available than in the past, he began asking Lotar to pose for him. The former photographer, who had long been a shadowy presence around the bars in Montparnasse, cadging drinks, revealed extraordinary qualities as a model that Alberto discovered with mounting excitement. Half comatose from alcohol and misfortune, Lotar seemed to inhabit the same enigmatic space between life and death as Alberto's most moving sculptures. More than anyone before, this last model was a breathing likeness of a Giacometti figure, with the extra advantage that he could hold a pose, motionless, for hours on end – as if, the writer Giorgio Soavi noted, he were indeed dead.

Ailing artist and destitute sitter became locked into the strangest symbiosis, as if an electric current had passed between them, rendering each desperately dependent on the other (which in several ways they soon were). The three magnificent busts that evolved out of this almost supernatural complicity resembled both of them, an amalgam of suffering and resilience that, seemingly communicating from beyond the grave, stands at the very peak of Giacometti's achievement. All executed in 1965, the busts have that unearthly quality that underlines the role Genet ascribed to them as 'guardians of the dead', but stylistically they remain separate, with the first retaining quite naturalistic traits (especially the hollow cheeks and the thin, wide, downturned mouth of the disenfranchised drunk), while the two later ones, their bony heads surmounting a pyramid of closely kneaded flesh, have the absolute authority of Egyptian or Sumerian funerary figures. Both completely contemporary and harking back to the earliest times, past and present meet in the busts to form an extraordinary conjunction. Here Alberto rises to mingle with the greatest artists not only through the reach of his sculptural genius but the depth of his humanity. What other poet of the human condition could take a vagrant sodden with drink from the Paris gutter and transform him into a high priest of such spiritual dignity as to accompany great rulers into the afterlife? One thinks of the most poignant images in history, from ancient pharaoh to rough-hewn Christ, or even King Lear, his wits turned, defying the

Tony Evans, Alberto, Louis Clayeux [centre] and Robin Campbell preparing the Tate retrospective, July 1965

storm on the heath. Through the transmutation of art, the down-and-out assumes the grandeur of an Egyptian statue, the tramp in disguise is revealed as a Sumerian prince.

Alberto had fond memories of London where his work had already been the subject of a highly appreciated small exhibition organised at the Institute of Contemporary Art in 1955; he had stayed at the elegant Stafford Hotel in St James's and been well fêted. Now the Tate Gallery proposed a full retrospective for spring 1965, and Alberto had already made a couple of trips over the Channel by train and ferry to see the space and start planning the best choice of work and layout for the event. He already knew several artists in the capital, including Henry Moore, Barbara Hepworth and Ben and Winifred Nicholson, who had bought Alberto's *Woman* (1928–9) in the mid-1930s. He was also in contact with his erstwhile mistress, Isabel Rawsthorne, Lisa and Robert Sainsbury and Roland Penrose.* Gratifyingly, Alberto was provided with a space in the basement of the Tate where he could work, remodelling certain plasters, notably *Four Figurines on a Stand*, and generally touching up and fine-tuning the works as he liked to do once an exhibition came into view. For sculptures like *Suspended Ball* that were not available for loan, he simply created a copy, and with David Sylvester, the critic who had curated his previous London show and whose portrait he had painted in 1960, he hit on the idea of exhibiting a number of Surrealist works facing each other in both their plaster and bronze versions. As with the Venice Biennale, Diego and Clayeux made the journey to advise while the work was being installed. Once the show had been laid out and the lighting fine-tuned, Alberto walked through it with Sylvester, looking at everything silently, then he said, 'Well, it's all shit, but it's the best shit there is.'[12]

As the opening approached and other supporters, like Michel Leiris and Pierre Matisse, joined the throng, Isabel organised epic dinners at Wheeler's fish restaurant in Soho and the White Tower in Fitzrovia to show Alberto the London art scene at its most convivial. Francis Bacon, who had begun painting portraits of Isabel, ably assisted in the celebrations, taking Alberto on a tour of the private drinking clubs he

*Penrose was an artist, collector and co-founder of the Institute of Contemporary Arts, London.

knew, accompanied by Lucian Freud, who had met Alberto in 1946 and even sat for him. On one such evening, aware that they might not meet again, Alberto and Bacon stayed out drinking and talking about art, life and love until dawn.[13]

Annette joined Alberto at the discreet St Ermin's Hotel beside St James's Park, but the relative harmony between them was disrupted when Caroline appeared out of the blue, demanding to speak to a discomfited Alberto in private. She then disappeared as quickly as she had come, without troubling to go to the Tate where no fewer than eight portraits of her were prominently displayed. The artist remained delighted nevertheless with the way the exhibition had been received and made a point of allowing the Tate to purchase a group of his works at a highly discounted rate. As usual, Alberto gave himself no respite, meeting scores of new admirers and giving numerous interviews, including two lengthy, detailed conversations with Sylvester for the BBC.[14] Among the friends he made was Robin Campbell, the director of the Arts Council, who, having accompanied him to several museum and gallery shows in London, left a telling memoir of the time they spent together:

> The exhibition closed at the end of August and Giacometti returned to London for the last time. He told us it was the best exhibition he had ever had and he was pleased that it had been a success. Giacometti went to the exhibitions of Henry Moore and Francis Bacon which opened while he was here. He laid his hand on a huge reclining figure and said: 'It's like the side of a mountain,' and in self-mockery: 'I could do some little figures here, maybe a shepherd with a flock of sheep.' I remember he said: 'Compared with Francis Bacon's my paintings look as if they had been done by an old spinster…' He was excited most of all by a tall T'ang tomb figure of a woman in the King Edward VII gallery [of the British Museum]. He said he found this a supreme masterpiece and he spent at least half an hour walking round it, away from it and coming back to it again. The T'ang figure led him to say that more and more he preferred to anything else the impersonal and objective quality in early art: he had less and less liking for the kind of art where the artist puts his own feelings and attitudes into what he was doing: 'Modern artists are frantic egomaniacs – myself included, of

Graham Keen, Alberto and Francis Bacon in London, 1965

> course.' At lunch afterwards … he made me, as he spoke no English, tell the girl who brought the food how pretty he thought her. 'One living girl like that is worth more than anything in any museum.'[15]

The more fragile and exhausted Alberto became, the more he appeared to push himself. London had been amusing and he had enjoyed some novel experiences, like exploring a few of the city's secret homosexual haunts with Bacon. But all that, with the frantic socialising and the banqueting, was taking its toll. He was barely back in Paris before he was planning his next major trip, this time to a city he had dreamed of but never imagined actually visiting. Preceded by a show of carefully selected drawings at Pierre Matisse in the autumn of 1964, the artist's big, new retrospective at the Museum of Modern Art in New York virtually coincided with the exhibition at the Tate in the summer of 1965. Having missed the opening, Alberto took the momentous decision to make his first trip across the Atlantic just before the retrospective closed in October. Before leaving, he allowed a camera crew headed by his faithful Swiss photographer Scheidegger and his good friend Dupin to invade the inner sanctum of his studio and film him while he worked (as Picasso had done for Henri-Georges Clouzot, director of *The Wages of Fear*). Although he grumbled at having to put up with the cumbersome technical equipment and the wires trailing across the studio floor, Alberto lent himself to the proceedings, not least because it gave him the chance to converse with Dupin as he painted his portrait. He also modelled a figure in clay for the benefit of the film, a process he was so practised at by now that, unbelievably, he could complete it in about two minutes.[16] Filmed in colour, the result has a contemporary feel, lending a new reality to an artist and studio that had hitherto been portrayed only in grainy black and white.

By a continuing process of osmosis, artist and studio, having come to resemble and represent each other, had also grown increasingly famous together. One of the best descriptions of the man and his lair – his refuge, his shell – at this time has come down from Robert Craft, the American conductor and writer who accompanied Igor Stravinsky when he met Giacometti for the final time in 1965. While CBS was recording the encounter between the two artists live, Craft jotted down the following succinct portrait of the sculptor in his studio:

> [Giacometti] is thinner than last year but otherwise looks the same, ie, like an unmade bed. Apart from the rumpled clothes and dishevelment, his skin is coriaceous, like a piece of old luggage, his hair has apparently never been trained by a comb, his fingernail dirt is paleozoic, and his tartared teeth alternate yellow, black, and absentees, like the keyboard of a broken harpsichord. In the street, when he comes to greet us and see us off, he blends into the *quartier*; or, at any rate, the *blousiers* who pass by, *baguettes* under arm and talking about food, do not notice him.
>
> The clutter in his studio gives an impression of sparseness, like the art it contains. Giacometti has fitted the walls of the alleyway entrance with a Della Robbia (?) and other reliefs.* In the room, small, with a high skylight, one notices the graffiti first: all of the

*It seems most unlikely that Giacometti would have installed the 'reliefs' – casts of Donatello's (not Della Robbia's) *Cantoria*, designed originally for Santa Maria del Fiore, Florence – in the courtyard: that kind of embellishment would have come almost certainly from other, earlier hands.

> walls are scratched, scribbled on, painted, like those of a catacomb or cave. Next we are aware of the sculptured figures, a hundred or more of them, it seems, some as small as lead soldiers, two or three larger than life. Several of them appear to walk about the room, but most are gathered in a corner where their thin gray trunks look like trees after a forest fire. Two others are wrapped in canvas tied with rope; from time to time Giacometti sprinkles these newest creations from a watering can, as if he were tending flowers.
>
> We sit on a cot, after clearing it of paints, bottles, papers, books, sketches, canvases, palettes; these last are remarkable in that the daubs are bright colors, the paintings all dark gray. The other furniture consists of a battered table, a potbellied stove, and a small tree which comes up through the floor like a medieval miracle ...[17]

Just before Craft and Stravinsky left the studio, Alberto, who had as usual been repeatedly lamenting his failure to accomplish any worthwhile work, produced a bottle of whisky and poured some farewell drinks. The liquid, Craft notes, tasted exactly like turps.

In the final months of his life, Alberto appeared almost footloose, as if, with his mother now dead, he sensed all too clearly that the attachment anchoring his existence from its very inception was no longer there. Given that the exhibition opening, with all the accompanying razzamatazz of a major New York event, was long past, there remained little real need to undertake the trip across the Atlantic, particularly since the passage took a week either way out of an already demanding schedule. Nevertheless, Annette warmed to the luxury of an ocean liner, and the reassuring company of Pierre and Patricia Matisse allayed some of the boredom and fear that gripped Alberto mid-ocean. Patricia's photographs show him hunched against the cold on deck, peering abstractedly across the water as the unreal silhouette of New York comes into view. Once on dry land, he visited his own exhibition and several museums dutifully, attending a reception organised especially in his honour to meet Manhattan's art stars, notably De Kooning, Rothko and Rauschenberg. As 'manic' as ever, what seemed to interest Alberto most, although surrounded by miracle architecture and treasure houses of art, was Chase Manhattan Plaza, where he might have sited (where he thought he might still site) a whole group of oversize figures. Accordingly, he visited the space several times at night, when it was empty, positioning Annette, the architect Bunshaft and James Lord, at various intervals to gauge the effect the figures would have in different locations, eventually determining that a single female figure, towering between six and eight metres over the daily bustle of bankers, would best suit the Plaza. On returning to Paris, Alberto did indeed get Diego to run up an outsize armature for the huge figure, but the project was destined to go no further.

During the return trip to Le Havre on SS *France*, Alberto tried to make the most of the crossing by staying in his cabin and attempting to finish a text for a book consisting of his 'interpretive drawings', or 'copies', of various works of art he admired from Egyptian sculpture through the Old Masters to Cézanne.[18] Thinking over the variety of works he had copied since childhood, he suddenly stops mid-text and exclaims: 'How can one describe all that? The entire art of the past, of all periods, of all civilizations rises before my mind, becomes a simultaneous vision, as if time had become space.' In any case, he finds it difficult to focus on anything while at sea:

> I have hardly looked at the ocean since the moment, two days ago, when I saw the distant point of New York dissolve, disappear – delicate, fragile, and ephemeral – at the horizon, and it is as if I were witnessing the beginning and the end of the world. My chest is tight with anguish, I can only feel the sea around me, but there is also the dome, the immense vault of the human head.
>
> … Impossible to concentrate on anything, the ocean encroaches upon it all, it has no name for me although today it is called the Atlantic. For millions of years it had no name, and one day it will again be without name, without end, blind, wild as it appears to me today. How can one talk here about copies of works of art, frail and ephemeral works of art that exist here and there on continents, works of art that decay, disintegrate, that wither away day after day, and many of which – among them those that I prefer – have already once been buried, hidden beneath sand, earth, and stones?

> … I don't know if I am a comedian, a rascal, an idiot or a very scrupulous fellow. I only know that I have to try to draw a nose from life.[19]

Shortly after returning to Paris, Alberto set off yet again, this time to see his work on display at the Louisiana Museum, a trip possibly prompted by the need to avoid Caroline and her colleagues, whose extortionate demands had begun to irk him. And yet, although exhausted, he was still passionately involved with Caroline, working on a new portrait of her and being driven around Paris in the car he had given her so that he could sketch further scenes for the *Paris Without End* project he had promised Tériade. He pushed himself, time and time again, to keep up, to keep going on the treadmill of endless work and next to no rest, smoking and talking and still going out on the town. His friends saw to their alarm that he now looked like a mere memory of himself. On his last visit to Alberto in 1965, Brassaï found 'an emaciated, bent Alberto Giacometti, tottering around in his old clothes, his face lined more than ever by suffering. Yet the gleam in his eyes, which were red with sleeplessness, is still there, and his voice is still compellingly certain, as warm as ever.' And he recalls that Alberto said to him:

> Brassaï – photograph me like this. I'm a wreck. The future looks dark. I ask myself for how long I can keep on working. I am on a dead-end street. I honestly don't know how I can get myself out of it. And in spite of everything, as you can see, I keep working, keep doing my stuff. Yesterday evening I worked till midnight on this bust, which I still owe Maeght, then I went to the Coupole. I came back at three in the morning and, instead of going to bed I worked until seven. I have had almost no sleep. I'm under such pressure to keep working on this bust that I haven't even had a cup of coffee.[20]

Towards the end of 1965 Alberto himself began talking more often about death and about his need to go on living in order to take his work further. Making notes for the text he wanted to have as a preface to *Paris Without End*, he seems almost to be moving in and out of consciousness, as his mother had done before she died:

> Now it's past three in the morning. Before, in the Coupole, when I had eaten and wanted to read, I fell asleep; my dream-thoughts distorted and transformed what I was trying to read – a line, two lines in the newspaper, and my eyes kept falling shut. The cold outside, the cold and sleep drove me home; going to bed and sinking into sleep in spite of fear … silence. I am alone here, outside is the night, nothing is stirring and sleep is overcoming me. I don't know who I am, what I'm doing, what I want; I don't know whether I am old or young, maybe I still have a few hundred thousand years to live until I die; my previous life is sinking into a gray void.[21]

That void had begun to open all around him. Everything began to indicate that his health was failing and that he needed complete rest as well as a full medical examination, for which he had chosen to return to Switzerland. Undaunted, he followed his usual routine, staying up late with friends in Montparnasse on his last night before leaving Paris. Scheidegger, who was with him, noted down all the details of what was to be their final meeting:

> Except for his coughing, which interrupted our conversation from time to time, he seemed to be in good spirits, full of energy, interested in all the problems that occupied us … We met, as we had so often, after midnight in the bar of the Dôme. Alberto was already there with his two models Caroline and Lotar. They were alone on the heated terrace of the restaurant and sat there without speaking, as if something extraordinary had happened. Finally Alberto's departure for Chur, Lord's departure for New York, and my departure for Zurich got us talking. It was one of the saddest nights I ever spent with Alberto. We spoke of nothing important, nothing intimate, very unlike the times we usually spent together. We all sat there, silent again. Around four o'clock we said our goodbyes – as so often in the last years. It was Alberto's last night in Paris. The same day, at ten o'clock that night, he left for Chur for his examination.[22]

Although no recurrence of his cancer was detected at the hospital in Chur, Alberto was diagnosed with chronic bronchitis and exhaustion. He remained undaunted, hoping that given time to recuperate he would be able to go back to Paris and resume work. Both Annette and

Caroline visited him, which led to scenes in the hospital between the two women. As New Year 1966 got under way, Alberto's condition worsened, and to one of the nurses looking after him, he said, 'I am going mad, I no longer recognize myself, I no longer want to work.' A pleural tap revealed an advanced swelling of the tissue around the heart, and Alberto's close relatives were contacted. When he saw his whole family gathered in his room the following day, 11 January, Alberto murmured, 'You're all here. That means I'm going to die.' Later that evening, he fell into a coma, dying shortly thereafter. He was sixty-four.

Diego left Chur the next day on the night train to Paris. He had wanted to go back earlier, fearing that the last clay bust of Lotar might burst if left for too long in the freezing studio, but Alberto had dissuaded him, saying that he wished to work on it further. When he arrived, Diego found that the damp rags wrapped around the bust were indeed frozen stiff, so he lit a low fire in the stove and waited for them to thaw gently. Once the work had been cast in bronze, Diego had it placed on Alberto's grave.

In 1969, long after the last of hundreds of tributes to the memory of the artist had been made, Alberto Giacometti springs vividly back to life when his book, *Paris Without End*, is finally published. Made up of one hundred and fifty lithographs, with snatches of text in between, these sketches are the freest, most spontaneous images the artist ever made, partly because lithographic pencil on transfer paper allows no erasures or fresh starts, partly because they were made on the hoof – walking, looking out of the window, from a café table – and partly because Alberto suspected that he had little time to live, that he didn't much care and that whatever came from his hand-eye coordination after half a century of recording the world around him – with infinite effort, infinite revision, infinite accuracy – would be as good or as bad as anything else he had done.

These drawings, sometimes the merest notations, the scruffiest of strokes, the quickest of blobs, at other times closely orchestrated and heavily scored, are the essence of the artist, of his life and his truth, evoking all aspects of his career. They are done too quickly to strive for effect, or even to be seen as suggesting contemporary anguish or the solitude of modern man. With every thought of perfection thrown to the winds, they batter the eye with their immediacy. Here is the bar at Le Select, there a bridge arching over the Seine, a naked woman stripped to a few, vertical strokes or the massive dinosaur skeletons at the Muséum d'histoire naturelle so fleshed out with black, lithographic pencil they seem about to charge. A cobweb of pencil marks, with the white of the paper shining through, and an avenue of trees, a terrace of tables, the twin towers of Saint-Sulpice, a jukebox in a bar come instantly into focus. If there is a breakneck speed to them, like slides spilling over each other onto a screen, it's because they were done at speed, one after the other, dropping to the floor, dripping with rain or lost out of the window of the car that Caroline was driving, barrelling through the city. He was back in the red sports car he gave her, racing around Paris, making sketches as she drove faster and faster, laughing recklessly, with the breeze blowing off the Seine through her hair and the transfer paper fluttering out of control. And he was there, with his two loves, Paris and Caroline, who understood him, excited him, in as far as an old, sick man deep in the dregs of life could still be excited.

And everything, all unending Paris, going past, like a movie speeding up faster and faster as she sped across the city, pushing the limits, like he did, always wanting more, wanting better, the raids on the unknowable and unachievable, the light on the eye, the curve of the cheek, being almost there but not quite there, as the flux that you lived in but could never record rushed by. And in the flux it all returned, the Jardin des Plantes, the solemn nineteenth-century monuments filled with historic remains, the cafés and their shiny zinc counters, the trees overarching the streets, the faces and figures glimpsed and gone. All endless, and if he could get back to the studio, to the old life, it would all come back again, the same ceaseless striving and the rare, perverse pleasure of pitting oneself against impossible odds. He would work again and see the streets and trees of Paris again. Paris stretching out before him, with the boulevards reaching towards the sky, and the sunlight coming through the trees beside the cafés and the terraces, and people talking together, where he had sat and argued and laughed with Breton and Aragon, Genet and Beckett, Sartre and Beauvoir, with elegant ladies and old tramps, moving and merging, scenes from a life lived in sketches, unfurling page by page, silhouettes and silences, as vivid and as insubstantial as a dream.

Paris without end, art without end, Giacometti without end ...

Envoi

Weeks before his death, Giacometti wrote a few lines in a notebook that put his entire life into perspective:

> All that doesn't amount to much
> all the painting, sculpture, drawing,
> the writing or rather literature.
> All that has its place
> and no more than that.
>
> Only trying matters.
>
> How marvellous!

Since Giacometti died, little seems to have changed in Alésia. Wandering through the modest grey streets, you still hear the hammering and sawing of artisans in their workshops, restoring parquet floors, welding a balustrade. If the streets are rather less shabby, the area retains its humble, provincial atmosphere. Push open the door on any down-at-heel building and the courtyard has a similar air of neglect, weeds among the cobblestones, a rusting bicycle, feral cats. So much so that, a century after he first arrived in Paris, you might still expect to see Giacometti come round the corner, slouched over, scruffily dressed, with an ancient face no one would forget – deeply lined, deeply human – that had looked unflinchingly into the void, suffered and survived.

Then the illusion fades. The old Alésia is only a memory now. When Giacometti died, a certain idea of Paris, indeed a certain Paris, died too.

Even under scrutiny, Giacometti remains a will-o'-the-wisp, there, then not there, fixed and fluctuating, like his work, forever beginning, forever unfinished. So much information from so many sources crowds in, but none of it definitive: a mass of detail that never quite adds up. An improbable, manic existence utterly committed to pinning down what could never be pinned down: the flicker of life, the human mystery, the breath on a mirror.

I arrived in Paris in January 1966, clutching a letter of introduction to Alberto Giacometti. The letter was never handed over because Giacometti had just left Paris for the hospital in Switzerland where he died. Over the decades that I lived in the city thereafter, he became a vital part of my existence, a source of strength and a symbol of survival, his work a talisman that protected me through the best and the worst of times.

That letter has now been delivered.

Notes

INTRODUCTION

1 Michael Peppiatt, *Francis Bacon: Anatomy of an Enigma*, London, 1996.
2 James Lord, *Giacometti: A Biography*, New York, 1985.

1 MAGIC CITY (1922–26)

1 Luis Buñuel, *My Last Sigh: The Autobiography of Luis Buñuel*, New York, 2013, p. 85.
2 'Pourquoi je suis sculpteur', entretien avec André Parinaud, *Arts*, Paris, 13–19 June, 1962.
3 Quoted in Reinhold Hohl, *Giacometti: A Biography in Pictures*, Ostfildern/Stuttgart, p. 56.
4 Annetta Giacometti, letter to Alberto Giacometti, 16 December 1922, Fondation Giacometti Archives, Paris.
5 Alberto Giacometti, *Ecrits*, Paris, 2008, p. 311.
6 Alberto Giacometti, letter to his family, 31 January 1925, SIK-ISEA (Swiss Institute for Art Research) Archives, Zurich, 274.A.2.1.57.
7 Giacometti, *Ecrits*, p. 230.
8 Alberto Giacometti, 31 January 1925, *Lettres d'Alberto Giacometti à ses parents*, Giacometti Foundation, Paris, 2021, p. 47.
9 Giacometti's text on Derain was published in *Derrière le miroir*, no. 94–95, the catalogue to Derain's exhibition at the Galerie Maeght, Paris, February–March 1957; on Braque, an obituary in *Les Lettres françaises*, Paris, September 1963; and on Laurens, in *Labyrinthe*, no. 4, Geneva, January 1945.
10 Alberto Giacometti, letter to his family, 28 April 1927, Alberto Giacometti Foundation Archives, Zurich.

11 Letter to Alberto Giacometti from his father, 8 February 1924, Alberto Giacometti Stiftung Archives, Zurich.
12 Jean Clay, 'Alberto Giacometti: Le dialogue avec la mort d'un très grand sculpteur de notre temps', *Réalités*, no. 215, Paris, December 1963.
13 'Hier, sables mouvants', originally published in *Le Surréalisme au service de la Révolution* in May 1933. Quoted in Michael Peppiatt, *In Giacometti's Studio*, New Haven and London, 2010, pp. 45–6. Unless attributed otherwise, translations, particularly of the longer texts, have been made from the original French by the author.
14 Giacometti, 'Interview with Jean Clay', *Ecrits*, p. 313.

2 RUE HIPPOLYTE (1926–30)

1 Letter to his parents, 30 December 1926, SIK-ISEA Archives, Zurich.
2 Michael Peppiatt, 'Interview with Diego Giacometti', *Connoisseur*, New York, April 1987.
3 Quoted in Hohl, *Giacometti: A Biography in Pictures*, p. 58.
4 Alberto Giacometti interviewed by Jean-Marie Drot in *Giacometti, un homme parmi les hommes*, a film made in November 1963.
5 See Georges Bataille, *The Solar Anus*, illustrated by André Masson, Paris, 1931.
6 *Documents*, no. 4, September 1929, pp. 209–14.
7 Michel Leiris, *Journal 1922–1989*, Paris, 1992, p. 196. Leiris had several consuming passions at this time, including a fascination with jazz and Lew Leslie's *Black Birds Revue*, then a great hit at the Moulin Rouge, which Leiris reports on enthusiastically in the same issue of *Documents*.
8 *Aujourd'hui* (a short-lived review published in French-speaking Switzerland), 9 January 1930.
9 Letter from Ottilia Giacometti to her parents, 3 May 1929, SIK-ISEA Archives, Zurich, 274.A.3.2.23.
10 Man Ray, *Self-Portrait*, London, 2012, p. 250.
11 Quoted by Véronique Wiesinger, *Giacometti: La figure au défi*, Paris, 2007, pp. 32–3.
12 *Le Surréalisme au service de la révolution*, no. 3, December 1931, pp. 15–17.
13 Hohl, *Giacometti: A Biography in Pictures*, p. 65.

3 A FANTASTIC PALACE AT NIGHT (1930–33)

1 Letter from Alberto Giacometti to his family, 5 December 1929, SIK-ISEA Archives, Zurich, 274.A.2.1.97.

2 Letter from Alberto Giacometti to Bruno Giacometti, 27 November 1929, SIK-ISEA Archives, Zurich, 274.A.2.1.102.
3 Letter from Alberto Giacometti to his family, 27 November 1929, *Lettres d'Alberto Giacometti à sa famille: Les débuts, 1920–29,* Paris, 2021, p. 82.
4 Letter from Giovanni Giacometti to Alberto and Diego Giacometti, 11 December 1929, Fondation Giacometti Archives, Paris.
5 Buñuel, *My Last Sigh*, p. 119.
6 Julien Levy, *Memoir of an Art Gallery*, New York, 1977, p. 14.
7 In his writings on Giacometti, James Lord frequently hints that the artist had homosexual leanings.
8 See Michael Peppiatt, *Bacon/Giacometti: A Dialogue*, London, 2020. The remark was probably partly a joke and partly out of sympathy for people with unorthodox tastes.
9 Giacometti, *Ecrits*, p. 387.
10 Casimiro di Crescenza, '*On ne joue plus* (1932) di Alberto Giacometti', *Venezia Arti*, Venice, 1992, p. 6.
11 Original in Italian in a notebook dated 1932–3. Reproduced in Giacometti, *Ecrits*, pp. 462–3.
12 Giacometti, *Ecrits*, p. 464.
13 David Sylvester, *Looking at Giacometti*, London, 1995, p. 233.
14 'Carnets' (2000–0053), Fondation Giacometti Archives, Paris. With the earliest entries in Italian, then later in French, these little notebooks form an invaluable resource for information about the artist.
15 Alberto Giacometti, letter to his parents, January 1931, SIK-ISEA Archives, Zurich, 274.A.2.1.106.
16 Correspondence of Vicomte Charles de Noailles, sale notice, *La Gazette de Drouot*, Paris, no. 3, 22 January 2020.
17 Brassaï, 'My Last Visit to Giacometti', *Le Figaro littéraire*, 20 January 1966. Brassaï later remarked that 'All [Alberto] needed to be happy was a mound of clay within easy reach, some plaster, some canvases and a few sheets of paper.'
18 Letter to his family, December 1930, SIK-ISEA Archives, Zurich, 274.A.2.1.107.
19 Christian Zervos, 'Quelques notes sur les sculptures de Giacometti', *Cahiers d'art*, nos 8–10, 1932.
20 Letter to his family, undated (autumn 1932), Alberto Giacometti-Stiftung Archives, Zurich.
21 Hohl, *Giacometti: A Biography in Pictures,* pp. 72–3. Perhaps Alberto had a less violent form of seduction in mind when, in 1933, he and Arp invited Meret Oppenheim, who would become known chiefly for her

'fur' teacup, to exhibit with the Surrealists in 1933; she later reciprocated with a small sculpture entitled *Giacometti's Ear*.

22 Letter from Alberto Giacometti to André Breton, 8 August 1933, Breton Archives, Bibliothèque Jacques-Doucet, Paris, BRT.C.832.

23 Letter from André Breton to Alberto Giacometti, 2 February 1934, Fondation Giacometti Archives, Paris, 2003–4502.

4 CONVULSIVE BEAUTY (1933–37)

1 Leiris, *Journal 1922–1989*, p. 309.

2 Giacometti, *Ecrits*, p. 514.

3 Jean Clay, 'Alberto Giacometti', *Réalités*, Paris, December 1963, pp. 135–45.

4 Alain Jouffroy, 'Portrait d'un artiste: Giacometti', *Arts – Lettres – Spectacles*, Paris, December 1955.

5 René Crevel, 'Discours aux peintres', *Commune*, June 1935.

6 Letter dated 24 October 1934, Fondation Giacometti Archives, Paris, 2000–0021.

7 André Parinaud, Entretien avec Giacometti, 'Pourquoi je suis sculpteur', *Arts – Lettres – Spectacles*, Paris, June 1962.

8 Giacometti, *Ecrits* (dated c. 1933–4), pp. 514–16.

9 Ibid., p. 512.

10 See Alexandre Kojève, *Introduction to the Reading of Hegel: Lectures on the Phenomenology of Spirit* (Ithaca, NY, 1980); and for a brief overview of Kojève's ideas on art, see *Kandinsky: Incarnating Beauty* (New York, 2022).

11 Ibid. Giacometti slightly misquotes Heraclitus here.

12 Interview with Michel Conil-Lacoste, *Le Monde*, Paris, November 1962.

13 Alberto Giacometti, letter to his mother, 14 February 1935, SIK-ISEA Archive, Zurich, 274.A. 2.1.131.

14 Parinaud, Entretien avec Giacometti, 'Pourquoi je suis sculpteur', p. 34.

15 Ibid., pp. 34–5.

16 Quoted in Hohl, *Giacometti: A Biography in Pictures*, p. 83.

5 REALITY UNVEILED (1937–44)

1 Giacometti, *Ecrits*, c. 1934, p. 174.

2 Isabel Rawsthorne, 'Memoirs', Tate Gallery Archive, London.

3 Giacometti, *Ecrits*, p. 249.

4 David Sylvester, 'The Residue of a Vision', *Alberto Giacometti: Sculpture, Paintings, Drawings*, exhibition catalogue, London, 1965.
5 Giacometti, 'Interview with Jean Clay', *Ecrits*, p. 317.
6 Lord, *Giacometti: A Biography*, p. 207.
7 Alberto Giacometti, letter to his mother, 1946, Alberto Giacometti-Stiftung Archives, Zurich. Alberto adds that he dined often with Picasso who had invited him to drop in whenever he wanted.
8 Rawsthorne, 'Memoirs', Tate Gallery Archive. Lord confirms this, *Giacometti: A Biography*, p. 323. The English sculptor Raymond Mason recounts that Alberto came to see him once in order to avoid a visit from Picasso who, he said, had eyes that photographed his latest works and reproduced them the next day tenfold (Raymond Mason, *Art et Artistes*, Moncalieri, 2000, p. 80).
9 Lord, *Giacometti: A Biography*, p. 251.
10 Rawsthorne, 'Memoirs', Tate Gallery Archive. Also mentioned in Lord, *Giacometti: A Biography*, p. 207.
11 'Giacometti dessine Stravinski', Documentary on Igor Stravinsky, produced by Metropolitain, Munich in association with Schweizer Fernsehen, 2001.
12 Alberto Giacometti, letter to his mother, 1 January 1945, Alberto Giacometti-Stiftung Archives, Zurich.
13 See Jean Starobinski, 'A Genève avec Giacometti', in 'Alberto Giacometti, retour à la figuration, 1933–47', exhibition catalogue, Geneva, 1986, p. 14.
14 Balthus on Giacometti, 'Alberto Giacometti', exhibition catalogue, Goulandris Foundation, Museum of Contemporary Art, Andros, 1992.
15 Albert Skira, 'Giacometti à "Labyrinthe"', *Les Lettres françaises*, Paris, 20 January 1966.
16 Quoted in Reinhold Hohl, *Giacometti: Sculpture Painting Drawing*, London, 1972, p. 134.
17 See Isaku Yanaihara, *Avec Giacometti* (French edition), Paris, 2015, p. 58.

6 POST-WAR PARIS (1945–46)

1 Rawsthorne, 'Memoirs', Tate Britain Archive, London.
2 Quoted in Sylvester, *Looking at Giacometti*, p. 144.
3 Ibid., pp. 144–5.
4 Hohl, *Giacometti: Sculpture Painting Drawing*, p. 144.
5 Lord, *Giacometti: A Biography*, pp. 258–9.

6 Alberto Giacometti, letter to Pierre Matisse, 1947, Pierre Matisse Gallery Archives, Morgan Library & Museum, New York, box 11, folder 7, item 14.
7 Georges Limbour, 'Le charnier de plâtre d'Alberto Giacometti', *Action*, 24 September 1947). Reprinted in Georges Limbour, *Dans le secret des ateliers*, Paris, 1986.
8 Quoted in John Russell, *Matisse: Father and Son*, New York, 1999, p. 152.
9 Ibid.
10 Simone de Beauvoir, *La Force de l'âge*, vol. II, Paris, 1960, p. 321.
11 Beauvoir's relationship with Algren is amply recorded in their correspondence, published as *Beloved Chicago Man: Letters to Nelson Algren, 1947–64*, London, 1998.
12 Simone de Beauvoir, *Force of Circumstance*, Paris, 1965; London, 1968, p. 39.

7 THE DREAM, THE SPHINX AND THE DEATH OF T. (1946–47)

1 Michel Leiris, *Giacometti oral et écrit*, in *Alberto Giacometti: Ecrits* (original edition), Paris, 1990, p. ix.
2 Quoted by Laurie Wilson, *Alberto Giacometti: Myth, Magic and the Man*, New Haven and London, 2003, p. 226.
3 Alexander Liberman, *The Artist in His Studio*, New York, 1988, p. 278.
4 First published in 1945, then translated into English as *The Blood of Others*.
5 Simone de Beauvoir, *Beloved Chicago Man*, pp. 97–8.
6 My thanks to James Chadwick for allowing me to quote from his research on the building.
7 Quoted by Jean Genet, *L'Atelier d'Alberto Giacometti*, Paris, 1966 (unpaginated).
8 Notably in Lord, *Giacometti: A Biography*, and Wilson, *Alberto Giacometti: Myth, Magic and the Man*.
9 Letter from Alberto Giacometti to Pierre Matisse, mid-October 1947, Pierre Matisse Gallery Archives, Morgan Library & Museum, New York, box 11, folder 7, item 15.

8 CUTTING THE FAT OFF SPACE (1947–50)

1 Quoted in Russell, *Matisse: Father and Son*, p. 155.
2 Thomas B. Hess, *Barnett Newman*, New York, 1969, p. 39.
3 Russell, *Matisse: Father and Son*, p. 161.
4 Jacques Dupin, *Alberto Giacometti*, Paris, 1962, p. 77.

5 See Lord, *Giacometti: A Biography*, pp. 299–303.

9 ALL THE POWER OF A HEAD (1950–55)

1 'Un Sculpteur vu par un sculpteur', *Labyrinthe*, no. 4, 15 January 1945.
2 See the art critic Carola Giedion-Welcker's memoir of meeting Alberto at that moment published in *Neue Zürcher Zeitung*, 16 January 1966.
3 See Yanaihara, *Avec Giacometti*, p. 80.
4 Letter from Alberto Giacometti to Pierre Matisse, 28 December 1950, Pierre Matisse Gallery Archives, Morgan Library & Museum, New York.
5 John Russell, *Matisse: Father and Son*, p. 168.
6 In an autobiographical essay, 'Curriculum Vitae', Sylvester calls Giacometti 'the saintly knight without armour who had come to redeem art from facility and commercialism'. David Sylvester, *About Modern Art: Critical Essays 1948–2000*, London, 2002, p. 15.
7 Quoted by Gérard Regnier, 'Une vision infernale', *Les Nouvelles littéraires*, Paris, 23 October 1969.
8 *Worstward Ho!*, Beckett's penultimate novella, published in 1983.
9 Giacometti, *Ecrits*, p. 599.
10 Hohl, *Giacometti: Sculpture Painting Drawing*, p. 148.
11 Originally published in Samuel Beckett, 'Three Dialogues', *transition* magazine, Paris, 1949.
12 Ibid.
13 Samuel Beckett, *The Unnameable*, New York, 1958.
14 Giacometti, *Ecrits*, p. 166.
15 Alberto described Sweeney visiting him in the studio and telling him how much he liked the *Spoon Woman* and the drawings of Henri Matisse among other works. See *Lettres d'Alberto Giacometti à sa famille: La Consécration*, Paris, 2021, p. 53.
16 Recorded interview of the artist discussing his career with Georges Charbonnier, RTF (Radiodiffusion-télévision française), Paris, 3 March 1951.
17 Interview with François Weyergans, 'Weyergans, du pitre au fakir', RTBF (Radio-télévision belge de la Communauté française), 27 October 1993.

10 THE SECRET WOUND (1955–59)

1 See Lord, *Giacometti: A Biography*, p. 360.
2 See Peppiatt, *Bacon/Giacometti: A Dialogue*, p. 30.
3 Alberto Giacometti, handwritten text in a sketchbook, around 1950. See Giacometti, *Ecrits*, p. 547.

4 Published and accompanied by three lithographs by Giacometti in Maeght's *Derrière le miroir* series. The text was reworked by Genet and republished with photographs by Scheidegger in a paperback edition by L'Arbalète, Paris, 1958.
5 Genet, *L'Atelier d'Alberto Giacometti*, translated by the author.
6 Ibid.
7 For a fuller account, see Edmund White, *Genet*, London, 1993, p. 471.
8 Ibid., p. 772.
9 See Lord, *Giacometti: A Biography*, p. 352.
10 As early as 1929, Alberto mentions that he has met Stravinsky, who likes his work. See *Lettres d'Alberto Giacometti à sa famille*, op. cit., p. 80.
11 See Igor Stravinsky, 'Stravinsky as seen by Giacometti – Giacometti as seen by Stravinsky', *Vogue*, New York, 15 August 1958.
12 Letter from Alberto Giacometti to Pierre Matisse, late April 1952, Pierre Matisse Gallery Archives, Morgan Library & Museum, New York, box 11, folder 19, item 99.
13 Jean-Paul Sartre, *Les Mots*, Paris, 1964, p. 213.
14 See Yanaihara, *Avec Giacometti*, p. 216. Other accounts claim that it was Camus' *The Outsider* that he translated.
15 Ibid., quoted in Catherine Grenier, *Alberto Giacometti: A Biography*, Paris, 2018, p. 285.
16 Quoted in Grenier, *Alberto Giacometti: A Biography*, p. 217.
17 Marlene Dietrich, *Marlene*, New York, 1987, pp. 162–3.

11 A LONGING FOR DARKNESS (1959–63)

1 Raymond Mason singles this point out in his memoir, *Art et Artistes*, p. 78.
2 See Lord, *Giacometti: A Biography*, p. 432.
3 Quoted in Hohl, *Giacometti: Sculpture Painting Drawing*, p. 170.
4 Ibid., p. 169.
5 Letter from Samuel Beckett to Barbara Bray, 21 April 1961, quoted in Samuel Beckett, *Lettres*, III, Paris, 2016, 485, n. 3. Bray also worked with Harold Pinter on a film adaptation of Proust's *Remembrance of Things Past*.
6 Michael Peppiatt, 'Remembering Alberto Giacometti – An Interview with Jacques Dupin', *In Giacometti's Studio: An Intimate Portrait*, New York, 2010, p. 36. With Leiris, Dupin edited and introduced the first edition of Giacometti's collected writings, *Ecrits*, Paris, 1990.
7 Herbert Lust, *Alberto Giacometti: Friendship and Love*, Tel Aviv, 2003, p. 32.

8 See Lord, *Giacometti: A Biography*, p. 425. Lord identifies the hotel where these assignations took place as the Villa Camellia, conveniently situated in the Montparnasse area on rue Jules-Chaplain.
9 Letter from Caroline (Yvonne-Marguerite Poiraudeau) to Alberto Giacometti, 1960, Beinecke Library, James Lord Papers, Yale University, New Haven.
10 Letter (photocopy) from Alberto Giacometti to Caroline (Yvonne-Marguerite Poiraudeau), 6 May 1960, Fondation Giacometti Archives, Paris.
11 Lust, *Alberto Giacometti: Friendship and Love*, pp. 82–3.
12 Yanaihara, private diary, 1961, Yanaihara Archives, p. 269.
13 Gotthard Jedlicka, 'Alberto Giacometti zum 60. Geburtstag', *Neue Zürcher Zeitung*, Zurich, 10 October 1961, p. 4. When Jedlicka died in 1965, Giacometti published a brief tribute to him in the same Zurich newspaper.
14 Sylvester, *Giacometti: A Biography*, p. 218.

12 PARIS WITHOUT END (1963–66)

1 Alberto Giacometti, *Paris sans fin*, Paris, 1966; new edition, Paris, 2018, n. p.
2 Alberto Giacometti, quoted in Grenier, *Alberto Giacometti: A Biography*, p. 285.
3 Alberto Giacometti, 'Interview with Jean Clay', *Ecrits*, p. 323.
4 Quoted in Hohl, *Giacometti: Sculpture Painting Drawing*, p. 181.
5 Brassaï, *The Artists in My Life*, London, 1982, p. 54.
6 Alberto Giacometti, *Hotel Room* I–V, 1963, Alberto Giacometti-Stiftung, Zurich.
7 Quoted in Hohl, *Giacometti: Sculpture Painting Drawing*, p. 189.
8 Samuel Beckett, *Disjecta*, ed. Ruby Cohn, London, p. 134.
9 Jean-Marie Drot, 'Alberto Giacometti', *Les heures chaudes de Montparnasse*, television series, ORTF, Paris, November 1963.
10 Alberto Giacometti: 'Georges Braque vient de mourir', *Les Lettres françaises*, Paris, September 1963. Reprinted as 'Hommage à Georges Braque' in *Derrière le miroir*, Paris, May 1964.
11 Interview with Gotthard Jedlicka, *Ecrits*, p. 333.
12 Quoted in *Giacometti: Critical Essays*, ed. Peter Read and Julia Kelly, Farnham, 2009, p. 14.
13 Peppiatt, *Bacon/Giacometti: A Dialogue*.

14 Published in David Sylvester, *Looking at Giacometti*, London, 1994, pp. 211–39. A new translation of these talks by Paul Auster was published in the *Guardian*, London, 21 June 2003.
15 Robin Campbell, 'A Personal Reminiscence', *Studio International*, no. 2, London, 1966, p. 47.
16 See David Sylvester, 'Giacometti: An Inability to Tinker', *Sunday Times Magazine*, London, 4 July 1965.
17 Robert Craft, *Stravinsky: Chronicle of a Friendship*, Nashville and London, 1994, pp. 400–1.
18 *Giacometti: A Sketchbook of Interpretative Drawings*, texts by the artist and Luigi Carluccio, New York, 1967.
19 Ibid.
20 Hohl, *Giacometti: Sculpture Painting Drawing*, p. 188.
21 Giacometti, *Paris sans fin*, quoted in Hohl, *Giacometti: Sculpture Painting Drawing*, p. 187.
22 Ernst Scheidegger, 'Die letzte Nacht in Paris', *Die Weltwoche*, Zurich, 21 January 1966, quoted in Hohl, *Giacometti: Sculpture Painting Drawing*, p. 193.

Index

Acknowledgements

Special thanks to Catherine Best, Mike Butcher, Ben Chisnall, Richard Collins, Jonny Coward, Shanika Hyslop, Youssef Khaireddine, Ian Marshall and Lauren Whybrow at Bloomsbury for their help in publishing *Giacometti in Paris*.

I am particularly grateful to my research assistant, Michael Kurtz, for enriching and editing the text as well as for his encouragement and unfailing good humour.

My wife, the art historian and exhibition curator Jill Lloyd, has not only contributed her invaluable knowledge and skills to this book, as she does to everything I write; she has also given me ideal conditions in which to write it.

For their advice, support and friendship, I should also like to record my gratitude to Fiamma Arditi, Katharine Arnold, Charles Asprey, Alice Bellony, Philippe Bern, Thérèse Tigretti Berthoud, David Blow, Anne and Yves Bonavero, Miel de Boton, Viscount and Viscountess Bridgman, Adam Brown, Ben and Louisa Brown, Richard Bucht, Marlene Burston, Charles and Natasha Campbell, Guillaume Cerruti, Neil and Narisa Chakra Thompson, Charles Cholmondely, Kieron Connolly, Patrice and Mala Cotensin, Casimiro Di Crescenzo, Sir Howard and Lady Davies, Hugh Marlais Davies, Cécile Debray, Adrian and Jamie Dicks, Christopher Eykyn, Michael Fishwick, Lady Elena Foster, Colin and Sophie Gleadell, John Gordon, Nicholas Goulandris, Catherine Grenier, Andrew Hochhauser, David Hockney, Max Hollein, Henry and Alison Meyric Hughes, Mark Inglefield, Christina and Richard Ives, Bill and Janet Jacklin, Sam Keller, Toby Kidd, Alastair

King, Antony and Zarrina Kurtz, Ulf Küster, Andrew Lambirth, Mingwei Lee, Mark and Lucy Lefanu, Memoria Lewis, Albert Loeb, Tessa Lord, Daniella Luxembourg, Alan and Christina Macdonald, Nicholas Maclean, Gillian Malpass, Graham Marchant, Tim Marlow, Thérèse Meier, Lucy Mitchell-Innes, Bona Colonna Montagu, Serena Morton, David Nash, Hughie and Clare O'Donoghue, Francis Outred, Alex Peppiatt, Ann Peppiatt, Clio Peppiatt, Elliott Power, Renée Price, Lesley Ramos, John Rivett, Christopher and Carmel Shirley, Frank and Pauline Slattery, Alex Stavrakas, Arturo di Stefano, Sir Ian and Lady Stoutzker, Stanley Tucci, Ortrud Westheider, Thomas Williams and Michael Ziegert.

Illustration credits

P3: Photo © Pierre Vauthey/Sygma/Sygma via Getty Images; P6: Photograph by Ernst Scheidegger © 2023 Stiftung Ernst Scheidegger-Archiv, Zurich; P20: Photo by Albert Harlingue/Roger Viollet via Getty Images; P23: Photo from The Met, New York: Purchase, Mr. and Mrs. John A. Moran Gift, in memory of Louise Chisholm Moran, Joyce F. Menschel Gift, Joseph Pulitzer Bequest, 2016 Benefit Fund, and Gift of Dr. Mortimer D. Sackler, Theresa Sackler and Family, 2016 (2016.614); P27: Photo by Apic/Getty Images; P38: Fondation Horst Tappe / Bridgeman Images; P43: Brassai prostitute © 2023 Estate Brassaï - RMN-Grand Palais /Dist. Photo SCALA, Florence; P52: Photo by ullstein bild/ullstein bild via Getty Images; P53: Photo by Roger Viollet via Getty Images; P58: PVDE / Bridgeman Images; P63: ©Man Ray Trust / ADAGP/ Telimage - Paris, 2008; P67: Untitled (Self-Portrait with Camera), 1930 (printed 1935/36). Solarized gelatin silver print, 4 3/4 x 3 1/2 in. (12.1 x 8.9 cm) © Man Ray 2015 Trust / DACS, London 2023. Purchase: Photography Acquisitions Committee Fund, Horace W. Goldsmith Fund, and Judith and Jack Stern Gift, 2004-16 2004-16; RMN-Grand Palais /Dist. Photo SCALA, Florence; P67: PVDE / Bridgeman Images; P70: Photo by adoc-photos/Corbis via Getty Images; P71: Members of the Surrealist Group, 1935 - Suede, Stockholm © Anna Riwkin/Moderna Museet, Stockholm and DALI foundation. © Archives Charmet / Bridgeman Images. P72: © Man Ray 2015 Trust / DACS, London 2023, RMN-Grand Palais /Dist. Photo SCALA, Florence; P79: © Man Ray 2015 Trust / DACS, London 2023; photo from Musee National d'Art Moderne - Centre Pompidou, Paris, France; P85: © The estate of James Boswell / Tate;

P97: Brassaï self-portrait © 2023 Estate Brassaï - RMN-Grand Palais / Dist. Photo SCALA, Florence; P101: © Man Ray 2015 Trust / DACS, London 2023. RMN-Grand Palais /Dist. Photo SCALA, Florence; P103: Photopress-Archiv/RIA/Keystone / Bridgeman Images; P106: Photo by Apic/Getty Images; P109: © Archives Charmet / Bridgeman Images; P136: Photo by Keystone/Hulton Archive/Getty Images; P143: © Tallandier / Bridgeman Images, artwork in photo © Succession Picasso/DACS, London 2023; P148: Photo by Roger Viollet via Getty Images; P150: Photo by ullstein bild/ullstein bild via Getty Images; P171: ©John Deakin / John Deakin Archive / Bridgeman Images; P177: Photo by adoc-photos/Corbis via Getty Images; P184: STF/AFP via Getty Images; P188: Photo by Roger Viollet via Getty Images; P190: Photo by Roger Viollet via Getty Images; P217: Photo by Roger Viollet via Getty Images; P219: Photo by Keystone-France/Gamma-Keystone via Getty Images; P226: © Michel Sima / Bridgeman Images; P230: Photo by Edie Adams and Ernie Kovacs Estate/Getty Images; P233: © Fondation Henri Cartier-Bresson/Magnum Photos; P246: Photo by Roger Viollet via Getty Images; P247: © 2023 Estate Brassaï - RMN-Grand Palais /Dist. Photo SCALA, Florence; P262: © Fondation Henri Cartier-Bresson/Magnum Photos; P269: Photo by Davis/Getty Images; P271: Photo by RDB/ullstein bild via Getty Images; P292: Photo by Wolfgang Kuhn/United Archives via Getty Images; P296: RMN-Grand Palais / Dist. Photo SCALA, Florence; P299: Photo by Roger Viollet via Getty Images/Roger Viollet via Getty Images; P312: Photopress Archiv/Keystone / Bridgeman Images; P316 © Ida Kar / National Portrait Gallery, London; P321: Musei Civici - Museo d'arte Antica, Sala degli Scarlioni; P326: Photograph by Ernst Scheidegger © 2023 Stiftung Ernst Scheidegger-Archiv, Zurich; P331: Photo by Tony Evans/Getty Images; P334: © Graham Keen/ Topfoto.

A Note on the Type

The text of this book is set in Adobe Garamond. It is one of several versions of Garamond based on the designs of Claude Garamond. It is thought that Garamond based his font on Bembo, cut in 1495 by Francesco Griffo in collaboration with the Italian printer Aldus Manutius. Garamond types were first used in books printed in Paris around 1532. Many of the present-day versions of this type are based on the *Typi Academiae* of Jean Jannon cut in Sedan in 1615.

Claude Garamond was born in Paris in 1480. He learned how to cut type from his father and by the age of fifteen he was able to fashion steel punches the size of a pica with great precision. At the age of sixty he was commissioned by King Francis I to design a Greek alphabet, and for this he was given the honourable title of royal type founder. He died in 1561.